NETSCAPE™
PLUG-INS
DEVELOPER'S KIT

que®

NETSCAPE™ PLUG-INS DEVELOPER'S KIT

Written by Michael Morgan

QUE®

Netscape™ Plug-Ins Developer's Kit

Copyright© 1997 by Que® Corporation.

Library of Congress Catalog No.: 96-70765

ISBN: 0-7897-0844-2

98 97 99   6 5 4 3 2 1

Interpretation of the printing code: the rightmost double-digit number is the year of the book's printing; the rightmost single-digit number, the number of the book's printing. For example, a printing code of 97-1 shows that the first printing of the book occurred in 1997.

Credits

PRESIDENT
Roland Elgey

PUBLISHER
Joseph B. Wikert

DIRECTOR OF MARKETING
Lynn Zingraf

PUBLISHING MANAGER
Jim Minatel

EDITORIAL SERVICES DIRECTOR
Elizabeth Keaffaber

MANAGING EDITOR
Sandy Doell

STRATEGIC MARKETING MANAGER
Barry Pruett

PRODUCT DIRECTOR
Stephen L. Miller

PRODUCTION EDITOR
Don Eamon

COPY EDITOR
Judith Goode

PRODUCT MARKETING MANAGER
Kristine Ankney

ASSISTANT PRODUCT MARKETING MANAGERS
Karen Hagen
Christy M. Miller

TECHNICAL EDITOR
Sunil Hazari

TECHNICAL SUPPORT SPECIALIST
Nadeem Muhammed

ACQUISITIONS COORDINATOR
Jane K. Brownlow

SOFTWARE RELATIONS COORDINATOR
Patty Brooks

EDITORIAL ASSISTANT
Jennifer L. Condon
Andrea Duvall

BOOK DESIGNER
Ruth Harvey

COVER DESIGNERS
Ruth Harvey
Barbara Kordesh

PRODUCTION TEAM
Stephen Adams
Melissa Coffey
Amy Gornik
Tammy Graham
Jason Hand
Kay Hoskin
Clint Lahnen
Tony McDonald
Laura Robbins
Sossity Smith
Marvin Van Tiem

INDEXER
Joy Dean Lee
Tim Tate

Composed in *Century Old Style* and *Franklin Gothic* by Que Corporation.

To Chris. Yes, God is *in the details.*

About the Author

Michael Morgan is founder and president of DSE, Inc., a full-service Web presence provider and software development shop. The DSE team has developed software for such companies as Intelect, Magnavox, DuPont, the American Biorobotics Company, and Satellite Systems Corporation, as well as for the Government of Iceland and the Royal Saudi Air Force. DSE's Web sites include the prestigious Nikka Galleria, an on-line art gallery. DSE's sites are noted for their effectiveness—one of the company's sites generated sales of over $100,000 within 30 days of being announced.

During Academic Year 1989-1990, Mike was invited by retired Navy admiral Ron Hays to serve as the first Fellow of the Pacific International Center for High Technology Research (PICHTR) in Honolulu. PICHTR is a spin-off of the the University of Hawaii and bridges the gap between academic research and industrial applications. Mike directed the first technology-transfer initiatives at PICHTR, and helped PICHTR win its first industrial contract. Mike assisted Admiral Hays in presenting PICHTR and its mission to the Hawaii research community, the Hawaii legislature, and Hawaii's representatives to Congress.

Mike is a frequent speaker at seminars on information technology, and has taught computer science and software engineering at Chaminade University (the University of Honolulu) and in the graduate program of Hawaii Pacific University. He has given seminars for the IEEE, National Seminars, the University of Hawaii, Purdue University, and Notre Dame.

Prior to founding DSE in 1988, Mike was a member of the technical staff at Magnavox Electronic Systems Company in Fort Wayne, Indiana. As a Magnavox engineer, he developed the first expert system for use in airborne AntiSubmarine Warfare. As a member of the Magnavox Industrial Modernization Team (IMIP), he identified and performed the conceptual design of three information-technology projects with a total value in the tens of millions of dollars.

In the early 1980's Mike was employed by the City of Virginia Beach, where he completed the development of the world's first automated municipal water distribution system. He is credited with saving the City several hundred thousand dollars in connection with that system.

Mike was an Army Signal Corps officer with active duty in the 5th Infantry Division and Reserve duty with the U.S. Rapid Deployment Force. He was among the youngest officers ever awarded the Meritorious Service Medal.

The author of over twenty technical papers and presentations on various aspects of information technology, he is the co-developer of the Project Unit Costing Method, which allows project managers to construct justifications for information technology projects based on cost savings and cost avoidance. He is also the inventor of GAELIC, the Gallium Arsenide Experimental Lisp Integrated Circuit, an ultra-high-speed processor optimized for artificial intelligence applications, and the co-inventor of MEND, a Multiple Expert iNtelligent Diagnostics system.

Mike is the co-manager of the CGI archives of the HTML Writers Guild, and is a member of the Help Team for Matt Wright's Script Archive. In these capacities, he works with programmers around the world helping set up advanced solutions on the Web.

He holds a Master of Science in Systems Management from the Florida Institute of Technology, and a Bachelor of Science in Mathematics from Wheaton College, where he concentrated his studies on computer science. He has also taken numerous graduate courses in computer science through the National Technological University. Mike is a member of the IEEE Computer Society.

Mike usually can be found in his office at DSE, drinking Diet Pepsi and writing Perl and C++. He lives in Virginia Beach with his wife, Jean, and their six children.

Acknowledgments

While my name appears on the cover of this book, many people worked together to produce the manuscript, and to turn the manuscript into the book you are now holding. If you find this book useful, you have them to thank.

Miguel Pating, Director of Development at Visionary Systems, Inc. (**http://www.visi.net**) and Ed Fang, Director of that organization, provided invaluable assistance and key resources throughout the development process.

As with all my books, I am again indebted to my colleague, Christopher Kepilino, and to my wife, Jean. Chris and Jean attended to the myriad of details that are needed to turn an idea into a book. They produced screen shots, reviewed the manuscript, and made sure that files and e-mail moved smoothly between my desk and the publisher's.

As always, the folks at Que have been capable and professional. Stephen Miller reviewed the entire manuscript, providing insight into many new technology topics. Don Eamon (with copy-edit help from Judith Goode) production edited the entire manuscript—a monumental task, calling for incredible patience. Thanks, guys.

I am also indebted to the readers of this and my previous books for your feedback. Please feel free to visit my Web site (**http://www.dse.com/General/2.MLM_Home.shtml**) or send me e-mail at **morganm@mail.dse.com**. I look forward to hearing from you.

As always, any errors or omissions are my responsibility.

Michael Morgan

Virginia Beach

October 16, 1996

We'd Like to Hear from You!

As part of our continuing effort to produce books of the highest possible quality, Que would like to hear your comments. To stay competitive, we *really* want you, as a computer book reader and user, to let us know what you like or dislike most about this book or other Que products.

You can mail comments, ideas, or suggestions for improving future editions to the address below, or send us a fax at (317) 581-4663. For the online inclined, Macmillan Computer Publishing has a forum on CompuServe (type **GO QUEBOOKS** at any prompt) through which our staff and authors are available for questions and comments. The address of our Internet site is **http://www.mcp. com** (World Wide Web).

In addition to exploring our forum, please feel free to contact me personally to discuss your opinions of this book: I'm **76103,1334** on CompuServe, and I'm at **slmiller@que.mcp.com** on the Internet.

Thanks in advance—your comments will help us to continue publishing the best books available on computer topics in today's market.

Stephen L. Miller
Product Development Specialist
Que Corporation
201 W. 103rd Street
Indianapolis, Indiana 46290
USA

Contents at a Glance

I Introduction to Plug-Ins

1 Bridging the Gap from CGI and
   Helper Applications to Netscape Plug-Ins   11
2 A C++ Primer   39
3 Integrating Plug-Ins into Web Site Design   75
4 Building a Simple Plug-In   101

II Design Issues

5 Design Issues   135
6 NPP Methods: Starting the Plug-In   161
7 NPP Methods: Handling Interaction   189
8 NPP Methods: Other Tasks   215
9 Understanding NPN Methods   237
10 Example: Simple Plug-In   269
11 Example: CharFlipper Plug-In   289
12 Example: npAVI Plug-In   309

III Plug-In Compatibility

13 Getting Back on the Network   337
14 If All the World Used Microsoft...   363
15 ActiveX and Plug-Ins in Other Browsers   391
16 Spanning the Windows World   411

IV Plug-In Foundations

17 Using Class Libraries and Frameworks   437
18 Plug-Ins as a Programming Resource   455
19 Installing the Plug-In   479

Appendixes

A Glossary   495
B What's on the CD-ROM   507

Index   513

Table of Contents

Introduction   1

    Who Should Read This Book?   2

    What This Book Is About   3

    What Will I Learn In This Book?   3

    How This Book Is Organized   4

    How to Use This Book   5

    Conventions Used in This Book   6

    What Technical Assumptions Does This Book Make?   7

I | Introduction to Plug-Ins

1 Bridging the Gap from CGI and Helper Applications to Netscape Plug-Ins   11

    The World Before Plug-Ins   12

    How Helper Applications Work   15

        MIME   15

        How Web Servers Select a Media Type   17

        How Web Browsers Handle Media Types   18

        What Helper Applications Can and Cannot Do   20

    Extending the Functionality of Netscape   22

        Your Own MIME Media Type   24

        Migrating Applications to the Web   26

        Building Programming Resources for HTML and JavaScript Programmers   27

    Building Your Plug-In   28

        Downloading the Navigator Plug-Ins SDK   29

        Unpacking the SDK   30

        Configuring the SDK   31

    From Here...   37

2 A C++ Primer   39

Understanding Classes and Instances   40
Inheritance   40
Polymorphism   41
Classes in C++   41

Introduction to Members and Methods   47
Data Members and Access Methods   50
Templates   57
Container Classes and the STL   59

Design Issues   67
Virtual Methods and Abstract Classes   67
Public versus *Private* Inheritance   69
Using Instances as Class Members   70
Style Guides and Naming Conventions   71
GUIs—the Graduate Course of Object-Oriented Methods   72

From Here...   73

3 Integrating Plug-Ins into Web Site Design   75

Patterns for Plug-Ins   76
What are Patterns?   76
Introduction to Plug-In Architecture   80

What Can You Do with a Plug-In?   90
Multimedia   90
Document Viewers   91
A Plug-In-Based Application   91

Control Issues in Asynchronous Plug-Ins   98
Threads   98
Processes   99
Reentrant Code   99

From Here...   99

4 Building a Simple Plug-In   101

Overview of the Development Process   102

Getting Ready to Build a Plug-In   102
Installing the SDK   102

Generating the Project Code   103
Adding Files from the SDK   108

Putting the Pieces Together   108
Modifying the Version Information Resource   109
Setting Up the DLL Configuration   113
Modifying npshell.cpp   114
Modifying npChap04.h   118
Modifying npChap04.cpp   120
Modifying npChap04Dlg.h   121
Connecting the Dialog Resource to the Message
Handlers   123
Modifying npChap04Dlg.cpp   124
Setting Up the Module Definition File   127

Building, Installing, and Testing the New Plug-In   128
Testing with about:plugins   129
Testing with Sample Data   129

From Here...   130

II | Design Issues

5 Design Issues   135

The Run-Time Model   136
NPP Methods   136
NPN Methods   139
Moving Existing Applications to the Web   145
Threads and Processes   146

Accessing the Data   146
Streaming   147
AsFile   148
Seekable Streams   148

The Hollywood Principle   150
Starting the Plug-In   152
Handling Interaction   154
Printing   154
Destroying the Instance   155

Designing for Debug   155
  Get the Compiler to Flag Defects   156
  Use Lint and Warnings   157
  Use the ASSERT macro   157
  Work with the MFC ASSERTs   158
From Here...   158

6 NPP Methods: Starting the Plug-In   161

Launching the Plug-In   162
  Advertising a MIME Media Type   162
  Loading the Plug-In   168
  Instantiating a Copy of the Plug-In   174
Using *NPP_NewStream()*   177
  Reading the Data as a Stream   179
  Reading the Data as a File   180
  Calling for the Data in a Seekable Stream   180
Presenting the Data   181
  Using Macintosh GrafPorts   182
  Programming on UNIX in the X Window System   183
  What to do in *NPP_SetWindow()*   186
From Here...   186

7 NPP Methods: Handling Interaction   189

Once You Have the Keyboard Focus   190
  Getting Events   190
  Reading the Keyboard Events in Windows   198
  Watching the Mouse   202
A Better Way of Managing Message Mapping   206
Processing the Stream   209
  Handling Streams with the Windows API   210
  An Example of Streaming Data   210
  Handling Streams in MFC   213
Starting Additional Streams   213
From Here...   214

8 NPP Methods: Other Tasks 215

   Understanding *NPP_Print()* 216
       Embedded Mode 216
       Full-Page Mode 219

   Using *NPP_Destroy()* 230
       Freeing Dynamic Memory 230
       Saving Instance Data 231
       Destroying the Window 234

   Using *NPP_Shutdown()* 234

   From Here... 235

9 Understanding NPN Methods 237

   Using *NPN_GetURL()* 238
       The Essence of Hyperlinking 241
       Loading an URL 241
       Sending to the Current Instance 244
       Migrating Existing Applications to the Web 244
       Thinking About Asynchronous Processing 246

   Determining the *NPN_Version()* 247
       Using the Plug-In API Version 247
       Using *NPN_UserAgent()* 248

   Accessing the *NPN_PostURL()* 249
       Sending a File of Data 249
       Sending a Buffer 250
       Special Considerations for Older Versions of Navigator 250
       Setting up a Distributed System 252
       Coupling with CGI or LiveWire 257

   NPN_RequestRead() 259
       Understanding Seekable Streams 259
       How to Use *NPN_RequestRead()* 262

   Using *NPN_NewStream()* 262
       Streaming into Navigator 263
       NPN_Write() 263
       NPN_DestroyStream() 264

Using *NPN_Status()*   264
    A Progress Indicator   265
    Reporting Time Remaining   266
Understanding *NPN_MemAlloc()* and *NPN_MemFree()*   267
From Here...   268

10   Example: Simple Plug-In   269

"Simple" in Action   270
    Compiling the Plug-In   270
    Moving the Files into Position   270
    Running the Plug-In   270
Understanding Flow of Control   271
    Follow Navigator   272
    NPP_Print()   281
LiveConnect Details   282
    Examining the Java Code   282
    How the JavaScript and HTML are Connected   284
    Closing Down the Plug-In   286
From Here...   287

11   Example: CharFlipper Plug-In   289

Introduction to CharFlipper in Action   290
    Compiling the Plug-In   290
    Moving the Files into Position   290
    Running the Plug-In   290
Flow of Control   291
    Follow Navigator   292
LiveConnect Details   302
    Examining the Java Code   302
    Triggering the Plug-in with Periodic Events   304
    How the JavaScript and HTML Are Connected   306
    Closing Down the Plug-In   307
From Here...   307

12 Example: npAVI Plug-In 309

npAVI in Action 310

Installing the Sun JDK 310

Compiling the Plug-In 310

Moving the Files into Position 313

Running the Plug-In 313

Putting npAVI into a Project 314

Flow of Control 316

Follow Navigator 316

LiveConnect Details 330

Examining the Java Code 331

How the JavaScript and HTML are Connected 333

Closing Down the Plug-In 333

From Here... 333

III | Plug-In Compatibility

13 Getting Back on the Network 337

Introduction to Multitasking 338

Understanding Processes and Threads 338

Processes 340

Threads 341

Synchronization and Critical Sections 342

Deadlocks 344

Platform Capabilities and Limitations 348

UNIX 349

Macintosh 349

Windows 351

Multitasking on the Cheap 353

Returning to the Net 355

Lack of a "Yield" Function 355

Separate Threads 356

Synchronization of Access to Global Data with a
Semaphore 357

Managing Thread Termination Through Events 359

Timers   361
Reentrant Calls   361

From Here...   362

14   If All the World Used Microsoft...   363

It's Not Just Object Linking and Embedding Anymore   364
What Are Compound Documents?   364
Introducing OLE 2   365
Clipboard Transfers   366
Drag-and-Drop Transfers   370
In-Place Activation   372
OLE Automation   375

Integration the Microsoft Way   381
Using ODBC   381
Custom Controls with Active X   387

What about OpenDoc?   388

From Here...   389

15   ActiveX and Plug-Ins in Other Browsers   391

ActiveX Controls   392
Installing ActiveX Controls   394
Native Support for Network Protocols   397
The "Active" in ActiveX   398
How to Write an ActiveX Control   398

ActiveX Documents   404

ActiveX Scripting   405

The ActiveX Server Framework   408

From Here...   409

16   Spanning the Windows World   411

Special Considerations for Classic Windows   412
Why Do They Spell it "Windoze?"   413
The Burden of 16-Bit-Hood   416
Memory Models   417
Multitasking in Classic Windows   425
Deciding Whether to Use Win32s   425
The Best of Both Worlds   426

Some Known Problems with Windows Plug-Ins   427
   Problems with the 16-Bit Version of Navigator   427
   Problems with an Easy Workaround   428
   Problems with Full-Page Plug-Ins   429
   General Problems with the Windows Navigator   429
From Here...   432

IV | Plug-In Foundations

17 Using Class Libraries and Frameworks   437

Class Libraries   438
   Using a Class Library   438
   Accessing Microsoft Foundation Classes   445
   Using Symantec's ObjectWindows Library   446
   Class Libraries for UNIX   449
   TCL from Symantec   450
Introduction to Frameworks   450
   MacApp   451
   Taligent's CommonPoint   451
From Here...   454

18 Plug-Ins as a Programming Resource   455

Compound Documents... Again   456
   Document-Centric Computing Meets the Web   456
   The UNIX Way   457
   The Microsoft Way   457
Integrating Plug-Ins with HTML   459
Integrating Plug-Ins By Using LiveConnect   460
   What is LiveConnect?   461
   How Much Java Do I Need to Know?   462
   Using LiveConnect to Talk to JavaScript   464
   Talking to the Plug-In   468
   Putting It All Together   476
From Here...   476

19 Installing the Plug-In 479

The Installation Process: A User Perspective 480

    Manual Installation 480

    Assisted Installation 481

    Installation Scripts and Pages 485

LiveConnect and Installation 486

    How Navigator Loads Plug-Ins 487

    MIME Type Conflict 487

    The *plugins* and *mimeTypes* Arrays 488

    The *embeds* Array 489

Navigator 4.0 490

From Here... 490

Appendixes

A Glossary 495

B What's on the CD-ROM? 507

Browsing the Contents of the CD-ROM 508

Electronic Versions of other Que Publications 508

Source Code 508

Plug-Ins 509

Helpers 509

    Audio 509

    HTML Editors & Utilities 510

Java 510

CGI & Perl 511

VRML 511

Web Utilities 511

Index 513

Introduction

Welcome to the world of Web browser plug-ins, and more particularly to the plug-ins for Netscape Navigator. Plug-ins are a powerful programming technique for extending Netscape Navigator 2.0x and beyond to deal with non-native types and offer new functionality. The demand for Web page designers has grown at an extraordinary rate. Although many talented people have entered the field of HTML authoring, the demand for specialty programs such as plug-ins promises to keep professional programmers busy for years to come.

Using plug-ins, programmers can build code resources that allow HTML programmers to embed new media types such as audio, video, and specialty graphics in their Web pages. With advanced plug-ins, the programmer can write a complete application, including calls back to the server and communications with multiple clients.

Netscape Plug-Ins Developer's Kit shows how to make your site come alive—first with high-quality static content, and then with full interaction between the browser and the native graphical environment, which gives users access to all the features of their PC, Macintosh, or UNIX workstations from inside Navigator. ■

Who Should Read This Book?

This book is for you if you already know how to program and if you develop or maintain a site on the World Wide Web. This book will help you decide whether the plug-in capabilities of Netscape's latest browsers can benefit your site.

If you have been building pages with static HTML, *Netscape Plug-Ins Developer's Kit* shows you how to start by mixing existing plug-ins with code you write in Java and JavaScript. You'll want to read Chapter 1, "Bridging the Gap from CGI and Helper Applications to Netscape Plug-Ins," to learn what plug-ins can do for your site. You also will want to review Chapter 18, "Plug-Ins as a Programming Resource," which explains how to connect plug-ins and Java to JavaScript by using LiveConnect, and Chapter 19, "Installing the Plug-In," to learn about the latest techniques in auto-installation.

If you're a programmer new to C++, go to Chapter 2, "A C++ Primer," which starts with object-oriented concepts, and then moves through templates and the Standard Template Library.

If you support an intranet or other Windows-only environment, pay particular attention to the discussion of Microsoft's OLE capabilities in Chapter 14, "If All the World Used Microsoft…." You also may want to see Chapter 15, "ActiveX and Plug-Ins in Other Browsers," for a comparison between plug-ins for Navigator and in the Microsoft Internet Explorer's ActiveX technology.

If you are new to HTML, the author recommends *Special Edition Using HTML* by Mark Brown and John Jung.

If you are new to running a Web site, you may benefit from *Webmaster Expert Solutions* (Que, 1996).

If you're not (yet) a programmer, or if you're new to C++, see *SE Using Borland C++*, *SE Using Microsoft Visual C++*, and *Borland C++ by Example*, all by Que Corporation.

Netscape Plug-Ins Developer's Kit picks up where these books leave off, and describes the features available in plug-ins that allow you to increase the quality of your site by reusing platform-specific code.

What This Book Is About

Netscape Plug-Ins Developer's Kit is a "how-to" book. It starts with a description of the methods of a plug-in and shows, step-by-step, how to produce pages on the World Wide Web that take advantage of the features in Netscape's newest browsers. The following list catalogues a few capabilities offered by Navigator through plug-ins:

- Displaying new media types on the client computer
- Drawing into a part of the Navigator window
- Interacting with the user through keyboard and mouse events
- Obtaining data from the network via URLs
- Posting data to CGI scripts or server-side JavaScript programs
- Adding hyperlinks or hotspots to link to new URLs

The primary focus of this book is helping you become familiar with the plug-in internals, so that you can build effective, high-quality pages with reusable components, resulting in a lower development cost. These pages include both static multimedia content, document viewers, and advanced interactive applications with platform-specific code.

What Will I Learn In This Book?

Although *Netscape Plug-Ins Developer's Kit* contains many examples and "cookbook" solutions, there also is a component of "understanding" in each chapter. We describe why things work as they do. This level of understanding helps the reader adapt to different configurations, change with new technology, and troubleshoot problems when their site is not working correctly.

Most chapters contain two to three sections on "understanding" as well as examples and sample code. Many chapters also describe a step-by-step process that programmers can use to ensure high-quality results in their plug-ins.

How This Book Is Organized

The Netscape sample plug-ins that come with the software development kit are notorious for their lack of clear instructions. Only a handful of people have built plug-ins based on the example code alone—indeed, several sites have sprung up on the Web to "correct" misimpressions left by the sample plug-ins.

Netscape Plug-Ins Developer's Kit places the best of on-line information together with material unavailable from any other source—the source code and discussion of real plug-ins, which can be used as a starting point for your own applications. The first chapter meets the needs of programmers who are ready to download the Netscape samples and start writing plug-ins. This part warns you of the limitations of the Netscape sample, and shows how to download the Software Development Kit (SDK) and configure it for the platform.

Chapters 2, "A C++ Primer," is designed if you are new to C++ or if you need a refresher to come up to speed on new techniques such as exceptions, templates, and the Standard Template Library.

Chapters 3, 4, and 5, "Integrating Plug-Ins into Web Site Design," "Building a Simple Plug-In," and "Design Issues," focus on issues that get you, as a programmer, started quickly—the architecture of a basic plug-in.

Chapters 6, "NPP Methods: Starting the Plug-In," through 9, "Understanding NPN Methods," serve as a reference, with examples of each basic plug-in method. Chapters 10, "Example: Simple Plug-In," through 12, "Example: npAVI Plug-In," show how to code various plug-ins by using the methods presented in earlier chapters.

Chapter 13, "Getting Back on the Network," shows how the plug-in can call Navigator and have it access the Net on behalf of the plug-in.

Chapters 14, "If All the World Used Microsoft…," 15, "ActiveX and Plug-Ins in Other Browsers," and 16, "Spanning the Windows World," highlight the features of

Microsoft Windows and OLE as they apply to both Navigator and Microsoft Internet Explorer plug-ins.

The book concludes with three chapters on reusable code: Chapter 17, "Using Class Libraries and Frameworks," shows how to take advantage of the thousands of lines in Microsoft Foundation Classes and other commercial libraries. Chapter 18, "Plug-Ins as a Programming Resource," shows how to use Netscape's LiveConnect technology to integrate Java, JavaScript, and plug-ins. Chapter 19, "Installing the Plug-In," shows how to automate the installation process so that plug-ins become transparent (or nearly so) to the end user.

The book is organized to ease your transition from experienced programmer to plug-in developer. To get started quickly, read the first chapter, then go right to Chapter 4, "Building a Simple Plug-In." If you are new to C++, reading Chapter 2, "A C++ Primer," is a must do before moving into the chapters on plug-in methods. Before you write plug-ins for serious applications, you'll want to have Chapters 3, "Integrating Plug-Ins into Web Site Design," through 9, "Understanding NPN Methods," and at least one of the "Example" chapters (10, 11, and 12) under your belt. If your plug-ins will be used mostly on Windows platforms, make sure that you read Chapters 14, "If All the World Used Microsoft…" through 17, "Using Class Libraries and Frameworks." To build integrated client applications by using LiveConnect, see Chapter 18, "Plug-Ins as a Programming Resource."

Finally, Appendix A is a glossary of terms to help those of you who are unfamiliar with some of the territory covered in this book. Appendix B describes the amount of material contained on this book's companion CD-ROM.

How to Use This Book

This book assumes that you are an experienced programmer, and that you know both HTML and the architecture of the Web. For more information about programming in C++ on various platforms, see *SE Using Borland C++*, *SE Using Microsoft Visual C++*, and *Borland C++ by Example*, all by Que Corporation.

To write LiveConnect applications, you want to have Java and JavaScript to integrate with your plug-ins. See *Special Edition Using Java*, *Special Edition Using JavaScript*, and *Java by Example*, Que Corporation.

If you already know how to program in JavaScript, you are ready for Chapter 18 on LiveConnect. If most of your plug-ins will be used in a Windows environment, start by reading the first nine chapters, then read at least one Example chapter (Chapters 10, 11, and 12), and then move on to Chapters 14, "If All the World Used Microsoft…," through 17, "Using Class Libraries and Frameworks." Pay particular attentions to the section on Microsoft Foundation Classes in Chapter 17.

Conventions Used in This Book

Within each chapter you find italicized text, bulleted lists, and numbered lists. *Italics* are used to mark important words or phrases and to introduce new technical terms. An italicized term is followed by a definition or an explanation.

Bulleted lists are used when the order of the items isn't important. The items represent related concepts that are explained in the list.

Numbered lists are used when the numbering, or sequence, is important. Steps in a procedure appear in numbered lists. Follow the steps from beginning to end. Make sure that you understand each step—don't just skip one because you don't understand it.

The chapters also contain figures (which often are screen shots that show what to expect on your computer) and code listings (which contain complete programs, usually in JavaScript, to illustrate a technique).

Code fragments are contained in the text and set in `monospace font`. These fragments illustrate a technique, but they are not by themselves a complete program.

Sometimes in these code listings a line runs beyond the page width of this book. When this happens, you see a small arrow, ➥, at the beginning of the new line. When you see this arrow, it means that all of this material can actually be entered into the program on a single line.

Characters that you are asked to type are set in **bold** font. If you must substitute a file name or other element into the line, a placeholder for the file name or element is used and is set in ***bold italics***.

The syntax of a particular command or tag is shown with a special kind of code fragment. A syntax form looks like the following example:

```
<P [ALIGN=Left|Center|Right]>
```

Here, optional elements appear in [square brackets]. Variants are separated by the vertical bar |. Monospaced font must be typed exactly as it appears. According to the preceding syntax form, all of the following HTML is legal:

```
<P>
<P ALIGN=Left>
<P ALIGN=Center>
<P ALIGN=Right>
```

The following HTML, however, is illegal:

```
<P ALIGN=Center
<P ALIGN=CenterRight>
<P COLOR="#110000">
```

Tables are used when appropriate.

Icons appear in the margins of this book to indicate either that a file or application exists on this book's companion CD-ROM or that an Internet address appears within the adjacent text.

On the CD

What Technical Assumptions Does This Book Make?

The plug-in SDK is available for nearly every modern operating system: Macs, Windows machines, and a variety of UNIX computers. *Netscape Plug-Ins Developer's Kit* uses Microsoft Visual C++ on Windows 95 for many of its examples, and provides notes that show the differences between that environment and Macintosh, UNIX, and non-Microsoft Windows compilers. Most readers will find it easy to adapt this standard description to the configuration on their development platform.

This book also emphasizes direct writing and debugging of the plug-in with a text editor. Although advanced development environments can build much of the plug-in with little guidance from the designer, there is no substitute for learning about each method by writing it yourself. ●

Introduction to Plug-Ins

1 Bridging the Gap from CGI and Helper Applications to Netscape Plug-Ins   11

2 A C++ Primer   39

3 Integrating Plug-Ins into Web Site Design   75

4 Building a Simple Plug-In   101

CHAPTER 1

Bridging the Gap from CGI and Helper Applications to Netscape Plug-Ins

Netscape Navigator is a well-designed, highly functional product. Netscape's innovations have catapulted the company to its position as leader of the Web browser vendors. Navigator provides native support for a variety of graphics formats, as well as Hypertext Markup Language (HTML), the language of Web pages.

Netscape, however, recognizes that the needs of the Web community change faster and grow wider than it can support in Navigator. Starting with version 1 of the product, Netscape provided ways to extend Navigator with "helper applications," which support data formats beyond the built-in graphics and HTML.

How helper applications work

After you understand the limitations of helper applications, you might not want to use them. This chapter describes the strengths and weaknesses of helper applications.

About MIME media types

This Internet-standard way of identifying data is the basis for loading plug-ins. This chapter describes how to find existing MIME media types and how to register your own type.

How plug-ins work

Many Web users consider them to be superior to helper applications. This chapter lists five ways in which plug-ins are superior to helper applications.

Where to get the plug-in Software Development Kit (SDK)

This chapter shows you how to download it.

How to set up the SDK

Whether you use OS/2 Warp, a Macintosh, a Windows computer, or a UNIX machine, Netscape has an SDK for your computer. This chapter shows how to set up the SDK for your machine.

Starting in Netscape Navigator Version 2, Navigator supports "plug-ins," another way to extend the range of data types that can be presented on or with a Web page. ■

The World Before Plug-Ins

To see why plug-ins are useful, go to the "desktop" of your computer and double-click a few documents. If you choose a document that your system associates with a particular application, that application is launched. But if you double-click a document whose type isn't associated with a known application, you see a dialog box like the one shown in Figure 1.1.

> **N O T E** Most of the examples in this book were developed using Netscape Navigator 3.0. If you are using an older version of Navigator, your results may differ markedly from the figures and examples given here.

ON THE WEB

The latest versions of Netscape Navigator for all platforms (Mac, UNIX, and the various members of the Windows family) are available on-line at the Netscape home site, **http://home.netscape.com/**. ■

On the whole, Apple and Microsoft have developed workable schemes for mapping documents to applications. Even most UNIX vendors provide similar schemes with the X Windows system.

FIG. 1.1
A Windows 95 user is invited to "associate" a file extension with an application.

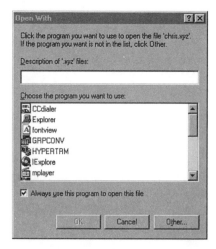

The users' world today, however, goes far beyond their local hard drive. They may have files on a file server on the local area network. They may access files on a coworker's machine on the other side of the room or, through a company intranet, the other side of the world. They also may use a variety of files from the Internet.

FIG. 1.2

A Navigator user attempts to open an unrecognized file type.

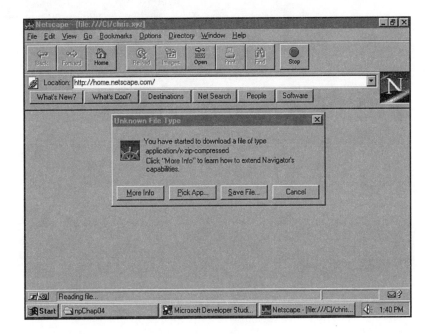

When a Netscape Navigator user attempts to open a document that Navigator does not recognize, the dialog box shown in Figure 1.2 appears. This dialog box allows the user to select an external viewer application through the "Pick App…" button, or save the file.

External viewers, also known as *helper applications*, allow the Web user to see a variety of data types that are not built into Netscape Navigator or other popular browsers. Figure 1.3, for example, shows a graphic stored in Computer Graphics Metafile (CGM) format—a format popular with the Computer-Aided Design (CAD) community. This image is viewed from Netscape by using FIGleaf, a plug-in from Carberry Technology.

FIG. 1.3
CGM graphics can
be viewed through
helper applications
or plug-ins.

The downside of helper applications is that they are, indeed, applications. To view
a file with a helper application the user's machine must start an entirely new program, which means that:

- They have to wait while the new program loads.

- They may run out of memory and not be able to launch the new program.

- If the helper application launches, they see the document in its own window,
  out of context from the Web document.

- No interaction exists between the Web document and the external file—for
  example, if the external file is a movie, similar to that shown in Figure 1.4, no
  provision is available to allow the user to use buttons on the Web page to
  control the movie viewer.

FIG. 1.4
This Macintosh
QuickTime movie
viewer has its own set
of controls—the user
cannot run it from the
Web page.

How Helper Applications Work

To understand helper applications you must first understand *MIME* types. *Multimedia Internet Message Extensions*, or MIME, was developed to allow users to exchange files by e-mail. Although the Web doesn't use the full MIME standard, it is convenient to use media types (formerly known as MIME types) to tell a Web browser how the file is formatted.

MIME

MIME is described in detail in Request for Comments (RFC) 1590. RFC 1590 updates the registration process originally described in RFC 1521. Although MIME was originally intended for use in e-mail systems (and RFC 1521 was written with this application in mind), today's user encounters MIME in a variety of multimedia settings.

ON THE WEB

For more information on MIME, check out the Frequently Asked Questions list at **ftp://ftp.uu.net/usenet/news.answers/mail/mime-faq** or **http://www.cis.ohio-state.edu/text/faq/usenet/mail/mime-faq/top.html**.

MIME is designed to have a limited number of top-level types, such as "application," "text," and "video," which can be extended by subtypes. Table 1.1 shows some typical MIME-compliant media types. As the table shows, MIME types consist of a type and a subtype.

Table 1.1   MIME Types and Subtypes

Type	Subtype	Meaning
application	msword	Format of Microsoft Word documents
application	rtf	The "Rich Text Format" for word processors
application	octet-stream	A "catch all" type for a collection of bytes
application	zip	The compressed-file format of PKZIP and its kin
application	pdf	Adobe's Portable Document Format
audio	aiff	An audio interchange format developed by Apple Computer
audio	midi	A music format based on instruments
audio	wav	The RIFF WAVE sound format developed by Microsoft and IBM
image	cgm	Computer Graphics Metafile image format
image	gif	Graphics Interchange Format image format
image	jpeg	File interchange format of the Joint Photographic Experts Group
text	plain	ASCII text
text	html	The Hypertext Markup Language
video	mpeg	Video format of the Motion Picture Experts Group
video	quicktime	Format developed by Apple Computer

When a Web browser requests a document from a server, the server sends several header lines before it sends the document. One header is "Content-type." This header line contains the MIME type and subtype, separated by a slash. Therefore, most Web pages are preceded by the following line:

```
Content-type: text/html
```

How Web Servers Select a Media Type

Most Web servers have a file that associates file extensions with MIME types. On NCSA, Apache, and similar servers the file is named `mime.types`. A typical line in `mime.types` says the following:

```
text/html html
```

This line tells the server that if the file has an extension of ".html" the server should send `text/html` in the `Content-type` header.

Suppose that you wanted to serve Microsoft Word documents, in their proprietary format, directly from your Web server. If your MS-Word documents use the file extension `.doc`, and if they are the only documents with this extension, you can add the following to `mime.types`:

```
application/msword    doc
```

Equivalently, you could put the following line into the configuration file `srm.conf`:

```
AddType    application/msword    doc
```

TIP After changing a configuration file such as `mime.types` or `srm.conf`, you need to either restart your server or explicitly tell the server to reread the configuration files. In UNIX, you can tell the server to reread the configuration files by sending the following SIGHUP signal:

```
kill -SIGHUP processID
```

Here, *processID* is the process number of the parent server *daemon*.

N O T E Under UNIX, many processes are detached from any terminal and run in the background, waiting for user requests. These processes are known as *daemons*. A typical UNIX machine being used as a Web server may have several instances of the `httpd` daemon (the Web server software) running, as well as an `ftp` dameon, a

continues

continued

telnet daemon, and various service daemons such as timed and whois. By convention, many daemon names end in the character 'd.' ▪

How Web Browsers Handle Media Types

Start Netscape Navigator and go to Options, General Preferences. From this screen choose the Helpers tab. The result should resemble the screen shown in Figure 1.5. (Fig. 1.5 shows the screen in the Macintosh version of Navigator. The exact appearance of your screen may vary slightly due to platform and version variations.)

FIG. 1.5
Navigator allows the user to associate applications with media types.

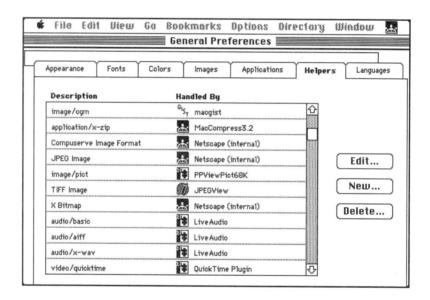

Note that if Navigator recognizes the media type it uses the common name (such as CompuServe Image Format for image/gif). Some formats, such as GIF and JPEG, are handled internally by Navigator. Others are handled by helper applications or plug-ins (which are discussed throughout the rest of this book).

Select a media type that is handled by a helper application and click the Edit button. The resulting dialog box is shown in Figure 1.6. Note that in this dialog, the user can specify the MIME-compliant media type and subtype, as well as a file extension. The information in Figure 1.6 says that if Navigator encounters a header from the server that identifies the content type as image/cgm or if it is asked to open a file that has a file extension of .cgm, Navigator should launch the helper application, MacGIST.

N O T E Recall that plug-ins, by definition, are platform-specific. The example in this chapter shows a Macintosh plug-in, MacGist. The Macintosh version of Gist was created by Steve Langer (**shl@icf.llnl.gov**), from the UNIX version written by Dave Munro. Plug-ins for various media types and platforms are available on this book's companion CD-ROM. ■

FIG. 1.6
Navigator allows the user to specify an application with a MIME type and subtype and a file extension.

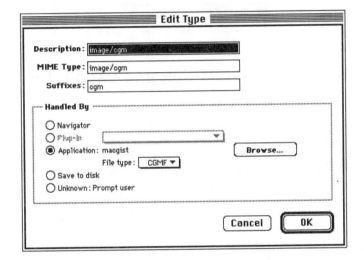

To add a new media type to the list that Navigator recognizes, go to the Helpers tab under the Options, General Preferences menu item, and click the New button. The resulting dialog is identical to the one used by the Edit button. Fill in the fields and click OK.

N O T E The Macintosh operating system doesn't use file extensions to associate documents with applications. Instead, each file has two four-character fields, known as "Creator" and "Type." Most applications can handle more than one file type. Microsoft Word can recognize 18 file types—Figure 1.7 shows a few of these types.

Using the New... dialog, Navigator users on the Mac can specify which file type to associate with the media type. "MSWD" is the "Creator" of a native MS-Word document. "W6BN" is the type for Word 6.0. ■

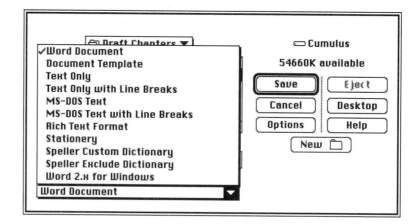

FIG. 1.7
Microsoft Word 6.0.1 for Macintosh recognizes 18 different Macintosh file types.

What Helper Applications Can and Cannot Do

Helper applications represented a good first-step at extending Navigator to non-native data types, but there are limitations. This section explores some reasons that helper applications by themselves may not meet the needs of many Web users.

Many Different Applications Recall that common applications such as Microsoft Word can be configured as helper applications to read their own proprietary formats. Many of these applications occupy tens of megabytes and cost hundreds of dollars. Although intranet users may have a standardized set of applications, Internet users are unlikely to buy the full application in order to read a document in a proprietary format.

What is needed is a reader application that allows the user to see the data, without necessarily having the capability to change the data.

Separate Windows Helper applications are, after all, applications. As shown in the example with Microsoft Word, they do not need to be written in a special way—Navigator downloads the file from the Web, and then invokes the application. The application opens the file and displays it in its own window, with its own menu bar, just as though a user had launched the application and chose File, Open.

When the application launches, it takes several seconds to load into memory. If the computer memory is already full (with Navigator and other applications), the application may not load at all. If it loads, the user is quite aware that he or she no longer is interacting with Navigator—the user now is in the helper application.

Many Webmasters wish they could embed files from a variety of formats in their documents and keep the user in the Navigator window and menu bar. Navigator needs a way to reference a file from inside an HTML document, and have Navigator invoke a reader to display the file inline.

No Interaction with Navigator Many data types require more interaction than just "reading." Audio and video data can be started and stopped, played at normal speed, or faster or slower. Navigator is being positioned as the "universal client"—to live up to that name, it should take control of embedded data.

Many Webmasters would appreciate the capability to hook buttons or other controls on an HTML page to the helper application, so that a user can interact with the application and the data through controls on the page.

Waiting for the File *Hypertext Transport Protocol* (HTTP)—the protocol of the Web—is designed to allow browsers to request an entire file from the server. When the file contains HTML, it usually downloads in only a few seconds with a 14.4 modem. A graphic image such as a GIF or JPEG may take half-a-minute or more, but multimedia files such as sound and video can take many minutes—so long that most users aren't pleased with having to wait. This "dead air" that accompanies large files is one reason that more multimedia is not displayed on the Web.

Some vendors, such as Progressive Networks, makers of RealAudio, developed alternative protocols that allow their clients to present the data as it downloads. A user listening to RealAudio begins to hear sound a few seconds after he or she connects, while the rest of the file continues to download.

Users would welcome a byte-oriented protocol, rather than a file-oriented protocol, which allows them to begin to display, play, or listen to the data as soon as it is available, rather than being forced to wait until the entire file has downloaded.

No Interaction with the Web Site Much data on today's Web is static—the file is stored on the server until it is requested, then it is downloaded to the browser. But some applications would benefit from more interaction. An application, for example, that displays video data as it downloads benefits from a "Fast Forward" control that can tell the server to skip part of the video.

Application programmers could use a mechanism that allows them to communicate (through Navigator) back to the server.

Extending the Functionality of Netscape

In Navigator 2.0, Netscape introduced inline plug-ins as an alternative to helper applications. Plug-ins are platform-specific pieces of code that display their contents inside the Navigator window, in much the same way as the HTML <IMG> tag displays an image "inline" rather than in a separate window. This technology affords the following features:

- Plug-ins are small code resources, not full applications. They are run in the Navigator process. Consequently, they cost less to develop, take up less disk space, and load more quickly than full applications.

- Because plug-ins share address space with the Netscape application, they can run in the Navigator window. The HTML coder can embed references to the data directly in the HTML file, and the plug-in will open inline in the Navigator window. The coder still can get a full window if he or she chooses. There also is a provision to run in the background, when no graphical interaction is required, such as for an audio application.

- The plug-in is activated as soon as the data begins to flow from the server. The programmer has the option of waiting for the data to be stored as a file, but the recommended programming technique is to present the data as it arrives.

In mid-1996 Netscape released Navigator 3.0. Navigator 3.0 supports additional plug-in capabilities. In particular, it includes a technology Netscape calls LiveConnect, which integrates plug-ins with client-side JavaScript and Java. Figure 1.8 illustrates LiveConnect.

FIG. 1.8
LiveConnect is Netscape's approach to integrating all of the client-based programming techniques.

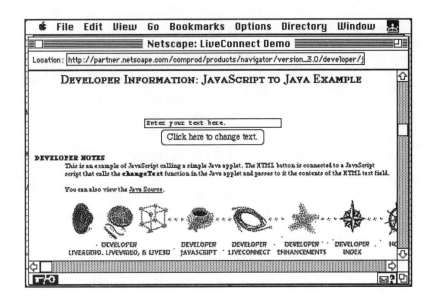

JavaScript is a high-level object-oriented language, principally designed for use in the browser. (There also is a server-side version of the language that works with Netscape's second-generation servers and the LiveWire toolset.) JavaScript is an approachable language, and many programs have been written in JavaScript by people who do not consider themselves professional programmers.

Java is a powerful object-oriented language. Java programs can be compiled into *applets* and stored on the server. When the browser requests a page that references these applets, the applets are downloaded and run on the browser.

Although plug-ins are written in the native code of the client platform (OS/2, Windows, Macintosh, or a specific version of UNIX), Java is platform-independent. A Java applet can run on any platform that supports the Netscape Navigator browser.

With LiveConnect, a JavaScript programmer can include data that requires a plug-in and Java applets on a page, and can issue calls to both entities to control them or send them information. Plug-ins and applets can also call JavaScript functions to determine how they should proceed. This level of integration means that applets and plug-ins, which are usually written by skilled programmers, become a code resource for use by page designers, extending the reach of page designers who do not necessarily have to be able to write sophisticated programs.

Your Own MIME Media Type

Unlike Java applets, which are mini-applications, plug-ins are intended to be built around data. Before you can build a plug-in, you (the developer) must specify the MIME media type(s) that the plug-in handles. Many plug-ins will be able to work with an existing MIME media type such as the Computer Graphics Metafile format shown previously in this chapter (in the section "The World Before Plug-Ins"), or those listed in Table 1.1, but sooner or later, you will need to give users access to data that has no MIME-compliant media type. This section explains two ways of dealing with this situation, depending upon whether your data will be distributed privately or publicly.

Private MIME Types   If you develop a plug-in strictly for an intranet, or for a limited Internet audience, you may decide to specify your own type of MIME media. Usually, you can use an existing type, and only need to select a sub-type. By convention (and in accordance with RFC 1590) unregistered types and subtypes begin with the "x-" characters. Therefore, you may see "application/x-zip," "audio/x-mpeg," and "image/x-png".

TIP Many developers do not take the time to register their media type, so you see common formats such as the Portable Network Graphic (PNG) with "x-" subtypes. The RFC 1590 registration process is streamlined compared with the requirements of RFC 1512. To avoid conflict with other types, and to "stake your claim" on a name, register your type if there is a possibility of your data being distributed publicly.

N O T E   MIME media types are intended to reflect data formats rather than applica-
tions. Therefore, "application/msword" may be better named "application/msword6" to reflect the version of the proprietary MS-Word data format. Some types were registered or came into general use early in the life of the standard and don't reflect the latest thinking in naming standards. ▪

On the CD

Registering a MIME Type   The procedure for registering MIME media types is given in Part 2 and Appendix A of RFC 1590, which updates RFC 1521. RFC 1590 was issued in March 1994. Before starting the registration process, always check the list of RFCs to see if there is a newer RFC that updates RFC 1590. You can find a complete list of RFCs on this book's companion CD-ROM.

T I P The Internet Assigned Numbers Authority (IANA) is the central registry for MIME types. They are set up primarily to process new sub-types. If you believe that you have a justification for a new top-level type, you should write an RFC on the new type and publish it in accordance with the current Internet standards process. Only if your RFC is approved should you use it as a top-level media type.

To register a new media type, first select a top-level type from the current list (such as application, image, video, or audio). Then select a unique name for the sub-type. Send a message to the mailing list **ietf-types@cs.utk.edu**—readers of this list will comment on the appropriateness of your choice. A typical message format would be as follows:

```
To: ietf-types@cs.utk.edu
Subject: Proposed new Media Type content-type/subtype

Media Type name:
Media Subtype name:
Required parameters:
Optional parameters:
Encoding considerations:
Security considerations:
Published specification:
Person and e-mail address to contact for further information:
```

If the `Media Type name` field doesn't contain an existing top-level Media Type, the IANA needs an explanation of why an existing top-level Media Type cannot be used.

The `Published specification` field should contain a reference to a publicly available specification. If the request is for a new top-level Media Type, the field should reference the RFC or RFC-to-be specifying the new type.

The `Security considerations` field is the place to list all known security risks. The IANA doesn't require that your application be secure, only that all known risks be identified.

Allow two weeks for comments and feedback. If, based on the comments, you decide to change the name of your type, it's a good idea to send the amended proposal back to the mailing list.

After your proposal is reviewed by the `ietf-types` mailing list, send a message to **IANA@isi.edu** to start the registration process. Use the same format as the `ietf-types` mailing list, but make the subject "Registration of new Media Type *content-type/subtype*."

ON THE WEB

The IANA will ensure that your proposal has been reviewed by members of the Internet Engineering Task Force through the `ietf-types` mailing list. Then they will register your new type, assign an Object Identifier (OID) under the IANA branch, and post the registration on their ftp server, at **ftp://ftp.isi.edu/in-notes/media-types**.

Your media type also will be published in RFC 1340, "Assigned Numbers." If you expect that the Internet public will want to put data into your new format or will write plug-ins or other applications to read your data, put the full spec into an informational RFC.

T I P   To publish an informational RFC, follow the guidelines given in RFC 1543, "Instructions to RFC Authors." This document serves as a checklist of sections and elements to include. Then send the completed RFC to **rfc-editor@isi.edu**. Remember that an RFC is, literally, a Request For Comments. Before making a final commitment to a format, consider releasing a Draft RFC, and then modifying it in accordance with the feedback you get from the Net community.

Migrating Applications to the Web

Many software publishers have developed applications that generate and read documents that can be sent over the Web. Plug-ins are an excellent way to extend the viability of an application. Get a media type assigned for each data format your application produces, and then write a plug-in that reads and presents your data to the user. You may even want to use JavaScript and LiveConnect to allow the Web user to interact with the data.

One example of this approach is Adobe's Portable Document Format, PDF. Adobe makes the plug-in (and before that, the helper application) available at no charge

Part

I

Ch

1

from its Web site. Adobe sells Acrobat, which writes these PDF files, through commercial channels. The result? The Internet community has a huge demand for PDF files, and sales of Acrobat are brisk.

N O T E If you are registering a MIME media type based on a commercially available software package, you don't need to release an RFC with the data format. In the Published specification field, name the software package and version number. ■

Building Programming Resources for HTML and JavaScript Programmers

In the late 1970s, when the first desktop computers were being offered, thousands of people who didn't consider themselves professional programmers learned BASIC, an interpreted language that was built into most desktop machines. Teachers, insurance agents, and bankers all wrote small BASIC applications that met specific needs in their industry. The same phenomenon occurred again in the early 1980s when spreadsheets appeared.

During the late 1980s and the early 1990s, the computer industry realized that the number of trained programmers would fall far short of the demand. Many companies are building on the BASIC and spreadsheet models—they are making it possible for professional programmers to build reusable components, which then are used by sophisticated users to build complete systems. A skilled user can use client-side and server-side JavaScript to stitch together data, plug-ins, and Java applets into a complete solution for use on an intranet or the Internet.

For plug-ins to be used as components, they must have the following three characteristics:

- A well-documented data type.
- A well-documented interface (both with the Netscape EMBED tag and with JavaScript).
- A high tolerance for errors—the plug-in should recover or exit with a message that explains the error, rather than crash.

> **CAUTION**
>
> Because plug-ins run in the address space of Navigator, failures in plug-ins can crash the browser. Moreover, users may not know that a page they are trying to access contains data that is displayed by a plug-in—they may conclude that their browser is crashing because of defects in Navigator. At a minimum, this conclusion makes it unlikely that you will get timely defect reports. Therefore it is important that plug-ins be thoroughly exercised by in-house testers and knowledgeable reviewers before release to the general public.

Building Your Plug-In

Unlike Java applets, plug-ins are written in platform-specific code. Netscape Navigator is available for OS/2 Warp, Windows 3.*x*, Windows 95, Windows NT, 680*x*0-based Macintoshes, PowerPC-based Macintoshes, and a variety of UNIX platforms. If you want your data to be readable by any Navigator user, you need to develop versions of your plug-in for all of these platforms.

The good news is that the code for plug-ins is quite similar across platforms. In some cases you can use the same code and compile for different targets. Microsoft's Visual C++, for example, can generate code for Intel processors (running all manner of Windows), the Macintosh (both 680*x*0 and PowerPC), and even the DEC Alpha chip (running Windows NT). MetroWorks CodeWarrior Gold for the Macintosh can generate code for both types of Mac processor, as well as Windows 95 and Windows NT.

Differences between platforms usually have more to do with the Graphical User Interface (GUI) than with the interface between Navigator and the plug-in. Windows applications will call the Windows API (possibly through Borland's Object Windows Library, OWL, or Microsoft's Foundation Classes, also known as MFC). Macintosh applications use the Macintosh toolbox, built into every Mac. UNIX programmers can choose from a wide variety of "widgets"—pre-built objects that fit into an X-Window environment.

Because a complete plug-in should be available on all platforms, this book contains information relevant to all four major operating systems. Where the operating system is irrelevant, most examples are drawn from the Windows 95 platform and are shown in Microsoft Visual C++.

N O T E Users sometimes complain that, in Navigator 2.0 and 3.0, they must explicitly download the plug-in before they can view non-native data. Starting in Navigator 4.0, Netscape is offering the capability to automatically download and install a plug-in. The HTML programmer can identify the URL of the plug-in, and allow the browser to fetch the plug-in and install it. ■

Downloading the Navigator Plug-Ins SDK

ON THE WEB

Netscape distributes its plug-in Software Development Kit on its Web site, at **http://home.netscape.com/eng/mozilla/3.0/handbook/plugins/index.html**, shown in Figure 1.9.

FIG. 1.9
You may eventually develop plug-ins on all major platforms. Choose one platform on which to learn. This book uses Windows 95 and the Microsoft Visual C++ compiler for most of its examples.

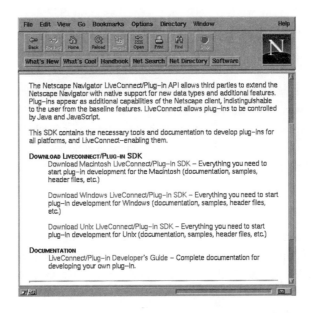

> **N O T E**   Although you may eventually write plug-ins for all four platforms, pick one
> platform to learn on first. Most examples in this book are given for develop-
> ment on Windows 95 and Microsoft Visual C++. If you don't have access to this platform,
> follow along on your own system, and pay close attention to the notes that discuss OS/2
> Warp, Macintosh, and UNIX development. ▨

Visit the Netscape site and download the version of the SDK appropriate for your
development platform.

Unpacking the SDK

Each version of the SDK is compressed in a way that is appropriate for the platform (for example, the Windows version is zipped, the Macintosh version is a
Stuff-it archive, and the UNIX version is compressed using tar). Copy the SDK to
the directory of your choice and unpack it.

You can get WinZip and StuffIt Expander from the CD-ROM that accompanies this
book. Use WinZip or PKUNZIP with Windows and OS/2. Use StuffIt Expander on
the Macintosh.

ON THE WEB
If you use UNIX, your machine probably came with the compression utility, `tar`. For an
even better version, check out GNU `tar`, which comes from the Free Software Foundation.
GNU software is widely available on-line. Visit **http://www.cs.pdx.edu/~trent/gnu/
sites.html** for a starting point. The "official" site of the Free Software Foundation, **http://
www.gnu.ai.mit.edu/**, is almost as useful as the unofficial site (**http://
www.cs.pdx.edu/~trent/gnu/**).

 If you're distributing your files or plug-ins through the Net, you also should learn about
`gzip`. This product is the Free Software Foundation's leading compression utility and is
available on the standard GNU sites. Because `gzip` is available on all common platforms, you can store a single gzipped file which can be downloaded by Mac, Windows,
OS/2, or UNIX users.

Configuring the SDK

You need a C++ compiler to build Navigator plug-ins. Netscape's SDKs are built from its engineers' computers and do reflect the software tools that Netscape uses internally. On Windows, Netscape uses Microsoft's Visual C++. On the Mac, it uses Metrowork's CodeWarrior. Most versions of UNIX come with a native C/C++ compiler. IBM recommends IBM's Visual Age C++ 3.0 for building plug-ins for OS/2 Warp.

 T I P The Free Software Foundation has a C++ compiler, g++, which runs on nearly all versions of UNIX. You can download the source from any GNU site but, of course, you need a compiler to compile the source. Some GNU sites have precompiled binaries of g++ for various versions of UNIX, to get you started.

For information about precompiled binaries online, visit the "Precompiled GNU Binaries" section of **http://www.cs.pdx.edu/~trent/gnu/**. This page also contains links to information about g++, including the Frequently Asked Questions list at **http:// www.cis.ohio-state.edu/hypertext/faq/usenet/g++-FAQ/plain/faq.html**.

If you don't have a compiler and cannot find (or don't want to download) the precompiled binaries online, visit Ready-to-Run Software, Inc. at **http://www.rtr.com/**. Ready-to-Run specializes in packaging the binaries of publicly available software into "ReadyPacks," which include an intelligent installation system that allows you to quickly select the programs you want to install and where to install them. Often, GNU software has dependencies—to run Program A, you need Program B. Ready-to-Run's ReadyPacks include a cross-reference utility to show just which programs you need to load from the ReadyPack.

g++ is part of Ready-To-Run's "Language Pack #1," described in detail at **http:// www.rtr.com/rtr01/lp1.htm**.

In addition to their online information, you can order a printed Ready-to-Run catalog from their Web site, or by phone at **800-743-1723** or **508-692-9922**.

Although you can build plug-ins with any C++ compiler, you have less work to do if you use the same compilers as Netscape. For example, some portions of the Windows example plug-in rely on Microsoft Foundation Classes. The Symantec compiler comes with MFC—the Borland compiler is bundled with OWL, which offers similar capabilities. The Borland compiler also can be used to recompile MFC, if you get this library from Microsoft. Visual C++, however, is available in versions starting at under $100—for learning to build plug-ins, a copy of Visual C++ shortens your learning time.

Figure 1.10 illustrates the process of turning a high-level language, such as C or C++, into a executable file. The compiler produces object code, often signified with a file extension of .obj or, occasionally, .o. The linker puts together these object files with platform-specific code like the code that makes up the Windows or Macintosh API. The finished product is an executable file. On either a DOS or a Windows computer, this executable has a file extension of .exe.

FIG. 1.10
Source files are compiled, then linked with other object files to make an executable image.

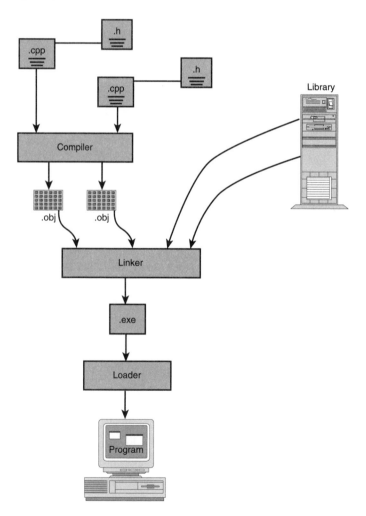

N O T E The use of the term "object file" as the output of a compiler has nothing to do with object-oriented programming. The use of these two terms is completely coincidental. ■

For years all linking was done by the developer when the product was built. Today, all major platforms allow programmers to build code resources that can be linked into applications when the application loads or even during run-time. Libraries designed to be linked on the user's computer are known as *dynamic libraries*; libraries designed to be linked on the developer's machine are *static libraries*.

When an application statically links a library, the object files from the library become a permanent part of the application, and the size of the application grows. Dynamic libraries are attractive when the libraries probably will be used by more than one application. Then applications take up less disk space and memory because they share the library. Figures 1.11 and 1.12 illustrate this difference.

FIG. 1.11
Static libraries are built into the application when it is developed.

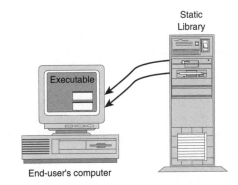

CAUTION

If you deliver an application that relies on a dynamic library, you must make sure that each end user has a copy of the library. For example, Windows applications that dynamically link MFC fail if the end user doesn't have a copy of MFC*xxx*.dll (where *xxx* represents the localized version of the Microsoft Foundation Classes library).

Each SDK comes with a copy of Netscape's documentation in HTML files. After the kit is unpacked, use Navigator to open the doc/index.html page, and then to bookmark it. You use this page as the starting point to the online documentation.

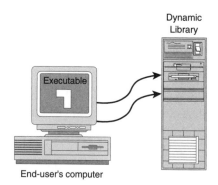

FIG. 1.12
Dynamic libraries are linked in as they are needed, either at run-time or as the application is loaded.

Dynamic Library

Executable

End-user's computer

Windows   Microsoft Windows allows programmers to write code either as applications or as Dynamic Link Libraries (DLLs). The principal difference is that applications have a function named WINMAIN() that serves as their starting point, and DLLs do not. This design makes it easier to build a DLL that can, with few changes, be readily compiled into an executable application—a technique demonstrated in Chapter 4, "Building of a Sample Plug-in." Rather than defining a WINMAIN() function, Windows DLL programmers must explicitly export function names from the DLL to the calling program.

Netscape plug-ins keep information about which MIME types they handle in their VERSION resource. When Navigator starts, it looks in the directory that holds the Navigator executable for a directory labeled "Programs." Inside this directory, it looks for a directory labeled "Plug-ins." It examines the VERSION resources of each file in the plug-ins folder and reads out the MIME type.

Later, when it encounters a Content-type header with a type it does not recognize, it scans the list of MIME types registered by the plug-ins. If it finds a match, it loads that plug-in DLL into memory and calls the exported functions.

OS/2 Warp   Early in the life of the Web, IBM announced their own browser (Web Explorer) for OS/2. In mid-1996 IBM announced that it was adopting Netscape 2.02 as the standard browser for OS/2 (although they have adapted it to include some of the nicer features of Web Explorer, such as speech input). IBM and Netscape also took a different approach to integrating Java. Because OS/2 version 4 already has Java integrated into the operating system, Navigator call's OS/2's Java rather than its own Java interpreter. These differences should be transparent to the user and the developer.

Part

I

Ch

1

N O T E If the end user is working with OS/2 Warp version 3, encourage them to get the adapter kit from IBM so they can use Java with Navigator 2.02. ■

IBM probably will not offer Netscape 3.0 for OS/2. Rather, they are working with Netscape to bring Netscape 4.0 (Galileo) to OS/2 Warp. Look for Netscape 4.0 in OS/2 early in 1997.

ON THE WEB

Unlike the SDKs for the other platforms, the OS/2 Warp Plug-Ins SDK is stored on the IBM site, rather than on the Netscape site. You get it from **http://www.internet.ibm.com /browsers/netscape/warp/**.

If you develop OS/2 Warp plug-ins before Galileo is released for OS/2, remember that you have only Netscape 2.02 features. Most important, this fact means you have no LiveConnect capabilities, so you cannot integrate Java and JavaScript with your plug-in.

Be sure to download the plug-in documentation that comes from the IBM site. This version is almost identical to the version on the Netscape site, but includes the instructions specific to OS/2 Warp development.

T I P The OS/2 Warp version of the plug-ins SDK is compressed with PKZIP. If you use PKUNZIP to decompress the files, make sure that you use the -d switch to maintain the directory structure.

Visual Age C++ relies heavily on makefiles. To specify the MIME media type and file extensions in your plug-in, use the compiler's editor to modify the makefile. The easiest way to do this is to make a working directory in the SDK directory and copy the contents of the npshell directory into your new working directory. (You may want to name the working directory myplugin.) Now open the makefile copied in from npshell and change the RCDATA lines to reflect values appropriate for your plug-in. If, for example, you are writing a plug-in that plays AVI movies, the makefile should include the following:

```
#include "npapi.h"
        RCDATA NP_INFO_ProductVersion { 1,0,0,1}
        RCDATA NP_INFO_MIMEType        {"video/x-msvideo\0"}
```

```
RCDATA NP_INFO_FileExtents    {"avi\0"}
RCDATA NP_INFO_FileOpenName   {"OS/2 Video Plugin\0"}
```

To include multiple MIME types in the plug-in, use a vertical bar to delimit each value in the MIME type. For example, `VALUE "MIMEType", "video/x-msvideo ¦ video/quicktime\0"` specifies that the plug-in will handle both AVU (`x-msvideo`) and `QuickTime` video types.

TIP While you have the makefile open, you may want to specify `OPT=DEBUG` and `CRT=DYNAMIC`. These options give you a debug version with dynamic linking (comparable to a Windows DLL), respectively. The makefile gives the plug-in the ".dll" file extension.

In OS/2, Netscape looks for plug-ins by starting at the directory that holds netscape.exe and looking "down" for a "plugins" subdirectory. You don't have to start the plug-in name with "np" unless you want to for consistency with the Windows versions of the plug-in.

TIP Try to avoid putting non-plug-in files in the OS/2 plugins directory. If you need to provide your plug-in with additional files, put them in a subdirectory inside the plugins directory.

CAUTION

Be sure to check the "Known Problems" section of the OS/2 version of the plug-ins SDK. (In the initial release, it's at **file://*path-to-sdk*/ht4.htm#C3**.) For example, the initial release doesn't support printing, and doesn't properly handle two instances of the same data. Most of these problems should be eliminated when IBM and Netscape release Navigator 4.0 for OS/2 Warp, expected in early 1997.

Macintosh   Applications in the Macintosh operating system are based on resources. Each Macintosh application has two CODE resources. (It may have more, but it must have these two.) CODE resource 1 is known as the "main segment." This segment is loaded when the application starts, and isn't unloaded until the application exists. (CODE resource 0 is used for housekeeping and is not a concern here.)

Not all code is kept in CODE resources. The Mac has a lot of little code resources tucked into resources like CDEFs (Control Definition Functions, for drawing controls) and MDEFs (Menu Definition Functions, for drawing menus). It switches from one printer to another by switching PDEFs (Printer Drivers) at run-time.

When Navigator is launched on the Macintosh, it looks for the folder that contains the Navigator executable—then it looks for a subfolder named Plug-ins. Finally, it searches each file in the Plug-ins folder for a resource named NSPL with an ID of 128. If it finds this combination, it knows that file contains a plug-in. Navigator then looks for a string resource (STR#) with ID 128. Macintosh STR# resources contain lists of strings. STR# 128 contains the MIME types that this plug-in recognizes.

Later, when Navigator encounters a stream from a server, it compares Content-type headers with the MIME types it read from the plug-ins. If it finds a match, it loads the resources of this plug-in into memory and calls functions in the plug-in.

UNIX   Most versions of UNIX allow a program to build what are named .so libraries—shared object files that function like Windows DLLs. The instructions for building a shared object library vary slightly between UNIX versions. Significantly, AIX (IBM's version of UNIX) supports shared object libraries by using the same export mechanism as Windows. This process is sufficiently different that Netscape doesn't yet support plug-ins on its AIX version of Navigator.

UNIX uses a mechanism similar to the mechanism described for Windows and Macintosh. It looks through the shared objects in the Plug-ins directory for librar-ies that advertise Netscape plug-in functions. When UNIX finds these libraries, it looks up the MIME types they handle, and then links and loads the correct plug-in at run-time.

From Here...

From the beginning, Netscape Navigator has supported helper applications that allow users to access data types other than the ones built into Navigator. The mechanism for describing these data types is the MIME-compliant media type.

Starting with Navigator 2.0, Netscape supports inline plug-ins, which allow pro-grammers to write native code to read data and to present it inside the Netscape window.

With Navigator 3.0, Netscape introduces LiveConnect, which integrates plug-ins, JavaScript, and Java. Now all of the programming techniques for the client can be brought together into an integrated solution.

Starting with Navigator 4.0, Netscape will support automated downloading and installation of plug-ins, making the use of plug-ins even more transparent to the end user.

The programmer who wants to field a complete plug-in solution needs to build his or her plug-in on all major platforms. This book presents solutions for the OS/2 Warp, Macintosh, and UNIX machines, while emphasizing Windows 95 and the Microsoft Visual C++ compiler as an appropriate and readily available learning environment.

- Because Navigator plug-ins must be written in C++, Chapter 2, "A C++ Primer," lays a foundation of object-oriented methods, C++ syntax, and language-specific topics such as templates and the Standard Template Library (STL).

- Chapter 3, "Integrating Plug-Ins into Web Site Design," shows how plug-ins fit into the "grand scheme" of Web design, which includes client- and server-side JavaScript, Java, CGI scripts, and the integrating technology of LiveConnect.

- Chapter 18, "Plug-Ins as a Programming Resource," returns to the subject of LiveConnect and describes the LiveConnect methods in detail.

- Chapter 19, "Installing the Plug-In," covers user-level plug-in issues, including installation.

CHAPTER 2

A C++ Primer

The Web development community is populated by C programmers, Perl programmers, and Visual Basic programmers, as well as Java, JavaScript, and even UNIX shell programmers. When you choose to write a Netscape Navigator plug-in, you become a C++ programmer.

When it was released, object-oriented programming was hailed as the next great step forward, but it has a reputation for a learning curve that runs six to twelve months. C++ is an object-oriented version of C—and C is a language with its own reputation for a steep learning curve.

Fortunately, many of the object-oriented aspects of a plug-in are already built into the shell that Netscape provides. By understanding how a C++ program is put together, a programmer with experience in another language can begin to write plug-ins. ■

About classes and instances

The ability to view the problem as a set of classes and instances of those classes is the foundation of object-oriented programming.

How inheritance works

Object-oriented applications can be much smaller and simpler by inheriting from class libraries.

The difference between methods and data members

Learn how to use access methods to protect variables from their programmer.

Some recommendations on design

Learn some rules of thumb about when to use inclusion versus inheritance, and how to design for easy debug.

How to protect your code against run-time errors

Use C++'s exception-handling mechanisms.

Understanding Classes and Instances

Object-oriented analysis, design, and programming (collectively known as the *object-oriented methods*) are based on the observation that the real world is made of classes of objects, and that each class has certain things (known as *functions*) that it allows people to do to it. Each class also has attributes (data) that may remain relatively constant and can be changed by exercising functions.

For example, the class of chairs can be sat on. Chairs also have an associated color. The color of some chairs, such as wooden chairs, can be changed by paint. These chairs have a function, `paint()`, that changes their color. Other kinds of chairs—upholstered chairs—can have their color changed only by running the function, `reupholster()`.

One big advantage of thinking about software in terms of objects is that the people who pay for software think in terms of objects. If you write a banking application, it is useful to be able to talk to the banker about objects like ATM machines, checks, and loans, rather than describing the "DebitAccount Module."

In this discussion (and in most of the object-oriented literature), a set of related objects is known as a class. As a programmer, when you make a new instance of a class, you call it *instantiation*. Given a `chair` class, you can make a whole roomful of chairs by repeatedly calling the class constructor, instantiating chair after chair.

Inheritance

Real-world objects are related by "a-kind-of" relationships. A wooden chair is "a-kind-of" chair. So is an "upholsteredChair." Figure 2.1 illustrates these "a-kind-of" relationships among chairs. "A-kind-of" relationships are sometimes abbreviated to AKO-relationships or are called IS-A relationships.

FIG. 2.1
An inheritance hierarchy shows how each class is related to others by "a-kind-of" relationships.

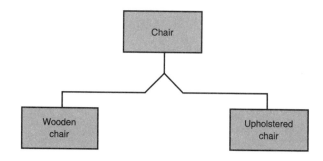

Polymorphism

Developers also noted that related classes tend to allow the same kinds of functions. Figure 2.2 shows an inheritance hierarchy of dancers. Each dancer understands the function dance(), although the ballerina executes that function in a way that the line dancer may scarcely recognize.

FIG. 2.2
Related classes have similar functions, although they may use them in different ways.

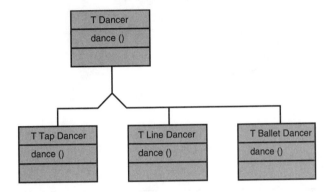

This capability to call a function on an instance without worrying about exactly how the instance executes the function is referred to as *polymorphism*. A program could conceivably fill a room with dancers of all kinds, and then call the function dance() on each dancer. The calling program doesn't have to know the difference between tap and soft-shoe—the dancers know.

Here's a software example of polymorphism. Suppose that a software engineer is designing a computerized telephone switching system. The system will include many kinds of telephone lines: various types of digital line (including the Integrated Services Digital Network, or ISDN) as well as analog lines. When a request arrives to ring a number, however, the software can send a Ring() message to any line, with confidence that the software implementing this line will handle Ring() in the appropriate manner.

Classes in C++

Modern software engineering practice suggests that it's a good idea to separate the specification of a piece of software from its implementation. This practice allows the designer to change his or her mind about implementation without affecting calling code—only the specification needs to remain stable.

C and C++ programs usually are divided across two files—header files, with an .h file extension, and source files, which often have a .cpp file extension in C++. It is customary to keep the class specification in a header file and the implementation in the source file.

In the following example shows the header of a class that stores a queue of characters. The file name might be charQueue.h.

```
class charQueue
{
    public:
            charQueue();
            ~charQueue();
            void add(char c);
            char remove();

    class QueueEmpty
            {
            };
};
```

 TIP When you write class definitions, you can easily forget the trailing semicolon after the final curly brace. To avoid this mistake, take advantage of any automated layout features in your development environment. Microsoft's Visual C++, for example, has ClassWizard and Borland's C++ has ClassExpert; both of these features lay out templates for classes.

This specification says that there are four publicly available functions. (Functions that are members of a class are also known as *methods*.) Two of these functions have special names.

- charQueue() is the class constructor. Constructors have the same name as the class, and they allocate the memory for the new instance, perform an initialization called for by their implementation, and return a pointer to the new instance.

- ~charQueue(), the class destructor, is called when an instance is deleted or goes out of scope. Destructors should free any dynamic memory allocated by the instance. Destructors always have the same name as the class, preceded with a tilde (~).

- add() adds the character passed as a parameter to the queue. It does not return anything. If it cannot add the character, it raises an exception (described later in this chapter).

- remove() takes a character from the queue and returns it to the calling function.

Besides these public functions, the class also declared an additional class, used during exception processing (see "Exception Handling" later in this chapter).

The class also has some private or protected components needed for the implementation. We add these components later—they aren't important to the user of the class.

On the CD

To use charQueue, a calling function makes a new instance by calling the C++ new operator with the class constructor. Then the user can add and remove characters. Finally, the user would delete the instance. This sequence (in the /source/chap02 directory on the companion CD-ROM) is shown in Listing 2.1.

Listing 2.1 *main.cpp*—Demo of *charQueue*

```
#include <iostream.h>
#include <stdlib.h>
#include "charQueue.h"
#include "main.h"
// defines kMaxBufferSize to be a constant short integer of size 81

void main()
{
    charQueue* theQueue;
    try
    {
      theQueue = new charQueue();
      theQueue->add('f');
      theQueue->add('o');
      theQueue->add('o');
    }
    catch (...)
    {
      cout << "Internal error: Could not put characters into the
    ➥queue." << endl;
      exit(0);
    }

    // now lets copy the contents of the queue into an array
    char buffer[kMaxBufferSize];
```

continues

Listing 2.1 Continued

```
      short i=0; // an index into buffer
      try
      {
        for (i=0; i < kMaxBufferSize; i++) // a C++ idiom for "do forever"
        {
          // when queue is empty, remove throws a queueEmpty exception
          buffer[i] = theQueue->remove();
        }
        throw BufferFullException();
      }
      catch (charQueue::BufferFullException )
      {
        cout << "Internal error: buffer full." << endl;
        exit(0);
      }
      catch (charQueue::QueueEmpty )
      {
        cout << "Buffer contains " << buffer << endl;
      }
      catch (...)
      {
        cout << "Internal error while reading character queue." << endl;
        exit(0);
      }
      delete theQueue;
    }
```

C++ Main   Like C programs, C++ programs have a top-level calling routine known as main(). Like C, C++ main routines can take parameters. Unlike C, when the parameter list is empty, it is customary to put nothing between the parentheses and not to specifically put void there.

Also like C programs, C++ files usually start by including some header files. The compiler looks for files whose names are bounded by angle brackets (<, >) in the system include directories. The compiler looks for files whose names are bounded by quotes ("") in the current directory.

The main.h file shown in Listing 2.2 is used to declare a single constant. const in C++ provides a type-safe way to declare constants and is preferred in favor of old-style C macros. The main header file also holds an exception class definition needed by main. You can find main.h on the companion CD-ROM in the /source/chap02 directory.

Listing 2.2 *main.h*—The *main* Specification

```
#ifndef MAIN_H
#define MAIN_H
const short kMaxBufferSize = 81;

class BufferFullException
{
};

#endif
```

The first line in `main.cpp`, `charQueue* theQueue;` declares a pointer to a `charQueue`. The pointer is named `theQueue`. In C it's customary to put the asterisk next to the variable. This practice also is common in C++ but it's often clearer to have the asterisk follow the type name so that the line can be read "declare a `charQueue` pointer named `theQueue`."

Exception Handling   Many programs are written as a series of calls to the operating system libraries. Typically, these calls either return data or an error code if there is a problem. This design means that the programmer has two choices—either to check the result of every call for an error (which takes time and clutters up the code) or to check the only errors that "can really occur." Of course, the second option leaves the program open to unexpected defects.

With the newest versions of C++, the programmer has a third choice: write the code in a straightforward way—one call after the next—but `catch` errors (known as *exceptions*) that are thrown by the code.

The general syntax of the C++ exception-handling mechanism is as follows:

```
try
{
  // do something in here
  // throw an exception if there is a problem
}
catch (which exception to catch)
{
  // handle exceptions out here
}
```

There are two `try...catch` sequences in this code. The first sequence handles exceptions that occur when setting up the queue and filling it. The second sequence handles exceptions that occur while reading from the queue—the most common exception should be "Queue Empty."

The expression `catch (...)` is used to denote code that catches any exception not already caught.

TIP Make your code less likely to cause a run-time failure by ensuring that all code is protected by a `catch (...)` clause. In this way, unexpected exceptions can be handled in the `catch (...)` clause rather than crashing the program.

Note, too, that this class `charQueue` has its own exception classes. Building exception classes for every class that can throw exceptions is a good idea.

TIP Most class libraries use an exception hierarchy. If you use Microsoft Foundation Classes, consider deriving your exceptions from `CException`.

CAUTION

Don't confuse the C++ exception-handling described here with the so-called "C exceptions," "MFC exceptions," and "structured exceptions" offered by early versions of the MFC. These older styles were introduced before exception-handling was part of the C++ language. New code should use the C++ style shown in this chapter.

Calling a Constructor   Recall that a constructor allocates memory, performs any initialization called for in the implementation code, and returns a pointer to the new instance. The line `theQueue = new charQueue();` calls the `charQueue` class constructor and puts the address of the new instance into the pointer variable `theQueue`.

Calling a Member Function   C++ gives the programmer two ways to call a member function. When you have a pointer to an instance (such as `charQueue`), use the arrow notation (for example, `charQueue->add('f');`). If you have the instance itself (a dereferenced pointer), use dot notation: `theActualQueue.add('f');`.

Recall that `add()` return no value. (It is of type `void`.) The `remove()` function call returns a char, so the following assignment calls the member function and puts the resulting character into the i[sup]th slot in the `buffer` array:

```
buffer[i] = theQueue->remove();
```

I/O Through *iostreams* Note that the example includes <iostream.h>. This class defines the C++ bindings to standard input, standard output, and standard error (cin, cout, and cerr) as well as numerous other stream-oriented I/O classes and methods. Streams are useful when you are writing to disk files and other devices— in the context of plug-ins, the programmer generally uses native graphical user interface (GUI) objects and methods to interact with the user.

Introduction to Members and Methods

If you save the code fragment from charQueue.h as charQueue.h and try to build the application, you find that it fails during the link step because it cannot find any implementation of the charQueue methods. To turn this code into a runnable program, you need to make three changes:

- Develop an implementation and put it into a file named charQueue.cpp

- Add private members to the class specification to support the implementation

- Add an additional class, private to charQueue, to support the implementation

The source code that implements charQueue.cpp is in Listing 2.3.

Listing 2.3   *charQueue.cpp*—One Way to Implement the Class

```
#include "charQueue.h"
#include <assert.h>

charQueue::listNode* charQueue::listNode::kNull = (listNode*) 0;

charQueue:: charQueue()
{
    fHead = fTail = listNode::kNull;
}
charQueue::~charQueue()
{
    if (listNode::kNull != fTail)
    {
        listNode* aPointerFromTail = fTail;
        while (listNode::kNull != aPointerFromTail->fNext)
        {
            aPointerFromTail = aPointerFromTail->fNext;
            assert (listNode::kNull != aPointerFromTail->fPrevious);
            delete aPointerFromTail->fPrevious;
```

continues

Listing 2.3 Continued

```
            }
            assert (listNode::kNull != aPointerFromTail);
            delete aPointerFromTail;
            fTail = fHead = listNode::kNull;
        }
}
void charQueue::add(char aChar)
{
    if (listNode::kNull == fTail)
    {
        fTail = new listNode();
        fTail->fChar = aChar;
        fHead = fTail;
    }
    else
    {
        listNode* aPointerFromHead = fHead;
        while (listNode::kNull != aPointerFromHead->fPrevious)
        {
            aPointerFromHead = aPointerFromHead->fPrevious;
        }
        aPointerFromHead->fPrevious = new listNode();
        aPointerFromHead->fPrevious->fChar = aChar;
        aPointerFromHead->fPrevious->fNext = aPointerFromHead;
        fTail = aPointerFromHead;
    }
}


char charQueue::remove()
{
    char theResult;
    if (listNode::kNull != fHead)
    {
        theResult = fHead->fChar;
        listNode* thePreviousNode = fHead->fPrevious;
        if (listNode::kNull != thePreviousNode)
            thePreviousNode->fNext = listNode::kNull;
        else
            fTail = listNode::kNull;
        delete fHead;
        fHead = thePreviousNode;
    }
    else
    {
        throw QueueEmpty();
    }
    return theResult;
```

```
}

charQueue::listNode::listNode()
{
     fPrevious = fNext = kNull;
}
```

Skip over the declaration of kNull for a moment and examine the implementation of each of the four public functions. This file reveals that charQueue is implemented as a double-linked list built from dynamic memory. The constructor initializes a head and tail pointer to null. The destructor starts from the tail and works its way to the head, deleting list nodes as it goes.

The add() method builds a new list node and clips it into the growing list. Figure 2.3 shows the list as it grows from no nodes to one, two, and three nodes.

FIG. 2.3
charQueue::add()
attaches list nodes to
the linked list.

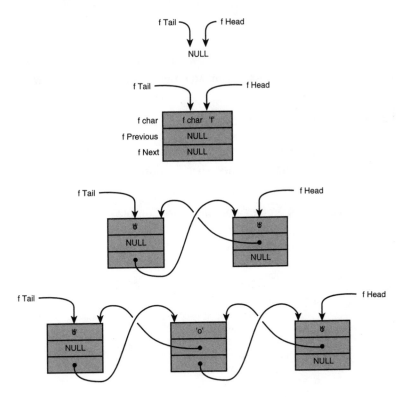

The remove() method goes to the head of the queue and reads out the character, then it deletes the head node and points the head at the next node in the queue. Figure 2.4 shows the sequence as nodes are removed from the list.

FIG. 2.4
charQueue::
remove() takes
nodes off the list
from the head.

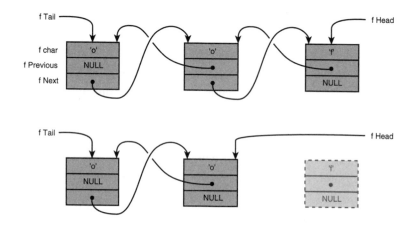

The remove method can throw one kind of exception. If a user of the class attempts to remove a character from an empty queue, remove throws QueueEmpty.

Data Members and Access Methods

Classes have two kinds of members: functions (known as *methods*) and data. Listing 2.4 shows the finished specification of the charQueue class.

Listing 2.4   *charQueue.h*—The Complete *charQueue* Class Specification

```
#ifndef CHARQUEUE_H
#define CHARQUEUE_H

class charQueue
{
    public:
        charQueue();
        ~charQueue();
        void add(char aChar);
        char remove();

    class QueueEmpty
        {
        };
```

```
      private:
            class listNode
            {
                  friend class charQueue;
                  static listNode* kNull;
                  public:
                        listNode();
                        char fChar;
                        listNode* fPrevious;
                        listNode* fNext;
            };
            listNode* fHead;
            listNode* fTail;

};
#endif
```

Access Restrictions and Friends   The complete specification has two major sections—public and private. The language allows each member to be specified as public, protected, or private. *Public members* can be accessed by any other class or by stand-alone functions such as main. Public members represent the class's interface to the outside world.

Protected members are not available to outsiders, but they are accessible from descendants of the class. *Private members* are accessible only by the class itself.

There is one exception to this rule. If a class or a class method is declared to be a friend, this class or method can access private and protected members just as though they were public. This approach is useful when you need the protection of private or protected members, but want to "poke a hole" in the security shield to give a small number of outsiders access.

Note that this specification includes an embedded class, listNode. Because listNode is used only by charQueue, the entire class definition was embedded as a private member, and charQueue is a friend to listNode. This statement means that listNode is not known outside of charQueue, and that charQueue can only get at listNode's internals because of its status as a friend.

Access Methods   Unless the class is very simple, it is common practice to make data members inaccessible from the outside world and force outsiders to use *access methods*. For example, listNode has three public data members: fChar, fPrevious, and fNext. The class could have been specified with these members private and access methods such as Char(), SetChar(), and so on.

Class Variables   Data members are associated with each instance. If you make three different list nodes, each can have a different character in fChar. For this reason, data members are often referred to as *instance variables*—one set of variables is available for each instance.

Sometimes it is necessary to define *class variables*. There is one set of class variables for each class. To specify that a variable is a class variable, declare it to be static. kNull is declared to be a class variable and is initialized at the top of charQueue.cpp.

On Constructors and Destructors   If the programmer does nothing but define a class, the compiler handles building constructors and destructors. The *default constructor* takes no parameters—it builds an instance of the class and initializes the data members with default values.

You often want a version of the constructor that takes parameters so that you can initialize the instance with specific values. If you pass an object as the parameter to a constructor, you can build a constructor that uses the value of the parameter as the basis for the new instance.

A special type of constructor, known as the *copy constructor*, takes an instance of the class as a parameter. Therefore, the programmer can write the following:

```
class X
{
  X();
  X(const X& x);
  X(const Y& y);
  .
  .
  .
}
```

> **NOTE** The notation const means that the programmer intends that the specified item not be changed throughout the scope of the const. In the context of a function call, X(const X& x); means that the programmer intends to pass a reference to an instance of class X to the constructor and promises not to use this reference to change the data members of x. The compiler enforces the programmer's promise, helping the programmer make sure that whatever he or she does to that reference later doesn't inadvertently change the contents of the const object. ■

The first constructor shown is the default constructor, which can be used to make static or dynamic instances of the class. The second constructor takes an instance of class X and makes a new instance with the same values as the original. The third constructor makes a new instance of X based on the values in an instance of class Y. These constructors allow the programmer to write code like the following example:

```
main()
{
   X theX; // invoke the default constructor.
   Y theY; // the default constructor of another class
   X anX = theY; // run the Y-to-X constructor
   X anotherX = theX; // run the copy constructor
}
```

If the programmer doesn't provide an implementation of the copy constructor, the compiler generates one. Sometimes this version is acceptable—sometimes it can lead to disaster. Consider the situation in Figure 2.5.

The compiler's "shallow copy" constructor reuses the same dynamic data from the original. Here's how such a constructor behaves:

```
X theX("Object 1");
X anotherX = theX;
anotherX.SetName("Object 2");
cout << theX.Name() << endl;
```

This code fragment outputs "Object 2"—probably not what the programmer intended. The problem is that the "shallow copy" copied the pointer to the string. When the copy changed the string, the name of the original also changed.

Figure 2.6 illustrates what the programmer probably intended.

FIG. 2.5
Using a compiler-generated "shallow copy" on a class with dynamic data members.

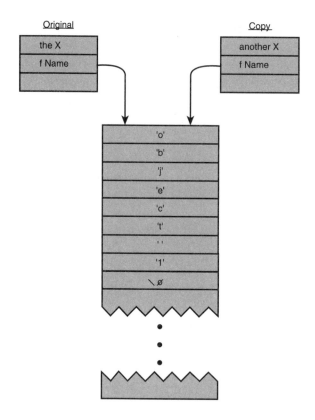

FIG. 2.6
Using "deep copy" on a class with dynamic data members.

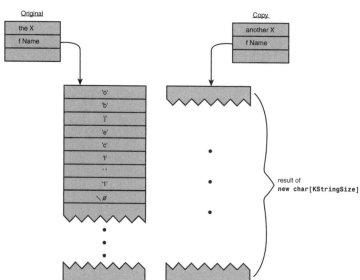

To implement "deep copy," the programmer should write a copy constructor that makes new dynamic data members:

```
X::X(const X& x)
{
  fName = new char[kStringSize];
  strcpy(fName, x.Name());
}
```

TIP Whenever you define a new class, consider whether you need to define your own copy constructor. If the class has data members that are pointers or references, the answer is "Yes"—define your own "deep copy" constructor.

NOTE If you're new to C++, you may be surprised to see more than one version of a function with the same name. For example, all of the constructors of class X are named X—they differ only in their parameters.

This technique is known as *overloading*. C++ allows you to have as many versions of a function as you like—as long as their *signature* is different. The signature includes all of the parameters but *not* the function's return type. Therefore, you can have

```
int X::foo ();
int X::foo (int);
char X::foo(char);
```

but you cannot have

```
char X::foo(int);
```

because int X::foo (int); and char X::foo(int) have the same signature. ■

If you allocate memory in the constructor or during the life of the instance, you should deallocate this memory explicitly in the destructor. For example, in class X used in the preceding paragraphs, the constructors make a new array of chars on the heap. The constructor should read as follows:

```
X::~X
{
  delete fName;
}
```

Don't Forget the Operators Whenever you define a copy constructor, you also nearly always need an assignment operator. The copy constructor takes care of code like the following:

```
X anotherX = theX;
```

It is not invoked, however, when you write the following:

```
X anotherX;
anotherX = theX;
```

In this case, the first line runs the default constructor. The second copy assigns the values from theX to the existing instance anotherX.

TIP After you build an assignment operator, building a copy constructor is easy, so its usually a good idea to write the assignment operator first, and then define the copy constructor in terms of the assignment operator.

The assignment operator looks just like the preceding copy constructor except that it first tests to make sure that the user is not assigning an object to itself:

```
X& X::operator=(const X& rhs)
{
   if (this == &rhs)
     return *this;
   // copy all the members in an appropriate way
   strcpy(fName, rhs.fName);
}
```

Operators are usually called by using their symbol (for example, +, ++, =). Here the author takes the rather unusual but quite reliable approach of calling the assignment operator function directly as the copy constructor:

```
X::X (const X& rhs)
{
this->operator=(rhs);
}
```

NOTE The copy constructor could have been implemented as follows:

```
X::X(const X& rhs)
{
  *this = rhs;
}
```

This implementation implicitly calls the copy constructor. Paul Kimmel points out in Chapter 17 of his book, *Special Edition Using Borland C++ 5* (Que, 1996), that the implicit call is too vague and may be error-prone. Kimmel's book is an excellent reference on modern C++, whether you are using Borland C++ 5 or some other compiler. ▪

Templates

One problem with the `charQueue.cpp` shown previously is that it's limited to characters. C++ is regarded as a type-safe language (although a programmer can easily overcome type-checking with typecasting). Suppose that you define a class `TString`. To provide a queue for strings based on class `charQueue` you would have to reimplement `charQueue` as `stringQueue`.

If you then wanted a queue of `Tcustomers`, you would need yet another queue class. Building new utility classes to deal with each new class quickly becomes tiresome, and you find yourself asking if you can somehow let the computer do the work.

In C++ the answer is "Yes." C++ allows the programmer to build templates that defer the type until compile time. Templates are based on the concept of parameterized types, which was added to C++ after the rest of the language had been developed.

Most popular implementations of C++ started using templates in 1992 or 1993, so some books on the subject call parameterized types an "advanced topic." They are not particularly "advanced" or complex, however—in fact, they are essential for many kinds of real-world applications.

Here's the `remove` method from `charQueue`, reworked so that it accepts the type as a parameter. Note that the data member `fchar` was renamed `fdata` to better reflect its new role.

```
template <class T>
<T> charQueue::remove()
{
    T theResult;
    if (listNode::kNull != fHead)
    {
        theResult = fHead->fdata;
        listNode* thePreviousNode = fHead->fPrevious;
        if (listNode::kNull != thePreviousNode)
            thePreviousNode->fNext = listNode::kNull;
        else
            fTail = listNode::kNull;
        delete fHead;
        fHead = thePreviousNode;
    }
    else
    {
        throw QueueEmpty();
```

```
        }
        return theResult;
    }
```

Listing 2.5 shows how to declare a parameterized class.

Listing 2.5   charQueue.H—The Parameterized *Queue* Class Specification

```
#ifndef QUEUE_H
#define QUEUE_H

class Queue
{
    public:
        Queue();
        ~Queue();
        void add(T theData);
        T remove();

    class QueueEmpty
        {
        };

    private:
        class listNode
        {
            friend class Queue;
            static listNode* kNull;
            public:
                listNode();
                T fData;
                listNode* fPrevious;
                listNode* fNext;
        };
        listNode* fHead;
        listNode* fTail;
};
#endif
```

To instantiate a template class, just pass the type to the template:

```
theCharQueue = new Queue<char>();

theStringQueue = new Queue<TString>();

theCustomerQueue = new Queue<TCustomer>();
```

The CD-ROM has a complete parameterized implementation of the queue class in the `Queue.h`, `Queue.cpp`, and `QMain.cpp` files.

T I P Templates can be used for other parameters besides type. For example, if you want to build a static vector such as `buffer` from `main.cpp`, you could specify its size as a parameter.

> **CAUTION**
>
> Some C++ compilers have a difficult time deriving new classes from template classes. The classic example is a stack class derived from a vector class. Microsoft Visual C++ 4.0 does *not* have this problem; Borland C++ 5 does. The CD-ROM includes a program you can use to test your compiler (at /source/chap02/tmpinst/). This code also shows a fix that works in the Borland compiler.
>
> For more information about this problem and about the fix, see Chapter 19, "Using Template Classes," of *Special Edition Using Borland C++ 5* (Que, 1996).

Container Classes and the STL

Container classes are classes like the queue from the example, which has instances of other classes or of native data types (like char). The need for well-written container classes comes up over and over in all kinds of programs, and the parameterized types of C++ allow reusable libraries of template classes.

Most C++ compilers now come with the Standard Template Library (STL), which is just such a library of template classes. Figure 2.7 illustrates the five types of components in the STL.

T I P Plug-ins are likely to be implemented across more than one platform, so you can lower overall costs and implementation time by building portable code. If you have STL on all of your development platforms, use it and avoid writing your own container classes.

FIG. 2.7
The STL uses
container classes and
the classes that
manipulate them.

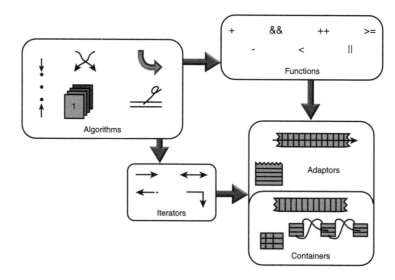

Containers   STL offers both *sequence containers* and *associative containers*.
Sequence containers are similar to the conventional array available in C, C++, and
most other languages. In a sequence class, the order in which data is stored
directly reflects the order in which it was added to the class. The sequence
containers are as follows:

■ Vectors

■ Deques

■ Lists

Table 2.1 shows how these classes differ from each other.

Table 2.1   Choose an STL Sequence Class Based on Program Needs

Class	Can grow at run-time	Random access
Vector	Yes, from one end	Yes
Deque	Yes, from both ends	Yes
List	Yes, from both ends	No

Each class is tuned for a particular type of performance. If your program does not need random access, for example, you may get a performance boost by using the list rather than the deque (pronounced "deck").

Associative containers store data based on some attribute of the data, known as a *key*. Using a key, the associative container class returns the data. Many associative classes are implemented by using a binary tree or a hash table, which allow data to be looked up faster in an associative class than in a sequence class.

The down side? Associative classes take up more space because they must hold the data structure that holds their keys and the pointers to the data.

Associative classes allow fast access, but require more memory than sequence classes. Table 2.2 summarizes the features of the various associative container classes.

Table 2.2 Associative Classes

Class	Key == Data	Allows Duplicate Keys
Set	Yes	No
Multiset	Yes	Yes
Map	No	Yes
Multimap	No	Yes

A set is a good class to use if you are implementing a spell-checker dictionary. The data *is* the key. When the program retrieves the word from the set, there's nothing else to look up.

On the other hand, an in-memory database might be implemented by using a map. The map *uses* the key to fetch the data, but the data includes information not found in the key. A customer record can contain an address, buying history, and other information. The customer ID can serve as the key.

Adapters   Occasionally, the nature of a problem needs a special kind of container. STL provides three adapters that use one of the existing sequence container classes to implement a container with special functions. Table 2.3 shows which sequence containers can be used as the basis for each adapter.

Part
I

Ch
2

Table 2.3 When Choosing an Adapter Class, Select an Underlying Sequence Container Class			
Adapter Class	**Vector**	**Deque**	**List**
Stack	✔	✔	✔
Queue	✔	✔	
Priority Queue	✔	✔	

There also are adapters for the iterator classes, described at the end of the following section, and function objects, described at the end of the section on function objects.

Iterators   To apply an algorithm to a data collection, the STL provides classes that iterate over the containers, retrieving one object at a time. These classes are referred to as *iterators*. STL defines five types of iterators.

- Input
- Output
- Forward
- Bidirectional
- Random Access

Input iterators use a simple model of the data. Consider the container as a tape, with data stored in cells along the length of the tape. The tape can only move in one direction. As it moves, the data in the cell under the read-head is read out. Figure 2.8 illustrates this model.

FIG. 2.8
An input operator is
read-only and
unidirectional.

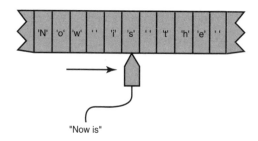

An output operator uses the same model but is write-only.

Forward iterators are similar to input and output iterators, but objects may be dereferenced more than once. Bidirectional iterators further extend the model, allowing the "tape" to move both forward and backward.

The most powerful iterators are random access iterators. They can do everything a bi-directional iterator can do. They also support the [ ] operator, which allows random access to any element in the container.

STL defines adapters for the iterator classes—classes that extend the functionality and are based on one of the five iterators described in this section. There are three iterator adapters:

- Reverse iterators
- Insert iterators
- Raw Storage iterators

Reverse iterators are just like forward iterators, but they move backward through the container. Insert iterators are specialized output operators. Continuing the tape analogy, insert operators push new cells into the middle of the tape.

The raw storage iterator is an output iterator that writes to uninitialized memory. Typically, a programmer calls new to get a chunk of raw memory, and then fills it with the raw storage iterator.

All of these iterators form a hierarchy, as shown in Figure 2.9. If an algorithm calls for, say, an input iterator, any of the "higher" iterators (that is, forward, bidirectional, or random access) work.

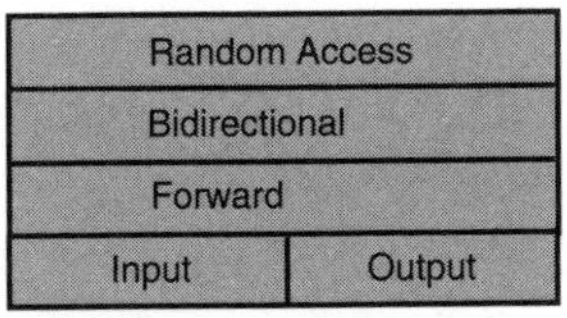

FIG. 2.9
STL iterators form a hierarchy—any iterator can be substituted for one below it in the hierarchy.

Random Access	
Bidirectional	
Forward	
Input	Output

> **CAUTION**
>
> Not all containers support all iterators. Random access iterators, for example, are defined on vectors but not on deques.

Function Objects   C++ has a wealth of knowledge about native types, but this information is missing when algorithms are applied to user-defined classes. Suppose that the programmer is applying the sort algorithm to a list of TCustomer objects. There is no "natural" way to order customers. The programmer must supply a function object that can be invoked to tell the sort algorithm how to compare two different TCustomers.

STL's built-in function objects are available in three categories: arithmetic, comparison, and logical. The arithmetic operators include the following:

- plus
- minus
- times
- divides
- modulus
- negate

The built-in comparison function objects are as follows:

- equal_to
- not_equal_to
- greater
- less
- greater_equal
- less_equal

The logical function objects are shown in the following list:

- logical_and
- logical_or
- logical_not

STL also provides adapters for function objects. These adapters include negators, binders, and adapters (for pointers to functions).

Algorithms   STL has over 100 built-in algorithms that can be applied to data in the containers through iterators. These algorithms are divided into four categories:

Part
I
Ch
2

- Non-mutating sequence operations—Operations that work on the sequence container classes vector, deque, and list, and that do not change the contents of the container. Examples include `find`, `count`, `equal`, and `search`.

- Mutating sequence operations—Operations that work on sequence container classes and *do* change their contents. Examples include `copy`, `swap`, `replace`, and `partition`.

- Sorting and related operations—Operations that include `sort`, `binary_search`, `merge`, and `lexicographical_compare`.

- Generalized numeric operations—Operations that include `accumulate`, `inner_product`, `partial_sum`, and `adjacent_difference`.

Putting It All Together—the *charQueue* Example in STL   Listing 2.6 (on the CD-ROM in the /source/chap02directory) shows the same function as `main.cpp` but with STL.

Listing 2.6   *stlMain.cpp*—Using STL Lists, Iterators, and the Copy Algorithm

```
#define NOMINMAX
#include <iostream.h>
#include <algo.h>
#include <list.h>
#include <iterator.h>

typedef std::list<char> charQueue;
int main()
{
    // make and populate the queue
    charQueue* theQueue = new charQueue();
    theQueue->push_back('f');
    theQueue->push_back('o');
    theQueue->push_back('o');

    //associate an iterator with cout
    std::ostream_iterator<char> theOutStream(cout);
```

continues

Listing 2.6 Continued

```
    //finally, copy out the list to stdout using iterators and the copy
    algorithm.
    std::copy (theQueue->begin(), theQueue->end(), theOutStream);
    cout << endl;
    delete theQueue;

    return 0;
}
```

Note that Listing 2.6 proceeds in three steps. First, a list (with parameterized type char) is instantiated and populated. You could easily have used a deque or vector for this same purpose.

Next, a special output iterator called the ostream_iterator was set up, also parameterized for char.

Finally, copy was invoked. Copy expects input iterators as its first two parameters—these parameters define where in the container the copying begins and ends. The third parameter is an output iterator—ostream_iterator qualifies, so the contents of the list are written directly to cout.

T I P

STL is shipped with Microsoft's Visual C++ but without technical support. Some of the names conflict with names in Microsoft Foundation Classes. To use STL and MFC in the same program, put STL in a separate namespace—by convention, std.

If you follow Microsoft's instructions, wrap the declarations of the STL headers in a namespace declaration. If you use the FTP version, just include the STL files in the usual way. Teris has already built the namespace declaration (std) into the include files themselves.

ON THE WEB

Microsoft includes directions on how to modify the STL source so that it can be used with MFC, but a version online was modified even more thoroughly. See **ftp://ftp.rahul.net/ pub/teris/readme.stl** and **ftp://ftp.rahul.net/pub/teris/stl.zip**.

You also can get mstring.h from this site—mstring is a portable string class that you can use until strings are added to the standard library.

Design Issues

When you are designing real-world classes, the following several issues become apparent:

- Some classes have parents that are "abstract." For example, there are thousands of different models of airplanes, each of which can have instances, but there is no such thing as a "generic transport aircraft" or a "generic fighter."

- Sometimes, it's useful to copy the behavior of a class into a new class without copying any of the internal details.

- Classes can be related by other links besides "a-kind-of." One of the most common is "is-part-of."

Virtual Methods and Abstract Classes

Suppose that a programmer is writing code for a motor controller. The motor controller uses two types of position sensors, which are read in completely different ways. (In this example, these two types of sensors are *resolvers* and *encoders*.)

The programmer may decide that the TPositionSensor class must have a Read() method but to leave its implementation up to the derived classes. In C++, the programmer shows that a derived class can override a method by using the keyword virtual. A method is specified to have no implementation—the C++ term is *pure virtual*— by putting = 0 after the function declaration. Therefore,

```
class TPositionSensor
{
.
.
.
  virtual TPosition Read() = 0;
.
.
.
}
```

tells the compiler to require all classes derived from TPositionSensor to define Read(). Because the compiler can never instantiate the TPositionSensor class (what would it do when someone called Read()?) TPositionSensor becomes an *abstract class*. (Classes that *can* be instantiated are called *concrete classes*.)

By convention, abstract classes get the word "abstract" added to their name, so `TPositionSensor` becomes `TAbstractPositionSensor`. The finished class hierarchy is shown in Figure 2.10.

FIG. 2.10

`TAbstract Position Sensor` is the abstract base class for the TResolver and Tencoder classes.

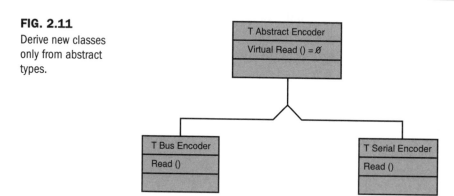

 T I P It's a good idea to derive new classes only from abstract classes. Therefore, if the designer introduced a new kind of encoder (such as a serial encoder), he or she might change the inheritance hierarchy to the one shown in Figure 2.11 rather than the one shown in Figure 2.12.

FIG. 2.11

Derive new classes only from abstract types.

FIG. 2.12
Deriving from concrete types is permitted by the language but can lead to unexpected behavior at run-time.

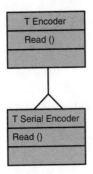

 TIP In every abstract class, the programmer should declare all the methods except constructors as virtual. This technique allows all future derived classes to override the method, incorporate it into their own version, or use it "as is" (unless it is pure virtual). Note that you can (and should) have virtual destructors, but you cannot define virtual constructors (because each class gets its own constructors anyway.)

Public versus *Private* Inheritance

Usually inheritance is based in a real-world relationship between two classes. The class of wooden chairs, for example, really is a subset of the class of chairs. But occasionally, the relationship is more accidental.

A furniture manufacturer may have TSeat, TLegSet, and Tback classes. Clearly, TChair should not be derived from these classes because a chair isn't a subset of the classes of seats, legs, and backs. On the other hand, the programmer who already worked out methods such as TSeat::Upholster and TLegSet::Paint() may want to reuse this code in the TChair class.

One way to reuse code is to derive the new class privately from the parent classes. Therefore, the programmer might write the following:

```
class TChair: TSeat, TLegSet, TBack
{
public:
  TChair(TSeat s, TLegSet l, TBack b) :
    TSeat(s), TLegSet(l), TBack(b)
  {
  }
```

```
        private:
          // private data members are used to characterize the state of
          // objects of the new class
          TDecor fDecor;
          TLoadCapacity fLoad;
        }
```

Now the programmer can paint the legs or upholster the seat or back by reusing the methods in the base classes, but the private derivation doesn't imply that a chair is a kind of seat, back, or legs.

 TIP Often a composite class has one dominant base class and one or more modifying bases. You can recognize this situation when the customer begins to use adjectives to modify nouns.

The noun may correspond to the dominant base class and could be instantiated by itself. The adjectives add new features or capabilities, and do not stand alone.

By convention, the dominant base class in this situation takes a T prefix. The "adjective" classes are referred to as *mix-in classes* and take an M prefix. Therefore, you might write the following:

```
        class TWindsorChair : private TAbstractChair, MColonialPeriod
        {
          .
          .
          .
        }
```

Using Instances as Class Members

Private derivation is most commonly used when the composite object needs to be capable of overriding virtual methods in the base classes. For example, calling myChair->Upholster() may cause TChair to invoke a modified form of upholster for TSeat and TBack, and to invoke Paint() on the TLegSet.

Sometimes private derivation goes too far—the derived class can access protected members of the private base class. The programmer may choose to place instances of related classes into data members, clearly indicating a "has-a" relationship rather than an "is-a" relationship. The new class still can call public methods of the embedded classes, and various methods (or even the whole class) can be specified to be friends of the embedded class.

Hybrid methods, which incorporate private derivation *and* embedded instances, also are possible, as follows:

```
class TWindsorChair : private TAbstractChair, MColonialPeriod
{
public:
  TWindsorChair(TBack* theBack, TLegSet* theLegSet, TSeat* theSeat);
private:
  TBack* fBack;
  TLegSet* fLegSet;
  TSeat* fSeat;
}
```

Style Guides and Naming Conventions

The added complexity of managing objects and classes of many different sorts has lead to the adoption of design and coding style standards for C++. Little widespread agreement exists among programmers—some programmers preface class names with C, others prefer T and M as shown in this chapter. Some programmers use underscores to separate words in names—others use mixed case.

Many programmers append the so-called "Hungarian notation" to the front of their variable names. Others believe this notation unnecessarily reveals implementation details. These naysayers prefer to define classes to represent major types, such as using TAltitude to represent the altitude in feet rather than, say, an int.

The exact set of style- and naming-conventions is less important than the consistency with which they are used. For example, many programming teams adopted the rule that data members have names starting with a lowercase f.

These teams denote local variables and parameters with a and the. For example, a local variable might be called theCount or anEntry. These teams also agree among themselves that they never abbreviate and they devise consistent rules on capitalization. In this way they don't need to guess whether the variable name is fTimePeriod, ftimePeriod, ftimePd, or fTime_Period.

The code shown in this book can be readily adapted to a variety of style- and naming-standards, or can be used as a basis for a standard if an organization doesn't yet have a standard.

GUIs—the Graduate Course of Object-Oriented Methods

The examples in this chapter use simple, character-based interfaces. Real programs on Microsoft Windows, Macintosh, and UNIX systems with the X-Window System all spend much more time and attention on the user interface. Their designs reflect windows and window managers, message queues and event lists, and numerous containers, iterators, and algorithms.

The good news is that most development environments have programs like AppWizard (in Microsoft Visual C++) and AppExpert (in Borland C++) to help lay the foundation of an application, and ClassWizard and ClassExpert to fill out many of the details. Even better news is that many of the details of interfacing with the user are handled by Navigator for the programmer who writes a plug-in. Nevertheless, for a programmer new to GUIs, there is a steep learning curve.

Programmers new to one of the platforms that support Navigator plug-ins or readers who need to come up to speed on a new platform quickly may profit from one or more of the books in the following lists.

Some Windows books that can help you learn more are:

- Microsoft Visual C++—*Special Edition Using Visual C++ 4* (Que, 1996)
- Borland C++ 5—*Special Edition Using Borland C++ 5* (Que, 1996) and *Borland C++ By Example* (Que, 1995).

Some Macintosh books that can help you learn more are:

- Symantec C++—*Symantec C++ Programming for Macintosh, 2nd Edition* (Sams, 1994)
- Metroworks CodeWarrior—*Programming Starter Kit for Macintosh* (Hayden, 1995)

For UNIX, use one of the preceding books to learn the basics of C++; character-oriented programs for UNIX resemble "console" applications under Windows or the Macintosh.

An X Windows book that can help you learn more is:

- *Using X* (MIS Press, 1992) to learn how to write graphics-oriented programs in the X Windows System.

From Here...

Many programmers have successfully worked on Internet applications and even Web applications without using C++—or at least without using some of the more powerful features of C++, such as parameterized types, overloading, and the STL.

This chapter provided an overview of C++ for programmers coming to the language from other development environments and a review of some of the newer features for those who learned C++ early on.

For more information about related topics, see the following:

- Chapter 3, "Integrating Plug-Ins into Web Site Design," continues the discussion of design by introducing design patterns and showing how patterns apply to plug-in design.
- Chapter 4, "Building a Simple Plug-In," visits the concrete world of the "Hello, world" plug-in.
- Chapter 5, "Design Issues," revisits many topics of this chapter, but in the detail possible after the analysis in Chapter 4.
- Chapter 17, "Using Class Libraries and Frameworks," revisits object-oriented libraries, this time dealing with vendor-specific libraries such as Microsoft Foundation Classes and Borland's Object Windows Library (OWL).

Integrating Plug-Ins into Web Site Design

The team needed to build an effective Web site includes the site designers, HTML writers, and, sometimes, plug-in programmers. This chapter describes the use of plug-ins by Web site designers. You as a plug-in programmer can use this information to improve your plug-ins and make them integrate better into Web pages.

As you observed in Chapter 1, "Bridging the Gap from CGI and Helper Applications to Netscape Plug-Ins," the Web site designer has many options. He or she can use static HTML, programs on the server (such as CGI and server-side JavaScript), and programs on a client (including Java applets, client-side JavaScript, and plug-ins). With LiveConnect, a designer can integrate all of the client-side techniques to give the user a seamless experience.

About design patterns

This chapter describes an online repository of some of the best patterns available.

How a plug-in works

Learn about the two objects in every plug-in: one built by you, and one built by Netscape.

About the two kinds of plug-ins

You can use Netscape's <EMBED> tag to emulate a third.

How to start background tasks in a plug-in

This chapter describes how to handle new processes and new threads.

How to write reentrant code

By ensuring that your code is reentrant, you gain new flexibility to interact with Netscape Navigator from your plug-in.

To lay out the end user's overall experience, the designer follows a series of defined steps. In recent years the industry has come to capture such processes at all levels, from analysis and design to coding. When these process definitions are presented with context, rationale, and examples, they are known as *patterns*.

This chapter shows how to select and design plug-ins to the Web site based on patterns. Chapter 4, "Building a Simple Plug-In," provides patterns in detail at the code level. Then Chapter 5, "Design Issues," returns to the design level to look at the patterns the designer and you, the programmer, can use to implement the plug-in. ■

Patterns for Plug-Ins

Patterns are among the hottest topics in software engineering today. The concept is simple—find techniques that work and document them in a standard format. This section describes patterns in general, shows the standard formats for patterns, and shows several sources for patterns.

Next, this section shows the architecture of a Netscape Navigator plug-in and lays the foundation for writing patterns that can be used with these kinds of plug-ins.

What are Patterns?

The history of software engineering is a progression from chaos to structured methods, object-oriented methods, and an emphasis on defined, repeatable processes. Patterns are the logical next step in that progression. They represent a "customary practice" that has been documented to provide context, rationale, and additional information.

The term was coined by architect Christopher Alexander. In his 1977 book, *A Pattern Language* (Oxford University Press), Alexander describes patterns as recurring themes in architecture. The "Window on Two Sides of Every Room" pattern describes a general rule with specific benefits but does not prescribe the size of the windows, their height from the floor, or the distance between them. (Some other patterns address some of these issues, however.)

In his 1991 doctoral theses at the University of Zurich Institut fur Informatik, Erich Gamma seized on the concept of patterns and brought them to the software engineering community. Gamma, along with Richard Help, Ralph Johnson, and John Vlissides, later authored *Design Patterns: Elements of Reusable Object-Oriented Software* (Addison-Wesley, 1995). Collectively, these authors are called the "Gang of Four."

Alexander's Patterns   Patterns are characterized by three elements in pattern documentation:

- *An issue in system design.* This often is a problem to solve or a situation that you may encounter. This issue serves as the trigger that tells the designer a particular pattern is appropriate.
- *A description of a solution.* Although concrete examples should be given, the heart of the description is abstract (because the system design issue is abstract).
- *The consequences of applying the abstract structure to a system architecture.* These consequences can be described in terms of trade-offs. They help the system designer determine whether or not the pattern is appropriate in light of the system's overall constraints.

Various models exist for design patterns. This section shows Alexander's template. The next section shows the template adopted by the Gang of Four.

Alexander's patterns typically are written in a narrative style. They include a concrete example of a problem the pattern solves, in context, and then a solution. A typical Alexandrian pattern mapped into the software domain has seven sections:

1. Pattern Name
2. Problem
3. Context
4. Forces
5. Solutions
6. Force Resolution
7. Design Rationale

Part
I

Ch
3

The "forces" referred to by Alexander correspond to the "-ilities" of software engineering (such as portability, reliability, maintainability, and readability). Force resolution describes how these trade-offs are made in a particular pattern and leaves the door open for other patterns in the same problem with different weights to the various forces.

The "Gang of Four" Template   The Gang of Four provides a more formal structure for documenting patterns. This template serves as a checklist for the pattern author and provides a convenient reference for users of the pattern. The thirteen elements of the Gang of Four's pattern template, along with their section numbers, are as follows:

1. *Name*—A succinct identifier that becomes part of the design vocabulary. Typical names include "Builder," "Proxy," and "Walker."

2. *Intent*—A statement of the issue the pattern addresses and a description of how the pattern improves the design.

3. *Also Known As*—Synonyms for the pattern.

4. *Motivation*—A concrete scenario of the issue described in the Intent section. The scenario shows the classes and objects used in the pattern that addresses the issue.

5. *Applicability*—A short statement of the problem or conditions that trigger the use of this pattern.

6. *Structure*—Typically, a graphical representation of the pattern, using a notation based on the Object Modeling Technique (OMT), with pseudocode for the methods.

7. *Participants*—A description of the classes and/or objects of the pattern, showing their responsibilities and collaborators. The standard information on CRC cards (Classes/Responsibilities/Collaborators) is an appropriate model for this section.

8. *Collaborations*—A description of the collaboration relationships among the collaborators named in the Participants section.

9. *Consequences*—A discussion of the trade-offs of using this pattern. What system design objectives are met and at what cost in terms of other objectives? The software engineering "-ilities" are a good starting point for listing design objectives.

10. *Implementation*—Concrete tips and hints that may be useful to the users of the pattern.

11. *Sample Code*—Whenever possible, at least two examples from different domains.

12. *Known Uses*—Well-known problems that are solved using this pattern.

13. *Related Patterns*—Other patterns that might be used along with this one, including patterns with an alternative approach to the same issues.

The first three sections are used to unambiguously identify the pattern. Section 4 captures most of the content of an Alexandrian pattern and sets a context for the pattern. Section 4 also includes a concrete example to set the scene for the sections that follow.

Sections 5 through 9 define the pattern in abstract terms. Sections 10 and 11 return to the concrete. Section 12 could be a bibliography, and Section 13 could be a cross-reference within a pattern catalog or even a cross-reference to other well-known catalogs and repositories.

One way of thinking about patterns is in the context of Figure 3.1. This figure, from the paper, *Design Patterns: Abstraction and Reuse of Object-Oriented Design,* by the Gang of Four, shows a design space that encompasses all of the patterns in their pattern catalog.

In the context of this figure, each pattern lives at the intersection of a "jurisdiction" and a "characterization." Jurisdiction has to do with whether the pattern works on classes, objects, or more complex structures such as peer objects.

Creational characterization is used for patterns that make new elements of their jurisdiction. Structural characterization means that the pattern adds functionality. Behavioral characterization patterns are used to show how elements cooperate to fulfill their semantics.

The Observer pattern, for example, abstracts the synchronization of state or behavior. The Strategy pattern provides a way to capture an algorithm in an object. Many STL-style algorithms are examples of Strategies. STL-style iterators are examples of patterns with object jurisdiction and behavioral characterization.

As an example of a typical pattern, consider the problem of the pointer in C and C++. C and C++ programmers are plagued because dereferencing a null pointer

Part
I

Ch
3

usually causes a program to exit unexpectedly. One pattern that addresses this issue is the protected proxy (a member of the Proxy family of patterns).

FIG. 3.1
Most patterns for object-oriented development fit somewhere on this map.

Jurisdiction		Characterization		
		Creational	Structural	Behavioral
	Class	Factory Method	Adapter (class)	Template Method
			Bridge (class)	
	Object	Abstract Factory	Adapter (object)	Chain of Responsibility
		Prototype	Bridge (object)	command
		Solitaire	Flyweight	Iterator (object)
			Glue	Mediator
			Proxy	Memento
				Observer
				State
	Compound	Builder	Composite	Strategy
			Wrapper	Interpreter
				Iterator (compound)
				Walker

A protected proxy can be dereferenced at any time—if it doesn't point to anything, it raises an exception. Proxies are associated with specific objects. Structural characterization has to do with adding new functionality. Consequently, the Proxy pattern lives at the intersection of Object jurisdiction and Structural characterization.

For completeness, the jurisdiction and characterization should appear at the top of a pattern description, near the name.

Introduction to Plug-In Architecture

This section introduces three ways of starting a plug-in: embedded, hidden, and full-page. It then moves into a high-level look at plug-in design. This chapter points out patterns that are associated with the plug-in architectures.

Three Ways of Invoking a Plug-In   Plug-ins fit into HTML in three different ways: embedded, hidden, or full-page. Although these terms are sometimes used as though they are types of plug-ins, they actually are just ways of calling the plug-in. There are coding differences, however; if the plug-in is designed to be embedded, check when it is started to see how it was invoked and warn the user if it was called improperly. The HTML writer will see this warning when testing the page, so the warning should give the HTML writer enough information to fix the problem.

Embedded Plug-Ins   Netscape has added the <EMBED> tag to the set of extensions recognized by Navigator. The <EMBED> tag includes the SRC attribute, so an HTML writer can write the following line, and the browser attempts to get the requested entity:

```
<EMBED SRC="http://www.some-server.com/aMovie.avi">
```

As described in Chapter 1, "Bridging the Gap from CGI and Helper Applications to Netscape Plug-Ins," the server uses the file extension (.avi) to select a MIME content type. When the server sends the Content-type header line back to the browser, Navigator selects the plug-in that handles this media type.

The HTML writer can also use the TYPE attribute of the <EMBED> tag to force Navigator to look for a plug-in to handle the specified type. The TYPE attribute makes sense when a plug-in doesn't need a data stream, or when the data is generated dynamically and doesn't have a well-defined MIME media type.

Navigator defines a rectangle in the Navigator window to hold embedded data. The HTML writer can use the HEIGHT and WIDTH attributes of the <EMBED> tag to specify the size of the rectangle.

Hidden Plug-Ins   A plug-in also may be hidden. Use the <EMBED> tag, but specify a HIDDEN attribute. (You can say HIDDEN=true if you prefer—true is the default.)

Full-Page Plug-Ins   Sometimes you want to allocate a whole window to the plug-in content. Rather than using the <EMBED> tag, just link to the file. For example, an HTML writer can write the following:

```
Examine <A HREF="http://www.some-server.com/myFile.xyz">my file</A>
```

When the site user follows this link, the server looks up the MIME media type based on the xyz file extension and begins streaming the data to the browser. Navigator looks up the media type from among its registered plug-ins—if it finds a match, it loads the plug-in and starts an instance.

Introduction to Plug-In Architecture   As described in Chapter 1, "Bridging the Gap from CGI and Helper Applications to Netscape Plug-Ins," Navigator plug-ins are implemented as code resources that execute in the same address space as Navigator. They are distinguished from other applications by the fact that they call and are called by Netscape Navigator. Figure 3.2 shows the context of a Netscape Navigator plug-in.

FIG. 3.2
A Navigator plug-in lives in the space between Navigator and the native operating system.

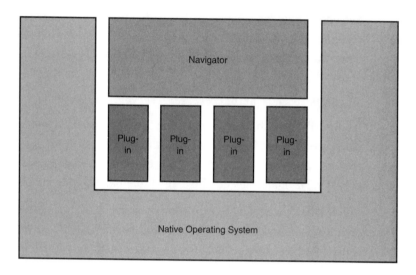

Most plug-ins have examples of patterns with object jurisdiction and behavioral characterization. Recall that when Navigator starts, it registers the MIME media types used by the plug-ins and waits until it's called on to process one of those types.

When Navigator reads a content type that it doesn't handle internally, it looks at the list of registered plug-ins to see if the type can be handled by one of the plug-ins. If so, it loads the plug-in code, instantiates two classes (one in the plug-in and one in Navigator), and makes a series of calls to the plug-in object.

Figure 3.3 illustrates these two objects. All calls from Navigator to the plug-in start with the characters "NPP_." Calls from the plug-in to Navigator start with "NPN_."

All of the methods that are part of the plug-in Application Program Interface (API) are defined in the npapi.h file.

FIG. 3.3
Within its context, a
Navigator plug-in is
defined by two
objects.

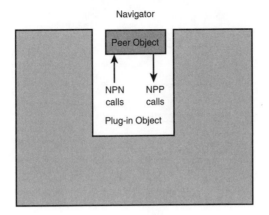

Navigator

Peer Object

NPN
calls

NPP
calls

Plug-in Object

 TIP You can use C++ exceptions to signal conditions within your plug-in. Error conditions to
and from Navigator are passed through result codes from the methods. `npapi.h` has
definitions of the result codes in `NPError` type.

Figure 3.4 illustrates the calls Navigator makes to the plug-in. When the plug-in is
loaded (and before it is instantiated), Navigator calls `NPP_Initialize()`. As soon as
a copy of the plug-in is instantiated, Navigator calls `NPP_New()`. If more copies of
the plug-in are opened while the plug-in is loaded, `NPP_New()` is called for each new
instance.

When `NPP_New()` is called, Navigator sets its `pluginType` parameter to either
`NP_EMBED` or `NP_FULL` to reflect the way in which the plug-in was invoked.

N O T E The original plug-in documentation from Netscape described three types of
plug-ins: embedded plug-ins, full-page plug-ins, and hidden plug-ins. In the
current implementation, Netscape supports embedded plug-ins and full-page plug-ins
as `pluginType` types in `NPP_New()`. If the HTML writer uses an `<EMBED>` tag with the
`HIDDEN` attribute to make a hidden plug-in, Netscape sets `pluginType` to `NP_EMBED`
but does not call `NPP_SetWindow()` to tell the plug-in to draw into the window. ■

When the instance window is closed, Netscape calls `NPP_Destroy()` on that instance, and then deletes the instance. When the last instance of a plug-in is destroyed, Netscape calls `NPP_Shutdown()`, and then unloads the plug-in.

FIG. 3.4
During its life, Navigator makes a series of calls to a plug-in.

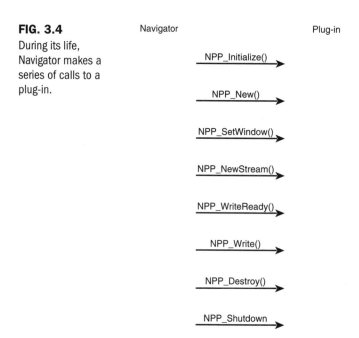

You, as the plug-in programmer, are free to take any appropriate action when Netscape calls your plug-in. Generally, NPP_New( ) is used to do all initialization not done by the constructor. NPP_Destroy() can delete any objects instantiated during initialization.

You also may want to use NPP_Destroy() to save information related to an instance. When possible, Navigator restores that information to a new plug-in instance that is instantiated on the same content.

Suppose that a user opens the myMovie.avi file. Navigator starts an AVI-reading plug-in that begins playing the movie. Before the movie is finished, the user closes the plug-in window. If the user later opens myMovie.avi again, the plug-in could use stored information to return the user to the exact frame where he or she left off.

The Plug-In Object Most plug-ins interact with windows in the native environment. A plug-in that draws into a rectangular space in the Navigator window is known as an *embedded plug-in*. A plug-in that opens its own window is referred to as a *full-page plug-in*.

At one time, Netscape envisioned a third type of plug-in, which would run in the background and have no open window. Their latest thinking is that functionality should be provided with the existing types of plug-ins, but that the HTML writer should pass the HIDDEN attribute to the plug-in through the <EMBED> tag.

After it is instantiated, Netscape calls the plug-in's method NPP_SetWindow(). As a parameter for this method, Netscape passes the handle for the native window provided for the plug-in's use.

N O T E On Windows and UNIX, window->window is a handle to a subwindow of the Netscape window hierarchy. On the Macintosh, this field points to a NP_Port structure. ■

N O T E If the plug-in is running on Windows or UNIX, Netscape filters messages and only sends the plug-in messages destined for the plug-in's window. On the Macintosh, the Mac OS and the plug-in share the event stream. The Macintosh programmer should write a method NPP_HandleEvent() that picks off the events the plug-in can handle and refers the rest back to the operating system. ■

Unless you make other arrangements, the plug-in's methods are part of Navigator's main thread of control, which means that if a plug-in seizes control for a long time, Navigator looks to the user as though it has stopped responding. (Methods of handling substantial asynchronous work are described under "Control Issues.")

After the plug-in instance is instantiated and has a handle to its window, Navigator can pass data to it. Navigator signals the plug-in that a stream of data is available by calling the plug-in's NPP_NewStream() method.

When the stream is no longer available, Navigator calls NPP_DestroyStream(). Netscape recommends that plug-ins wait while Navigator buffers data, and then calls NPP_WriteReady() and NPP_Write() to "write" the data into the plug-in.

When Navigator calls NPP_NewStream(), the plug-in sets up a buffer to receive incoming data. Before actually writing the data to the plug-in, Navigator calls NPP_WriteReady(). That method reports back to Navigator the space remaining in the buffer and clears the way for Navigator to write that number of bytes.

Part

I

Ch

3

After Navigator puts data into the buffer, the plug-in is free to process this data asynchronously. Before Navigator writes to the plug-in again, it calls `NPP_WriteReady()` to see how much buffer space is available. `NPP_WriteReady()` is an example of an Observer pattern, providing synchronization and coordination between two objects.

> **CAUTION**
>
> The terms "read" and "write" as used in plug-in methods are written from the point of view of whichever object is making the call. This convention may lead to some confusion. Data flows to the plug-in because Navigator writes it. The plug-in also can issue a "read request" that solicits data on a seekable stream. In both cases the direction of data flow is *to* the plug-in.
>
> The plug-in also can be written so that Navigator saves the stream to the hard drive (in its cache), and then calls `NPP_StreamAsFile()` to process the entire stream at once. Netscape strongly discourages using this method. (Trade-offs between `NPP_Write()` and `NPP_StreamAsFile()` are described in Chapter 5, "Design Issues.")

In addition to the `NPP_New()`, `NPP_NewStream()`, and the other methods already described, Netscape can call the following methods on the plug-in object:

- `NPP_Print()`
- `NPP_URLNotify()`

> **N O T E** Netscape Navigator 3.0 and beyond allow methods related to LiveConnect. These methods are described in Chapter 18, "Plug-Ins as a Programming Resource." ■

The plug-in printing mechanism is an example of a Mediator pattern. The printing mechanism is decoupled from Navigator by the plug-in object. If the plug-in is using a full window, Navigator even offers the plug-in control of the print dialogs.

`NPP_Print()` is used when Navigator wants the plug-in to print itself. If the instance is full-page, `NPP_Print()` is first called with `platformPrint->mode` set to `NP_FULL` before Netscape displays any print dialogs. This technique gives the plug-in an opportunity to put up its own dialogs and to control the printing process. If it does this, it should set `pluginPrinted` to true before returning.

If you want to allow Navigator to set up the printing process, set `pluginPrinted` to false and return. Navigator calls `NPP_Print()` again, this time with `platformPrint->mode` set to `NP_EMBED`. The plug-in that sees `platformPrint->mode` set to `NP_EMBED` knows that it is responsible only for drawing its representation into the native window. Navigator sends this window in the member `platformPrint->embedPrint.window`.

N O T E If the plug-in is running on the Macintosh and `platformPrint->mode` is set to `NP_FULL`, `platformPrint` contains a handle to the standard Macintosh print record. The handle is referred to as a `THPrint` in Mac-speak; the print-record itself is named `TPrint`. ▪

T I P If you opt to control your own full-screen printing, save the user's choices from the Print and Page Setup dialogs with the instance data. If the user prints this instance again, restore this data as the new defaults.

Windows programmers should note that the coordinates of the window rectangle are in *TWIP*s—a Microsoft-coined term that means "twentieth of a point." Make sure that you use the `DPtoLP()` method of the `CClientDC` object to convert the coordinates from device coordinates to logical coordinates before drawing text into the window.

`NPP_URLNotify()` is used in connection with methods on the Netscape peer to tell the plug-in that an URL-related request to Netscape has completed. This method is described in greater detail in the next section, "The Netscape Peer."

The Netscape Peer   Recall that when Navigator instantiates a plug-in object, it also instantiates a peer object of its own. You can make calls to the peer with methods that begin with "NPN_." These methods represent services that Navigator performs for the plug-in.

Some of these services are rather mundane. `NPN_UserAgent()`, for example, returns the browser's ID string. `NPN_Version()` returns the version numbers of the browser and the plug-in SDK. There is platform-specific code (in `npmac.h` and `npwin.h`) to compare the browser's major version number with the plug-in's version—if the user tries to load a version 3.x plug-in with a version 2.x browser, the plug-in exits.

> **CAUTION**
>
> Netscape only increments the major version number of the SDK when they release a version that is incompatible with older browsers. Netscape has promised to increment the *minor* version number when the browser offers new plug-in features. Your plug-in should compare the browser minor version number with its own minor version number to ensure that all new features it uses are available.

A principal use of the Netscape peer object is to reach out through Navigator back to the Net. You can ask Netscape to open a new stream by calling `NPN_GetURL()`. To open a new stream and be notified when the request is completed, call `NPN_GetURLNotify()`. When Navigator completes the request, it calls `NPP_URLNotify()` and tells the plug-in the result of the request. These methods can be used to implement links.

> **TIP**
>
> If your plug-in includes buttons or hot spots, put the destination in the status line, as Navigator does. This technique keeps your plug-in consistent with Navigator's look and feel.
>
> Use `NPN_Status()` to write to the Navigator status line.

The `NPN_PostURL()` is the reverse of `NPN_GetURL()`. It allows the plug-in to package up and send data to a Web server, where a CGI script or server-side JavaScript program can process it. The plug-in API also offers a `NPN_PostURLNotify()` that provides notification through `NPP_URLNotify()`.

> **TIP**
>
> You can use `NPN_PostURL()` to send data to non-Web servers (specifically FTP, mail, and news). If you are sending a file, however, and the plug-in is running on a Windows or Macintosh machine, the file must be a text file with UNIX-style line breaks (*newlines*, also known as *linefeeds*).

> **CAUTION**
>
> Each protocol has its own needs for headers. Some protocols, such as HTTP, need a blank line between the headers and the body. If you don't need headers for a particular file but the protocol requires that headers be separated from the body by a blank line, start the transmission with a blank line.

You cannot use NPN_PostURL() to send separate headers (even a blank line) from a memory buffer—only from a file. To send a memory buffer with separate headers, use NPN_PostURLNotify().

When a plug-in handles NPP_NewStream(), it tells Navigator how to handle the stream. It can specify that the data be delivered as a stream (the recommended technique) or as a file. If the stream is seekable, the plug-in can tell Navigator that it doesn't want data sent—the plug-in asks for data as needed. If the stream was set up in this way, the application calls NPN_RequestRead() to get the data.

CAUTION

Only two kinds of streams are inherently seekable—files on the local hard drive and streams from Web servers that allow byte-range requests. If you use NPP_NewStream() to set a stream to NP_SEEK mode even though it isn't inherently seekable, Navigator must download the entire file to the cache so it can fulfill NPN_RequestRead().

Trying to seek on a stream that isn't inherently seekable therefore forces the user to wait while the whole file downloads. If this download takes a long time (remember that a 28.8-kbps modem can only fetch about 40 kbytes in 15 seconds), warn the user before starting the download.

Not only can the plug-in open a new stream for reading, it also can open an URL for writing. Use the NPN_NewStream() to open the stream and write to it with NPN_Write(). The call to NPN_NewStream() allows you to specify the target. These targets are the same ones Netscape uses with their <frameset> tags.

After the plug-in is done with the stream, it should call NPN_DestroyStream().

TIP A plug-in can make a new instance of itself by opening a new stream with the one of the MIME media types that it handles. If the target is the same window or frame in use by the current instance (such as _current), the old instance is destroyed as soon as it completes NPN_Write().

Recall that when NPP_Destroy() is called by Navigator, you can set an NPSavedData parameter and store data for use by future instances that are called on the same URL. The memory for this parameter must be owned by Navigator because the plug-in is gone after `NPP_Destroy()` completes. Allocate a chunk of memory in Navigator with `NPN_MemAlloc()`.

T I P   The Macintosh version of Navigator uses a memory cache that can fill memory. If your Macintosh plug-in tries to allocate memory with `NewPtr()` (part of the Macintosh's Memory Manager) and `NewPtr()` returns a `memFullErr`, request the memory through `NPN_MemAlloc()`.

For easier implementation and greater portability, just call `NPN_MemAlloc()` in the first place. `NPN_MemAlloc()` forces Navigator to purge enough of its memory cache to satisfy the request, so it is more likely to succeed than `NewPtr()`.

N O T E   The Macintosh API also offers `NPN_MemFlush()`, which asks Navigator to free a block of memory. In general, use `NPN_MemAlloc()` to get memory. `NPN_MemFlush()` is useful only if you need to make a call that allocates memory indirectly. If you need as much memory as possible, write a loop to repeatedly call `NPN_MemFlush()` until it returns 0 (indicating that no more memory can be freed). ■

When you are done with a block of memory allocated with `NPN_MemAlloc()`, release it with `NPN_MemFree()`.

Additional methods are available on the Netscape peer object that are used with LiveConnect. These methods are described in Chapter 18, "Plug-Ins as a Programming Resource."

What Can You Do with a Plug-In?

ON THE WEB

A visit to **http://home.netscape.com/comprod/products/navigator/version_3.0/ plugins/index.html** reveals dozens of plug-ins, which fall into three groups: multimedia, document viewers, and applications.

Multimedia

One major use of plug-ins is to extend Navigator to handle new media types as though they were native. By using the `<EMBED>` tag as though it were, say, an `<IMG>`

tag, the HTML programmer can place advanced graphics and movies on the page. The plug-in is responsible for reading the incoming data stream and drawing a representation of the data directly to the window.

If the `<EMBED>` tag is called with the `HIDDEN` attribute set to true, no window appears. The plug-in designed to play a sound may be used in this way.

Document Viewers

Sometimes the non-native media type is best thought of as a document rather than as a component to an HTML page. The Adobe Acrobat PDF viewer is an example of this type. When a user follows a link to a PDF document, Navigator starts the Acrobat plug-in in a full window and displays the document.

It still is possible to observe the Netscape look and feel in a full-page plug-in. When the user moves the cursor over a link, call `NPN_Status()` to show the link. When the user selects a link, call either `NPN_GetURL()` to open a new window or `NPN_NewStream()` with `current` in the target. Then call `NPN_Write()` to overwrite the old contents of the current window.

T I P Use `NPN_GetURL()` when the link takes the user to an existing entity on the Web. Use `NPN_NewStream()` and `NPN_Write()` when the plug-in generates the new content. In either case, cue the user about what will happen by marking the link with `NPN_Status()`.

A Plug-In-Based Application

Although most plug-ins are multimedia-type viewers or document viewers, plug-ins give the programmer the potential of building a full client-server application.

ON THE WEB
This section shows an example of such an application, using the "Early Development" design patterns from the Portland Pattern Repository at **http://c2.com/ppr/early.html**.

The Story Pattern   The Story pattern is triggered when someone decides to computerize something. The key element of Story is to encourage the customer to talk about ways the end user will use the application.

For this example, your customer is a manufacturer of lawn tools. The vice president of sales tells you stories about the sales staff. The company distributes its products through distributors such as hardware stores, garden supply stores, and department stores. Here is one of their stories.

The sales staff is expected to review their accounts looking for customers who haven't bought for a while or whose purchase volume has declined. The staff members are also encouraged to keep in touch with their accounts—they try to call every customer at least three times a year, even if their volume is high.

Sales are highly seasonal—the summer months are the best, but sales of rakes, leaf blowers, and work gloves are good in the fall. Snow blowers make up the bulk of the winter sales.

Every day each account rep makes a list of which customers to call. In larger firms customers usually speak to someone in purchasing. At smaller firms they try to speak to the owner. Most of the accounts are smaller firms.

When account reps have the customer on the phone, they talk about the customer's recent purchases. They are often called on to answer simple technical support questions about the products or to describe features. They also like to have on hand a complete record of the customer's buying history.

The account reps have several problems with the current manual system. The product catalog is often out of date—by the time the summer catalog is out, the fall selling season has begun.

Technical support notes are packaged separately from the catalog—often, account reps can find the product in the catalog (they can describe the features) but cannot find the tech support notes (so they cannot answer questions about the use of the product).

Calls from account reps often come as an interruption to their customers, so time is of the essence. Sometimes they are asked to call back. More often the owner can give them a few minutes and may even place an order if the account rep has the necessary information on hand.

Another problem the account reps have is that orders are sometimes put on hold by the credit department. This practice has led to some hard feelings and lost accounts: the account rep takes the order and is often unaware that the order has been held up for days waiting for the credit manager to approve it.

The User Decision Pattern   After you have a set of stories, you can begin to map them to the elements of a user interface. Figure 3.5 shows a graphical representation of this mapping. The best user interfaces show consistency.

For example, users can imagine that they are in a "virtual world," such as a desktop. They may access applications like timers and word processors, but they perceive these tools as scheduling calendars and notepads.

The User Decision pattern calls for the designer to make a list of every decision the user must make during the stories. For each decision, the designer writes down the information the user needs to make a good decision.

FIG. 3.5
Mapping stories
to user interface
elements requires a
transformation from
chronological order to
spatial organization.

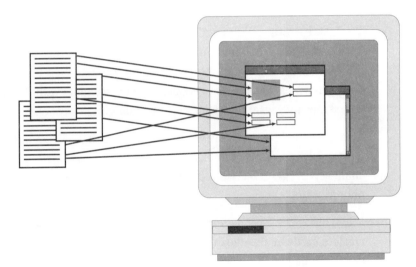

Using the User Decision pattern, make a list of every decision the user makes during the stories and identify the information they need to make a good decision. Table 3.1 shows some of the decisions and information associated with the story of the lawn tools manufacturer.

Table 3.1   The User Decision Process

Decision	Information
Which customers to call	Customer's purchase history Record of previous calls
Which products to recommend	Catalog of products with feature lists
What information to give customer	Catalog, tech support notes
When to tell customer order will ship	Complete order Credit approval
Whether to approve credit	Customer's payment history Size of order

The Task Pattern   With the list of decisions in hand, the designer turns to the Task pattern. The hallmark of the Task pattern is that different account representatives can work in the order that best suits their needs. Some representatives may prefer to concentrate on accounts with declining sales. Other reps may want to concentrate on calling their best customers frequently.

Management, however, may want to make sure that all customers are called—not just the best accounts. Some companies go so far as to write a script for their account reps. A good interface design helps account reps structure their work, without requiring that every account rep work in exactly the same way as every other.

When using the Task pattern, the designer writes each task on an index card and clusters cards by the information they need. Figure 3.6 shows what some of these clusters look like in the case of the lawn tool manufacturer. Each cluster becomes a candidate task and gets a name.

The Task Window Pattern   The purpose of the Task Window pattern is to find an acceptable design point somewhere between the extremes of "everything in one window" and "a window for every element."

When using the Task Window pattern, the designer reviews the list of tasks with the users. After there is some agreement about which tasks the users perform (and which users perform which tasks), the designer develops one window for each task.

FIG. 3.6
When using the Task pattern, the designer clusters user decisions by the kind of information needed.

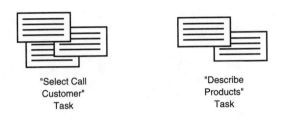

"Select Call Customer" Task

"Describe Products" Task

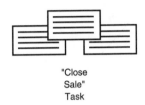

"Close Sale" Task

The available actions in each window are the visible functions of each task. Sometimes, it makes sense to divide the window into related panes.

The Early Program Pattern Soon after the stories are complete and the user interface is defined, it's time to build a prototype. For Web-based applications with sophisticated user interfaces, a prototype of the user interface is key to ensuring that the end user's needs are met.

ON THE WEB

For a technically literate client, you may choose to build an architecture prototype. Patterns for all of these early programs are available in the Portland Pattern Repository at **http://c2.com/ppr/**.

Figures 3.7 and 3.8 show how portions of the lawn tools manufacturer's application may look if implemented by using an intranet with Windows 95 clients.

An application such as the one described in this section can be implemented as a combination of static HTML, client-side and server-side JavaScript, Java, and plug-ins. Plug-ins are particularly attractive when the application will be fielded over the intranet because the solution may be needed only on a single platform, and the organization may be able to draw on existing applications and code.

Part

I

Ch

3

FIG. 3.7
The account rep uses a customer list pane, a customer information pane, and a phone pane to do the Call Customer task.

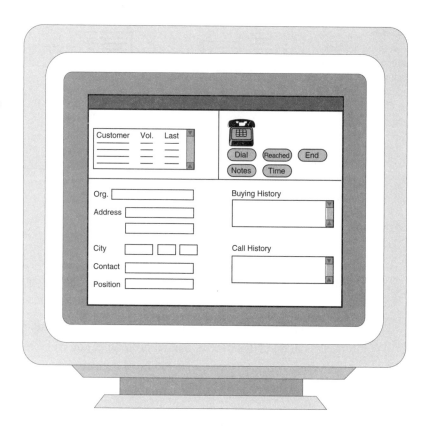

The following components of the solution are candidates for implementation as plug-ins for these reasons:

- *Customer List*—The server sends an in-house media type application/
  x-customer-list, which can be displayed as a table in a scrollable window. The table enables drag and drop. When the account representative is ready to open a customer's file he or she drops the customer ID on the customer information pane.

- *Phone Application*—This plug-in needs to access the local hardware. When the user chooses Dial, the plug-in dials the phone, and then waits while the account representative either schedules a time to call back, logs the fact that the customer was not in, or completes the call.

- *History*—This plug-in uses the Win32 control named Tree List to display a history of the customer's purchases. An item can be dragged from the history to the catalog to open the catalog to the proper page, revealing features, competitive information, and troubleshooting tips (implemented as static HTML pages).

FIG. 3.8
While talking to the customer, the account representative can access an integrated electronic catalog and set of technical support notes.

- *Notify*—A client-server application. When the account representative finalizes the order, an application on the server runs it and—if possible—issues credit approval. If the application is unable to issue credit approval, it looks for a logged-in credit manager and uses server-push to notify the manager that a request for approval is pending. The Credit Approval pane is written as a form by server-side JavaScript.

Control Issues in Asynchronous Plug-Ins

Some plug-in methods are inherently asynchronous. For example, when your plug-in calls the URL methods of the Netscape peer object, control is returned to the plug-in immediately, and the plug-in is notified of the results later by NPP_URLNotify() (if you used the Notify version of the URL call).

At other times the plug-in may need to proceed asynchronously and allow Navigator to resume processing while the plug-in does its work. There are two methods for doing asynchronous work: threads and processes. Threads and processes are similar—one name for a thread is a "light-weight process." The principal difference between the two is that a thread runs in the same address space as its parent (so that it can access data structures allocated by the parent), while a process runs in a separate address space and communicates with its parent by using InterProcess Communications (IPC) mechanisms.

Threads

Until the mid-90s, most high-end operating systems (such as UNIX and Windows NT) gave the programmer only one way to put the processor to work on more than one task: *process forking* (also known as *spawning*). Forking a new process is a CPU-intensive step because the process has its own set of kernel entries and its own address space.

Separate processes also presented complexities for the programmer since direct communication between different address spaces needs signals, pipes, or other forms of interprocess communication (IPC) rather than simple function calls.

Many programmers felt a need for a "lightweight process" that could run asynchronously in the same address space as its parent. Both UNIX and Windows NT now offer *threads*—a mechanism of starting a separate processing sequence without the overhead of a separate process.

ON THE WEB

Macintosh programmers can expect similar facilities in the next generation of Mac OS, System 8. See the latest information on Apple's site (**http://www.macos.apple.com/ macos8/**) for details.

When the programmer needs to start asynchronous work during an NPP_call, he or she should start a new thread and return control to Navigator.

Processes

Sometimes the programmer has an existing application or a package of easy-to-assemble modules that do the asynchronous work. (These easy-to-assemble packages are particularly common in UNIX, where shell, awk, and perl programs are common, and pipes make it easy to put together tools.)

In these cases, the programmer should consider calling system(), which transfers control to a new process and allows it do the work. Various IPC mechanisms, ranging from simple pipes to sophisticated TCP and UDP solutions, allow communications between the plug-in and the separate process.

Reentrant Code

In general, Navigator instantiates a new plug-in object from the plug-in code when it needs one to deal with a stream or an <EMBED> tag. One important exception exists to this rule: Netscape warns that if the plug-in calls Navigator through NPN calls, Navigator may make reentrant calls to the plug-in.

Most of the STL classes are reentrant. If you use a commercial version, the vendor can show you which classes are not reentrant. If you use one of the off-the-Net versions, examine the classes you use for static variables. Either use a different class or devise your own version of the class, which moves the class variables into instance variables or singleton objects.

From Here...

This chapter described the use of design patterns—an important new topic in software engineering. Then, in the context of the design patterns of the Gang of Four and the Portland Pattern Repository, the chapter described the architecture of Navigator plug-ins.

Plug-ins are based on a pair of collaborating objects—one, the plug-in, representing the native operating system. The other, the Netscape peer object, representing Netscape and the Net itself.

Plug-ins are only one part of the design of a complete application. A Web-based application, such as the example with the lawn tools manufacturer, may include static HTML, client- and server-side JavaScript, and Java, as well as plug-ins. Using LiveConnect, you can integrate all of the client-side techniques.

- Chapter 4, "Building a Simple Plug-In," presents the "Hello, World" of plug-ins—loaded with instrumentation to make the calls from Navigator visible.
- Chapter 5, "Design Issues," returns to the high-level issues of plug-ins in the context of the calls explained in Chapter 4. Several design patterns are presented, using trade-offs that are typical in the plug-in environment.
- Chapter 6, "NPP Methods: Starting the Plug-In," shows several alternate ways of starting a plug-in instance.
- Chapter 7, "NPP Methods: Handling Interaction," provides examples of how to interact with the user while the plug-in is running.
- Chapter 8, "NPP Methods: Other Tasks," completes the discussion of NPP methods, taking up `NPP_Print()` and `NPP_Destroy()`.
- The NPN methods are described in Chapter 9, "Understanding NPN Methods," showing how the plug-in can get back to Navigator and the Net.

CHAPTER 4

Building a Simple Plug-In

The sample applications included with the Windows version of the Netscape plug-in Software Development Kit (SDK) are a *tour de force* of plug-in programming. They include calls to Java code and enable the user to play AVI movies. Unfortunately, so much is going on in these sample applications that the new plug-in programmer can be overwhelmed.

Traditionally, the first program a C or C++ programmer writes in a new environment is one to put up the words, "Hello, world!". Such a simple program serves to check out the compiler and development environment, because the code itself is trivial. This chapter shows you how to build a "Hello, world!" plug-in—a plug-in that just shows these words to the user.

After "Hello, world!" is working, you can use this plug-in as a foundation for showing more of the calls a plug-in and Navigator can exchange. ■

How to use Visual C++ AppWizard to set up a plug-in

Careful design can make the plug-in runnable as either an application or a dynamic link library. This chapter shows how to set up the code this way.

Which pieces of the SDK include in a new plug-in project

This chapter shows how to "stub out" LiveConnect pieces so that you can better understand basic plug-in programming.

How development on a Mac is different from Windows

This chapter shows how to write code to be used on either platform.

How to test a new plug-in for correct installation

This chapter describes the difference between installation and loading.

How to test a new plug-in for correct loading

This chapter shows how to use a sample document with the correct file extension to verify that the plug-in is loading properly.

Overview of the Development Process

This chapter uses Microsoft's Visual C++ 4.0 Standard Edition under Windows 95 as the sample development environment. You can use this environment to develop applications for Windows computers as well as for the Macintosh.

This chapter concentrates on the plug-in rather than the application environment. There are some notes showing how Macintosh plug-ins differ from plug-ins for Windows. For more information on writing plug-ins for Windows environments other than Windows 95, see Chapter 16, "Spanning the Windows World."

 Visual C++ 4.0 Standard Edition does not allow the developer to link Microsoft Foundation Classes (MFC) statically. The consequences are that you must provide (or the user must already have) the MFC dynamic link library (DLL) on the target machine.

If you are developing plug-ins for general release, you may prefer to link MFC statically. You can use the linker in the Visual C++ 4.0 Professional Edition as well as in some non-Microsoft development environments to link the MFC library to your plug-in.

If you are developing plug-ins for an intranet that only has Windows computers, you may be able to get by with a Windows-only plug-in. If you are developing for the Internet in general, consider releasing versions of your plug-in for all major platforms. This chapter shows how to develop a generic plug-in, using Windows 95 and Microsoft's Visual C++ as the development environment.

Getting Ready to Build a Plug-In

This section lists the steps to set up a project so that you can build it either as a plug-in or as an executable. If you follow these steps, at the end of this section, you will have a project directory that you can tailor to be a plug-in DLL.

Installing the SDK

Start by getting the latest copy of the Windows version of the Netscape plug-in Software Development Kit. The example in this chapter is built by using nspi30.zip.

ON THE WEB

The latest version of the SDK is available online at the Netscape site. The SDK for Navigator 3.0 is available at **http://home.netscape.com/eng/mozilla/3.0/handbook/plugins/index.html**.

You need WinZip to unzip the kit and install it on your hard drive. WinZip is available online at **http://www.winzip.com/winzip/winzip_f.htm**, and also is on the CD-ROM. WinZip provides a convenient front-end to the popular PKZIP and PKUNZIP utilities.

When you prepare plug-ins for distribution, you will often want to compress them before placing them on a site. **http://www.yahoo.com/Business_and_Economy/Companies/Computers/Software/Systems_and_Utilities/Compression/** contains many links to sites that discuss compression. One site on this list, **http://members.aol.com/flashptdev/html/pageone.htm**, is loaded with tips and utilities regarding zip archiving and compression under Windows.

TIP Chapter 1, "Bridging the Gap from CGI and Helper Applications to Netscape Plug-Ins," also contains information on `gzip`, a platform-independent compression utility, available from the Free Software Foundation.

Part
I
Ch
4

Figure 4.1 shows WinZip in action. Note that you can install the SDK anywhere on your hard drive—it need not be in the Visual C++ project directory.

Generating the Project Code

A plug-in is a combination of code you write and code Netscape has written. Most modern development environments have templates that help you write the common parts of many programs.

The template-driven process in Visual C++ is *AppWizard*. You can use AppWizard to make standalone executables, DLLs, or static libraries. You also can choose whether you want to include Microsoft foundation classes in your project.

Launch the Visual C++ Developer Studio and choose File, New. Specify a new Project Workspace from the dialog box that appears. The screen you see next is shown in Figure 4.2.

FIG. 4.1
WinZip provides a convenient front-end to the popular PKZIP and PKUNZIP utilities.

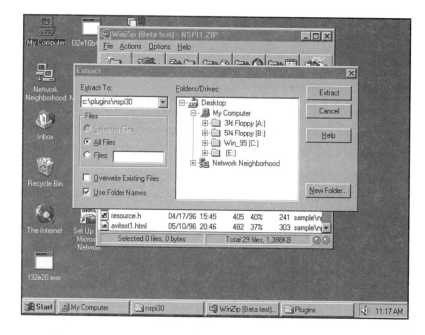

FIG. 4.2
Using the Microsoft Developer Studio, you can have AppWizard build the skeleton of an MFC Executable, an MFC DLL, an OLE Control, or a variety of non-MFC programs.

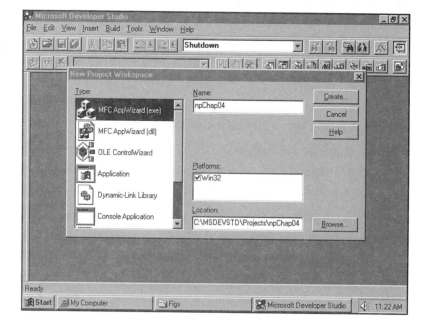

When you develop your own plug-ins, you should enter a name of your choice in the Name field. For now, type **npChap04** in the Name field and confirm that the path in the Location field is a reasonable place to keep the files associated with this project.

TIP Under Windows, Navigator only recognizes a DLL as a plug-in if its name starts with the letters "np." To simplify development, give all your plug-ins a name that follows this convention. Also remember to follow the MS-DOS naming convention (no more than eight characters in the name, followed by a three-character file extension, often referred to as the "8.3 naming convention") if your finished plug-in will be used in an older Windows environment such as Windows 3.x or Windows for Workgroups.

N O T E AppWizard builds classes for your new plug-in that use the name you enter here as the basis for the class names. Remember that although Windows file names are not case-sensitive, C++ is. For example, if you name your project npAVIvu, your application class becomes `CNpAVIvuApp`.

Although a plug-in is a DLL (under Windows), choose MFC Application Wizard (exe) on the New Project Workspace dialog. This technique allows the plug-in to be compiled as either a DLL or a standalone application, which makes some debugging steps easier.

The dialog entitled MFC AppWizard - Step 1 asks what kind of application you want to build. For embedded plug-ins, the Single Document Interface (SDI) often is appropriate—this interface makes it easy to subclass the Netscape window.

For the "Hello, world!" plug-in, choose Dialog based. This choice causes the plug-in to display a dialog box when it is invoked. We use this dialog box to illustrate the use of controls such as push buttons.

Continue through the AppWizard by clicking the Next button. The next screen is MFC AppWizard - Step 2 of 4. Leave About box checked, but uncheck 3D controls. Change the title for the dialog to Chapter 4 Demo Plug-In. Figure 4.3 shows the screen you see next.

FIG. 4.3
Be sure to turn off 3D
Controls in Step 2 of
the AppWizard.

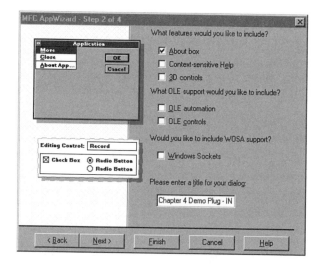

After Step 2, use the default values on the remaining steps. As a shortcut, just click
the Finish button from the Step 2 screen.

N O T E   If your version of Visual C++ gives the option (in Step 3) of linking the MFC
statically or in a shared DLL, choose the shared DLL for this demo. When
applications share the MFC library, each application is smaller than if they had to include
the whole library in their executable file. But if your plug-in may end up on a machine
that doesn't have the MFC DLL, you need to ship the MFC DLL with your plug-in or link the
MFC library statically.

The Standard Edition of Visual C++ doesn't give the option of linking the MFC library
statically—you need the Professional Edition of Visual C++ or a different development
environment if you decide to link statically. ■

After you arrive at the Finish screen, look over the choices you made. Your screen
should resemble Figure 4.4. When you select OK, AppWizard builds the code for a
standalone application with the options you selected.

   Right now, before you change a thing, Build npChap04.exe from the Build menu. You
should expect no errors—because this code was written by Microsoft's AppWizard, all
errors will be errors in AppWizard. This double-check ensures that everything in
AppWizard worked correctly.

FIG. 4.4
Double-check your
selections before
allowing AppWizard
to generate the code
for your plug-in.

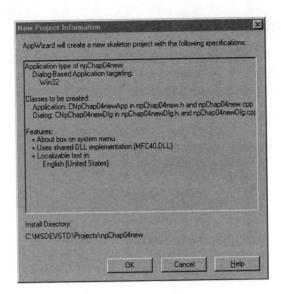

 For a more rigorous check of AppWizard, choose $\underline{S}$ettings from the $\underline{B}$uild menu. Then
choose the C/C++ tab and change the Warning level from Level 3 to Level 4. In general,
you should strive to write code that does not generate any warnings even when the
warning level is set as high as it can go. As a minimum, you should understand any
warnings your code generates and consciously choose to allow the warning to stand.

When you have a working standalone application, you can run it. (Remember, it's
not a plug-in or even a DLL yet.) Choose $\underline{E}$xecute npChap04.exe from the $\underline{B}$uild
menu. You should see the dialog box shown in Figure 4.5.

FIG. 4.5
Although the controls
don't do anything yet,
this application has
the same user
interface as your
finished plug-in.

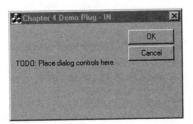

Part
I

Ch
4

Adding Files from the SDK   *win temp.c*

Before starting to write code, you should make this application look more like a plug-in. Copy the file npshell.cpp from the SDK directory into the npChap04 project directory. You also should move the following header files into the project directory:

- jri.h
- jri_md.h
- npapi.h
- npupp.h

If you prefer, you can make a new directory for header files. (It's customary to call this directory "include".) You can put project-specific header files in an include directory in the project files, and leave SDK include files in the include directory of the SDK directory.

Back in Developer Studio, choose Insert, Files into Project and add `npshell.cpp` into the project. Also add npwin.cpp into the project. You can leave npwin.cpp in the SDK directory—you won't be changing that file and can share it between all your plug-in projects.

> **N O T E** The npwin.cpp file holds platform-specific code for Windows. There are similar files (such as npmac.cpp) that you should include to build plug-ins on other platforms. ∎

Now that all the components are in the project, it's time to turn this generic application in the "Hello, world!" plug-in.

Putting the Pieces Together

The components are in place and you can begin to change them. This section shows the changes you need to make to turn the application into a DLL and the DLL into a plug-in.

Modifying the Version Information Resource

From inside the Project Workspace pane of Developer Studio, open the ResourceView. From there, open the Version resource and select the VS_VERSION_INFO. Figure 4.6 shows the screen you see next.

FIG. 4.6

The Developer Studio's ResourceView gives you direct access to the program's resources.

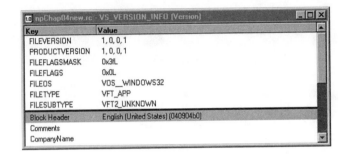

Open the VS_VERSION_INFO resource. (By convention, Windows programs have only one VS_VERSION_INFO resource.) Find the line that reads FILETYPE VFT_APP. ✓ The field is a drop-down menu. Double-click VFT_APP to get a list of file types. Choose VFT_DLL and allow the menu to close.

Next, double-click English (United_States) (040904b0) in the Block Header line and select the Code Page drop-down menu. The code page is an ordered set of the characters available to the program.

It is critical that you change the code page from Unicode to Windows, Multilingual ✓ for the code to function correctly as a plug-in. When you close the dialog, you should see English (United States) (040904e4) as the new Block Header.

While you are here, feel free to change the Comments, CompanyName, LegalCopyright, LegalTrademarks, OriginalFilename, and ProductName fields. These fields hold string information that can be read by the program with the GetFileVersionInfo() and VerQueryValue() Windows API functions. Figure 4.7 shows a typical version information resource.

Use File, Save to save the resource file, and then close the Version Info Editor with the close box. Now choose File, Open. Set the Open As: field to text, and then open npChap04.rc.

Part

I

Ch

4

FIG. 4.7
Many fields of the
version information
resource can be set
to reflect your
organization and its
needs.

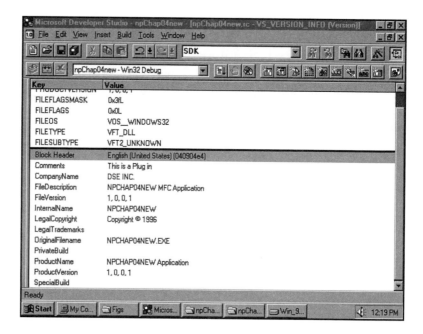

CAUTION

If you open the resource file in with Open As: set to Auto, the file is opened by the Resource
Editor rather than the text editor. You need to use the text editor to add three lines to the
version resource.

N O T E AppWizard sets up your resource file so that it includes `res\npChap04.rc2`. To
add resources that the Resource Editor doesn't know how to edit, use the text
editor to open the `rc2` file. These three lines aren't resources, however, so they must be
added in the .rc file. ■

Find the place in the .rc file that mentions BLOCK StringFileInfo—inside that
block is a series of lines of the form VALUE *key*, *value*. Add the following lines to
the bottom of that list:

```
VALUE "MIMEType", "application/x-chapter4\0"
VALUE "FileExtents", "ch4\0"
VALUE "FileOpenName", "Chapter 4 Plug-In (*.ch4)\0"
```

The first of these lines adds the MIMEType string to the version information. When Navigator launches, it looks for plug-ins in the plug-ins directory. In each plug-in, Navigator looks for a list of MIME-compliant media types in the MIMEType string of the version information. It uses this information to determine which plug-in to invoke when a stream has a particular content type.

Navigator uses the MIMEType field when it receives a stream from the server. It uses the FileExtents field when it opens a local file. This line says that if the user uses the File, Open File menu item to open a file with extension .ch4, Navigator invokes this plug-in.

The last line is used by Navigator in the File, Open File dialog box—it enables the user to filter the files in a directory to see only those which can be read by the plug-in. Figure 4.8 shows this file type being selected in Navigator.

FIG. 4.8

The FileOpenName string in the version info tells Navigator which filter to offer the user on the Open File dialog.

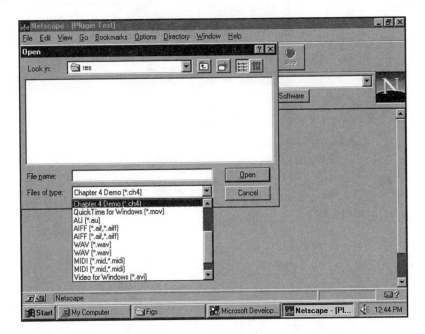

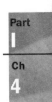

Part

I

Ch

4

TIP   If your plug-in will support more than one MIME media type, separate the entries with a vertical bar. For example, some media types are present on the Web in both registered and unregistered forms. To support both a registered and an unregistered version of the media type used in the example application, your entries might read:

```
VALUE "MIMEType", "application/chapter4|application/x-chapter4\0"
VALUE "FileExtents", "ch4|ch4\0"   ?
VALUE "FileOpenName", "chapter 4 plug-in (*.ch4)|Chapter 4 Plug-In
(*.ch4)\0"
```

Double-check the manual editing by reopening the resource file with the Resource Editor. You should see the three new entries, as shown in Figure 4.9.

FIG. 4.9
Use the Resource Editor to verify that the resource file has the three new entries.

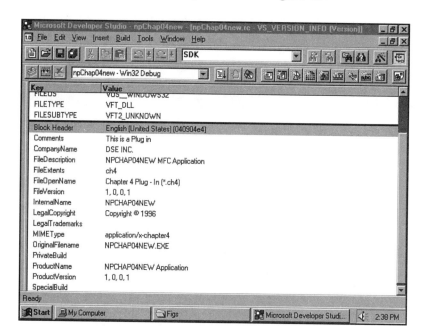

Recall that we told AppWizard to make this program an application rather than a DLL so that we could build this program as either a DLL or a standalone executable. We are now at the point where we begin to build the DLL from the application.

Setting Up the DLL Configuration

This approach takes advantage of the fact that DLLs are like applications. In many cases, the only difference is that an application has a WinMain() function, whereas the DLL has DllMain().

When a user launches an application, Windows opens the executable image and finds the place where WinMain() begins. When a Windows 95 or Windows NT program calls a function in a DLL, it first calls DllMain(). In fact, DllMain gets called under four circumstances, each of which has a symbolic name:

- DLL_PROCESS_ATTACH—When a new process attempts to access the DLL.

- DLL_THREAD_ATTACH—When an existing process starts a new thread that accesses the DLL.

- DLL_THREAD_DETACH—When a thread detaches from the DLL, but at least one thread still remains attached.

- DLL_PROCESS_DETACH—When the last thread of a process detaches from the DLL.

To build a configuration of the project that includes DllMain() instead of WinMain(), choose Build, Configurations. On the resulting dialog, click the Add button. Name the configuration DLL. Allow it to copy its settings from the Debug configuration. Leave the platform at its default, Win32. (Microsoft supports other versions as add-on modules in the Professional Edition of Visual C++.)

Figure 4.10 shows the finished Add Project Configuration dialog. Click the OK button to save the new configuration, and then close the Configurations dialog box.

Part

I

Ch

4

FIG. 4.10
Add a DLL configuration to the project.

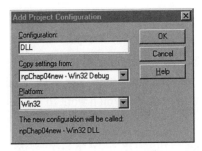

Now choose <u>B</u>uild, <u>S</u>ettings and select the DLL Configuration in the Settings For field. The tabs at the right list various parts of the project, each of which has several setting options.

These options are used by the Developer Studio to set up command lines for the compiler, linker, and other tools. The resulting settings are stored in the makefile, npChap04.mak. When you build your project, these command lines are run from the makefile.

> **N O T E**   If you are using the Professional Edition of Visual C++, you have a choice on the General tab of how to link the MFC library. Be sure the setting is consistent with your earlier choices.
>
> If you are using the Visual C++ Standard Edition, the MFC library is linked in a shared DLL and the option is not available to you. ▪

On the General tab of the Project Settings dialog, set the Category menu to Preprocessor. In the Preprocessor definitions list, add _WINDLL—this entry tells the linker that you intend this module to be a DLL.

If you are using include directories in the SDK directory or the project directory, add them to the Additional include directories field now. Specify the complete path to each include directory.

Click the OK button to store the new definitions and close the Project Settings dialog.

Now that the DLL configuration is set up, switch to that configuration as the new default. Figure 4.11 shows the drop-down menu to change.

Modifying npshell.cpp

npshell.cpp contains a template for a plug-in. You modify the methods in that file to build specific functionality into your application. For most applications, you have other files with classes and functions, and you'll want to call that code from the methods in npshell.cpp.

Except for npshell.cpp, no files in the SDK need to be changed by the plug-in programmer. These files provide the "glue" between Navigator and the plug-in.

FIG. 4.11
Set the default
project configuration
from the Build
toolbar.

Default Configuration—

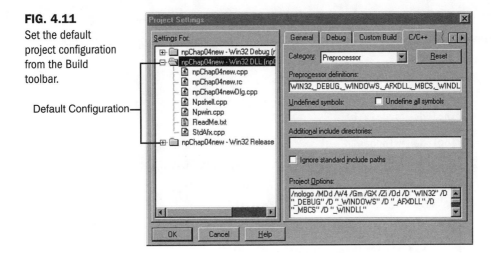

TIP   Leaving common files such as npwin.cpp in the SDK directory not only saves disk space
but also simplifies maintenance. If Netscape issues a new (and backward-compatible)
version of npwin.cpp, you only need to replace one copy rather than visiting the project
directory of each plug-in project.

Updating Header File Dependencies   Choose Build, Update All Dependencies.
Make sure that the DLL configuration is checked in the Projects field and click
OK. You should expect a series of warnings that Macintosh files Quickdraw.h and
Events.h are not present.

You also should expect a warning that Visual C++ cannot find X11/Xlib.h, a file
used on UNIX systems that run the X-Window System. If any other warnings appear about missing header files, double-check the path names in the Additional
include directories field of the Preprocessor sheet of the C/C++ tab in the Project
Settings dialog box (available under Build, Settings).

Adding Code Specific to Plug-Ins   Now go to the Preprocessor sheet of the
C/C++ tab in the Project Settings dialog. Make sure that only the DLL
configuration is selected in the Settings For: field. Then add _PLUG_IN to the
list of preprocessor definitions. You can read this symbol yourself when you add
plug-in-specific pieces of code.

The following listing shows part of the modified version of npshell.cpp. The full version is on this book's companion CD-ROM, in /source/chap04/npshell.cpp.

```
// npshell.cpp
   .
   .
   .
#include "stdafx.h"
#include "npChap04.h"
#include "windows.h"
```

The include file stdafx.h supports the use of Microsoft Foundation Classes. npChap04.h is the include file for this chapter's example.

```
        .
        .
        .
// Global MFC CWinApp object
#ifdef _PLUG_IN
CNpChap04App theApp;
#endif
```

The DLL version of this plug-in defines the symbol _PLUG_IN. If that symbol exists then the application should have a DllMain() rather than a WinMain() routine. This design uses class CWinAppobject to encapsulate that difference.

```
// NPP_Destroy:
//-------------------------------------------------------------
NPError NP_LOADDS
NPP_Destroy(NPP instance, NPSavedData** save)
{
    .
    .
    .

    if (This != NULL)
    {
#ifdef _PLUG_IN
            theApp.EatPlugin();
#endif
```

This design calls various methods on the application, if the plug-in preprocessor variable has been defined.

```
        ..
        .
        .
        .
        .
}
```

```
//-----------------------------------------------------------------
// NPP_SetWindow:
//-----------------------------------------------------------------
NPError NP_LOADDS
NPP_SetWindow(NPP instance, NPWindow* window)
{
    .
    .
    .
    if((window->window != NULL) && (This->hWnd == NULL))
    {
        This->fWindow = window;
#ifdef _PLUG_IN
        theApp.PreparePlugin((HWND)window->window);
#endif
    .
    .
    .
        This->lpfnOldWndProc =
                (FARPROC)SetWindowLong(This->hWnd,
                (WNDPROC)SetWindowLong(This->hWnd,
                                GWL_WNDPROC,
                                (DWORD)SubClassFunc);
```

If you use Microsoft Foundation Classes, you should cast functions by using WNDPROC rather than the more general FARPROC.

```
        .
        .
        .
                if(This->hWnd != NULL) {
                    // subclass the new one
                    This->lpfnOldWndProc =
                            (FARPROC)SetWindowLong(This->hWnd,
                            (WNDPROC)SetWindowLong(This->hWnd,
                                            GWL_WNDPROC,
                                            (DWORD)SubClassFunc);
        .
        .
        .
        }
    .
    .
    .
}
// NPP_GetJavaClass
//
```

```
//      Return the Java class representing this plugin
//
jref NPP_GetJavaClass(void)
{

    // get the Java environment. You need this information pretty
    // much for any jri (Java Runtime Interface) call.
    JRIEnv* env = NPN_GetJavaEnv();
    //\\//\\//\\//\\//\\//\\//\\//\\//\\//\\//\\//\\//\\//\\//\\//.
    // init any classes that define native methods.
    // The following functions are generated by javah running on the
    // java class(es) representing this plugin. javah generates the
    // files <java class name>.h and <java class name>.c (same for
    // any additional class you may want to use)
    // Return the main java class representing this plugin (derives
    // from Plugin class on the java side)
//    return init_AviPlayer(env);
    // if no java is used
    return NULL;

}
```

When you run a plug-in under Navigator 3.0 or higher, Navigator asks your plug-in to return the results of a function named NPP_GetJavaClass(). This function is part of LiveConnect, which is described in more detail in Chapter 18, "Plug-Ins as a Programming Resource."

If your plug-in does not use LiveConnect, just return NULL.

Note that although this plug-in doesn't use LiveConnect, you must include at least a stub for the GetJavaClass() function to satisfy the linker because Netscape included this function in its header file. For the same reason, you include all of the jri header files. You will revisit these functions in Chapter 18, "Plug-Ins as a Programming Resource."

Modifying npChap04.h

On the CD

Recall that AppWizard built a number of files for us, such as the one shown in Listing 4.1, expecting you to use them in a standalone application. Your next task is to integrate these files with the SDK code. You find npChap04.h on the companion CD-ROM in the \source\Chap04directory.

Listing 4.1 npChap04.h—The Modified Version of the Header that AppWizard Built

```
// npChap04.h : main header file for the NPCHAP04 application
//
#ifndef NPCHAP04_H
#define NPCHAP04_H
#ifndef __AFXWIN_H__
    #error include 'stdafx.h' before including this file for PCH
#endif

#include "resource.h"          // main symbols
#include "npChap04Dlg.h"


/////////////////////////////////////////////////////////////////////////
// CNpChap04App:
// See npChap04.cpp for the implementation of this class
//

class CNpChap04App : public CWinApp
{
    CNpChap04Dlg dlg;
public:
    CNpChap04App();
    void PreparePlugin(HWND hwndPluginWindow);
    void EatPlugin();

// Overrides
    // ClassWizard generated virtual function overrides
    //{{AFX_VIRTUAL(CNpChap04App)
    public:
    virtual BOOL InitInstance();
    //}}AFX_VIRTUAL

// Implementation

    //{{AFX_MSG(CNpChap04App)
        // NOTE-the ClassWizard will add and remove member functions
        // here.
        //      DO NOT EDIT what you see in these blocks of generated code !
    //}}AFX_MSG
    DECLARE_MESSAGE_MAP()
};
/////////////////////////////////////////////////////////////////////////
#endif
```

Part

I

Ch

4

Modifying npChap04.cpp

Recall that a CNpChap04App object, theApp, was added to npShell.cpp. If _PLUG_IN is defined, you want to use that copy rather than the default copy in npChap04.cpp. You'll put the appropriate preprocessor directives in to make sure that only the standalone version gets theApp here. You also define PreparePlugin() and EatPlugin(), which were declared in the header file.

The listing below shows updates to the modified version of npChap04.cpp.

```
#include "stdafx.h"
#include "npChap04.h"
#include "npChap04Dlg.h"
```

Remove the reference to npChap04Dlg.h.

```
        .

        .

        .

#ifndef _PLUG_IN
CNpChap04App theApp;
#endif
```

Make the global CNpChap04App conditional—it's only defined here if this program is a stand-alone application, and not a plug-in.

```
        .

        .

        .

// PreparePlugin()
void CNpChap04App::PreparePlugin(HWND hwndPluginWindow)
{
    dlg.m_hWnd = (HWND)NULL;
    ASSERT(dlg.m_hWnd == (HWND)NULL);

    if (!(dlg.SubclassWindow(hwndPluginWindow)))
    {
        MessageBox(NULL,"SubclassWindow Failed","Error",MB_OK);
    }
    else
    {
        dlg.PrepareDialog();
        dlg.Invalidate(TRUE);
        dlg.UpdateWindow();
    }
}
```

```
// EatPlugin()
void CNpChap04App::EatPlugin()
{
    dlg.EatDialog();
    dlg.UnSubclassWindow();
}
```

Add two methods to manage the plug-in's messages and dialog box.

```
// CNpChap04App initialization

BOOL CNpChap04App::InitInstance()
{
#ifdef _PLUG_IN
    return CWinApp::InitInstance();
#else.
```

When the application is initialized, pass the request along to the parent class.

```
        .
        .
        .

#endif
}
```

Modifying npChap04Dlg.h

By default, AppWizard makes a dialog box but doesn't hook any code to the buttons. In this section and the one that follows it, we build the software to activate these two buttons. See Listing 4.2.

Listing 4.2   npChap04Dlg.h—The Modified Header for the Dialog Handler

```
#ifndef _npChap04Dlg_H
#define _npChap04Dlg_H

// npChap04Dlg.h : header file
//

/////////////////////////////////////////////////////////////////////
// CNpChap04Dlg dialog

class CNpChap04Dlg : public CDialog
{
```

continues

Listing 4.2 Continued

```
        CButton* cbExample;
        CButton* cbCancel;
        HWND hwndButtonHandle;

// Construction
public:
        CNpChap04Dlg(CWnd* pParent = NULL);      // standard constructor
        void PrepareDialog();
        void EatDialog();
        void UnSubclassWindow();

// Dialog Data
        //{{AFX_DATA(CNpChap04Dlg)
        enum { IDD = IDD_NPCHAP04_DIALOG };
                // NOTE: the ClassWizard will add data members here
        //}}AFX_DATA

        // ClassWizard generated virtual function overrides
        //{{AFX_VIRTUAL(CNpChap04Dlg)
        protected:
        virtual void DoDataExchange(CDataExchange* pDX); // DDX/DDV support
        //}}AFX_VIRTUAL

// Implementation
protected:
        HICON m_hIcon;

        // Generated message map functions
        //{{AFX_MSG(CNpChap04Dlg)
        virtual BOOL OnInitDialog();
        afx_msg void OnSysCommand(UINT nID, LPARAM lParam);
        afx_msg void OnPaint();
        afx_msg HCURSOR OnQueryDragIcon();
        virtual void OnCancel();
        virtual void OnOK();
        //}}AFX_MSG
        DECLARE_MESSAGE_MAP()
};
#endif
```

The header file npChap04Dlg.h defines the application/plug-in's dialog class—a subclass of MFC's class CDialog. The class has three members: two buttons and a window handle (HWND). The header defines a constructor and three other methods, which are used to manage the dialog and facilitate the process of passing messages to the dialog window. Implementations for these new methods are given in npChap04Dlg.cpp, coming up later in this chapter.

The most important method for a dialog box is DoDataExchange(). Typically, an application will put up a modal dialog and wait for the user to fill in the fields, select the buttons, and generally interact with the dialog. If the user finishes by clicking OK, the application calls DoDataExchange() to pull the data out of the dialog box's data structures into its own. Each dialog class should override the default DoDataExchange() to get its data.

This include file also includes declarations of the class's message handlers. The operating system generates messages that can be caught by these handlers and used to trigger runtime events. For example, OnPaint() is called in response to the Windows message WM_PAINT, and is used to redisplay the dialog box. The following section shows how to use Visual C++'s ClassWizard to connect handlers to resources such as buttons.

Connecting the Dialog Resource to the Message Handlers

Now that the handlers were declared for the OK and CANCEL messages from the buttons, you can hook the resource up to the code.

Use the ResourceView to open IDD_NPCHAP04_DIALOG, as shown in Figure 4.12. Double-click the OK button to show its properties.

FIG. 4.12
The Resource Editor gives direct access to dialog buttons and their associated IDs.

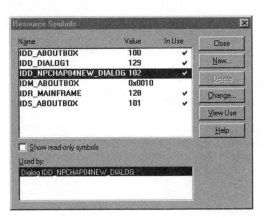

With the OK button selected in the Resource Editor, open the ClassWizard. The IDOK object is preselected in the Object Ids field. Select the BN_CLICKED message in the Messages field and associated it with the OnOK() method in the Member Functions field.

Repeat this process, associating the Cancelbutton's BN_CLICKED message with the OnCancel()method.

Modifying npChap04Dlg.cpp

Now you add the implementation of the new methods, as shown in npChap04Dlg.cpp.

```
.
.
.
#include "stdafx.h"
#include "npChap04.h"
#include "npChap04Dlg.h"
```

Again, take out the direct include of npCpah04.Dlg.h.

```
.
.
.
CNpChap04Dlg::CNpChap04Dlg(CWnd* pParent /*=NULL*/)
     : CDialog(CNpChap04Dlg::IDD, pParent)
{
.
.
.
#ifdef _PLUG_IN
     m_hIcon = AfxGetApp()->LoadIcon(IDR_MAINFRAME);
#endif
}
```

When an instance of the dialog class is constructed, load a default icon for the dialog.

```
void CNpChap04Dlg::EatDialog()
{
     ASSERT(cbExample != NULL);
     delete cbExample;
     ASSERT(cbExample != NULL);
     delete cbCancel;
}
```

As part of the clean-up process, the plug-in will call EatDialog(). When this occurs, delete the buttons, which were instantiated dynamically in the constructor.

```
void CNpChap04Dlg::UnSubclassWindow()
{
    // restore original Netscape WNDPROC
    WNDPROC* lplpfn = GetSuperWndProcAddr();
    if ( !*lplpfn )
    {
        ASSERT(0);
        return;
    }

    // Set the original window procedure using Windows AFI function
    (WNDPROC)::SetWindowLong(m_hWnd, GWL_WNDPROC, (LONG) *lplpfn );
}
```

Similarly, when the window is being closed, take the window procedure off the list and replace it with the original WNDPROC.

```
void CNpChap04Dlg::DoDataExchange(CDataExchange* pDX)
{
    CDialog::DoDataExchange(pDX);
    //{{AFX_DATA_MAP(CNpChap04Dlg)
        // NOTE: the ClassWizard will add DDX and DDV calls here
    //}}AFX_DATA_MAP
}
```

For starters, this function just calls its parent's DoDataExchange() function.

```
/////////////////////////////////////////////////////////////////
// CNpChap04Dlg message handlers

BOOL CNpChap04Dlg::OnInitDialog()
{
    CDialog::OnInitDialog();

    // Add "About..." menu item to system menu.

    // IDM_ABOUTBOX must be in the system command range.
    ASSERT((IDM_ABOUTBOX & 0xFFF0) == IDM_ABOUTBOX);
    ASSERT(IDM_ABOUTBOX < 0xF000);

    CMenu* pSysMenu = GetSystemMenu(FALSE);
    CString strAboutMenu;
    strAboutMenu.LoadString(IDS_ABOUTBOX);
    if (!strAboutMenu.IsEmpty())
    {
```

Part

I

Ch

4

```
                pSysMenu->AppendMenu(MF_SEPARATOR);
                pSysMenu->AppendMenu(MF_STRING, IDM_ABOUTBOX, ➡strAboutMenu);
        }

        // Set the icon for this dialog.  The framework does this
            // automatically when the application's main window is not a
        SetIcon(m_hIcon, TRUE);                    // Set big icon            dialog
        SetIcon(m_hIcon, FALSE);            // Set small icon

        // TODO: Add extra initialization here

        return TRUE;   // return TRUE  unless you set the focus to a
                            //control
}

void CNpChap04Dlg::OnSysCommand(UINT nID, LPARAM lParam)
{
    if ((nID & 0xFFF0) == IDM_ABOUTBOX)
    {
        CAboutDlg dlgAbout;
        dlgAbout.DoModal();
    }
    else
    {
        CDialog::OnSysCommand(nID, lParam);
    }
}

// If you add a minimize button to your dialog, you will need the code
//  below to draw the icon.  For MFC applications using the document/
//  view model, this is automatically done for you by the framework.

void CNpChap04Dlg::OnPaint()
{
#ifdef _PLUG_IN
    Cstring s = "Hello, world!";

    Crect rect;
    CPaintDC dcTmp(This);
    GetClientRect(rect);

    dcTmp.SetTextAlign(TA_BASELINE | TA_CENTER);
    dcTmp.SetTextColor(::GetSysColor(COLOR_WINDOWTEXT));
    dcTmp.SetBkMode(TRANSPARENT);
    dcTmp.TextOut((rect.right / 2), (rect.bottom / 2), s);
#else
    if (IsIconic())
```

```
        {
            CPaintDC dc(this); // device context for painting

            SendMessage(WM_ICONERASEBKGND, (WPARAM) dc.GetSafeHdc(), 0);

            // Center icon in client rectangle
            int cxIcon = GetSystemMetrics(SM_CXICON);
            int cyIcon = GetSystemMetrics(SM_CYICON);
            CRect rect;
            GetClientRect(&rect);
            int x = (rect.Width() - cxIcon + 1) / 2;
            int y = (rect.Height() - cyIcon + 1) / 2;

            // Draw the icon
            dc.DrawIcon(x, y, m_hIcon);
        }
        else
        {
#endif
            CDialog::OnPaint();
#ifndef _PLUG_IN
        }
#endif
    }
```

Much of the interesting work of a plug-in (or an application) is in OnPaint(). In this case, here is where the "Hello, world!" gets displayed.

Setting Up the Module Definition File

DLLs need to have their symbols explicitly exported to make them available to the calling program. Visual C++ uses a *module definition file* or just *definition file* (with file extension .def) to identify these and other elements for the library.

To make a definition file, choose File, New and select Text File on the dialog you see next. Put the lines in Listing 4.3 in the text file you see next and save it as npChap04.def.

Listing 4.3   npChap04.def—The Plug-in Definition File

```
LIBRARY npChap04

CODE  PRELOAD MOVEABLE DISCARDABLE
DATA  PRELOAD SINGLE
```

continues

Listing 4.3 Continued

```
EXPORTS
  NP_GetEntryPoints     @1
  NP_Initialize   @2
  NP_Shutdown           @3
```

Now go to Insert, Files into Project and add `npChap04.def` into the project.

When you write your plug-ins, you change the first line of this file to use the name you choose for your plug-in.

The elements of the second line give instructions to Windows about how to handle this DLL.

- PRELOAD—The code segment of the DLL should be loaded into memory as soon as Navigator calls for the plug-in.
- MOVEABLE—Windows is free to move the block of code around if it needs to consolidate blocks of free memory.
- DISCARDABLE—If Windows runs short on free memory, it can remove the code from memory and restore it later from the disk file as needed.

The third line passes similar information about the data segment.

- PRELOAD—The data segment, which contains global data, should be loaded as soon as the plug-in itself is loaded.
- SINGLE—Each copy of the plug-in shares the same data segment.

The final section of the definition file lists the entry points that Navigator needs to know about. These three entry points are the same for all plug-ins.

Building, Installing, and Testing the New Plug-In

Now, at last, we can build the plug-in. Choose Build, Build npChap04.dll. The DLL should build without errors or Level-3 warnings. (At Level 4, there are warnings about unused parameters in `npshell.cpp`.)

The finished plug-in is in the npChap04 project directory, in the DLL subdirectory. Move it from there to the plug-ins subdirectory beneath your copy of Netscape Navigator (version 3.0 or higher).

Testing with about:plugins

After the plug-in is installed, launch Navigator. In the Location/Go To field, type **about:plugins.** You should get a description of each installed plug-in. The description of this chapter's demo is shown in Figure 4.13. Make sure that the MIME type is correct and that the Enabled field says Yes.

FIG. 4.13
Use about:plugins to read the information Navigator found about the plug-in from the version information resource.

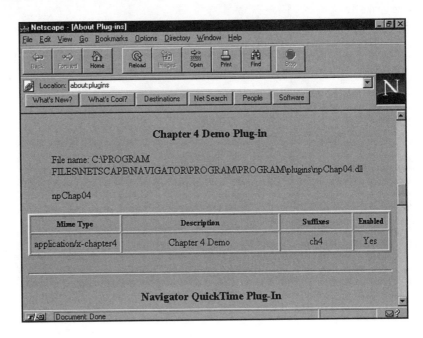

Testing with Sample Data

Recall that Navigator invokes a plug-in if the incoming content type matches the plug-in's MIME type. It also invokes the plug-in if the user opens a file with a matching file extension. In this section, we test the new plug-in by opening a file with the .ch4 file extension.

Use a text editor to make a file named test.ch4. Put any text into the file—it doesn't matter what, as long as the file is not empty.

T I P Save test files in the same directory as Navigator. In this way, you can test new plug-ins without wasting time by browsing back to a test directory.

Now use Navigator's File, Open File menu item. Select Chapter 4 Plug-In (*.ch4) from the Files of type drop-down menu. The test file, test.ch4, becomes visible in the dialog. Open the test file—the plug-in is invoked and opens the dialog, as shown in Figure 4.14.

FIG. 4.14
The plug-in starts and puts up the dialog box that you so carefully crafted.

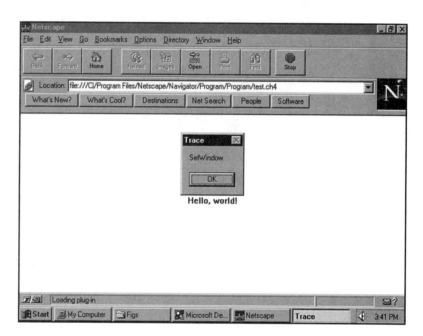

From Here...

In this chapter you saw how to build a simple Windows plug-in, using Visual C++'s AppWizard. You learned how the plug-in is built as an application and how it can be modified into a DLL. With this technique, you can use the Visual C++ debugger to trace much of the plug-in's logic without invoking Navigator.

You see another way to trace the plug-in's logic, with an emphasis on the Navigator interface, in Chapter 6, "NPP Methods: Starting the Plug-In"; Chapter 7, "NPP Methods: Handling Interaction"; Chapter 8, "NPP Methods: Other Tasks"; and Chapter 9, "Understanding NPN Methods."

- Chapter 5, "Design Issues," examines various options available to the plug-in programmer and makes specific recommendations about trade-offs.

- Chapter 6, "NPP Methods: Starting the Plug-In," provides an in-depth trace of the stream of control from the time the plug-in is invoked to the time it finishes displaying its data.

- Chapter 7, "NPP Methods: Handling Interaction," shows how the plug-in is notified of user actions, including actions that take place in Navigator and actions that take place in the plug-in window.

- Chapter 8, "NPP Methods: Other Tasks," shows how to print the plug-in contents. It also shows what happens when the user closes the plug-in window.

- Chapter 9, "Understanding NPN Methods," describes in detail the calls a plug-in programmer can make back to Navigator.

Part

I

Ch

4

Design Issues

5 Design Issues 135

6 NPP Methods: Starting the Plug-In 161

7 NPP Methods: Handling Interaction 189

8 NPP Methods: Other Tasks 215

9 Understanding NPN Methods 237

10 Example: Simple Plug-In 269

11 Example: CharFlipper Plug-In 289

12 Example: npAVI Plug-In 309

CHAPTER 5

Design Issues

Chapter 4, "Building a Simple Plug-In," introduced the mechanics of building a Navigator plug-in. But just as there is an enormous difference between a C "Hello, world!" program and a useful program that does real work, so too is there far more to a successful plug-in than the Chapter 4 demo.

Real plug-ins generally fall into three categories: plug-ins that display a specific data type, that display a document, and that give the user the ability to interact with the data (including LiveConnect plug-ins, which interact with JavaScript and Java programs).

This chapter reviews the tools available to the plug-in programmer, ending with the most sophisticated plug-in—the interactive plug-in. ■

About the plug-in run-time model

Navigator and the plug-in work together as a cooperating set of objects.

How to take advantage of native multitasking

Use threads and processes to move asynchronous work out of the user's view.

How to read data in a stream

Netscape prefers it this way—this chapter shows why.

The "Hollywood Principle"

This principle characterizes modern object-oriented programming. This chapter explains how to take advantage of object-oriented principles.

How to write a plug-in that helps debug itself

Make plug-ins "smarter" at compile time by using the techniques the authors of Microsoft Foundation Classes used.

The Run-Time Model

In Chapter 1, "Bridging the Gap from CGI and Helper Applications to Netscape Plug-Ins," you learned that plug-ins are a code resource loaded by Netscape Navigator at run-time. These resources have various names—under Windows and OS/2 Warp they are known as Dynamic Link Libraries. On a Macintosh, they are code resources. UNIX programmers call these resources shared objects. No matter what they are called by developers on the various platforms, plug-ins are software objects that are called by Navigator, and in turn they can call Navigator.

To keep the plug-in methods straight, Netscape uses the convention that the plug-in methods (which are called by Navigator) have names starting with "NPP_". Navigator offers programmers methods that they can call from their plug-ins— these methods all have names that start with "NPN_". As a plug-in programmer, you write the NPP methods. NPN methods are provided for you by Netscape.

NPP Methods

Chapters 6, 7, and 8, "NPP Methods: Starting the Plug-In," "NPP Methods: Handling Interaction," and "NPP Methods: Other Tasks," review the NPP methods in detail. This section provides an overview of those methods, and shows how they can be stitched together to form different plug-ins.

To see how the various NPP methods interact, load and build the plug-in on the CD-ROM known as zero. Although zero is designed for a Windows environment, it's a simple plug-in and can be easily ported to OS/2 Warp, the Macintosh, and the X-Window System.

Zero is a simpler plug-in than "Hello, world!". It answers the various calls from Navigator and returns. The significance is that each NPP method is instrumented with a call to the Windows method ::MessageBox(), so we can see when Navigator calls each routine.

Calling *zero* as a Full-Page Plug-In   Start by building a zero "document." Any text file will do, provided its file extension is .zer—the file extent recognized by zero. Use Navigator to open the file, and note the following chain of calls:

■ NPP_Initialize()—as the plug-in loads.

■ NPP_New()—when the first instance is loaded.

- `NPP_SetWindow()`—as Navigator passes in the information about the parent window.
- `NPP_NewStream()`—as Navigator starts the data streaming in from the file.
- `NPP_SetWindow()`—which can be called at any time, as the dimensions of the window change.

When the plug-in handles `NPP_Initialize()`, it should take all steps and initialize all memory required by the plug-in (as opposed to an instance of the plug-in). `NPP_New()` is the place to handle instance initialization.

Suppose that your plug-in object has class variables that need to be initialized. Initialize them in `NPP_Initialize()`. You should initialize instance variables in `NPP_New()`.

TIP When your plug-in is exiting, use the guidelines of what to initialize where in reverse. Memory allocated in `NPP_New()` should be freed in `NPP_Destroy()`. Memory allocated in `NPP_Initialize()` should be freed in `NPP_Shutdown()`.

After the plug-in is running, use the controls of the Navigator window to resize the window with the plug-in. Note that resizing the window triggers a call to `NPP_SetWindow()`—moving the window generally does not. Make the window small enough that a scroll bar appears. Scrolling the window triggers `NPP_SetWindow()`, too. Try printing the contents of the window, and see how `NPP_Print()` is called.

Now choose File, New Web Browser, and see that `NPP_New()` is called, but not `NPP_Initialize()`. The plug-in is already loaded, so Navigator just instantiates a new instance of the plug-in object (and its Netscape peer).

Now close one of the two Web browser windows, and observe that `NPP_Destroy()` is called. Recall that `NPP_Destroy()` is used alone on all instances of the plug-in (except the last instance). When you either close the last window or move off of this window to a different Web page, Navigator first calls `NPP_Destroy()` to clean up after the instance, and then calls `NPP_Shutdown()` to clean up after the plug-in.

Calling *zero* as an Embedded Plug-In Use Navigator to open `single.html`, shown in Listing 5.1. Experiment with various options and see how the plug-in is called. You can find this listing in the /source/Chap 05/single.html directory on this book's companion CD-ROM.

Part
II

Ch
5

Listing 5.1   *single.html*—A Single Instance of the Plug-In

```
<HTML>
<HEAD>
<TITLE>Single</TITLE>
</HEAD>
<BODY>
Here is the plug-in:
<EMBED TYPE="application/x-npZero" HEIGHT=100 WIDTH=100>
</BODY>
</HTML>
```

Notice that this HTML calls the plug-in by using the TYPE attribute of the EMBED tag because the zero plug-in doesn't use any of the contents of the source stream.

Starting a Second Copy of *zero*   The HTML file double.html, shown in Listing 5.2, has two calls to the plug-in. This listing can be found in the /source/Chap05/ double.html directory on this book's companion CD-ROM.

Listing 5.2   *double.html*—Two Instances of the Plug-In

```
<HTML>
<HEAD>
<TITLE>Single</TITLE>
</HEAD>
<BODY>
Here is the plug-in:
<EMBED TYPE="application/x-npZero" HEIGHT=100 WIDTH=100><BR>
Here is another instance:
<EMBED TYPE="application/x-npZero" HEIGHT=50 WIDTH=50><BR>
</BODY>
</HTML>
```

When this page loads, NPP_Initialize() is only called once, but NPP_New() is called twice—once for each instance. Notice that during resizing, *two* calls are made to NPP_SetWindow()—again, one for each instance. Similarly, when the window is closed, NPP_Destroy() is called twice, and then NPP_Shutdown() is called once.

Calling *zero* with No Visible Window   When Netscape first announced plug-ins for Navigator, they announced that three types of plug-in would be available: embedded, full-page, and background. There are still traces of the "background" or "hidden" type of plug-in in the SDK source code, but the implementation is simplified. To see how hidden plug-ins work, just load hidden.html, shown in Listing 5.3. You can find this listing in the /source/Chap05/hidden.html directory on this book's companion CD-ROM.

On the CD

Listing 5.3 *hidden.html*—A Hidden Plug-In

```
<HTML>
<HEAD>
<TITLE>Single</TITLE>
</HEAD>
<BODY>
Here is the plug-in:
<EMBED TYPE="application/x-npZero" HIDDEN>
</BODY>
</HTML>
```

Because the plug-in is hidden, Navigator declines to call NPP_SetWindow().

TIP

If your plug-in does any useful work without a window, call this work when you handle NPP_New(). NPP_SetWindow() is called only when the HIDDEN attribute either isn't present or is set to false.

NPN Methods

NPN methods are methods of the Navigator peer object that can be called by the plug-in. This section addresses the design consequences of calling various NPN methods.

NPN_GetURL Figure 5.1 shows what happens when a plug-in calls NPN_GetURL(). When the user opens a page that contains an <EMBED> tag, Navigator opens the stream and invokes the plug-in. The plug-in, in turn, opens a new URL, and directs the content to a specified target. When the new data streams in, Navigator reads the Content-type HTTP header, and potentially invokes a plug-in to read the stream.

When do you want to run such a sequence? Suppose that you have an existing business application that tracks material being delivered to a warehouse. You

Part
II

Ch
5

access the application, which serves up the data through a CGI or server-side JavaScript program. The first stream of data lists deliveries due in today and comes in with its own unregistered MIME media type, `application/x-expected re-ceipts`. The plug-in displays the data in its own window, with scroll bars and hot links. When the user passes the cursor over an expected delivery, the status bar shows link information, such as the order ID. If the user selects the link, the plug-in issues `NPN_GetURL()` to fetch detail information on that delivery. This request goes to a different server script, which returns the data under a different MIME media type, in turn triggering a different plug-in. Figure 5.2 shows the flow of information.

FIG. 5.1

`NPN_GetURL()` can be used to trigger new plug-ins, or new copies of the same plug-in.

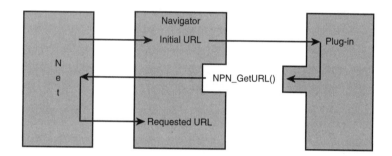

FIG. 5.2

`NPN_GetURL()` is used here to call for detail information on expected receipts.

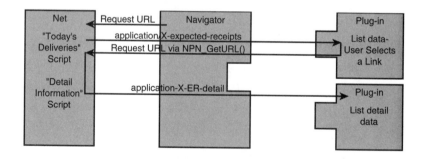

T I P To give intranet users ready access to an existing application, break this application into client and server portions. Write server scripts, such as CGI or server-side JavaScript programs, to access the server portion of the application. Write plug-ins to display the data on the client machine. Use in-house MIME media types and `NPN_GetURL()` to integrate the two halves of the application.

NPN_PostURL   Many client/server applications need to allow the end user to enter data on the client, which is later processed by the server. In the warehouse business application, for example, a user in the warehouse must inform the system that a particular delivery has arrived. The server then takes this delivery off the "Expected Receipts" list and opens a screen that enables the user to enter the quantity of each item actually received.

HTML forms are often used to post data to the server, but occasionally, this approach is a bit restrictive. In the case of the warehouse application, no one knows how many line items will appear on a given order, so the form can be designed to capture just one line item-quantity pair at a time. This design forces the user to endure network delays after each entry, and makes editing the data before sending it to the server for processing a difficult process. Here's a different design, based on plug-ins:

When the expected receipt arrives, the user opens a "Receive" page, which has a small plug-in waiting to read the Purchase Order number of the expected receipt. After the user enters this number, the plug-in accepts a series of item-number/quantity pairs. The item number is scanned in by a bar code scanner that hooks between the keyboard and the desktop computer (known in the bar code industry as a "wedge"). As each item is entered, it's stored in a data structure in memory on the client computer. It also can be written to the hard drive for added security, in case of a system failure.

If the user enters a line item ID a second time, the second quantity is added to the quantity already stored for this line item. In this way, if the same item comes off the truck on several different pallets, the total quantity is recorded.

When the truck is empty and all the items are counted, the user clicks the Done button, which displays a scrollable list of all items received. The user can review this list, edit it, and print it. Finally, the user selects Send, and the list is transferred from the desktop computer to the server by using a series of calls to `NPN_PostURL()`.

This design has the advantage that the data remains on the client as long as it's "local." That is, as long as the warehouse manager has control of the data and can edit it, update it, or print it, he or she has the data on a local computer. When the warehouse manager is ready to announce to the company that the material is now stored in the warehouse, he or she sends this information to the server. The client and the server cooperate to ensure the integrity and validity of the data.

The server, for example, might compare the list of items received with the list of items due in and tell the warehouse manager and the buyer that additional material is still expected on that purchase order (PO). The buyer might allow the PO to remain open, with the remaining items backordered, or she might close the PO, which allows the accounting system to issue a payment for the items which were actually received.

Figure 5.3 illustrates the flow of data through this system.

FIG. 5.3
As items are received, the warehouse manager logs them in by using a plug-in.

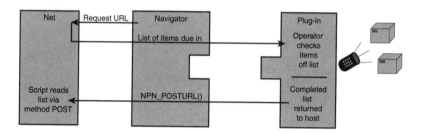

NPN_UserAgent and NPN_Version

Occasionally, you may need to enable certain plug-in features only if they are supported by the browser. By reading the browser's User Agent field, the plug-in can determine information such as the platform (such as 16-bit Windows, 32-bit Windows, or Macintosh) and the version of Navigator.

NPN_Version() returns the major and minor version numbers of both Navigator and the plug-in SDK. Navigator updates the major version number of the SDK every time a new SDK is not backward-compatible with its predecessor. Therefore, if a user attempts to load a version 3 plug-in with a Navigator 2.x, code in the SDK detects the mismatch and forces the plug-in to exit.

TIP You can use the *minor* number in the version to check for certain new features or maintenance fixes that, from time to time, may be added to Navigator.

NPN_MemAlloc and its kin

When the plug-in needs dynamic memory, you can use built-in routines (malloc() or new) or you can use NPN_MemAlloc(). The advantage of using NPN_MemAlloc() is that the memory is allocated by Navigator. This call has the following two benefits:

- Navigator can free up data structures of its own that are no longer needed, resulting in a smaller memory footprint for the combined Navigator/plug-in application.

- Navigator memory can be preserved by Navigator and made available to later copies of the plug-in.

TIP

Often, you know that a call will take memory but you don't know how many bytes the call may require. On the Macintosh, call NPN_MemFlush() to request that Navigator free up a block of memory. NPN_MemFlush() returns the number of bytes actually freed. Loop through the call until the number of bytes freed is zero (indicating that no more memory can be made available).

CAUTION

Make sure that you use NPN_MemFree() to release Navigator memory when you no longer need it. Failure to release memory leads to memory leaks and eventually crashes Navigator.

In C++ dynamic memory is allocated in two steps. The programmer calls new, which first allocates the memory and then runs the constructor to initialize the block. You can ensure that all calls to NPN_MemAlloc() are balanced with NPN_MemFree() by building these calls into new and delete.

Recall from Chapter 2, "A C++ Primer," that new and delete are operators, just like the arithmetic operators + and –. You can override C++'s built-in implementations of new and delete and write your own for your own classes. For example,

```
TMyClass::operator new(size_t)
{
 NPN_MemAlloc(size_t);
}

TMyClass::operator delete(void* theObject)
{
 NPN_MemFree(theObject);
}
```

Non-class entities (including arrays of objects) are allocated by using the global operator `::operator new( )`, and deallocated by using `::operator delete( )`. Override these operators if you need to use Navigator memory to store data structures other than objects.

NPN_NewStream   `NPN_GetURL( )` is used to open a new stream from the server to Navigator. `NPN_NewStream( )` is used to open a similar stream from the *plug-in* to Navigator. The stream can have its own MIME media type and is read in the current window. Navigator reads the content type of the new stream, and calls a plug-in or helper application if it cannot handle the media type internally.

`NPN_NewStream( )` occupies the same logical position as `Redirect( )` occupies in server-side JavaScript, `print "Location…\n\n"` in CGI scripts, and `exec( )` in UNIX programming. That is, it replaces the current instance with a new instance. When `NPN_NewStream( )` runs, it replaces the current contents of the plug-in window and (potentially) causes a new plug-in to load and be instantiated.

`NPN_NewStream( )` is used in connection with `NPN_WriteReady( )`, `NPN_Write( )`, and `NPN_DestroyStream( )`. These methods are described in greater detail in Chapter 9, "Understanding NPN Methods."

NPN_Status   One of the lessons learned by the programming community since the mid-1980s is that user interface issues are among the most important issues in program design. In the early days of the Macintosh, memory was tight and Apple provided a toolbox of user-interface routines in ROM. Nearly all Mac programs had the same "look and feel" because they all used the same interface routines. The File Open dialog box is the same on nearly all Macintosh programs.

As time passed Macintoshes with more memory became available, and some programmers tried to improve on the built-in routines. They discovered that Mac users preferred the built-in interface—programs that didn't provide the familiar menu bar and built-in dialogs didn't do well in the marketplace.

The lesson for plug-in developers is clear. Plug-ins are a creature of Netscape Navigator. The plug-ins that do best in the marketplace enable the user to believe that he or she has never left Navigator. The careful plug-in programmer will duplicate the Navigator interface wherever possible.

When a user moves the cursor over a hyperlink in Navigator, for example, the destination appears in the status bar. The plug-in programmer can give the plug-in the same behavior by using `NPN_Status()`, by tracking the mouse-movement messages.

Other *NPN* methods   The method `NPN_RequestRead()` is used to request data from a seekable stream. This method is described in greater detail in the section of this chapter, "Seekable Streams."

Navigator also provides four methods that may be used to send data back to the Net through Navigator. `NPN_GetURL()` and `NPN_PostURL()` generate the HTTP transfer methods `GET` and `POST` respectively. Each method has an associated `...Notify()` method; if you use the `...Notify()` method, your plug-in will be called when Navigator completes the transfer.

If you use the `...Notify()` versions of these methods Navigator will call your implementation of `NPP_URLNotify()` when the transaction completes. For more information on these methods see Chapter 9, "Understanding NPN Methods," and Chapter 13, "Getting Back on the Network".

Moving Existing Applications to the Web

Many plug-ins are built to "Web-enable" existing applications. The warehouse business application referred to previously in this chapter is one example. Often an existing application must be realigned in order to fit into the Web's look and feel. For example, an existing application typically does the following:

- Maps its menu items into the plug-in window because Netscape is already using the menu bar. Sometimes, pop-up menus or other controls are appropriate for this purpose.
- Allows the window to be resized—generally smaller than the full screen the application previously may have enjoyed.
- Is deployed as a shared library or DLL and installed in the Netscape plug-in directory—a rather different approach than is usual with applications.

The capability to link your application to the corporate intranet or World Wide Web can allow your application to take on whole new areas of functionality. Often, much of the cost of developing an application lies in analysis and design—the essence of an application can be "Web-enabled" as a plug-in for a fraction of the cost of the development of a full application.

Threads and Processes

Recall from Chapter 3, "Integrating Plug-Ins into Web Site Design," that many of the NPN methods do not return a result. Rather, they start Navigator processing and then return almost immediately. As mentioned in the section "Other NPN Methods," versions of the methods are available that call back the plug-in with a notification that the action is complete.

The plug-in programmer can use this same asynchronous behavior in the plug-in. Most operating systems give the programmer a way to start a lightweight process, or *thread*, that shares the address space with the parent process but follows a separate execution path.

For even more isolation from the other execution path, consider forking a whole new process. (This step is known as *spawning* in some operating systems.) This method frequently is convenient when the core of an existing application can be lifted out of its user interface and called as an asynchronous algorithm. Figure 5.4 illustrates this kind of design.

FIG. 5.4
The core of an existing application can be called as an asynchronous process.

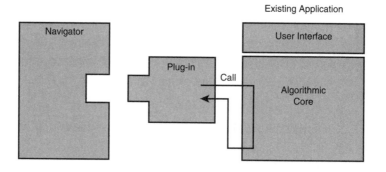

Accessing the Data

The essence of plug-ins is to take data from the Web and present it to the user, within the context of Netscape Navigator. One of the most important tasks for the plug-in is to access Web data.

Netscape provides three methods for accessing Web data from a URL. The programmer may choose to read and present the data as it comes in from the Net—a process known as *streaming*. Streaming is the preferred method because the user begins to see the data as soon as any of the data is available.

An alternate method of accessing the Web data is to allow Navigator to read the entire stream into the cache, and then read the data as a whole. This method has two disadvantages.

First, the user must wait until the entire stream is sent before any data is presented. With some file formats, such a design is difficult to avoid. The original JFIF (commonly known as the *JPEG image format* on the Net) stored some information at the end of the file that was needed to display it. The newer Progressive JPEG files are designed so that the viewer can start work as soon as it has received the first few bytes—a behavior much appreciated by users with a slow modem connection to the Net.

The second disadvantage is that the file may be too large for the cache. In this case Navigator may simply not deliver the file, giving the plug-in a null file name.

The newest and most innovative access method is called *seekable streams*. An understanding of seekable streams must be based on an understanding of conventional HTTP servers. This topic is taken up in the section of this chapter, entitled "Seekable Streams." To clarify the distinction between seekable streams and the more conventional kind, seekable streams are sometimes said to be in *pull mode*, in contrast with the more conventional *push mode*.

Streaming

When Navigator calls the plug-in's NPP_NewStream() method, it passes in a stream mode parameter. The plug-in sets this parameter before it returns. The default setting is NP_NORMAL, which means that the contents of the stream will be presented "one byte at a time."

When the stream is delivered in NP_NORMAL mode, Navigator delivers the data by using a series of calls to NPP_Write(). Navigator tells the plug-in how many bytes are available in the len parameter. Under some circumstances the buffer may actually contain more bytes than the len parameter advertises. Under these conditions the parameter should process as many bytes as possible, up to the number given in len, and should return the number actually processed to Navigator as the return value of the function.

To give Navigator permission to begin writing, the plug-in should respond to the Navigator's call to NPP_WriteReady(). Navigator will call NPP_WriteReady() to find out how much data the plug-in is ready to accept.

> **N O T E**   It's permissible for the plug-in to read fewer bytes in `NPP_Write()` than are actually available, but `NPP_Write()` should be sure to read at least as many bytes as was advertised by `NPP_WriteReady()`, or the number given in the `NPP_Write()` `len` parameter, whichever is smaller. ▪

For efficiency, nearly all of the links between the client and the server buffer their data, so the data probably will arrive in chunks. The plug-in should build these chunks into the data structures associated with this media type, and present the data it has as soon as possible.

AsFile

If the plug-in tells Navigator to save the data as a file (by setting the stream mode to `NP_ASFILE`), Navigator uses its disk caching mechanism as the basis for saving the data to the hard drive. Then it calls the plug-in's `NPP_StreamAsFile()` method and passes a pointer to the file name (referred to as `fname`).

If you want to process the stream as a file in a Navigator 3.0 plug-in, you should set the stream mode to `NP_ASFILEONLY`. This mode is more efficient than `NP_ASFILE` because it reads directly from the file (if the file is local) rather than saving it in the cache. `NP_ASFILE` remains in the specification to provide backward compatibility with Navigator 2.0.

> **CAUTION**
>
> Make sure that you compare `fname` with NULL before using it. If an error occurs while Navigator writes the stream to the hard drive, it still may call `NPP_StreamAsFile()` but sets `fname` to NULL.

> **N O T E**   After the file is in the disk cache, it remains there until the stream or the instance is destroyed. The plug-in can free up disk space by calling `NPN_DestroyStream()` when it has finished processing the file. ▪

Seekable Streams

A Web browser requests an entity from a Web server by using the *Hypertext Transport Protocol* (HTTP)—the protocol of the Web. With HTTP Version 1.0, the request was all-or-nothing. If the requested entity was a file, the entire file was sent. Over high-speed links this design caused few problems, but with modem-transfer rates sometimes falling below 1,000 bytes per second, the transfer of larger files can take too long for many user's needs.

Newer versions of HTTP support byte-range requests. A client can request just a portion of the file. This design also can be used to allow a client to seek records in a data file on the server, much in the same way that it may read a record from a local hard drive.

If the requested entity is on a server that recognizes the byte-range protocol, the call to NPP_NewStream() will have the Boolean parameter seekable set to true.

N O T E   Local disk files are always seekable and afford a good way to test code that depends on seekable streams. ∎

It isn't enough that a stream be seekable—the plug-in must explicitly request that the stream be set to mode NP_SEEK. Correspondingly, there is no guarantee of seekablity if the stream is not advertised as "seekable" by the call to NPP_NewStream( ).

When a stream is set up as seekable, the plug-in actively pulls data from the server. (Recall that seekable streams that are set to NP_SEEK mode are in "pull mode"). To request bytes from the stream, the plug-in calls NPN_RequestRead( ). Navigator responds by calling NPP_Write( ) and delivering as much of the data as is available.

Use seekable streams in much the same way as you use fseek() in a conventional application to read records from a hard drive. Suppose that you have a large file on the server stored as a binary tree. Tables 5.1 and 5.2 show the relative times required to fetch an entry from the server. These calculations assume that the file is 10M (megabytes), and that the client connects to the server at 1,700 bytes per second, a typical value for a 14,400bps (bits per second) modem. Records are assumed to be 100 bytes each. Hard drive access is assumed to take an average of 20 milliseconds. Because the file is organized as a binary tree of records, it takes an average of about eight seeks to find a given record.

Part

II

Ch

5

Table 5.1   Time to Retrieve a Record from a File, Accessed Through a Non-Seekable Stream

Step	Time
Client sends a GET request for the file	59 milliseconds
Server sends the file to the client	1.7 hours
Client looks up the record from the hard disk	170 milliseconds
Total Time	**1.7+ hours**

Table 5.2   Time to Retrieve a Record from the Server, Using a Seekable Stream

Step	Time
Client sends byte-range requests	502 milliseconds
Server sends the requested records to the client	6.875 seconds
Total Time	**7.377 seconds**

The advantage of seekable streams becomes stronger as the size of the data file increases. If the file is small or is organized poorly, it often is more efficient to send down the entire file rather than search it over the Net.

The Hollywood Principle

Most formal training in programming teaches students to write a complete application (similar to the "Hello, world!" application described in Chapter 2, "A C++ Primer"). Even applications, however, are often written today as callable routines (although with one entry point—main()). Plug-ins are written as callable libraries with multiple entry points.

Modern object-oriented programs such as Navigator plug-ins are sometimes known as being built with the "Hollywood Principle"—"Don't call us, we'll call you." This design can be confusing to programmers trained to follow the flow of control of a program.

Figure 5.5 illustrates classical program design. The program proceeds step-by-step, as though through a flowchart, from beginning to end.

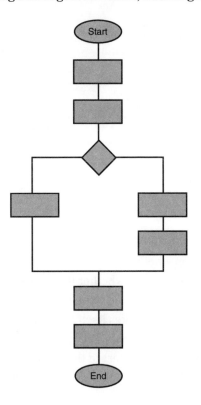

FIG. 5.5

Classical programs proceed through a series of steps and decisions from beginning to end.

Part
II

Ch
5

Modern programs with a graphical user interface have designs more like the one shown in Figure 5.6. The software loops continually looking for user actions. Depending on the platform, the loop may be part of the application or part of the operating system. When the user takes an action, such as pressing the mouse button, the loop dispatches a message to the underlying software object. (The Macintosh operating system calls these messages "events.") The underlying object handles the message and returns control to the loop. Typical responses to mouse-down messages include popping up a menu, changing the state of a check box, or moving the starting point for text entry.

FIG. 5.6
Modern programs consist of a loop that issues messages (also known as events) to the program.

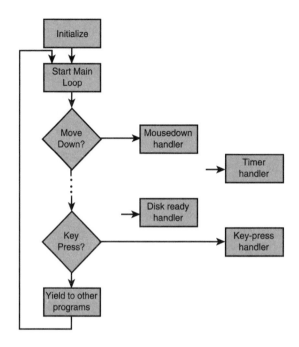

It doesn't matter to the main loop whether the software to handle the message was present when the application was built, or whether it was linked in at run-time, as long as the underlying object is there to handle the message when it is called. Therefore, when a plug-in is loaded, it makes itself available to handle messages that occur in the parts of the screen for which it is responsible. If the plug-in instance is deleted later, messages to that part of the screen are directed to the software object that replaces it. Figure 5.7 illustrates how a plug-in that loads at run-time handles messages.

Starting the Plug-In

Recall from Chapter 3, "Integrating Plug-Ins into Web Site Design," that plug-ins may be full-page, embedded, or hidden. Although these three options are often known as plug-in "types," they actually are three ways of calling a plug-in. The same plug-in may be called through a hyperlink (which results in a full-page plug-in), an <EMBED> tag with HEIGHT and WIDTH attributes (which results in an embedded plug-in), or an <EMBED> tag with the HIDDEN attribute set to true (resulting in a hidden or background plug-in). Navigator tells the plug-in how it was called by setting the mode parameter in the NPP_New( ) call.

FIG. 5.7
A software object doesn't need to be linked into the application statically in order to be available to handle messages from the main loop.

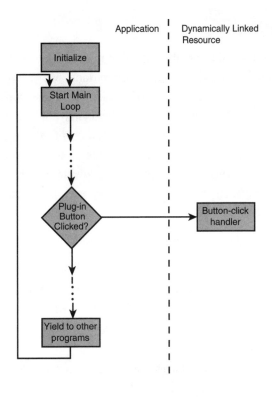

Application | Dynamically Linked Resource

Initialize

Start Main Loop

Plug-in Button Clicked?

Button-click handler

Yield to other programs

TIP Consider each of these three calling modes when designing your plug-in, and try to do something appropriate for each one. If your plug-in is designed to play an audio stream, for example, and the user calls it as an embedded plug-in, consider displaying a logo in the window and playing the sound anyway.

Similarly, if a video display plug-in is called as a background plug-in, consider popping up a model dialog that tells the user when the plug-in was called incorrectly, perhaps by adding a message that the attributes of HEIGHT and WIDTH in the <EMBED> tag for the URL must be set.

Also recall that the HTML coder may place additional parameters and values in an <EMBED> tag. These parameters are passed to the plug-in through the argc, argn, and argv parameters in much the same way as parameters are passed to C and C++ applications when invoked from a command line.

Handling Interaction

For type and document viewers, after the plug-in reads the contents of the stream and draws them into the window, its job is often done. More sophisticated plug-ins may display controls in the window. Scroll bars are a simple example. Pushbuttons, sliders, check boxes, radio buttons, and text fields may all be part of more sophisticated plug-ins. The plug-in programmer can interact with the user by using the mechanisms of the native operating system. Messages or events can be mapped to the parts of the window that serve as controls, allowing the plug-in to change the contents of the window, change an internal state, or communicate back to Netscape and to the network.

 Remember that plug-in windows tend to be small—especially for embedded plug-ins. Take care that your plug-in doesn't present so many controls that the user is overwhelmed. Rather, consider offering several plug-ins that communicate with one other. If these plug-ins may run on different machines, you can use the Net for communications. If they all run on a single desktop computer, you can use NPN_NewStream() in one plug-in to generate data for another.

If the plug-in requires many controls at the same time, consider setting the plug-in up as a full-page plug-in to ensure that you have room for all the controls.

Printing

One principal difference between full-page plug-ins and embedded plug-ins is in the way in which they handle printing. The page is the unit of printing, so Netscape allows full-page plug-ins to control their own printing if necessary.

When the user chooses File, Print while displaying an HTML page with one or more embedded plug-ins, Navigator puts up the printing dialog. It then calls NPP_Print(). The plug-in should respond by drawing into the print rectangle.

If the plug-in is full-page, NPP_Print() is called before the print dialog displays, which gives the plug-in an opportunity to modify the print dialog and preset various controls. If NPP_Print() handles the printing, it should set the parameter pluginPrinted (a component of NPFullPrint, which, in turn, is a component of NPPrint) to true before returning. Otherwise, Navigator itself presents the print dialog, and then calls the plug-in to print its contents.

TIP If your full-page plug-in handles its printing, remember the parameters for the dialog box and restore them the next time the user asks to print the same document.

Destroying the Instance

Recall from the beginning of this chapter that Navigator calls `NPP_Destroy()` when it leaves or closes the window associated with a plug-in instance. It occasionally may be attractive to associate information with the instance. If the user returns to the same URL, Navigator can provide this stored information back to the plug-in.

Information about printing defaults, for example, can be associated with a document URL. A plug-in that presents time-based data, such as audio or video, may retain information about the point in the file at which the presentation stopped. When the plug-in is later invoked on the same URL, Navigator restores the time index or frame number so that the plug-in can resume. This design can be attractive, particularly when using seekable streams.

To associate information with a plug-in instance, use `NPN_MemAlloc()` to set up a block of memory, and then store the data in that block. Pass a handle to the block of memory in the `save` parameter of `NPP_Destroy()`.

> **CAUTION**
>
> `NPN_MemAlloc()` returns a pointer to Navigator memory. This memory is not persistent—if the user exits Navigator, information in these blocks is lost. Do not use the `NPP_Destroy()` `save` parameter to store information essential for the plug-in. Rather, use native functions to save the data to the hard drive.

NOTE If you saved data about a specific URL with this plug-in by using the `save` parameter of `NPP_Destroy()` and that data is still available the next time the user visits that URL, the plug-in finds it in the saved parameter of `NPP_New()`. ■

Designing for Debug

Usually, plug-ins tend to be smaller than complete applications because much of their user interface is already provided by Navigator. Research reported by Steve

Part
II

Ch
5

McConnell in *Code Complete* (Microsoft Press, 1993) shows that up to 80 percent of the total development time on small programs (around 2,000 lines of code) is taken by the actual construction of the program: detailed design, coding, debugging, and unit testing.

To reduce costs and increase quality in plug-ins, use construction techniques that minimize defects in the code, and make it more likely that such defects are caught early.

Get the Compiler to Flag Defects

You can force some defects to be caught by the compiler. A common mistake in C and C++, for example, is to use the assignment operator, =, when you intended to use a comparison operator, ==. The following code is legal C++ but probably is not what the programmer intended:

```
if (myVariable = NULL)
{
 // take some action
}
```

The variable `MyVariable` is set to `NULL`. The assignment succeeds, so the `if` statement takes the "true" path. If the programmer reverses the order of the two elements of the comparison, as in the following example, the compiler will complain because you cannot assign a variable to a constant:

```
if (NULL = MyVariable)
{
 // take some action
}
```

TIP Use the C++ `const` capability to tell the compiler that variables are really constants. For example, the following line of code claims that `kFieldLength` will not be modified at run-time:

```
const short kFieldLength = 13;
```

If the programmer writes any code that attempts to change the value of `kFieldLength`, the compiler reports an error.

Many programmers use the convention that an initial lowercase 'k' on a variable's name means that it's a constant. The compiler doesn't care about this naming convention, but its use can help keep you (or the maintenance programmer who comes after you) from becoming confused.

> **TIP** Put const variables first in comparisons so that the compiler will complain if you accidentally forget the second equals sign in the comparison operator.

Use Lint and Warnings

Many examples of code are likely to be defective but nonetheless "legal" C and C++. Most development systems include a program named lint, which sometimes is built into the compiler as a high warning level. If you have lint, use it. If you don't, set the warning level to its highest setting. Set a goal of writing code that generates no warnings. Failing this, make sure that you understand each warning and are confident that it doesn't constitute a defect.

Use the ASSERT macro

Most C/C++ development environments include a macro named ASSERT. This macro takes an expression as a parameter. If the expression is true, the flow of control passes through the macro. If the expression is false, execution stops and the user is told that an ASSERT has failed.

Most environments set up ASSERT so that it's active only when the DEBUG flag is set. In Visual C++, for example, ASSERTS are compiled in when you build the Debug version of the program, but not when you build the Release version.

Part

II

Ch

5

> **TIP** Document your assumptions with the ASSERT macro. If you pass a pointer to a function, and the pointer should never be NULL, write the following:
>
> ```
> TMyClass::TMyMethod(TSomeClass* aPointer)
> {
>  ASSERT(NULL != aPointer);
>  .
>  .
>  .
> }
> ```
>
> During testing, if a chain of circumstances ever conspires to cause aPointer to be NULL, you see the message immediately.

Work with the MFC ASSERTs

If you use the Microsoft Foundation Classes, you have undoubtedly run into ASSERT failures coming up from MFC. MFC is loaded with asserts that document the developers' assumptions.

When you receive an ASSERT warning from MFC, note the file name and line number. MFC is a large, complex library, but Microsoft supplies the source code, so you can learn what the ASSERT is complaining about.

If you have Microsoft's Books OnLine, which come with Visual C++, you can search for ASSERT to see a list of each MFC assert and what it means. Use this list and also the MFC source code to understand why your code is triggering the ASSERT.

> **CAUTION**
>
> MFC runs slightly different initialization code, depending on whether it's called from an application or a DLL. Consequently, you may see an ASSERT warning when you call a routine from a plug-in, but not when you make the same call from an application.
>
> If you have this problem, write a test harness for your plug-in and follow the failing code in the debugger to see how your code got into the problem. Then go back and change your code so that it doesn't trigger the ASSERT.

From Here...

This chapter reviews the design issues that impact plug-ins—the types of plug-ins that exist, how to start them, how they handle user interaction, and how to debug them.

Plug-ins consist of two cooperating objects. One object, *the plug-in object*, has methods that you, as the plug-in programmer, write. Navigator calls these methods to get information from the plug-in or to give it information. The other object, *the Netscape peer object*, is written by Netscape and lives "inside" Navigator. You call the peer object to get information from Navigator or to ask Navigator to take certain actions. Methods of the plug-in object start with NPP_ and methods of the Netscape peer object start with NPN_.

- Chapter 6, "NPP Methods: Starting the Plug-In," provides an in-depth trace of the stream of control from the time the plug-in is invoked to the time it finishes displaying its data.

- Chapter 7, "NPP Methods: Handing Interaction," shows how the plug-in is notified of user actions, including both actions that take place in Navigator and actions that occur within the plug-in window.

- Chapter 8, "NPP Methods: Other Tasks," shows how to print the plug-in contents. It also shows what happens when the user closes the plug-in window.

- Chapter 9, "Understanding NPN Methods," describes in detail the calls a plug-in programmer can make back to Navigator.

Part

II

Ch

5

CHAPTER 6

NPP Methods: Starting the Plug-In

This chapter begins a three-chapter detailed description of the elements of the Navigator plug-in Software Development Kit (SDK), emphasizing the hooks to these elements (NPP methods) that need to be written by you, the programmer.

Specifically, this chapter begins at the point at which Navigator installs and inventories its plug-ins. It proceeds through the point at which Navigator loads the plug-in and makes a series of calls to it. This chapter concludes with the plug-in in control, displaying its data. ■

How Navigator knows which plug-in is associated with which MIME media type

By understanding the difference between installation and loading, you can distinguish between install failures and coding errors.

What happens when Navigator loads a plug-in

Adding a line of instrumentation to an NPP call helps isolate loading errors.

Which calls Navigator makes before sending data to the plug-in

Before sending data, Navigator and the plug-in negotiate the mechanism.

How Navigator links the plug-in to the data stream

Depending on the application, you may use one of three mechanisms—or no mechanism at all!

What options the plug-in programmer has about presenting the data

Your user may view the data as a document, an embedded image, or as a small application.

Launching the Plug-In

Recall that Navigator expects to find all plug-ins in a specific directory. In the case of the Windows version of Navigator, plug-ins must also begin with the letters np in their file name. When the user launches Navigator, Navigator looks at each candidate plug-in to see if it advertises a MIME media type that it handles. (During this process Navigator puts a message on-screen that says it's Loading plug-ins. As a programmer, you understand that it's only registering, or installing, the plug-ins. Later, when the plug-in is needed, Navigator actually loads the plug-in into memory.)

When Navigator encounters a request to handle a particular MIME media type, it looks at the list of plug-ins and selects the plug-in that handles this type. If the plug-in is already loaded (by a prior instance of this type) Navigator makes another instance of the plug-in. If Navigator is seeing this media type for the first time, it loads the plug-in code, and then makes the first instance.

The following section describes this start-up process in detail.

Advertising a MIME Media Type

Some software systems are designed so that a program announces to the world that it provides some service. These programs are said to "advertise" the service. For example, two computers communicating by using the Transmission Control Protocol (TCP) are said to advertise their available buffer space (known as "window size") to each other so that each computer knows how much data the other can handle.

Every Navigator plug-in must advertise at least one MIME media type and subtype. Netscape's documentation usually abbreviates "MIME media type and subtype" to "MIME type." This section shows how to put the MIME type identifiers into the plug-in. The method differs for each supported platform.

Setting Up a MIME Media Type in a Windows Plug-In   The MIME media type is specified in a Windows plug-in in the Version Information resource. The specific resource to change is named VS_VERSION_INFO. You should add three lines to the "StringFileInfo" section of the resource. These new lines resemble this example:

```
VALUE "MIMEType", "application/x-chapter6\0"
VALUE "FileExtents", "ch6\0"
VALUE "FileOpenName", "Chapter 6 Plug-In (*.ch6)\0"
```

To see a specific example of how to set the Version Information Resource, see the section "Modifying the Version Information Resource" in Chapter 4, "Building a Simple Plug-In."

TIP You can make your plug-in handle more than one MIME media type. Just separate the entries in the version information resource with vertical bars (for example, VALUE "MIMEType", "application/x-chapter6 | application/chapter-6\0").

The MIME media type you read should be selected in accordance with RFC 1590. A description of RFC 1590, and some examples of MIME media types, are given in the section, "MIME," in Chapter 1, "Bridging the Gap from CGI and Helper Applications to Netscape Plug-Ins."

TIP Remember that only registered MIME media types should be used without the leading x-. To make up a media type for internal use only, use the x-. To release a new media type for general use on the Net, go through the registration process described in the RFC.

See the "Registering a MIME Type" section in Chapter 1 for more information on the registration process.

Setting Up a MIME Media Type in an OS/2 Warp Plug-In   To specify the MIME media type and file extensions in an OS/2 Warp plug-in, modify the RCDATA lines in the makefile. To add the unregistered MIME media type used as this chapter's example, the makefile might include the following:

```
#include "npapi.h"
        RCDATA NP_INFO_ProductVersion { 1,0,0,1}
        RCDATA NP_INFO_MIMEType       {"application/x-chapter6\0"}
        RCDATA NP_INFO_FileExtents    {"ch6\0"}
        RCDATA NP_INFO_FileOpenName   {"Chapter 6 Sample Plugin\0"}
```

To include multiple MIME types in the plug-in, use a vertical bar to delimit each value in the MIME media type. For example, VALUE "MIMEType", "application/x-chapter6 | application/chapter6\0" specifies that the plug-in will handle both the unregistered and the registered version of the type.

Setting Up a MIME Media Type in a Macintosh Plug-In   Under Windows, each compiler vendor provides a tool to access Windows resources. On the Macintosh, Apple supplies ResEdit, which is included by nearly every compiler vendor in their development environment. ResEdit is the easiest way to change resources interactively—the technique used here to set the media type of a Macintosh plug-in. This section shows how to use ResEdit to specify the MIME media type(s) of the plug-in.

On a Macintosh, every file has a "resource fork" and a "data fork." These "forks" are simply two sections of the file. On some files the resource fork is empty. In an application, however, the code, the windows templates, the strings, and all the other resources are present in the resource fork.

Before the application is compiled, the resources are stored in a file with the extension .rsrc. Use ResEdit to open one of the .rsrc files that comes with the Macintosh version of the SDK—choose File, Open and use the dialog box to select the file. Figure 6.1 shows the two resources present in ViewText.rsrc.

FIG. 6.1
The resource files in the SDK contain a string resource and a version resource.

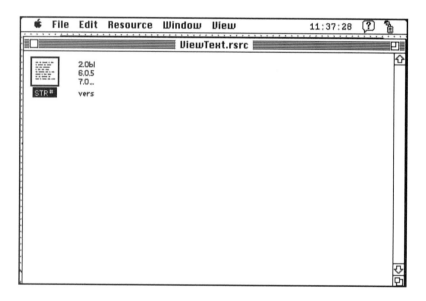

The vers resource contains information the Macintosh Finder shows the user if the user requests the **Get Info** menu item from the **File** menu. You should set the two version resources to meaningful numbers and release levels, although these resources are used only to provide information to the user. Figure 6.2 shows the range of information you can pass in a vers resource. Figure 6.3 shows the same information, viewed from the Finder.

FIG. 6.2
Using ResEdit, set up the vers resource.

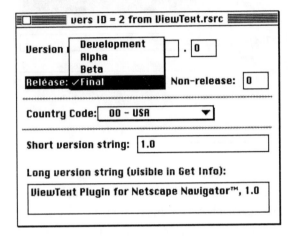

FIG. 6.3
The end user sees the vers information in the **Get Info** dialog box.

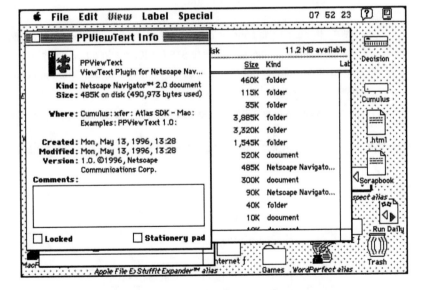

The resource used by Navigator to identify the MIME media type of a plug-in is the STR# resource, specifically STR# 128. Figure 6.4 shows STR# 128 open in ResEdit.

FIG. 6.4
Navigator reads STR#
128 to determine
which MIME media
types a plug-in
handles.

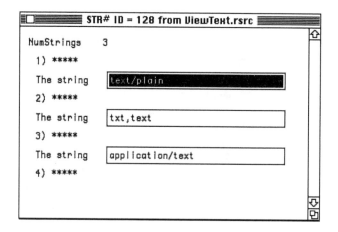

As far as ResEdit is concerned, STR# resources just contain lists of strings. Navigator, however, interprets the strings in STR# 128 as holding the MIME media type and file extensions associated with this plug-in. To specify a MIME media type and set of file extensions for a plug-in, set string 1 of STR# 128 to the MIME media type and string 2 to the file extension.

N O T E   If your plug-in handles more than one media type and file extension, add
additional pairs of strings to STR# 128. To add a new string, select the next
unused string number (for example, 3) *****) in ResEdit, and then choose **Resource,
Insert New Field(s)**.

Figure 6.5 shows how STR# 128 looks in Netscape's LiveAudio plug-in. ■

FIG. 6.5
Use ResEdit to set up
pairs of strings in the
STR# 128 resource.

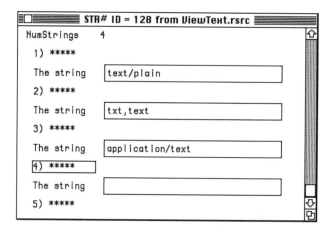

Figure 6.6 shows the corresponding list of types on the about:plugins page in Navigator 2.0. Navigator has read STR# 128 in each plug-in, add adds one line to the about:plugins page for each MIME type in STR# 128. (Newer versions of Navigator work in the same way, but their about:plugins page contains even more information.)

FIG. 6.6
Navigator interprets each pair of strings in STR# 128 as a separate media type and file extension.

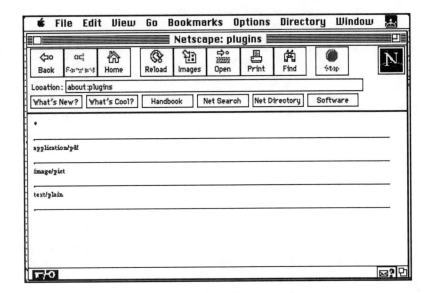

Setting Up a MIME Media Type in a UNIX Plug-In The X Window System doesn't have the concept of a "resource" in the same way as Windows, OS/2, and the Macintosh do, so if you are preparing a plug-in for use under UNIX you need to build the reference to the MIME media type into the program itself. Navigator calls your UNIX program with two new calls—NPP_GetMIMEDescription() and NPP_GetValue(). Use the following code as a model for implementing these two functions:

```
#ifdef XP_UNIX
char* NPP_GetMIMEDescription()
{
   return ("application/x-chapter6:ch6:Chapter 6 Sample Plug-in");
}

#define PLUGIN_NAME "Chapter 6 Sample Plug-in"
#define PLUGIN_DESCRIPTION "Demonstrates how to pass information
➥to Navigator from a UNIX plug-in"
```

Part
II

Ch
6

```
NPError NPP_GetValue(void* future, NPPVariable theVariable, void* value)
{
  NPError err = NPERR_NO_ERROR;
  if (variable == NPPVpluginNameString)
    *((char**)value) = PLUGIN_NAME;
  else if (variable == NPPVpluginDescriptionString)
    *((char**)value) = PLUGIN_DESCRIPTION;
  else
    err = NPERR_GENERIC_ERROR;
  return err;
}
#endif
```

Be sure to use the file `examples/UnixTemplate/source/UnixShell.c` (part of the UNIX SDK) as the model for your UNIX plug-in. You also will want to examine the files in `examples/Simple/Source` from the same SDK. In particular, look for conditionals based on `#ifdef XP_UNIX` to see how UNIX plug-ins differ from plug-ins built for other operating systems.

Loading the Plug-In

When Navigator is loaded, it goes through the available plug-ins reading MIME media types. If a user has two or more plug-ins loaded that both handle the same MIME type, Navigator registers the last type it finds.

Navigator finds media types in one of three ways:

- Navigator connects to a server that sends a `Content-type` header.
- Navigator reads a `TYPE` attribute in an `<EMBED>` tag.
- Navigator reads a local file with a file extension that matches the file extension advertised in a plug-in.

If the media type is one that Navigator handles itself (such as `text/html` or `image/gif`), Navigator calls its own internal routines. If the media type is not native to Navigator but there is no plug-in or helper application to handle the type, Navigator displays a dialog box similar to the one shown in Figure 6.7.

If Navigator finds a matching plug-in on the list, it next checks to see if the plug-in has already been loaded.

If the plug-in hasn't been loaded, Navigator makes a series of calls to the plug-in. The first of these calls is to methods provided by the SDK.

FIG. 6.7
If Navigator cannot find a plug-in or helper application to handle the media type, it announces that fact to the user.

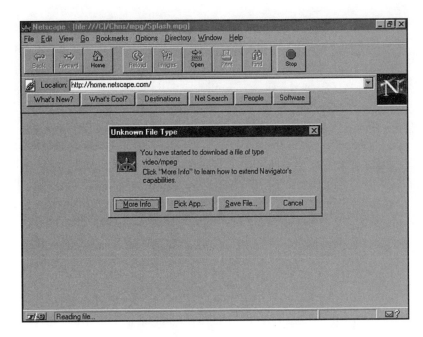

The Call to *main* To see how Navigator loads a plug-in, use the Macintosh SDK as an example. When Navigator is ready to load a plug-in, it first calls `main()`. In the Macintosh SDK, `main()` is located in the file `npmain.h`.

> **N O T E** Usually, C++ source code is stored in files with a special file extension such as `.C`, `.cc`, or `.cpp`. Headers are contained in `.h` files (sometimes referred to as `.hpp`). Netscape chose to put much of their source in the `.h` files. You can review files like `npmac.h`, `npwin.h`, and `npupp.h` to see how they implemented their part of the plug-in. ∎

Navigator passes three parameters to the plug-in via `main()`. First, it passes a table of pointers to various Netscape functions. Second, it passes a table of pointers to the plug-in functions. Finally, it passes a `UniversalProcPointer` (UPP) to an exit routine.

From `main()`, Netscape makes three checks:

1. Check the pointers passed by Navigator to ensure that they are valid. If any of these parameters is null, the plug-in exits with exit code `NPERR_INVALID_FUNCTABLE_ERROR`.

Part
II

Ch
6

2. Check the major version number of Navigator to ensure that it's compatible with this SDK. If Navigator has a newer version number than the SDK, the plug-in exits with exit code NPERR_INCOMPATIBLE_VERSION_ERROR.

3. Check the sizes of both function tables to be sure they are large enough to contain the functions this plug-in will be using.

> **N O T E**   In some beta versions of the SDK the third check, comparing the sizes of the function tables, is commented out. Check the latest version of the SDK for your platform if you think your plug-in may be overflowing one of the function tables. ◼

After the checks are completed, the plug-in copies the pointers in the Navigator plug-in table into its own local variables. These local variables point to the NPN_ functions. The plug-in likewise copies pointers of its own functions, the NPP_ functions, into the plug-in function table for use by Navigator.

Now that Navigator has copies of the pointers to the NPP_ functions, it can call these functions directly. The first function it calls is NPP_Initialize(), described later in this chapter, in the "The Programmer's Start-up Code: NPP_Initialize()" section.

Starting from *DllEntryPoint()*   Although the Macintosh views the plug-in as a code resource, the various versions of Microsoft Windows see the plug-in as a Dynamic Link Library, or DLL. The Win32 model (used in Windows NT, Windows 95, and the Win32s simulator) has two concepts of multitasking—processes and threads.

To load the plug-in from the disk into memory (in Navigator's address space) Navigator calls the Windows function LoadLibrary(). Navigator then uses the GetProcAddress() call to find the plug-in's DllEntryPoint() function, which performs the same tasks as the function more commonly named DllMain().

The first time Navigator needs the plug-in, it calls DllEntryPoint() and passes the DLL_PROCESS_ATTACH reason code. Subsequent instantiations pass the DLL_THREAD_ATTACH reason code. In either case (as well as in the corresponding DETACH cases), DllEntryPoint() returns TRUE.

Recall that Windows DLLs explicitly export entry points for use by the calling program. In the case of plug-ins, Netscape requests that the plug-in programmer export NP_GetEntryPoints(), NP_Initialize(), and NP_Shutdown(). Navigator calls each of these routines as part of the loading and unloading process. These Windows-specific functions are provided by Netscape in the file npwin.cpp.

NP_GetEntryPoints()   After the DLL load begins, the Windows version of Navigator calls NP_GetEntryPoints(). This function does some of the same work as main() did on the Macintosh version; it checks the incoming parameter (the pointer to the plug-in function table) to ensure that this pointer is not null. Next, it checks to ensure that the plug-in function table is large enough to handle all of the plug-in's functions. If either check fails, NP_GetEntryPoints() returns with exit code NPERR_INVALID_FUNCTABLE_ERROR. If no error exists, the function loads the function table with the pointers to the NPP_ functions.

NP_Initialize()   On a Windows machine, after Navigator copies the NPP_ function addresses into its own data structure, it calls the exported function NP_Initialize(). (Don't confuse NP_Initialize(), supplied by Netscape, with NPP_Initialize(), which you, the plug-in programmer, write.) NP_Initialize() completes the task started by NP_GetEntryPoints(). The combination of NP_GetEntryPoints() and NP_Initialize() corresponds to main() on the Macintosh SDK, as shown in Figures 6.8 and 6.9.

FIG. 6.8
In the Macintosh SDK, all Netscape-supplied initialization takes place in main().

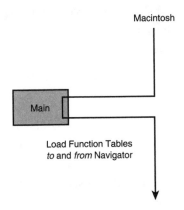

Macintosh

Main

Load Function Tables
to and *from* Navigator

Part
II

Ch
6

FIG. 6.9
On a Windows
machine, the
Netscape-supplied
initialization code is
divided between
NP_GetEntryPoints()
and
NP_Initialize().

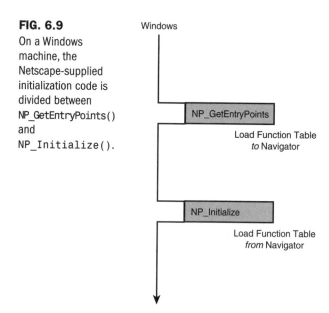

NP_Initialize() checks to ensure that its parameter is not null. Then
it checks to make sure that the SDK has at least as high a major version
number as Navigator. If the first check fails, the plug-in returns an exit code
of NPERR_INVALID_FUNCTABLE_ERROR. If the second check fails, the plug-in returns
NPERR_INCOMPATIBLE_VERSION_ERROR.

NP_Initialize() also ensures that the function table to hold the pointers to
the Netscape functions has enough room. If this check fails, code
NPERR_INVALID_FUNCTABLE_ERROR is returned.

Finally the standard (cross-platform) initialize function written by the plug-in
programmer is called. This function is named NPP_Initialize().

The Programmer's Start-up Code: *NPP_Initialize()*   What you do in
NPP_Initialize() is up to you and is largely determined by the design of your
plug-in. The general rule is that all static data members of your classes should
be initialized here. If you need to allocate disk files, memory, or other resources
that will be shared by all instances of the plug-in, do this work here. If you want
to check the platform to ensure that certain minimum resources are present,
do it now.

If, for example, your plug-in expects to find an ODBC-compliant database on the platform and all instances will share one connection to the database, NPP_Initialize() is the appropriate place both to ensure that the database exists and to establish the connection.

 TIP Prototypes for all the NPP functions are found in `npapi.h`. Make sure that you put `#include "npapi.h"` in any file that defines one of the NPP_ functions, such as `NPP_Initialize()`.

The specification of `NPP_Initialize()` is as follows:

```
NPError NPP_Initialize(void)
```

The function takes no parameters and returns an error code. If `NPP_Initialize()` is successful, it should return `NPERR_NOERR`. If a failure occurs, it should return the appropriate error code (listed in `npapi.h`). If the plug-in is unsuccessful in allocating memory, for example, it can return `NPERR_OUT_OF_MEMORY_ERROR`.

After you exit `NPP_Initialize()`, the next event is the instantiation of your plug-in. From this point, copies of this plug-in will be instantiated with no further calls to `NPP_Initialize()`.

Figure 6.10 emphasizes that, although instance variables are allocated to each instance, class variables (declared as `static` in C++) are shared across all instances.

FIG. 6.10
`NPP_Initialize()` is the place to initialize class variables—they will be shared by all instances.

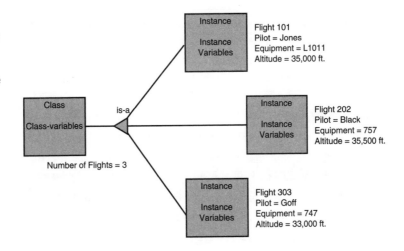

Instantiating a Copy of the Plug-In

At last, the executable image of the plug-in is loaded into memory, and Navigator and the plug-in know how to talk to each other. Any shared resources such as class variables or database connections are set up. The plug-in is ready to open its doors for business.

Recall that more than one copy of a plug-in may be present in memory at the same time. All copies will share the same code and the same class variables. Each instance will have its own instance variable. If the operating system supports preemptive multitasking, each copy may have its own thread of execution.

N O T E Most modern operating systems (OS/2 Warp, Windows 95, Macintosh's System 8, and UNIX) support preemptive multitasking with both processes and threads. Threads resemble processes, but more than one thread can run in the same address space.

Each task (regardless of whether it's a thread or a process) is assigned a certain amount of processor time by the operating system. When the time runs out, the processor stops the task and allows another task to run. The first task will start again when it is its turn, using a mechanism known as *round-robin* scheduling.

If a task is blocked (because it's waiting for an I/O operation to complete, for example), it can relinquish its position in the round-robin sequence. The operating system adds the task back to the sequence when the task becomes unblocked. ▪

 T I P Although processes are protected from one another by virtue of having discrete address spaces, two or more threads can share an address space and can potentially interfere with each other. If you are writing plug-ins for a multitasking operating system, bear this fact in mind and ensure that you think through issues of reentrant code.

NPP_New()   To instantiate your plug-in, Navigator calls the plug-in's NPP_New() function. NPP_New()'s specification is as follows:

```
NPError NPP_New(NPMIMEType *pluginType, NPP instance, uint16 mode,
➥int16 argc, char *argn[], char *argv[], NPSavedData *saved);
```

Recall that a plug-in can "sign up" for more than one MIME media type. The parameter pluginType is a pointer to the type actually specified by the stream or the <EMBED> tag. NPMIMEType is a typecast of a char pointer.

Note that, in the NPP_New() specification, the parameter instance is of type NPP. NPP is a C/C++ structure that has void pointer members named pData and nData. Navigator uses nData to store its private structures concerning this instance. You can use pData for your purposes. Just remember that it is a void pointer. You are responsible for allocating and deallocating any memory associated with pData. You also are on your own with respect to type safety. You may want to write a custom instance class and store a pointer to it in pData in order to get back some type safety.

The mode tells the plug-in whether it was called as an embedded or full-page plug-in. Valid values include NP_EMBED and NP_FULL.

Although it's tempting to think of mode as an enumerated type (enum) note that it's implemented as an unsigned 16-bit integer. If you write a switch statement to handle the various modes, make sure that you include a default case.

The three parameters argc, argn[], and argv[] are used to pass parameters in from the <EMBED> tag. Suppose the HTML writer writes the following:

```
<EMBED SRC="/path/to/data" HEIGHT=50 WIDTH=150 Foo=True Bar=False
Loop>
```

When Navigator calls NPP_New() it will pass the following:

- argc=6
- argn={ "SRC", "HEIGHT", "WIDTH", "Foo", "Bar", "Loop" }
- argv= { "/path/to/data", "50", "150", "True", "False", ""}

If you're coming to C and C++ from another language, remember that C and C++ use zero as the starting index for arrays. Therefore, in the preceding example, argn[0] is "SRC" and argv[1] is "50".

The type NPSavedData is a cast of a two-member structure, as follows:

```
typedef struct _NPSavedData
{
    int32  len;
    void*  buf;
} NPSavedData;
```

If you store data in NPSavedData when the plug-in is destroyed, Navigator associates this data with the current URL. If the same URL is requested later, Navigator attempts to restore your saved data here in NPP_New().

N O T E   The attempt to restore the NPSavedData associated with a URL will fail if
Navigator was shut down and restarted. The attempt also will fail if Navigator
needed to purge memory. Do not use NPSavedData to store any information your plug-in
cannot afford to lose. ■

A typical use of NPSavedData is to remember user selections. Another use is to remember how much of a data stream the plug-in had displayed. If, for example, the plug-in presents an audio stream, NPSavedData can be used to store an index into the stream. If the user stops the play before the recording is complete, and later loads a page that points to the same audio stream, the plug-in may resume at the point where the previous playback stopped.

Your plug-in should check instance to make sure that it is not null. If Navigator passes a null pointer to your plug-in, return code NPERR_INVALID_INSTANCE_ERROR.

Constructors   As part of NPP_New() you probably will want to allocate some memory and build initial instances of your plug-in's classes. Remember that calls to conventional new() or malloc()may fail even if memory is available because this memory may be controlled by Navigator and not the plug-in. Think about using NPN_MemAlloc() to allocate memory on the heap.

 You should use NPN_MemAlloc(), particularly when you write Macintosh plug-ins,
because the Macintosh version of Navigator uses a memory-based cache (in addition to
the conventional disk-based cache). If you allocate memory by using NPN_MemAlloc()
Navigator flushes the cache as required in an attempt to satisfy the request.

One approach to ensure that objects are allocated by using NPN_MemAlloc() is illustrated in the Macintosh SDK. Classes that require instance variables are derived from class CNetscapeMemObject. The Netscape programmers defined new() and delete() operators as follows:

```
void* CNetscapeMemObject::operator new(size_t size)
{
  return NPN_MemAlloc( size );
}
```

```
void CNetscapeMemObject::operator delete( void* theThing, size_t size
)
{
  NPN_MemFree( theThing );
}
```

 TIP In Netscape's example, they implement the new and delete operators as inline functions. You are advised to do the same. Implementing a function inline saves the overhead of a function call. This savings can add up if the function is called often (as new and delete tend to be).

Using *NPP_NewStream()*

After the instance and any standing classes are built, Navigator is ready to deliver the data to the plug-in. To determine how the plug-in prefers to receive the data, Navigator starts by calling NPP_NewStream().

Not all plug-ins have an associated data stream. If the plug-in doesn't need to read data, the HTML writer should call it as using the TYPE attribute of the <EMBED> tag. If your plug-in doesn't expect data, trap the call to NPP_NewStream and return a usage dialog if the plug-in is called incorrectly. ■

The specification for NPP_NewStream() is as follows:

```
NPError NPP_NewStream(NPP instance, NPMIMEType type, NPStream *stream,
➥NPBool seekable, uint16* stype);
```

The parameters instance and type have the same meaning they have when used in NPP_New(). Remember that, if you choose, you can read or change any data in instance->pdata.

The type NPStream is a cast of a structure, as follows:

```
typedef struct _NPStream
{
 void*   pdata;      /* plug-in private data */
 void*   ndata;      /* netscape private data */
 const char*  url;
 uint32 end;
 uint32 lastmodified;
 void*   notifyData;
} NPStream;
```

The members pdata and ndata have the same meaning they have in type NPP. You may store stream-specific data in pdata; you should leave ndata alone because it's private to Navigator.

The member url has the obvious meaning. The member end is the length of the stream, in bytes. If Navigator cannot determine the length of the stream, end is set to zero. This condition occurs if the server doesn't send a Content-length header, as, for example, if the output is being generated on-the-fly from a LiveWire application or CGI script.

The lastModified parameter should be interpreted as the date-time stamp of the stream, expressed in number of seconds after 12:00 AM, January 1, 1970 (a date and time known as the UNIX epoch).

The function parameter stype is set, by default, to NP_NORMAL. If your plug-in leaves this parameter at NP_NORMAL, Navigator sends the data to the plug-in by using a series of NPP_WriteReady() and NPP_Write() calls, as described in this chapter, in the following section, "Reading the Data as a Stream." You can change stype to NP_ASFILEONLY, which tells Navigator to save the entire stream into a file in its disk cache, then return the path name of this file (in NPP_StreamAsFile()). This technique is described in a following part of this chapter, in the section "Reading the Data as a File."

N O T E   Navigator also supports an stype of NP_ASFILE, for compatibility with older versions of the SDK. NP_ASFILEONLY is more efficient than NP_ASFILE, and should be used in all new plug-ins if file I/O is desired.

The inefficiency of NP_ASFILE stems from the fact that, in NP_ASFILE mode, Navigator delivers the data by using a series of calls to NPP_Write(), rather than a single call to NPP_StreamAsFile(). Also, if the file is local, NP_ASFILE tells Navigator to copy the file to the cache before calling NPP_Write(). When using NP_ASFILEONLY mode with a local file, Navigator gives the plug-in the path to the file itself, without copying the file to the cache. ■

If the parameter seekable is true, the plug-in can set stype to NP_SEEK. The parameter seekable is true if the stream is a local disk file, or is coming from a server that supports byterange requests. If seekable is false, the plug-in can still use NP_SEEK, but Navigator is forced to read the entire file from the server to a local file in the cache.

You find details of how to transfer data by using NP_SEEK mode in a following section, "Calling for the Data in a Seekable Stream."

Reading the Data as a Stream

If the plug-in sets stype to NP_NORMAL in NPP_NewStream(), Navigator next calls NPP_WriteReady() to determine how many bytes to send to the plug-in. Typically, you would allocate a buffer in NPP_NewStream() and store a pointer to that buffer somewhere in the structure maintained under stream->pdata. On each call to NPP_WriteReady(), the plug-in would just return the capacity remaining in the buffer.

The specification for NPP_WriteReady() is as follows:

```
int32 NPP_WriteReady(NPP instance, NPStream *stream);
```

After calling NPP_WriteReady(), Navigator calls NPP_Write(), in which it sends a buffer full of data. The buffer may be larger than the amount specified in the plug-in's return to NPP_WriteReady(). If so, the plug-in is obligated only to accept the amount it advertised in NPP_WriteReady(). It should copy that much data out of Netscape's buffer and into its own (or simply consume the data directly from Netscape's buffer), and then return the amount actually consumed as the return value of NPP_Write(). The specification for NPP_Write() is as follows:

```
int32 NPP_Write(NPP instance, NPStream *stream, int32 offset,
➡int32 len, void *buf);
```

The parameter offset is used to show where in the stream the current buffer fits. Offset zero is at the beginning of the stream. The parameter len indicates the length of the actual buffer.

If an error occurs while processing the stream, return a negative value from NPP_Write(). Navigator interprets this value as a request to destroy the stream, and calls the plug-in's own NPP_DestroyStream().

> **CAUTION**
>
> The buffer delivered by Navigator as part of NPP_Write() isn't persistent from one call to the next. If your plug-in doesn't copy the data into its own buffer before NPP_Write() returns, the data is irretrievably lost.

Reading the Data as a File

If the plug-in set `NPP_NewStream()`'s stype parameter to `NP_ASFILEONLY`, Navigator calls the plug-in's `NPP_StreamAsFile()` function. `NPP_StreamAsFile()`'s specification is:

```
void NPP_StreamAsFile(NPP instance, NPStream *stream,
➥const char* fname);
```

Parameters `instance` and `stream` have the same meaning they have in other NPP_ functions. The parameter `fname` is the path to the file, either in the cache or elsewhere on the local disk. Use this path name to perform I/O on the file by using the functions of the native operating system.

> **CAUTION**
>
> At the start of `NPP_StreamAsFile()`, check for the possibility that `fname` may be null. If `fname` is null, an error may have occurred while writing the file to the disk. If the file was local, it may not exist. In either case, error code `NPERR_FILE_NOT_FOUND` is a good choice for a return code.

Calling for the Data in a Seekable Stream

If you specify `NP_SEEK` as the `stype` mode in `NPP_NewStream()`, Navigator waits for your plug-in to request data. Call for the data by using the `NPN_RequestRead()` function:

```
NPError NPN_RequestRead((NPStream *stream, NPByteRange *rangeList);
```

An `NPByteRange` is a structure for accessing specific bytes in the stream. The structure is given by the following:

```
typedef struct _NPByteRange
{
    int32    offset;       /* negative offset means from the end */
    uint32     length;
    struct _NPByteRange* next;
} NPByteRange;
```

Note that the structure contains a pointer to other such structures. You can use this field to make an `NPByteRange` into a linked list, stringing `NPByteRange` structures together to request a series of discontiguous byte ranges.

NPN_RequestRead() is the first NPN_ function we have seen. Recall that NPN_ functions are calls made by the plug-in back to Navigator. You find more information on NPN_RequestRead() and also the other NPN_ functions in Chapter 9, "Understanding NPN Methods."

Presenting the Data

Unless the plug-in is called as a background plug-in, Navigator will call NPP_SetWindow() to pass the plug-in a pointer to the plug-in's window. NPP_SetWindow() is specified by the following, where the exact nature of an NPWindow depends upon the platform:

```
NPError NPP_SetWindow(NPP instance, NPWindow *window);
```

On a Windows or UNIX machine (running the X Window System), windows form a hierarchy. As shown in Figure 6.11, the window "owned" by Navigator can have subwindows. NPP_SetWindow() passes a handle to one of these subwindows to the plug-in. On Windows and UNIX platforms, these subwindows are native windows objects.

FIG. 6.11
On Windows and X Window UNIX machines, windows form a parent-child hierarchy.

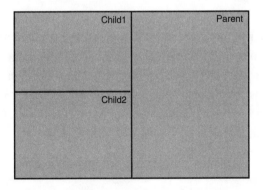

On a Macintosh, Navigator runs in a native window, but doesn't spawn a child window to pass to the plug-in. Rather, Navigator constructs a native Macintosh drawing area, known as a GrafPort, and passes a pointer to the GrafPort in a structure Navigator calls NPPort.

An `NPWindow` is defined by the cross-platform structure, as follows:

```
typedef struct _NPWindow
{
    void*    window;      /* Platform specific window handle */
    uint32   x;           /* Position of top left corner relative */
    uint32   y;           /*   to a netscape page. */
    uint32   width;       /* Maximum window size */
    uint32   height;
    NPRect   clipRect;    /* Clipping rectangle in port coordinates */
                          /* Used by Mac only. */
#ifdef XP_UNIX
    void *   ws_info;     /* Platform-dependent additional data */
#endif /* XP_UNIX */
} NPWindow;
```

Using Macintosh GrafPorts

On the Macintosh, `window` points to an `NPPort`. The `NPPort` is defined by the following:

```
typedef struct NP_Port
{
    CGrafPtr port;       /* GrafPort */
    int32    portx;      /* position inside the topmost window */
    int32    porty;
} NP_Port;
```

On the Macintosh, use the coordinates of the `clipRect` to limit drawing. In this way, if the user scrolls an embedded plug-in window to the edge of the screen, the plug-in will not overwrite the scroll bar or the menus. The Macintosh Toolbox call `ClipRect()` changes the clipping rectangle of the current `GrafPort`. This function takes a pointer to a `rect` as its parameter, and interprets the `rect` as a clipping rectangle in local coordinates.

CAUTION

Macintosh plug-ins share the `GrafPort` with other plug-ins and with Navigator itself. Make sure that you restore any port settings you change. For example, before calling `ClipRect()` to change the clipping rectangle of the port, call `GetClip()` to get a copy of the existing clipping rectangle. Upon exiting, restore that clipping rectangle with `SetClip()`, like this:

```
// make an empty region
rgnHandle theSavedClipRegion = NewRgn();
// copy the old clipping rectangle
```

```
GetClip(theSavedClipRegion);
ClipRect(&clipRect);
.
.
.
// restore the original clipping rectangle
SetClip(theSavedClipRegion);
// and free the region used to store the old clipRect
DisposeRgn(theSavedClipRegion);
```

Programming on UNIX in the X Window System

Note that the UNIX version of NPWindow contains an additional member: ws_info, which points to an NPSetWindowCallbackStruct allocated by Navigator. The structure's members, given in the following structure, are the standard pieces of information any program needs to know about a window in the X Window System.

```
typedef struct
{
    int32              type;
    Display*           display;
    Visual*            visual;
    Colormap           colormap;
    unsigned int       depth;
} NPSetWindowCallbackStruct;
```

The Callback Structure

To understand this callback structure, it's useful to understand what the X Window System is and how it works. Although Microsoft has its proprietary standard—Windows—and Macintosh has the Mac OS, the X Window System is an industry-standard software system that enables programmers to develop portable graphical user interfaces. Versions of the X Window System exist for all popular operating systems but the most common environment is UNIX.

The "plain vanilla" X Window System provides a C language interface known as Xlib. Although some programmers write programs that call Xlib directly, most find this interface tedious and difficult to use correctly. Xlib doesn't provide direct support for scroll bars, minimize and maximize buttons, or close buttons—the basic ingredients of most windows programming.

Many sets of tools were developed to provide an interface between the application program and Xlib. The X Toolkit, which includes the Xt Intrinsics layer and a set of high

Part
II

Ch
6

continues

continued

level *widgets*, is popular. ("Widgits" and "gadgets" are the names the X community has coined for reusable application-level objects.) Widgets implement the scroll bars, menus, buttons, and other controls so popular in a graphical user interface.) Most programmers also use a windows manager, such as Motif, to integrate widgets into a consistent look and feel. Figure 6.12 illustrates the relationship between these components. The top layer of the architecture shown in Figure 6.12 also includes *gadgets*, which are similar to widgets but have no associated window.

The X Window System is a hierarchical window system. A given output device (a monitor) is known as a *screen*. A *display* is a software process (an X server) that manages one or more screens, usually on a single workstation. *Client* software, such as Motif or Navigator, can run anywhere on the net, and can communicate with the server on the workstation by TCP/IP. Figure 6.13 shows how the pieces of the X Window System communicate with each other.

Navigator on a UNIX platform calls the plug-in, passing a `type`, `display`, `visual`, `colormap`, and `depth` through the `NPSetWindowsCallbackStruct`. Navigator and the plug-in, running as a client, are not necessarily running on the user's workstation, so the plug-in draws on the `display` and X handles getting these drawing commands to the user's computer. The pointer `display` contains the top level shell obtained by Navigator when Navigator called X Toolkit's `XtAppCreateShell()`.

Every screen supports one or more visual types, represented by the structure XVisual defined in Xlib. The visual types are:

- *PseudoColor*—Pixel values index a color map that stores independent red, green, and blue values.

- *StaticColor*—Similar to pseudocolor, but the colormap is predefined.

- *GrayScale*—Similar to pseudocolor, but only a single primary color (usually gray) is available.

- *StaticGray*—Similar to grayscale, but the colormap is predefined.

- *DirectColor*—The pixel itself stores the red, green, and blue values.

- *TrueColor*—Similar to directcolor, but the colormap is predefined.

If you were writing an X-based application rather than a plug-in, you would call `XCreateColormap()` when you initialized your application. If the default `visual` wasn't one of the static types, you can then begin to allocate colors to the colormap, and install the colormap.

Theoretically an application could allocate millions of colors in a colormap. In practice, the colormap is limited by the capabilities of the hardware. The parameter depth is provided by Navigator to tell the plug-in how many colors can actually be displayed by the screen.

Type, the remaining parameter passed by Navigator in the callback structure, isn't used by the plug-in programmer. Type is reserved for use by Netscape.

FIG. 6.12
The X Window System is a portable interface standard. Higher layers provide functionality such as scroll bars and buttons.

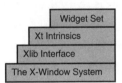

FIG. 6.13
Unlike conventional clients and servers, X servers reside on the workstation, and clients often run on a centralized processor.

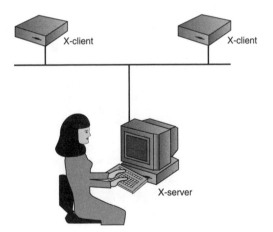

Part
II

Ch
6

CAUTION
Note that Navigator has already defined and installed the colormap. As a plug-in programmer, you should avoid overwriting Navigator's colormap. To do so causes the screen to flash into the new colors, a behavior considered undesirable by most users.

What to do in *NPP_SetWindow()*

Whether you are building a plug-in for a Windows computer, a Macintosh, or a UNIX machine, the most important step to take each time NPP_SetWindows() is called is to draw a representation of the data. Experiment with an instrumented version of the plug-in such as npZero.dll (introduced in Chapter 4, "Building a Simple Plug-In") to see when Navigator calls NPP_SetWindow(). You will find that NPP_SetWindow() is called when the window is resized, and may be called when the window is moved. You also may find that occasionally NPP_SetWindow() seems to be called for no reason. (Netscape is aware of this problem, but this behavior really doesn't hurt anything.) Your copy of the NPWindow pointer remains valid until the next time NPP_SetWindow() is called—you may want to store it in the instance so that you can compare the old window with the new one to see if NPP_SetWindow() was called spuriously.

Note, too, that if the HTML programmer specified your plug-in as hidden, you will never get an NPP_SetWindow() call. In this case your plug-in should be prepared to initiate its task of presenting the data as soon as the data becomes available, and not wait for a window.

From Here...

When your plug-in is started, Navigator initiates a series of calls that ensures that both Navigator and the plug-in know how to call each other. Then Navigator makes a series of calls to load the plug-in and make a new instance of it. Finally, Navigator offers data and a window, so that the plug-in can do what it was designed to do: transform an unknown data type into a representation visible from inside Navigator.

- Continue learning about NPP_ functions in the Chapter 7, "NPP Methods: Handling Interaction."

- Chapter 8, "NPP Methods: Other Tasks," concludes this discussion of NPP_ functions by looking at printing and plug-in shutdown.

- Many plug-ins do their work with some help from Navigator. Chapter 9, "Understanding NPN Methods," describes calls that the plug-in can make back to Navigator.

Also:

- If you're new to C++ and object-oriented programming, review Chapter 2, "A C++ Primer."

- To get started in plug-ins, see Chapter 4, "Building a Simple Plug-In," which shows the "Hello, world!" of plug-ins.

Part
II
Ch
6

NPP Methods: Handling Interaction

Chapter 6, "NPP_Methods: Starting the Plug-In," shows how Navigator loads the plug-in and starts an instance. By the end of that chapter the plug-in has access to its data and has a window open.

Recall that a plug-in, in its simplest form, transforms data from a nonnative MIME data type to some representation inside the Navigator window. Typically this representation is visual—Navigator opens a portion of its window, or even an entire new document, for use by the plug-in.

Less commonly, there is no data—the plug-in interacts with the user rather than with data. On other occasions, the representation may be non-visual. For example, a plug-in may be used to play a downloaded sound.

Whatever the plug-in's task, in many cases the programmer want to interact with the user as long as the plug-in is active. He or she may put up buttons, sliders, or pop-up menus in the plug-in's window. This chapter shows how to capture user events and make them available in the plug-in. ∎

How the three major operating systems pass events to the application

You can take advantage of the similarities between Windows, Macintosh, and UNIX to share more of your code between all three platforms.

How to map Windows messages to your plug-in

Use object-oriented design principles to select a destination for each message.

How Microsoft's Visual C++ helps maintain the message map

Use Microsoft's Developer Studio to relieve you of this tedious task.

About the Macintosh main event loop

The Macintosh passes events rather than messages; be sure your plug-in correctly forwards these events to your software objects.

About X Events

In this chapter, you learn that you can direct Windows messages from the server to widgets and gadgets in your plug-in.

Once You Have the Keyboard Focus

The HTML page has loaded. Navigator, seeing an <EMBED> tag, is retrieving data from the Web server and has loaded your plug-in. Your plug-in is receiving data and has displayed that data in its assigned window. For many plug-ins, the day is over—their work is done.

For more sophisticated plug-ins, however, tasks still await. You have included user controls in your window, and you must wait while the user clicks your buttons or types in your text fields. In short, you are waiting for an event.

Getting Events

The three major platforms supported by Navigator (Windows, Macintosh, and UNIX) each have different mechanisms for notifying a program of a user action.

Modern operating systems such as Windows NT, Windows 95, and the Macintosh operating system take complete control of the hardware. If the user moves the mouse, it is the operating system that tracks the cursor. If the user presses a key on the keyboard, it is the operating system that receives the character.

Each operating system provides a way for the programmer to register an interest in certain external events so that the application is notified by the operating system when these events occur.

N O T E   The discussion in this chapter about Microsoft Windows generally is applicable to all versions of this product. Where the versions differ, this chapter assumes that the Win32 model is used in Windows NT, Windows 95, and the Win32s simulator. (Strictly speaking, Windows 3.1 isn't an operating system but, rather, a sophisticated application that runs on top of MS-DOS.) ▪

Getting Events—the Windows Way   In Windows, all user input is translated by the operating system into messages that are placed in a data structure known as the *system queue*. The operating system periodically looks in the queue and redirects messages to the queue of the appropriate application. When an application is ready to process an input message, it reads the next message from its queue.

Messages can come directly from the application, from other applications, or from the operating system, as well as from the user (via the hardware). The user, for example, might click the close box of a window, which notifies the operating system to close this window. Before closing the window, the operating system sends the application a "close session" message, which gives the application a chance to finish tasks.

All Windows messages have four parameters, regardless of where they come from or what they are telling your program:

- A window handle (an unsigned 16-bit integer named an HWND)
- A message type (an unsigned 32-bit integer)
- An unsigned 32-bit integer to pass message-specific information
- A signed 32-bit parameter to pass message-specific information

The most common message types are Windows messages. In your documentation all of these messages begin with the characters, WM_.

> **N O T E** The Windows message queue has greater complexity than is described in this section. Windows, for example, can insert *asynchronous messages* from sources like the timer into the queue ahead of the usual *synchronous messages*. The queue also allows four different levels of message priority. For the purposes of plug-ins, however, it is sufficient to use the simplified model. ■

Remember that Netscape's call to NPP_SetWindow() passes a native window handle to the Windows plug-in. The operating system is prepared to dispatch events associated with this window to the plug-in. The plug-in just has to ask for them.

Here's a typical piece of code a plug-in can use to handle messages it receives. The full code appears on the CD-ROM as /source/chap07/msg1.cpp.

Listing 7.1   *msg1.cpp*

```
LONG theResult = -1;
switch(Message)
{
  case WM_PALLETTECHANGED:
  {
```

continues

Part

II

Ch

7

Listing 7.1   Continued

```
      .
      .
      .

    break;
  }
  case WM_PAINT:
  {
      .
      .
      .

    break;
  }
  default:
  {
    // this message was not for us; call old Window process
      .
      .
      .

    break;
  }
}
return theResult;
```

If the WM_PALLETTECHANGED message or the WM_PAINT message ever reaches
the plug-in, the plug-in now knows how to handle it. The question is, "How does
the plug-in tell Windows that it wants these messages?"

The answer is a *callback function*. Every window in the Windows operating system
has a list of functions, known as WindowProc functions, attached to it. A typical callback function contains the message-handling code just described.

Note that in the message-handling code fragment, the handler for default case
is missing. Windows expects a WindowProc to maintain a pointer to any WindowProc
it replaces so that if the new WindowProc cannot handle a message, it can forward
it to its predecessor.

Windows makes it easy to reserve space for these pointers in their function,
RegisterClass. Unfortunately, Navigator doesn't request this extra space, so
plug-ins for Navigator 3.0 on Windows also must maintain a linked list.

ON THE WEB

The code to implement this list is given in the `nspi30` SDK (which is available on-line at **http://home.netscape.com/eng/mozilla/3.0/handbook/plugins/index.html**).

Figure 7.1 illustrates the process by which Windows dispatches messages.

FIG. 7.1
Windows sends the message to the window's most recently attached callback function and expects the callback function to call its predecessor.

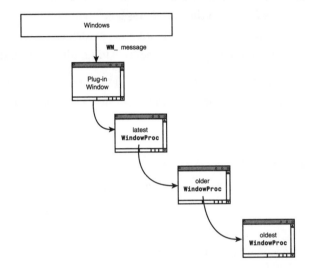

To install a new callback function, use the `SetWindowLong()` function, which you can use to change many different parameters of the window. For example, if `This` is a pointer to the current data structure that you stored in `pData`, you can put the following code in your implementation of `NPP_SetWindow()`:

```
This->hWnd = (HWND)(DWORD)This->fWindow->window;
This->lpfnOldWndProc =
   (FARPROC) SetWindowLong(This->hWnd,
                          GWL_WNDPROC,
                          (DWORD)myCallbackFunction);
AssociateInstance(This->hWnd, This);
```

When `NPP_SetWindow()` is called, this code sets the `WindowProc` of the window identified by `hWnd` to the callback function `myCallbackFunction`. Then it links the old `WindowProc`, carefully saved in `This->lpfnOldWndProc`, by calling `AssociateInstance()`.

Part

II

Ch

7

NOTE AssociateInstance() is part of the system that maintains a linked list of data structures associated with each of the plug-in's open windows. The code that implements this list is omitted here but is available in the Netscape Plug-In 3.0 SDK (nspi30). ■

When a message is sent to the window identified by hWnd, the callback function is invoked. If the message is on the list of messages handled by the switch statement, the appropriate action is taken and the function returns zero. Otherwise, the default case is taken and the old WindowProc tries to handle the message.

Here is a sample of the callback function, using the message handling code shown previously. The full code for this sample is on the CD-ROM, under the name /source/chap07/callback.cpp.

Listing 7.2   *callback.cpp*

```
LONG_NP_LOADDS WINAPI myCallbackFunction ( HWND hWnd,
                                            WORD Message,
                                            WORD wParam,
                                            LONG lParam)
{
  PluginInstance* This = GetInstance(hWnd);
  LONG theResult = -1;
  switch(Message)
  {
    case WM_PALLETTECHANGED:
    {

        .
        .
        .

      break;
    }
    case WM_PAINT:
    {

        .
        .
        .

      break;
    }
    default:
    {
      // this message was not for us; call old Window process
      theResult = CallWindowProc(This->lpfnOldWndProc,
                                 hWnd,
```

```
                              Message,
                              wParam,
                              lParam);
        break;
      }
    }
  }
  return theResult;
}
```

Look in the Microsoft-supplied file `winuser.h` to see the list of windows messages (WM_s) available. Which messages should your plug-in handle? You should certainly handle `WM_PAINT`. This message is sent whenever the window needs to be redrawn. It is sent once as the plug-in is starting, and then again whenever one of the following events occurs:

- A window needs resizing
- A portion of the window that was previously obscured becomes visible
- The contents of the window are scrolled
- The application invalidates the window by calling `InvalidateRect()` or `InvalidateRgn()`

Some of these events, like resizing, trigger `NPP_SetWindow()`, but play it safe and handle `WM_PAINT` directly.

You also may want to handle `WM_PALETTECHANGED`. This message is sent by Windows when a new window gets the keyboard focus. When the focus changes, the window with the focus sets its logical palette, which changes the system palette. The operating system sends `WM_PALETTECHANGED` to all visible windows, which gives them a chance to set their own logical palette.

Getting Events on a Macintosh   Recall from Chapter 6, "NPP Methods: Starting the Plug-In," that Windows and UNIX plug-ins get a native window, but Macintosh plug-ins get a `GrafPort`. One consequence of this implementation is that the plug-in sees all events, although it may handle very few. Otherwise, the practical effect of this difference is small.

When an event occurs, Netscape calls `NPP_HandleEvent()`. This function has the specification:

```
int16 NPP_HandleEvent(NPP instance, void *event);
```

Part

II

Ch

7

The second parameter is a pointer to a standard Macintosh `EventRecord`. Macintosh events are like Windows messages. Event types include the following:

- *Mouse events*: sent if the mouse is within the bounds of the instance
- *Key events*: sent if the instance has text focus
- *Update events*: sent if the instance needs to be redrawn
- *Activate events*: sent to all instances in the window being activated or deactivated
- *Suspend/Resume events*: sent to all instances in all windows
- *Null events*: sent to all instances in all windows

In addition to the usual Macintosh events, Navigator adds three custom events:

- `getFocusEvent`: the user has moved the keyboard focus onto the instance by clicking it or tabbing into it. All keystrokes entered now may reasonably be expected to be handled by the plug-in. Return `TRUE` if your plug-in handles keyboard events and `FALSE` if it does not.

- `loseFocusEvent`: the user has moved the keyboard focus away from the instance. Your plug-in no longer receives keyboard events. When you receive a `loseFocusEvent` you can validate any data the user entered or do any other processing that may be appropriate for your plug-in.

- `adjustCursorEvent`: the user has moved the mouse across the boundary of your plug-in. To give the cursor a special appearance while it is over your plug-in (for example, if the cursor should turn into an I-beam because the user may enter text), maintain the cursor state in your plug-in and toggle the cursor appearance when this event comes along.

  If your plug-in does something special with the cursor when the mouse enters its rectangle, return `TRUE` in response to this event. Otherwise, return `FALSE`.

You can read the event type from the `event->what` field. Generally, your implementation of `NPP_HandleEvent()` should return `TRUE` if your plug-in handles the event and `FALSE` if it does not.

T I P The definitive guide for Macintosh programming is *Inside Macintosh* (Addison-Wesley, 1994). The first edition of *Inside Macintosh* was organized chronologically. For example, Volume I dealt with the earliest versions of the operating system and Volume VI, published in 1991, dealt with System 7.0.

The second edition is has a topical organization and is much easier to use. For day-to-day use you want the volumes, *Overview*, *Macintosh Toolbox Essentials*, and *More Macintosh Toolbox*. Then you want selected volumes, depending on what your plug-in does. For example, you may need the volume on *QuickTime* to play video clips in this standard.

Most of the C/C++ compilers for the Macintosh come with CD-ROMs that contain much of the information in *Inside Macintosh*. If you prefer a paper copy, be sure to get the appropriate volumes of *Inside Macintosh*—otherwise, you may decide that you are perfectly satisfied with the CD-ROM documentation.

CAUTION

The events described in this section are known as *low-level events* in the Apple documentation. Do not confuse these events with Apple Events, which are high-level messages between applications.

Apple Events correspond to Microsoft Windows's Object Linking and Embedding (OLE) automation, in which one application can send messages to another, asking it to provide data or services. OLE is described in greater detail in Chapter 14, "If All the World Used Microsoft. . . ."

Typical code to implement `NPP_HandleEvent()` might include the following lines:

```
Bool theResult = FALSE;
switch (theEvent.what)
{
  case mouseDown:
  {
    Handle_Mouse_Down( &theEvent );
    theResult = TRUE;
    break;
  }
  case updateEvt:
  {
```

Part

II

Ch

7

```
      BeginUpdate( window );
      EraseRgn( window->visRgn );
      Update( window );
      EndUpdate( window );
      theResult = TRUE;
      break;
    }
  }
}
return theResult;
```

Which Macintosh events should your application handle? The updateEvt is analogous to the Windows message WM_PAINT, and should be handled in a similar fashion. Handle other events as needed by your plug-in.

What Happens in X?   The event model in Xlib is similar to the one used by Windows and the Macintosh. Remember that in the X Window System, the X server is associated with the user's workstation and the client may be on a separate processor. Nevertheless, X makes this distribution transparent to the programmer.

You can still think in terms of the server sending events to the client to tell the client that its window needs to be updated. (X calls this event *Expose*.)

Your plug-in should certainly handle Expose, just as the Windows plug-in handles WM_PAINT and the Macintosh plug-in handles updateEvt. Recall that X widgets are implemented as windows in their own right—don't forget to forward events received by your plug-in to any off-the-Net or commercial widgets your plug-in uses.

Reading the Keyboard Events in Windows

Microsoft Windows, the X Window System, and the Macintosh OS each generate a variety of events or messages associated with the keyboard. This section shows how to capture key-down messages in a Windows plug-in.

Recall that Windows messages are handled by a WindowProc function. Your window's WindowProc gets no keyboard messages, however, unless you assign it the keyboard *focus*.

To give your plug-in window the keyboard focus, call SetFocus(), passing it the HWND to your window. A good place to add this line is at the bottom of your NPP_SetWindow() implementation so that your window is given the focus when it is first instantiated, as well as after any resizing or repainting.

Here's a fragment of the revised `NPP_SetWindow()`:

```
NPError NP_LOADDS NPP_SetWindow(NPP instance, NPWindow* window)
{
  .
  .
  .
  This->hWnd = (HWND)(DWORD)This->fWindow->window;
  .
  .
  .
  // give our plug-in keyboard focus
  SetFocus (This->hWnd);
  return NPERR_NO_ERROR;
}
```

Next, add code to the window's callback function to handle the keyboard messages. Here's a portion of a `WindowProc` function to handle the Windows message `WM_KEYDOWN`:

```
LONG NP_LOADDS WINAPI SubClassFunc( HWND hWnd,
                                    WORD Message,
                                    WORD wParam,
                                    LONG lParam)
{
  PluginInstance* This = GetInstance(hWnd);
  int nVirtKey;
  LONG lKeyData; // not used in this example
  char buffer[2];
  switch (Message)
  {
  .
  .
  .
  case WM_KEYDOWN:
  {
    // Windows uses "virtual keys" to accommodate non-Roman character
    // sets.
    // Unicode is at the heart of Window's future.
    // When the message is WM_KEYDOWN, wParam holds the virtual key
    // and lParam holds extension information about the keypress
    nvirtKey = (int) wParam;
    lKeyData = lParam;

    // put the incoming character into a string
    buffer[0] = (char) nvirtKey;
    buffer[1] = NULL;

    // append the string into the instance's persistent buffer
    strcat(This->fBuffer, buffer);
```

Part
II

Ch

7

```
        // trigger a repainting of the window
        InvalidateRect(hWnd, NULL, FALSE);
        UpdateWindow(hWnd);
        break;
    }
    .
    .
    .
    case WM_PAINT
    {
        PAINTSTRUCT paint;
        HDC hDC = BeginPaint(hWnd, &paint);
        TextOut(hDC, 0, 0, This->fBuffer, strlen(This->fBuffer));
        EndPaint(hWnd, &paint);
        break;
    }
    .
    .
    .
    .
}
```

Note that this code collects the keystrokes in a structure named fBuffer, which is
a member of This. This is a pointer to an instance of class PluginInstance. Add
fBuffer to class PluginInstance by adding the line shown in bold.

```
typedef struct _PluginInstance
{
  NPWindow*      fWindow;
  HWND           hWnd;
  uint16         fMode;
#ifdef STRICT
  WNDPROC        lpfnOldWndProc;
#else
  FARPROC        lpfnOldWndProc;
#endif
  NPSavedData*   pSavedInstanceData;
  char           fBuffer[80];
  PluginInstance* pNext;
} PluginInstance;
```

Finally, initialize the fBuffer member to the empty string. Be careful where you
put this initialization. The callback function will be called on every keystroke, so
this clearly is not the right place. Likewise, NPP_SetWindow() gets called when the
window is resized or redrawn, as well as when the window is initially allocated.

You can put initialization code for instance variables in NPP_New(), or in
NPP_SetWindow(), inside the if statement that verifies that the window is new:

```
NPError NP_LOADDS NPP_SetWindow(NPP instance, NPWindow* window)
{
  if (NULL == instance)
    return NPERR_INVALID_INSTANCE_ERROR;
  PluginInstance* This = (PluginInstance*) instance->pdata;
  if ((window->window != NULL) && (This->hWnd == NULL))
  {
    This->fWindow = window;
    This->hWnd = (HWND)(DWORD)This->fWindow->window;
    .
    .
    .
    // empty the string
    This->fBuffer[0] = NULL;
  }
  .
  .
  .
}
```

Figure 7.2 shows the resulting plug-in in action.

FIG. 7.2
This simple plug-in translates every keystroke into a character in the plug-in window.

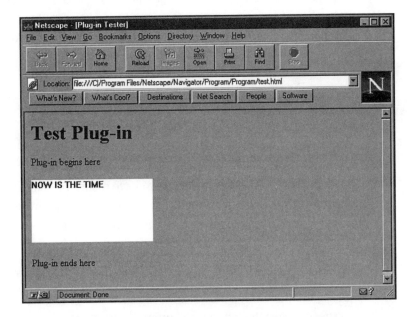

Several things are wrong with this plug-in, not the least of which is that fBuffer has a fixed length that will quickly overflow. If you want a quick fix to this problem, you might replace the char array with a dynamically sized container from the Standard Template Library (STL). Chapter 2, "A C++ Primer," describes the STL.

Part
II

Ch
7

The more immediate problem is that the program translates *every* keystroke to the screen—shift keys, delete keys, and also character keys. A better design adds a `switch` statement inside the `WM_KEYDOWN` case to handle noncharacter keys.

With this design, the program shows uppercase characters when the shift key is down. It deletes characters from the buffer when the backspace key is pressed.

This kind of keyboard behavior is so basic, however, that we shouldn't have to build it from scratch. Someone has written a generic keyboard and text buffer manager that we can incorporate into our program.

Microsoft has written classes to handle thousands of common Windows tasks and provides it as Microsoft Foundation Classes (MFC). Chapter 17, "Using Class Libraries and Frameworks," explores the general topic of class libraries and MFC in particular.

TIP

To implement a more sophisticated text editor in your plug-in, use the `CEdit` class from MFC. You can get even more functionality by using `CEditView`, which adds printing and find-and-replace capability. If you need to display text in more than one font or if you need special character formatting, use class `CRichEditView`.

Watching the Mouse

Handling mouse clicks is just as simple as handling key presses, but the amount of code is greater because users expect to be able to do more with the mouse.

You don't have to do anything special to have mouse messages sent to your window. Depending on the features you want to implement, however, you may need to handle more than one mouse message. This section shows how to implement a simple "scribbler" that allows the user to draw with the mouse.

The design of the scribbler is based on three mouse messages:

- `WM_LBUTTONDOWN`—Windows sends this message to your program when the user pushes the left mouse button down.
- `WM_MOUSEMOVE`—Windows sends this message every time the user moves the mouse.
- `WM_LBUTTONUP`—Windows sends this message when the user releases the left mouse button.

When Windows sends WM_LBUTTONDOWN, the plug-in records the mouse location and records that it is now in the "drawing" state. As the mouse is moved, the plug-in records the new mouse location, and calls InvalidateRect() and UpdateWindow() to force a WM_PAINT message.

The WM_PAINT handler draws a line from the old mouse location to the new mouse location if the plug-in is in the drawing state. When, finally, the user releases the left mouse button, the plug-in records the fact that it no longer is in the drawing state.

Here are the additions to the callback function to handle these three new messages, and the additional code for WM_PAINT:

```
LONG NP_LOADDS WINAPI SubClassFunc( HWND hWnd,
                                    WORD Message,
                                    WORD wParam,
                                    LONG lParam)
{
  PluginInstance* This = GetInstance(hWnd);
  switch (message)
  {
      .
      .
      .
    case WM_LBUTTONDOWN:
    {
      // Windows encodes the mouse position in the lParam parameter.
      This->newMouseLocation.x = LOWORD(lParam);
      This->newMouseLocation.y = HIWORD(lParam);
      This->oldMouseLocation = This->newMouseLocation;
      SetCapture(hWnd);
      This->bDrawTrail = TRUE;
      break;
    }
    case WM_MOUSEMOVE:
    {
      if (This->bDrawTrail)
      {
        This->oldMouseLocation = This->newMouseLocation;
        This->newMouseLocation.x = LOWORD(lParam);
        This->newMouseLocation.y = HIWORD(lParam);
        InvalidateRect(hWnd, NULL, FALSE);
        UpdateWindow(hWnd);
      }
      break;
```

Part

II

Ch

7

```
                        }
                        case WM_LBUTTONUP:
                        {
                          ReleaseCapture();
                          This->bDrawTrail = FALSE;
                          break;
                        }
                        .
                        .
                        .
                        case WM_PAINT:
                        {
                          HPEN hOldPen;
                          HPEN hPen;
                          long colorShade = 0x000001L;
                          int  penWidth = 2;

                          PAINTSTRUCT paint;
                          HDC hDC = BeginPaint(hWnd, &paint);
                          hPen = CreatePen(PS_SOLID, penWidth, colorShade);
                          hOldPen = (HPEN) SelectObject(hDC, hPen);
                          MoveToEx(hDC,
                                    This->oldMouseLocation.x,
                                    This->oldMouseLocation.y,
                                    NULL);
                          LineTo ( hDC,
                                    newMouseLocation.x,
                                    newMouseLocation.y);
                          SelectObject(hDC, hOldPen);
                          DeleteObject(hPen);
                          EndPaint(hWnd, &paint);
                          break;
                        }
                        .
                        .
                        .
                    } // end switch
                    .
                    .
                    .
                    return 0L;
                }
```

In this code fragment, three pieces of data must be preserved between invocations
of the plug-in: oldMouseLocation, newMouseLocation, and bDrawTrail. Add these
definitions to pluginInstance:

```
typedef struct _PluginInstance
{
  NPWindow*      fWindow;
  HWND           hWnd;
  uint16         fMode;
#ifdef STRICT
  WNDPROC        lpfnOldWndProc;
#else
  FARPROC        lpfnOldWndProc;
#endif
  NPSavedData*   pSavedInstanceData;
  POINT          oldMouseLocation;
  POINT          newMouseLocation;
  BOOL           bDrawTrail;
  PluginInstance* pNext;
} PluginInstance;
```

Note that this plug-in uses `SetCapture()` and `ReleaseCapture()` to ensure that all mouse movement is sent to this plug-in while the left mouse button is down, even if the mouse moves beyond the bounds of the plug-in's window.

Figure 7.3 shows the scribbler in action.

FIG. 7.3
This plug-in captures mouse movement while the left mouse button is down and uses this movement to draw lines into the plug-in window.

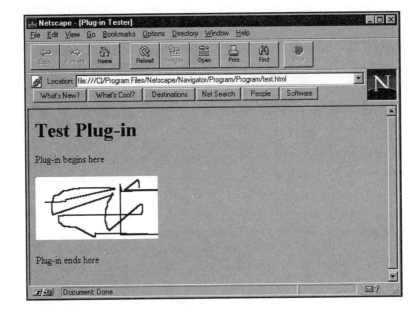

Part
II

Ch
7

A Better Way of Managing Message Mapping

As the plug-in becomes more sophisticated, the callback function becomes larger and more complex. You'll quickly want to pull the more elaborate handlers (such as WM_PAINT) into their own functions (such as onPaint).

Then, to handle a new message, you need to be sure to make *two* changes: add the new message to the switch statement in the callback function, where you call the handler, and implement the handler function itself.

Whenever you have to keep two things synchronized in software, you have a potential defect. Sometimes you struggle over a program in which you implemented a handler function but forgot to add the message in the callback function. At other times, the linker complains that you didn't supply a handler, even though you called one.

If you are using Microsoft Visual C++ or a similar compiler that supports Microsoft Foundation Classes, you can get the development environment to help you map messages onto their handlers, using a construct known as a *message map*.

Most MFC applications include the macro DECLARE_MESSAGE_MAP(); in their window definition. This macro works much like the virtual keyword in C++—it tells the compiler that the class overrides the handling of certain messages.

To complete the hookup of the message map, add the BEGIN_MESSAGE_MAP() macro to the body of the application, listing the messages your application is prepared to handle. To handle the WM_PAINT message, for example, your message map would include the following line:

```
ON_WM_PAINT()
```

The default name of the handler function for WM_PAINT is OnPaint(). When a plug-in with ON_WM_PAINT() in its message map receives the message WM_PAINT, OnPaint() is invoked. From here, processing goes on just as it did when you handled WM_PAINT explicitly in your WindowProc.

If you use Microsoft's Visual C++, the fastest way to set up a plug-in based on MFC is to use the MFC AppWizard. Open the Microsoft Developer Studio and choose

File, New. In the New dialog, choose Project Workspace, and in the New Project Workspace dialog choose MFC AppWizard (dll). Fill in a name and click the Create button.

> **CAUTION**
>
> Remember that under Windows, plug-ins need a name that begins with the letters "np". You will find it's difficult to change a project's name after it is set up. To keep your project internally consistent, put the "np" characters in the name right from the beginning—in the Name field of the New Project Workspace dialog.

The MFC AppWizard for dynamic Link libraries (DLLs) has only one step, and the default values give reasonable behavior for plug-ins. Click the Finish button, then click OK to approve the New Project Information.

 The Professional edition of Microsoft Visual C++ gives you the option of statically linking MFC into your DLL. This option is worth serious consideration.

If you statically link MFC in, your plug-in will be bigger but you don't have to worry that the end-user doesn't have the MFC DLL. If you dynamically link MFC, you save space but, undoubtedly, some users will not have the MFC DLL on their computer. They won't be able to run your plug-in without it.

Examine the application class produced by the AppWizard. If you named your plug-in npTest, this class is named `CNpTestApp`. At the bottom of the class declaration you find the following macro:

```
DECLARE_MESSAGE_MAP()
```

In the `.cpp` file where the class methods are implemented you find the following lines:

```
BEGIN_MESSAGE_MAP(CNpTestApp, CWinApp)
  //{{AFX_MSG_MAP(CNpTestApp)
        //NOTE - the ClassWizard will add and remove mapping macros here
        //DO NOT EDIT what you see in these blocks of generated code!
  //}}AFX_MSG_MAP
END_MESSAGE_MAP()
```

When AppWizard first builds your class, it reserves a message map but doesn't put messages into it. The comments have a special format—they are maintained by tools in the Developer Studio.

The macro BEGIN_MESSAGE_MAP() takes two parameters. The first (CNpTestApp in our example) is the target of the messages associated with this map. Any class derived from MFC's CCmdTarget can have a message map.

Note that CNpTestApp is derived from CWinApp. In MFC, the class CWinApp (or its descendent) provides the main event loop for the programmer. When the class's member function Run is invoked, the main event loop begins to spin, dispatching messages (or calling the idle function when there is nothing else to do).

Run dispatches messages to the application's windows. Each window has a WindowProc defined at the class level. A message map in that window class dispatches messages to their handlers.

Figure 7.4 shows the message-handling hierarchy of MFC. If your derived class gets a message it doesn't understand, it forwards the message up the hierarchy. The second parameter of the BEGIN_MESSAGE_MAP() macro in a given class implementation contains the name of the class directly "above" the current class. This class is the point at which your code interacts with MFC code to handle messages.

Each message macro (such as ON_WM_PAINT) is associated with a handler, such as OnPaint(). Note that the macros don't take arguments. The framework passes arguments to the handler if it needs them. Examine the MFC declaration of class CWnd. You will find the handler for ON_WM_PAINT declared as follows:

```
afx_msg void OnPaint();
```

The afx_msg keyword is a flag to the preprocessor, telling it that this function is associated with a message map. Its presence reminds the programmer that this function is special, in much the same way as the virtual keyword reminds a programmer about the special handling of virtual functions. (Message maps are *not* implemented using the virtual mechanism, although the effect is similar.)

TIP Can't find OnPaint() in the example MFC-based plug-ins?

Sophisticated applications benefit by having the data separated from the presentation of that data. In MFC, the data is stored in a *document* and presented by one or more *views*.

Views are ultimately derived from the MFC class CView, which handles WM_PAINT by calling the view's OnDraw() member.

You as the programmer are expected to implement OnDraw(). So when your MFC-based plug-in gets the WM_PAINT message, your window's message map forwards it up the hierarchy until it reaches Cview. Cview calls the OnDraw() member back in your own derived class.

FIG. 7.4
The message map for this example would be BEGIN_MESSAGE MAP(CNpTestApp, CWinApp).

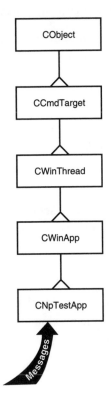

Processing the Stream

So far, these examples have ignored the major reason for building a plug-in—a server is sending you a stream of data that Netscape doesn't know how to handle. Recall from Chapter 6, "NPP Methods: Starting the Plug-In," that the preferred way to read your data is as a stream (stype is NP_NORMAL).

Part
II

Ch
7

If you accept the stream in NP_NORMAL stype, Navigator makes a series of NPP_WriteReady()—NPP_Write() calls until the stream is completely sent. If you're developing your own data type, consider placing information about the size of the file at the head of the file so that you can receive it as a stream.

Handling Streams with the Windows API

Here's a procedure for handling many types of streaming data:

1. In NPP_New(), allocate a buffer and store it in the data structure you associate with pdata. Consider using a container class from the STL or another class library so you don't have to worry about the details of buffer management.

2. In NPP_NewStream(), set the stype of the stream to NP_NORMAL.

3. In NPP_WriteReady(), report out the capacity of the buffer.

4. In NPP_Write(), copy the data into your local buffer. Record how much of the buffer capacity is left so the plug-in can return that information on the next invocation of NPP_WriteReady().

5. In NPP_SetWindow(), subclass the window and set up a WindowProc that handles WM_PAINT by painting a representation of the data in the buffer.

An Example of Streaming Data

Suppose that you define a data type that consists of positive numbers separated by new lines. Following the procedure given in the previous section, you might write the code described in the following sections.

Modifying the Persistent Data   Add the following members to PluginInstance:

```
short fBuffer[kBufferSize];
short fTopOfWindow;
short fBottomOfWindow;
```

Set kBufferSize to a reasonable size, with a line like the following:

```
const short kBufferSize = 32767;
```

Setting the Stream to *NP_NORMAL*   At the bottom of NPP_NewStream(), before the function returns, add the following:

```
*stype = NP_NORMAL
```

Reporting the Buffer Capacity   Provide an NPP_WriteReady() function:

```
int32 NP_LOADDS NPP_WriteReady(NPP instance, NPStream* stream)
{
  int32 theResult = 0L;
  if (instance != NULL)
  {
    PluginInstance* This = (PluginInstance*) instance->pdata;
    theResult = (kfBufferSize - (This->fBottomOfWindow) - 1);
  }
  return theResult;
}
```

Copying the Data into the Plug-In   Provide an NPP_Write() function, as follows:

```
int32 NP_LOADDS NPP_Write(NPP instance, NPStream* stream,
                          int32 offset, int32 len, void* buffer)
{
  if (instance != NULL)
  {
    PluginInstance* This = (PluginInstance*) instance->pdata;
    int i;

    // Start stripping off ASCII numbers
    char* theString = strtok((char*) buffer, "\n");
    if (NULL != theString)
    {
      This->fBuffer[offset] = atoi(theString);
      for (i=offset+1; i<kBufferSize && (i-offset < len); I++)
      {
        theString = strtok(NULL, "\n");

        // keep reading until we run out of room or data
        // don't trust len; it can overreport the data
        if (NULL == theString)
          break;
        This->fBuffer[i] = atoi(theString);
      }
      This->fBottomOfWindow = i;
      return (len);
    }
    else
      return 0L;
  }
  else
    return 0L;
}
```

Writing the Data to the Window   Finally, every time the window needs redrawing, plot out the data. This display routine is quite simple—a more

Part
II

Ch
7

sophisticated routine can include scroll bars, autoscaling, grid lines and axes, or even simple animation.

```
LONG NP_LOADDS WINAPI SubClassFunc( HWND hWnd,
                                    WORD Message,
                                    WORD wParam,
                                    LONG lParam)
{
  PluginInstance* This = GetInstance(hWnd);
  LONG theResult = 0L;
  switch (Message)
  {
    .
    .
    .
    case WM_PAINT:
    {
       HPEN hOldPen;
       HPEN hPen;
       long colorShade = 0x000001L;
       int penWidth = 2;

       PAINTSTRUCT paint;
       HDC hDC = BeginPaint(hWnd, &paint);
       hPen = CreatePen(PS_SOLID, penWidth, colorShade);
       hOldPen = (HPEN) SelectObject(hDC, hPen);
       MoveToEx(hDC, This->fBuffer(This->fTopOfWindow),
                     This->fTopOfWindow,
                     NULL);
       for (int i=This->fTopOfWindow+1;
               i<This->fBottomOfWindow;
               i++)
         LineTo(hDC, This->fBuffer[i], i); // autoscale here if desired
       SelectObject(hDC, hOldPen);
       DeleteObject(hPen);
       EndPaint(hWnd, &paint);
       theResult = 0L;
       break;
    } // end case
    .
    .
    .
  } // end switch
  fTopofWindow=0;
  fBottomofWindow=0;     return theResult;
}
```

The Result   Figure 7.5 shows the result plotted by the above plug-in.

FIG. 7.5

The simplest version of this plug-in plots data from the stream from the top of the window to the bottom of the window, without scrolling or animating.

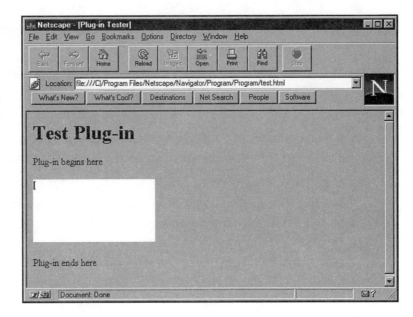

Handling Streams in MFC

If you are implementing in MFC, consider deriving a plug-in document that is instantiated in NPP_New(). Attach a view to this document in NPP_SetWindow() and implement that view's OnDraw() member so that it puts a representation of the document into the window.

The default memory map take cares of sending WM_PAINT to CView. CView, in turn, calls its implementation of OnPaint(), which calls your derived view's OnDraw().

Starting Additional Streams

During its interaction, your plug-in may produce data that should be shown to the user. Use the Navigator method NPN_NewStream() to send this data to a target in Navigator. Chapter 9, "Understanding NPN Methods," describes the various targets that you can choose.

As a result of the interaction, your plug-in can identify data that is still on the Web and that the user should see. For example, you can include buttons in your plug-in

Part

II

Ch

7

that function like links. If the user clicks one of these links, you want to call for the data from the associated URL.

Use NPN_GetURL() or, for notification, NPN_GetURLNotify() to open a new stream from the Web to Navigator. Note that this stream comes to Navigator, not to the plug-in (unless the content type matches one of the plug-in's content).

If you request the "Notify" version, Navigator calls your NPP_URLNotify() function when the URL transfer completes and reports whether the transfer was successful, unsuccessful, or was stopped by the user.

Finally, you can send data back to the Web by using NPN_PostURL() or NPN_PostURLNotify(). Like NPN_GetURLNotify(), Navigator uses your plug-in's NPP_URLNotify() function to report completion of the request. Again, see Chapter 9, "Understanding NPN Methods," for more detailed information on the NPN_ functions.

From Here...

After your plug-in is started, you may want to allow the user to interact with the data. At a minimum, you need to handle update events and messages such as WM_PAINT. Combine the user interaction with the NPP_WriteReady()—NPP_Write() loop, which delivers data from the server to your plug-in.

- Continue learning about NPP_ functions in the next chapter, "NPP Methods: Other Tasks."
- Review Chapter 6, "NPP Methods: Starting the Plug-In," to see how Navigator starts your plug-in and makes initial calls.
- Many plug-ins do their work with some help from Navigator itself. Chapter 9, "Understanding NPN Methods," describes calls the plug-in can make back to Navigator.

Also:

- If you're new to C++ and object-oriented programming, review "A C++ Primer" in Chapter 2.
- To get started in plug-ins, see Chapter 4, "Building a Simple Plug-In," which shows the "Hello, world!" of plug-ins.

CHAPTER 8

NPP Methods: Other Tasks

Chapter 6, "NPP Methods: Starting the Plug-In," shows how Navigator loads the plug-in and starts an instance. Chapter 7, "NPP Methods: Handling Interaction," describes additional tasks your plug-in may have to do to interact with the user and with the data stream itself.

Most plug-ins are also called on to print themselves, either as embedded content in a Navigator window or as a full document. All plug-in instances are eventually destroyed, and any associated window the instance has must be closed.

This chapter deals with these "additional duties" of the plug-in: printing, closing its windows, and destroying itself on request. ∎

About *NPP_Print( )*

Navigator can call your plug-in in two different ways, depending on how the HTML programmer is using your plug-in.

How to take control of the printing process

If your plug-in is called as a full-page plug-in, Navigator gives you the option of running the whole printing process.

How to print your content

Regardless of whether your plug-in is called as an embedded plug-in or a full-page document, you must draw your contents to the printer.

How to handle *NPP_Destroy( )*

If you're not careful, you can "leak memory" out of your plug-in and eventually crash the user's computer.

About saved instance data

Navigator tries to keep your data safe in case the user returns to it.

Understanding *NPP_Print()*

Recall that you, as the programmer, write all NPP functions. These NPP functions are called by Navigator. NPP_Print() is unique in that, under the right circumstances, Navigator calls it twice. NPP_Print() is Navigator's request that your plug-in print itself.

Embedded Mode

An HTML author can include a plug-in using an <EMBED> statement. Alternatively, the HTML author can put a link in his or her Web page that points to a whole new document.

If your plug-in is called through <EMBED>, it is an *embedded* plug-in. If your plug-in is invoked on a document, it is a *full-page* plug-in.

If your plug-in is embedded, Netscape calls the plug-in's NPP_Print() function once. If your plug-in is full-page, Netscape calls your plug-in's NPP_Print() once to find out if the plug-in handles the whole printing process. If it does not, Netscape calls your plug-in *again*, also through NPP_Print(), to have it handle the printing of the content.

Confused? NPP_Print() is a busy place, particularly for a full-page plug-in. This section shows an example of how to handle NPP_Print() in an embedded plug-in. NPP_Print() is defined by the following line:

```
void NPP_Print(NPP instance, NPPrint *platformPrint);
```

Here, instance is the usual instance that is passed from Netscape to nearly all NPP functions and platformPrint is a structure whose mode member can take on the NP_EMBED and NP_FULL values. When the user elects to print a page that has an embedded plug-in, Netscape calls NPP_Print() for the plug-in with platformPrint->mode set to NP_EMBED.

The full declaration of platformPrint is as follows:

```
typedef struct _NPPrint
{
    uint16      mode;            /* NP_FULL or NP_EMBED */
    union
```

```
{
    NPFullPrint fullPrint;   /* if mode is NP_FULL */
    NPEmbedPrint embedPrint;/* if mode is NP_EMBED */
    } print;
} NPPrint;
```

Note that the union statement says that the two data members fullPrint and embedPrint occupy the same space—only one member can be present in an instance at a time. If mode is set to NP_EMBED, the union print has embedPrint.

The structure of embedPrint is as follows:

```
typedef struct _NPEmbedPrint
{
    NPWindow    window;
    void*       platformPrint;  /* Platform-specific printing info */
} NPEmbedPrint;
```

The NPWindow in this structure is the window the plug-in should draw into for printing. Recall from Chapter 6, "NPP Methods: Starting the Plug-In," that an NPWindow is defined as shown in the following lines:

```
typedef struct _NPWindow
{
    void*       window;     /* Platform specific window handle */
    uint32      x;          /* Position of top left corner relative */
    uint32      y;          /*   to a netscape page. */
    uint32      width;      /* Maximum window size */
    uint32      height;
    NPRect      clipRect;   /* Clipping rectangle in port coordinates */
                            /* Used by Mac only. */
#ifdef XP_UNIX
    void *      ws_info;    /* Platform-dependent additional data */
#endif /* XP_UNIX */
} NPWindow;
```

Your plug-in should draw into the window member to print its contents.

> **CAUTION**
>
> On a Windows machine, the coordinates of the window rectangle are in *twips*. In the MM_TWIPS mapping mode the logical unit, twip, is 1/20 of a point or 1/1440 of an inch, and the base unit is in physical inches. This design is never used with a display (because displays come in all sizes and the physical inch is meaningless), but it is perfectly appropriate when drawing to a printer.
>
> *continues*

continued

Make sure that you call DPtoLP() to convert these points when you print text into the window. DPtoLP() converts device coordinates to logical coordinates using the current mapping mode.

Special Features on the Macintosh   The second field of NPEmbedPrint, platformPrint, says that it has Platform-specific printing info. Specifically, on the Macintosh, platformPrint has a THPrint, a handle to a TPrint. The TPrint, in turn, is an Apple-defined structure that includes the following:

- Printer driver version number
- Horizontal and vertical resolution in dots per inch
- Printable page size
- Physical page size
- Paper height and width (in 1/120th of an inch increments)
- Type of paper feed (such as cut sheet, fan-fold)
- Number of bytes in a printer band
- Height and width of a printer band in printer dots
- Number of bands per page
- Pattern-scaling factor
- Band-scanning direction code
- Page number of the first page to print
- Page number of the last page to print
- Number of copies to print

CAUTION

The TPrint structure is strictly read-only. Make sure that your code wraps reads of the structure in access methods—Apple changes the details of this structure from time to time to keep up with advances in printing technology. If you use access methods, you can take advantage of Apple's changes.

By the time Navigator is ready for your plug-in to print its contents, it has already given the user a Print... dialog. As a Macintosh user, you will recognize many of these parameters from the Page Setup or Print... dialogs. Navigator also fills in information it gets from the printer driver.

 TIP The TPrint has a rich array of detailed information about the printing job—more than most plug-ins will ever use. Unless your plug-in has special needs, don't access the TPrint record—simply draw the contents of your plug-in into the window provided, and let Navigator and the printer driver handle the rest.

This approach leaves your code more portable to other platforms and makes it more likely that your plug-in will work correctly with all printers (including future versions of the printer driver).

Full-Page Mode

When Navigator is ready to print your full-page plug-in, it first gives you an opportunity to take control of the printing process. Some documents benefit from this opportunity. For example, Figures 8.1 and 8.2 contrast the standard Print... dialog with the Print dialog provided by Microsoft Word.

FIG. 8.1
Unless you take control of the printing process, Navigator provides a standard Print... dialog for printing your full-page plug-in.

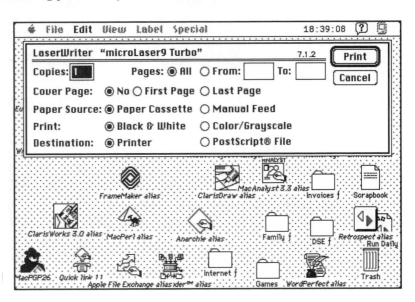

FIG. 8.2
Microsoft added
several items to the
Print... dialog to
supplement the
standard Print...
dialog.

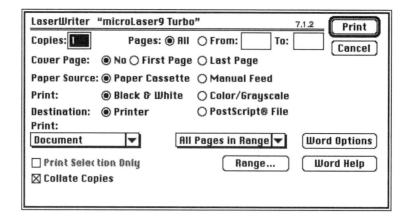

To allow you to take over the printing process, Navigator calls `NPP_Print()` with
`platformPrint->mode` set to `NP_FULL` and union member `print` filled with an
`NPFullPrint`. Navigator defines an `NPFullPrint` as follows:

```
typedef struct _NPFullPrint
{
    NPBool    pluginPrinted; /* Set TRUE if plugin handled fullscreen */
                             /*       printing */
    NPBool    printOne;      /* TRUE if plugin should print one copy */
                             /*       to default printer */
    void*     platformPrint; /* Platform-specific printing info */
} NPFullPrint;
```

The `platformPrint` member has the same information it has in `NPEmbedded`. Using
the `NPBool` `printOne` is self-explanatory and tells the plug-in that the user just wants
a quick, no-dialog print.

The `NPBool` `pluginPrinted` is the member that distinguishes full-page printing from
embedded plug-in printing. If you commandeer the printing process, providing
your own dialog boxes and driving the printer yourself, set `pluginPrinted` to true.
If Navigator sees this flag set to true, it bypasses its own Print dialog.

 Although Netscape allows your full-page plug-in to take over the printing process, you
need to use this option only if your plug-in has special needs. Most full-page plug-ins can
set `pluginPrinted` to false, allowing Navigator to handle the Print dialog.

If you set `pluginPrinted` to false, Navigator initiates the printing process. When it is ready for your content, Navigator calls your plug-in again—through `NPP_Print()`—with `platformPrint->mode` set to `NP_EMBED`.

TIP Your Macintosh plug-in may need access to information from the printer driver or the Print... dialog. But if you don't need to add items to the standard dialog or otherwise control the print process, simplify your design by returning false in `pluginPrinted`. Then, when Navigator calls `NPP_Print()` the second time, read `platformPrint` to get the information you need.

Alas, Netscape doesn't provide similar information for Windows or UNIX plug-ins in Navigator version 3.0. On these platforms you must take control of the printing process if you want detailed information about the printer or the print job.

If you save data with your full-page plug-in instance (using `NPSavedData`, described in a following section of this chapter, "Saving Instance Data"), consider including a copy of the `TPrint`. Then, if you are later asked to print again, you can reuse the `TPrint` to handle a `printOne` request.

Call `PrValidate()` to ensure that the user hasn't changed the active printer or printer driver since the last print request. If the `TPrint` changed—indicated by a TRUE return from `PrValidate()`—or if the user makes a `printOne` request before he or she has completed a Print... dialog, just call `PrintDefault()` to preset the fields of the `TPrint`.

Printing in Windows Printing is supported by the Microsoft Foundations Classes (MFCs) `CView` class. If your full-page plug-in handles multipage documents, override `CView`'s `OnPrint()` member in your own derived class.

In your view's version of `OnPrint()`, look up the size of the printer's page and use this information to adjust the clipping region of the device context associated with the print window. After the "page" is defined, call the view's `OnDraw()` member to output the content.

Even today, not all printers accept bitmaps. You can find out if the printer associated with your print window properly renders a bitmap by including the following code (in which `hDC` is the device context associated with the window):

```
if (!(GetDeviceCaps(hDC, RASTERCAPS)
    & RC_BITBLT))
{
  // printer cannot display bitmaps
  .
  .
  .
}
```

When you are ready to print, you will want to put up a Cancel dialog, in case the user decides to stop the print job before it completes. Putting up this kind of dialog box is a four-step process:

1. Set a Boolean flag that the abort procedure and the plug-in can share. The abort procedure reads this flag to see if it should allow the printing to continue.

2. Register an AbortProc function with the operating system.

3. Display the modeless Cancel dialog.

4. Disable the application window.

Here's the code for these four steps:

```
BOOL bContinuePrinting = TRUE;
SetAbortProc(hDC, AbortProc);
hdlgCancel = CreateDialog(hinst,
   (LPTSTR) "AbortDlg", hWnd, (DLGPROC) AbortPrintJob);
EnableWindow(hWnd, FALSE);
```

The abort procedure can be very simple, as follows:

```
BOOL CALLBACK AbortProc(HDC hDC, int nCode)
{
  MSG msg;
  while (PeekMessage((LPMSG) &msg, (HWND) NULL, 0, 0, PM_REMOVE))
  {
    // if the message isn't for us, send it on
    if (!IsDialogMessage(hdlgCancel, (LPMSG) &arg))
    {
      TranslateMessage((LPMSG) &msg);
      DispatchMessage((LPMSG) &msg);
    }
  }
  return bContinuePrinting; // set to FALSE by Cancel button
}
```

Use your development environment to construct a suitable Cancel dialog. Write a dialog procedure that includes the following code:

```
switch (message)
   .
   .
   .
   case WM_COMMAND: // the Cancel button is the only control
   {
     bContinuePrinting = FALSE;
     return TRUE:
     break;
   }
   .
   .
   .
}
```

Now when Navigator tells you to print, you can put up the common Print dialog (possibly with customizations). Verify that the printer you selected can print your document. Put the Cancel dialog box on-screen.

If the user clicks the Cancel button, the WM_COMMAND message is sent to the AbortPrintJob function, which sets bContinuePrinting to FALSE. When the plug-in sees bContinuePrinting go FALSE, it stops drawing pages and cleans up from printing.

After the Cancel dialog box is up, the plug-in calls StartDoc(), and then StartPage(). These Windows functions alert Windows that the print data is coming.

Then, based on the data returned from the Print dialog, you find the page(s) the user wants to print and draw their contents to the print window. Call EndPage() after each page is printed.

When all the data was sent (or bContinuePrinting becomes false), call EndDoc(). Finally, call EnableWindow() to return control to the plug-in window, call DestroyWindow() on the cancel dialog, and call DeleteDC() on the device context allocated by StartDoc().

For most plug-ins, this is all that's needed. But if your plug-in draws text, you may want to think about fonts and text metrics. Microsoft Windows comes with various fonts for the screen—Courier, Helvetica, and Times Roman, to name a few.

Most printers include most of these common fonts. But not all printers use all the standard fonts, and users can add fonts to their system. Therefore, a user may have text on the screen in a font that is unavailable in the printer.

N O T E Windows supports many font technologies. A Postscript printer uses, of course, a PostScript font. This font may be downloaded from the computer or stored in the printer's read-only memory (ROM).

Hewlett-Packard's PCL printers use HP's Printer Control Language (PCL). Both Microsoft and HP provide drivers for these printers, which offer good font quality.

On the PC screen, Windows can use bit-mapped fonts (known as *raster* fonts). If a user prints a document that is being viewed with raster fonts, Windows must try to match a printer font (such as PostScript or PCL) to the raster font.

TrueType technology is a compromise between raster fonts and printer fonts. TrueType fonts are built from mathematical models (like PostScript fonts) but can be displayed both on-screen and on the printed page.

For more information on Windows fonts see Chapter 8, "Working With Fonts," in *Platinum Edition Using Windows 95* (Que, 1996). ▓

Windows includes an elaborate *penalty weighting* algorithm based on ten font characteristics, including character sets, pitch, family, face name, height, width, and various styles. Windows uses this algorithm to choose a printer font that should be a close match to the screen font.

You, the programmer, should control which font the plug-in uses and match it with the available printer font. Otherwise, the printing may be done in a font that is quite unlike the font used on-screen.

T I P If your plug-in chooses the screen font, choose a TrueType font whenever possible. One big advantage of TrueType is that the printer version and the screen version match exactly.

For better control over the printed page, Windows programmers can call `GetTextMetrics()` to fill a `TextMetric` data structure with information about the currently selected font. The `TextMetric` structure includes information such as the following:

- Font height
- Average and maximum width
- Ascent and descent of characters above and below the base line
- Leading
- The font style (such as italicized, underlined, or struck out)

For pinpoint control of key pieces of text (such as titles), use `GetTextExtentPoint32()`. This function computes the width and height of a specified string in the current font. Use this information to center, scale, or align text with other elements.

Customizing the Print Dialog in Windows The most common reason for taking control of the printing process is to add items to the Print dialog. Microsoft provides a set of common dialog boxes, three of which apply to printing.

These three dialog boxes (Print Setup, Page Setup, and Print) get some information from the common dialog DLL (COMDLG32.DLL) and some information from the printer driver. Figure 8.3 shows the common Print dialog.

FIG. 8.3
Microsoft makes it easy to display the common Print dialog.

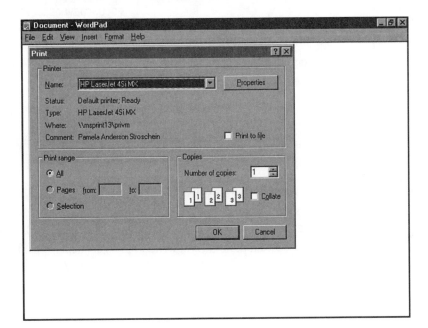

To customize the Print dialog, use MFC to write your plug-in. Then follow this procedure:

1. Copy the PRINTDLGORD dialog template from commdlg.rc to your plug-in's .rc file. If you have Microsoft Visual C++, commdlg.rc is located at \msvc\mfc\samples\apstudio\commdlg.rc.

2. Use the resource editor to add controls to your plug-in's copy of the PRINTDLGORD dialog template.

3. In your plug-in, derive a new C++ class from `CDialog`. For this example, call the new class `CPluginPrintDialog`. Use PRINTDLGORD as the dialog ID. If you use Visual C++, use the ClassWizard to build the class template. Where ClassWizard uses `CDialog` in the header and body files, substitute `CPrintDialog`.

   For example, your class declaration begins as follows:

   ```
   class CPluginPrintDialog : public CPrintDialog
   ```

4. Modify the class constructor. The `CPrintDialog` constructor is specified as follows:

   ```
   CPrintDialog(BOOL bPrintSetupOnly,
                DWORD dwFlags = PD_ALLPAGES |
                                PD_USEDEVMODECOPIES | PD_NOPAGENUMS |
                                PD_HIDEPRINTTOFILE | PD_NOSELECTION,
                CWnd* pParentWnd = NULL);
   ```

   Your constructor should set the second parameter, as shown here:

   ```
   CPluginPrintDialog(BOOL bPrintSetupOnly,
                DWORD dwFlags = PD_ALLPAGES |
                    PD_USEDEVMODECOPIES | PD_HIDEPRINTTOFILE,
                CWnd* pParentWnd = NULL);
   ```

   Make sure that you include the macro DECLARE_MESSAGE_MAP() at the end of your constructor's declaration.

5. If you follow the usual MFC design, your plug-in has a view (derived from the MFCs class `CView`), which displays your document. For this example, call this view `CPluginView`. In your view implementation file, `include` the header file for your custom dialog. Overwrite `CView`'s `OnPreparePrinting()` member as follows:

   ```
   BOOL CPluginView:OnPreparePrinting(CPrintInfo* pInfo)
   {
     // replace the default CPrintDialog with our own
     delete pInfo->m_pPD;
     pInfo->m_pPD = new CPluginPrintDialog(FALSE); //
        ➥FALSE for Print Dialog

     // set up some nice defaults
     pInfo->m_pPD->m_pd.nMinPage = 1;
     pInfo->m_pPD->m_pd.NMaxPage = 0xffff;
   ```

```
// point the view to our version of the print dialog
pInfo->m_pPD->m_pd.hInstance = AfxGetInstanceHandle();
pInfo->m_pPD->m_pd.lpPrintTemplateName =
➡MAKEINTRESOURCE(PRINTDLGORD);

// and turn on the template
pInfo->m_pPD->m_pd.Flags |= PD_ENABLEPRINTTEMPLATE;

// finally, call the parent's method to complete the task
return DoPreparePrinting(pInfo);
}
```

 TIP If you don't want some of the controls in the common Print dialog, disable them. Don't delete them—CPrintDialog expects to find them when it calls DoDataExchange(). You can hide them, but users may be confused if you make too many changes to the standard dialog. You can communicate your interface design more clearly by leaving the control present but disabled.

Customizing the Print... Dialog on a Macintosh   If your plug-in is designed for the Macintosh, you can add items to the standard Print... dialog. Delete no items from the standard dialog or change their position. (Not only can these kinds of changes confuse the software, they also can confuse the user.)

CAUTION

Don't use more than half the screen for your custom controls. Apple warns that future versions of their standard Print... dialog may use as much as half the screen, leaving only the bottom half for your customization. Remember, too, that many users still have older Macs with 9-inch screens.

As a practical matter, if your plug-in needs so many controls that it takes half the screen (even a 9-inch screen), it's probably too busy to be usable. Consider moving some of these controls to a separate dialog, and hooking this dialog to a pop-up menu or another control in your plug-in window.

If you want to understand how to change the Print... dialog, review how the standard dialog works. Your full-page plug-in puts up a Print... dialog by calling PrJobDialog(). This function calls the printer driver of the currently active printer. The printer driver, in turn, calls PrDlgMain(). PrDlgMain() has the following specification:

```
Boolean PrDlgMain(THPrint hPrtRec, ProcPtr pDlgInit)
```

The ProcPtr has the address of the dialog initialization procedure—for the Print... dialog. This procedure defaults to PrJobInit().

PrDlgMain() calls the pDlgInit, which sets up the dialog, dialog hook, and dialog event filter. Then PrDlgMain() calls ShowWindow() and ModalDialog() to make the dialog available to the user. As the user interacts with the controls, events are passed to the dialog event filter.

Figure 8.4 illustrates this calling sequence.

FIG. 8.4
The Macintosh operating system provides a hook, allowing applications to add controls to the Print... dialog.

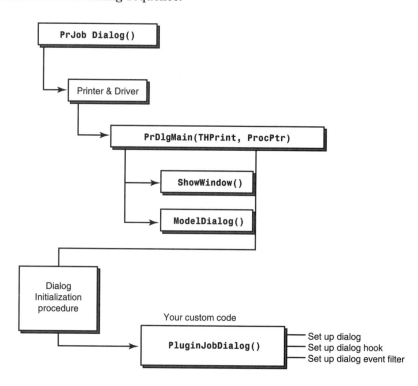

To add controls to the standard Print... dialog, use a resource editor such as ResEdit to make a new Dialog Item List (DITL) with the controls you want to add. Write your own dialog initialization routine, which appends the items from your DITL to the standard dialog and initializes those items. For example, you might write the following:

```
const short kPluginDITL=256;
```

```
.
.
.
pascal TPPrDlg PluginJobDialog( THPrint thehPrint)
{
  // Append the items in kPluginDITL to the DialogPtr PrtJobDialog
  .
  .
  .
  // save the old procedure; we'll need it if the user hits any of
  // the standard controls.
  prPItemProc = (long)PrtJobDialog->pItemProc;
  PrtJobDialog->pItemProc = (ProcPtr)PluginJobItems;
  return PrtJobDialog;
}
pascal void PluginJobItems(TPPrDlg theDialog, short theItemNo)
{
  // handle hits on our items
  // use a switch on the item number
  // If the item hit was not ours, call the standard handler
  CallPascal(theDialog, theItemNumber, prPItemProc);
}
```

TIP Symantec offers an electronic reference to the Mac toolbox functions, known as THINK
Reference. This product includes a nice function named AppendDITL() which can be
called to "Append the items in kPluginDITL to the DialogPtr PrtJobDialog" as required in
the preceding code.

ON THE WEB

For more information on THINK Reference, visit Symantec on-line at **http://
www.symantec.com/**.

Now, when you call PrDlgMain(), pass the address of your dialog initialization function. PrDlgMain() calls your function, which appends items from your DITL to the
standard Print... dialog.

When any item in the dialog gets a hit, your PluginJobItems() handles the event. If
the hit isn't on one of your plug-in's controls, you call the default handler.

When the user finally activates the OK button, ModalDialog returns, and your plug-
in can read the value the user set in the custom controls. If the user clicks Cancel,
your implementation of NPP_Print() should just clean up and exit.

Using *NPP_Destroy()*

It's said that "All good things must come to an end…". So it is with plug-ins. When the user leaves the page on which your plug-in content is displayed, Navigator calls your plug-in's NPP_Destroy() function, and then deletes the plug-in instance.

Freeing Dynamic Memory

In C++, every class has one or more constructors and one destructor. The constructors get called in response to instantiations. The destructor gets called when a stack-based instance goes out of scope or a dynamically allocated instance is deleted.

If a C++ class allocates memory in its constructor, it should deallocate that memory in the destructor. If you forget to deallocate the memory, the pointer to the allocated memory is lost, but the memory remains unavailable for use by other applications.

If the plug-in runs long enough, it eventually uses up all memory and crashes the Netscape client. Depending upon the operating system, the user may lose work in other open applications as well. The phenomenon of allocating memory and then failing to deallocate it is known as a *memory leak*, which can lead to subtle defects in your software.

Figure 8.5 illustrates a memory leak.

Recall that you should allocate dynamic memory for a plug-in by calling NPN_MemAlloc(). The corresponding routine to deallocate that memory is NPN_MemFree(). In C++, implement new and delete using NPN_MemAlloc() and NPN_MemFree() to ensure proper behavior. The section, "The Run-Time Model," in Chapter 5, "Design Issues," shows how to use NPN_MemAlloc() and NPN_MemFree() to implement custom versions of new and delete.

Besides deallocating dynamic memory allocated in constructors, you should make sure that you deallocate all memory you have reserved in the structure pointed to by instance->pdata. The rule of thumb to remember is "For every new, there must be a delete."

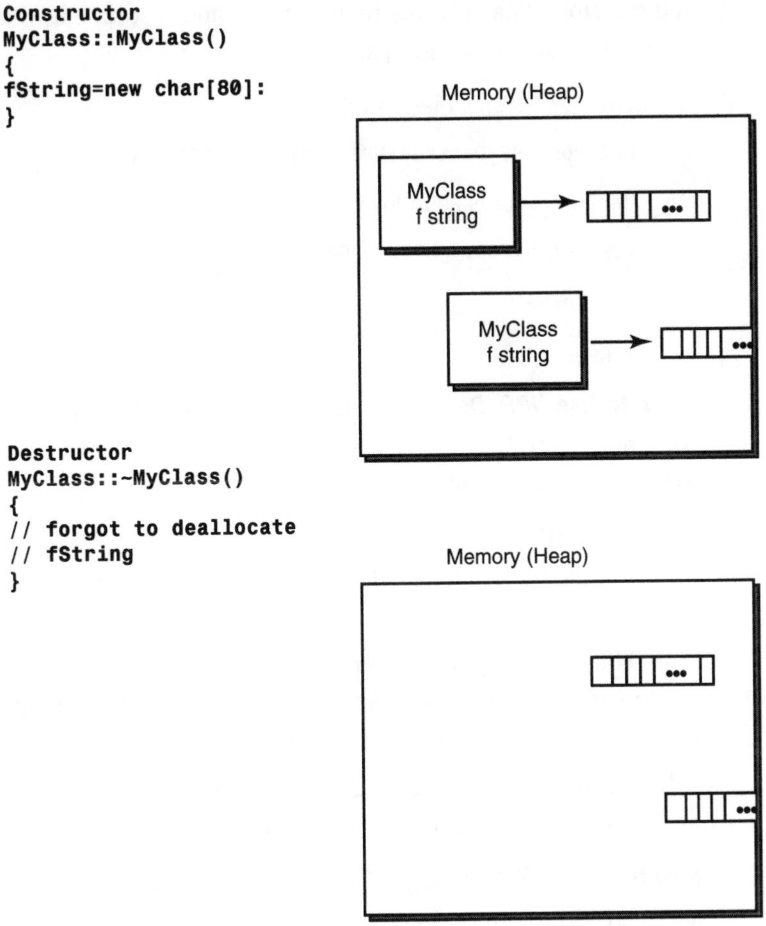

FIG. 8.5
If you forget to free memory that was allocated in the constructor, Navigator eventually runs out of memory and crashes.

```
Constructor
MyClass::MyClass()
{
fString=new char[80]:
}
```

Memory (Heap)

MyClass
f string

MyClass
f string

```
Destructor
MyClass::~MyClass()
{
// forgot to deallocate
// fString
}
```

Memory (Heap)

Saving Instance Data

Often, you want to associate some record of the user's activity with the URL they visited. For example, the user may have opened a video clip and played the first 30 frames. If the user leaves this URL and comes back later, perhaps play should resume at frame 31. Perhaps the user has printed the current document, specifying parameters such as page range and orientation. If he or she returns to this URL and prints the document again, you may want your plug-in to remember the parameters the user previously specified and use these parameters as the default settings.

You can store data in Navigator's memory and associate it with the current URL by saving this data in the save parameter of NPP_Destroy().

NPP_Destroy() is specified as follows:

```
NPError NPP_Destroy(NPP instance, NPSavedData **save);
```

Here, NPSavedData is as follows:

```
typedef struct _NPSavedData
{
    int32        len;
    void*        buf;
} NPSavedData;
```

When to Use *NPP_Destroy()*   If you allocate saved data in NPP_Destroy(), Navigator keeps this data in case the user returns to the same URL. You might want to save data if the following instances are true:

- Your MIME media type is time-based and you want to remember where to resume the sequence. If, for example, your data consists of a video clip, you might remember the frame number.

- The user has printed your full-page plug-in, and you want to remember the user's choices in the Print dialog so you can set them up as the new default the next time the user prints this document.

- The user has manipulated controls in your plug-in, and you want to be able to restore those controls the next time the user selects this URL.

How to Use *NPP_Destroy()*   To use saved data, follow these five steps in NPP_Destroy():

1. Design and use a C++ class or structure that has all the information you want to store. For this example, the class is named TStoredData.

2. Allocate a new instance of TStoredData (here named theStoredData) and fill its fields.

3. Allocate a new NPSavedData, with a line such as the following:

```
*save = (NPSavedData*) NPN_MemAlloc(sizeof(NPSavedData));
```

4. Assign sizeof(theStoredData) to (*save)->len.

5. Assign the address of theStoredData to (*save)->buf.

Now complete `NPP_Destroy()`. Navigator deletes your plug-in instance. Later, if the user visits the same URL as the earlier instance, Navigator passes `theStoredData` in the `saved` parameter of `NPP_New()`.

TIP Make sure that whatever structure you put into `(*save)->buf` (in this example, `TStoredData`) is flat—that is, none of its members are themselves dynamically allocated. If Navigator runs short on memory, it begins deallocating saved data to free space.

Because it doesn't know the internal structure of your storage class, it cannot deallocate internal dynamic memory. Figures 8.6 and 8.7 illustrate the wrong and right ways to design `TStoredData`.

FIG. 8.6
If any members of your storage class are dynamically allocated, that memory is lost when Navigator deletes the saved data, resulting in a memory leak.

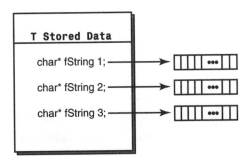

FIG. 8.7
Flatten your stored data before saving it, so that Navigator can get every field with a single call to `delete`.

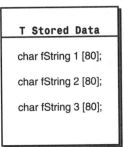

CAUTION

Remember that Navigator deletes saved data if it needs to free up memory. Remember also that all saved data is stored in RAM and is lost if the user exits Navigator. If your plug-in produces critical data that you don't want to lose, either save it on the user's hard disk, or use `NPN_PostURL()` or `NPN_PostURLNotify()` to send the data back to the server.

Note that some users are uncomfortable with the idea that a program they download from the Net may write to their hard disk. Be courteous—ask the user at runtime if it's okay, or at least put a conspicuous notice in your documentation that the file will be written to the user's hard drive.

Destroying the Window

If you are an experienced programmer, you are used to explicitly closing and deallocating all windows when the program exits. You don't need to do this in a plug-in. By the time `NPP_Destroy()` is called, the window is gone.

CAUTION

Do not do any graphics operations in `NPP_Destroy()`. Your window is no longer valid—it is gone!

Using *NPP_Shutdown()*

Recall from Chapter 6, "NPP Methods: Starting the Plug-In," that Navigator calls `NPP_Initialize()` when the plug-in is first loaded, before calling `NPP_New()` to make the first instance. `NPP_Initialize()` is the place to allocate any data that is used by all instances of your plug-in.

`NPP_Destroy()` corresponds to `NPP_New()` in that `NPP_Destroy()` is called whenever the instance is deleted. Similarly, `NPP_Shutdown()` corresponds to `NPP_Initialize()`.

When the last instance of a plug-in is deleted, Navigator calls `NPP_Shutdown()` so that it can delete any dynamic data allocated by `NPP_Initialize()`. Just as in

`NPP_Destroy()`, failure to free all the memory allocated in `NPP_Initialize()` leads to a memory leak.

From Here...

During the life of your plug-in, the user may want to print the contents of the plug-in. If the plug-in is embedded, Navigator calls the plug-in and requests that it draw its contents into the window provided.

If the plug-in is full-page, Navigator calls your plug-in and invites it to take over the printing process. You may choose to do so to customize the Print dialog or to access details of the printer driver.

If you choose not to run the printing process from the plug-in, Navigator calls your plug-in back when it is time to draw its content.

When the plug-in's life is over, Navigator calls `NPP_Destroy()`. In `NPP_Destroy()` you should deallocate all dynamic memory, including the memory allocated in the data structure pointed to by `instance->pdata`. To keep any data for use by the plug-in the next time it is called for this URL, you can save this data during `NPP_Destroy()`.

When the last instance of the plug-in is deleted, Navigator calls `NPP_Shutdown()`, giving your plug-in a chance to free any resources allocated during `NPP_Initialize()`.

- If you're new to C++ and object-oriented programming, review Chapter 2, "A C++ Primer."
- To get started with plug-ins, review Chapter 4, "Building a Simple Plug-In," which shows the "Hello, world!" of plug-ins.
- Review Chapter 6, "NPP Methods: Starting the Plug-In," to see how Navigator starts your plug-in and makes initial calls.
- Chapter 7, "NPP Methods: Handling Interaction," describes how events and messages are passed to your plug-in at runtime.
- Many plug-ins do their work with some help from Navigator itself. The next chapter, "Understanding NPN Methods," describes calls the plug-in can make back to Navigator.

CHAPTER 9

Understanding NPN Methods

Plug-in methods are divided into two sets—those that are *in* the plug-in and are called by Navigator, and those that are *in* Navigator and are called by the plug-in.

The first set of methods all begins, with the characters "NPP" for "Netscape Plug-in: Plug-in defined." The second set begins, with "NPN" for "Netscape Plug-in: Navigator defined."

This chapter describes the NPN methods your plug-in uses to make requests to Navigator. Using NPN methods, you can ask Navigator to post data back to a Web server, pull down a new stream of data, or display information in Navigator's status bar. ■

How to set up *hot spots* in your content window

By adding hyperlinks you make your plug-in more consistent with the rest of Navigator.

How to control the use of features based on Navigator's version

You can take advantage of the capabilities of Navigator 4.0 without giving up Navigator 3.0 compatibility.

How to send data from your plug-in to an HTML form

Use `NPN_PostURL()` and its kin to make your plug-in interact with the Web site.

About the `...Notify()` methods

By requiring Navigator to report the success or failure of its stream operations, your plug-in can report errors more reliably.

How to use `NPN_Status()`

Your plug-in can display its own progress indicator just like Navigator's.

Using *NPN_GetURL()*

Recall from Chapter 6, "NPP Methods: Starting the Plug-In," that Navigator and the plug-in exchange control information through the NPP and NPN methods. They exchange content through streams.

The Netscape definition of a *stream* includes the content (in a sequence of bytes), positioning information (showing where a current set of bytes fits in the overall stream), and when available, an overall size. Each stream also has an associated MIME media type that you can use to invoke an additional instance of the plug-in or a new plug-in.

N O T E When possible, Navigator reports the overall size of a stream, so that your plug-in can estimate how long it will take to download the entire stream. Use good judgment when interpreting the stream size. But if the stream is generated by a CGI script or server-side LiveWire program, the size may not be known until the stream is complete. ■

If you are developing your MIME media type for use with plug-ins and your content sometimes will be produced on-the-fly, consider placing a size field at the beginning of the contents. In this way your plug-in doesn't have to rely on the Netscape-supplied parameter.

Later in this chapter under "NPN_Status()," you learn how to put up a progress indicator in the status bar just like Navigator's.

If your plug-in is called as a full-page plug-in or if it's called by using an <EMBED> tag with a SRC attribute, Navigator calls the plug-in's NPP_NewStream() to associate a stream with the plug-in instance. During the life of the plug-in, Navigator sends the contents of the stream by using repeated calls to NPP_WriteReady() and NPP_Write() (if your plug-in sets the stream's stype to NP_NORMAL).

Recall from Chapter 6, "NPP Methods: Starting the Plug-In," that the plug-in can request that the stream be pushed by the server (if the stype is NP_NORMAL), pulled by the plug-in (if the stype is NP_SEEK), or read from a file (if the stype is NP_ASFILEONLY).

You can ask Navigator to open more streams for you by calling `NPN_GetURL()`. The specification for `NPN_GetURL()` is as follows:

```
NPError NPN_GetURL(NPP instance, const char *url, const char *window);
```

Here, `instance` is the NPP described in Chapter 6, "NPP Methods: Starting the Plug-In" and Chapter 7, NPP Methods: Handling Interaction. The `url` parameter is the Universal Resource Locator (URL) of the resource requested.

If the URL specifies a Web resource (http://...), Navigator uses the GET method to retrieve the resource. The parameter `window` is the target to which the results of the request are sent.

If `window` is `NULL`, the results of the request are sent to the plug-in by using the same protocol as is used on the initial stream: `NPP_NewStream()`, followed by `NPP_WriteReady()` and `NPP_Write()` or other calls, depending on the stream's `stype`.

If you want to show the results of the request to the user rather than processing them in the plug-in, send the stream to a named target. You can require the HTML coder to give a frame a specific name or you can use one of the targets shown in Table 9.1.

These targets are based on Navigator *frames*, which were introduced in Navigator 2.0. Figure 9.1 illustrates Navigator frames. You can steer the results of an `NPN_GetURL()` request to any of a number of windows by using the `window` parameter.

Table 9.1 Navigator Frames and Destinations

Target Name	Destination
`_self`	The same window in which the plug-in is displayed.
`_current`	Same as `_self`.
`_blank`	A new Navigator browser window.
`_new`	Same as `_blank`.
`_parent`	The window that holds the current frame.
`_top`	The full, top-level window that holds the current window.

FIG. 9.1
Navigator
frames form
NPN_GetURL()'s
basis for routing its
results.

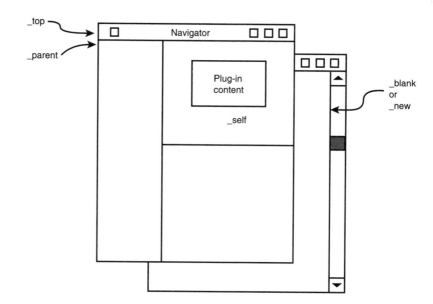

N O T E   HTML pages with Navigator frames have the following general syntax:

```
<HTML>
<HEAD>
</HEAD>
<FRAMESET>
</FRAMESET>
</HTML>
```

<FRAMESET> tags can be nested. If you direct NPN_GetURL() results to _self or
_current, the results are sent to the frame that holds the plug-in.

If you direct the results to _parent, the results are sent to the frame one level of
<FRAMESET> tags "higher" in the hierarchy than the current window. If you send the
results to _top, the new contents replace *all* current frames and fill the top-level
window. ▪

ON THE WEB

For the latest information on Navigator frames, visit **http://home.netscape.com/
assist/net_sites/frames.html**.

The Essence of Hyperlinking

Way back when you first learned about the Web, you discovered that when you moved your cursor over certain text or graphics, the name of a new destination— an URL—appeared in the status bar. In a graphical browser like Netscape, you can click this *link* and the contents of the new page replaces the old.

One of the reasons Netscape enables plug-ins is to keep the user interface as consistent as possible. You can provide hyperlinks in your plug-in. To be consistent with Navigator, you should show the destination in the status bar and be prepared to replace the contents of your plug-in window with the contents from the new URL.

This section describes loading new URLs via hyperlinks. Later in this chapter under "NPN_Status()," you'll see how to show the destination URL and a progress report in the status bar.

Loading an URL

Some data is inherently linked. Many documents are hierarchical and lend themselves to a linked presentation. If you are using Windows 95, Windows NT 3.51, or Win32s 1.3, you have access to the tree view, one of the common controls Microsoft introduced. The easiest way to put up a tree view is with Microsoft Foundation Classes (MFCs).

On the CD

The CD-ROM has code for a simple plug-in that includes an MFC tree view. You can use the tree view to present hierarchical data—the leaves provide links to HTML pages or pieces of data that could be interpreted by a plug-in.

In an intranet application, the tree might represent all material that is due in a warehouse. Each branch of the tree might represent a purchase order (PO). Each leaf under a PO might represent an item on the PO.

Figure 9.2 shows such a hierarchy.

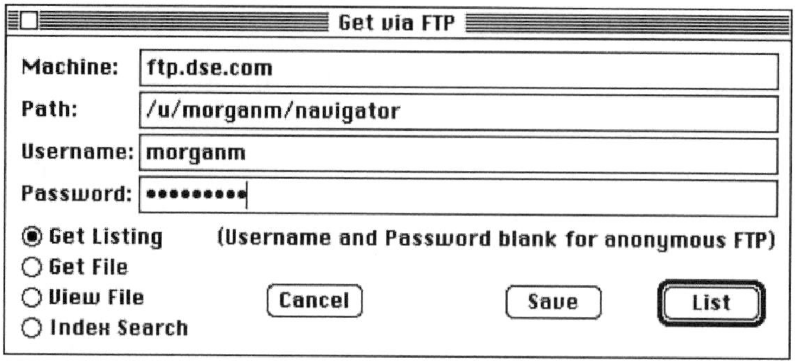

FIG. 9.2

Use an MFC tree view to represent hierarchical data in a Windows environment.

The MFC library has built-in messages generated by the tree view. You can arrange to get messages when an item is selected, or when a branch is expanded or collapsed. There is no built-in message to tell you when the cursor is over an item.

To have your tree view behave as much like Navigator as possible, consider tracking mouse movement while the cursor is over the tree view. Then call `CTreeCtrl::HitTest()` and pass in the cursor point. `CTreeCtrl::HitTest()` returns the `HTREEITEM` associated with that point or `NULL` if the point is not over a tree item.

After you know where the cursor is, you can determine if the tree item is a link and you can update the status bar to show what will happen if the link is followed.

To the Current Window   You can use `NPN_GetURL()`'s `window` parameter to direct the output to the plug-in itself (`window = NULL`), to the current window (such as `window = "_self"`), or to another window (such as `window = "_new"` or `window = "_parent"`). Note that if you direct the contents to the current window, your current plug-in instance is deleted.

Using this design, you can put up a tree view of the data. When the user moves the cursor over a hyperlink item, the item can be highlighted and the status bar can be updated to show the destination.

If the user clicks on an item, however, this design gets messy. Does the user expect to follow the link (as in Navigator) or to open a branch (as in the MFC tree view)?

TIP Whether you use the tree view or another control class, review the MFC documentation to see which built-in functions are available. With tree view, for example, use class's HitTest() member to determine whether a linked item has the mouse cursor over it. Then call the class's SelectItem() member to set the highlight.

Using the predefined methods not only saves you time, it also makes your interface more likely to have a look and feel familiar to users. This means the users are less likely to be confused.

You can work around this problem by having the user right-click the mouse to follow the link, or you could even have the right mouse button bring up a menu with other operations (as shown in Figure 9.3). A better design, however, will keep the tree view on the page and open a new window with the selected contents.

FIG. 9.3

Trap WM_RBUTTONDOWN and use it to start a handler that loads and tracks a pop-up menu.

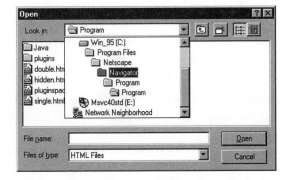

 TIP Macintoshes usually have only one mouse button. Rather than looking for a right-button click, the OS can look for a mouse-click in an empty part of the window. Therefore, if the user presses the mouse down in a part of the window that ordinarily would trigger no action, you might pop up a menu that shows the various operations available.

To Another Target—Navigator Style Some designers like to keep two frames open—one with navigational information (such as a list or a tree view) and one with the contents associated with the selected item.

This design enables you to make the interface like Navigator—always a plus if you can keep the user from being confused.

In this design, moving the mouse over a hyperlink item in the tree view highlights the item. Set the status bar to show the URL or other description of the destination.

If the user clicks the plus-minus button to the left of the item, the tree view expands or collapses the branches under the item. If the user double-clicks only the item, the tree view also expands or collapses the hierarchy.

If, however, the user single-clicks on the selection, you can trap the TVN_SELCHANGED message (which is generated every time a new item is selected). Then you can use this message to retrieve the contents from the Net and display them in the adjacent frame.

Sending to the Current Instance

If you set window to NULL, the results from NPN_GetURL() are sent via NPP_NewStream() and its follow-on methods. Remember that for the best performance, avoid stream types that need the data to be saved in a file—use NP_NORMAL to bring the data in as a stream with NPP_WriteReady() and NPP_Write().

 When you have more than one stream open to your plug-in, you must pay attention to the NPStream pointer that Netscape passes to your plug-in. Use this pointer to distinguish between the various streams and route each stream to the proper buffer.

Migrating Existing Applications to the Web

Many existing applications can easily be turned into plug-ins. Here are some rules of thumb to facilitate this transformation while maintaining most of the Navigator look and feel.

Subclass Your Application's Window to the Plug-In HWND A typical application opens a window, puts up a set of menus, then waits for user interaction. With your plug-in, Navigator already gave you a window. (On a Macintosh, Navigator gives you a portion of a window.)

On the Mac, you get all the events that occur in the Window—you can handle the events that make sense and return the rest.

In Windows, each window has a WindowsProc. You can make a new window (without displaying it) to set up a new WindowsProc. Then, by subclassing to the Navigator-supplied window, the whole message sent to the Navigator window is passed to your WindowsProc.

If you don't have MFC or prefer not to use it, use the *callback function* method of subclassing shown in Chapter 6, "NPP Methods: Starting the Plug-In."

Move the Application's Menu to a Pop-Up Menu   Your plug-in will not have access to the application menus. Many plug-in designers capture the right mouse button and use this mouse-down event or message to put up a pop-up menu like the one shown previously in Figure 9.3.

Typical items to put on such a menu include the following:

- Zoom (in and out)
- Flip, Rotate, Scale (and similar graphical transforms)
- Font changes (size, style, or the actual font)
- Copy (the contents)
- Copy the URL
- Reset
- Preferences (which you can store in pData, NPSavedData, or on the user's hard drive)
- Info (which can be displayed in a modal or modeless dialog, or in a Windows 95 Property Sheet control)
- Save (which copies the contents to the user's hard drive)
- Help
- About (the plug-in)

Don't Do Everything in a Single Plug-In   A typical application may have a number of windows, dialog boxes, controls, and menus. Because plug-ins already have the context of Navigator, each plug-in should be simpler than a full-blown application.

If you want to use Navigator to "Web-enable" a large application, break down the application by type of data. Associate a MIME media type to each data type and write a plug-in to handle each MIME media type.

Now use HTML and frames to build the "outside" of the user interface and use NPN_GetURL() to connect the components.

Thinking About Asynchronous Processing

NPN_GetURL() goes about its work asynchronously. When the plug-in calls Navigator, Navigator returns almost immediately from the function and proceeds on its own to process the request.

During this time, your plug-in doesn't know whether the request is still being processed or whether it failed. The more you depend on NPN_GetURL() to provide links between the components of your Web-enabled application, the more you need to know about the status of the NPN_GetURL() request.

Netscape provides the NPN_GetURLNotify() function to meet this need. The following line shows the syntax for NPN_GetURLNotify():

```
NPError NP_GetURLNotify(NPP instance, const char* url,
➥const char* target, void* notifyData)
```

This syntax is almost identical to NPN_GetURL(). The only difference is the addition of a private parameter, notifyData.

When NPN_GetURLNotify() completes, Navigator calls the plug-in's NPP_URLNotify() method and passes back the notifyData parameter. The plug-in uses this parameter to match up requests with notifications.

The specification for NPP_URLNotify() is as follows:

```
void NPP_URLNotify(NPP instance, const char* url,
➥NPReason reason, void* notifyData);
```

Note the reason parameter. Navigator returns one of the following three reason codes on completion of NPN_GetURLNotify():

- ■ NPRES_DONE—Indicating that the request was processed successfully.

- ■ NPRES_USER_BREAK—indicating that the request was canceled, typically by the user pressing the Stop button.

- ■ NPRES_NETWORK_ERR—Indicating that the server or network connection returned an error. Possibly, the URL was not found or the server returned a configuration error.

N O T E The `NPP_URLNotify()` reason codes are defined in the Netscape file npapi.h.
If Netscape decides to add additional reason codes, you find them listed here
in the latest version of the plug-in SDK. ▦

Determining the *NPN_Version()*

Since its earliest days, Netscape set a pace that few software developers can
maintain—they released a new major release every six months or so. Netscape's
goal is to maintain compatibility between plug-in versions, so that your Navigator
3.0 plug-in will run correctly on Navigator 6.0.

As Netscape adds features to their product, however, you may want to add corresponding capabilities to your plug-in. At some point, you will find your plug-in running and need to determine the version of Navigator "beneath" the plug-in.

You also may want to determine the version of the plug-in SDK with which the
plug-in was compiled. With a `switch` statement based on the SDK version number,
you can write code that uses advanced features in the SDK when they are available
and writes around them otherwise.

  The SDK major and minor version numbers are defined as preprocessor constants in the
Netscape file npapi.h. Their names are `NP_VERSION_MAJOR` and `NP_VERSION_MINOR`.
You can use this information with the preprocessor's `#ifdef` directive to conditionally
compile the code for advanced capabilities.

Always make sure that you check to make sure that an advanced API is present in both
the SDK and Navigator before calling it. You get a compile-time error if the prototype isn't
available in the SDK, but your user gets a runtime error if the API isn't available in
Navigator.

Using the Plug-In API Version

Call `NPN_Version()` to get the major and minor version numbers of both the plug-in
SDK and Navigator. The syntax is as follows:

```
void NPN_Version(int *plugin_major, int *plugin_minor,
➥int *netscape_major, int *netscape_minor);
```

Using *NPN_UserAgent()*

Although the Netscape plug-in is specific to Navigator, other vendors have shown an interest in duplicating Navigator's features as closely as possible. It's likely that, at some point, another browser vendor may support Netscape plug-ins.

The syntax for `NPN_UserAgent` is as follows:

```
const char* NPN_UserAgent(NPP instance);
```

NOTE At least one version of the plug-in SDK documentation incorrectly shows the specification for `NPN_Status()` rather than `NPN_UserAgent()` (and has the `NPN_Status` prototype wrong!). The syntax shown here for `NPN_UserAgent()` is based on the prototype in npapi.h.

> **CAUTION**
>
> Some releases of the 16-bit Windows Navigator crash with a General Protection Fault (GPF) when `NPN_UserAgent()` is called. If you use `NPN_UserAgent()`, test your plug-in with the versions of Navigator you expect your users to run and use `NPN_Version()` to provide alternative code where necessary.

A wealth of information is available in the browser's identifying string. For example, in Windows you can find out whether you are running on Win 95, Win NT, or Win 32s.

On the Macintosh, you can learn if the plug-in is executing on a 680X0 machine or on a Power PC. If your plug-in runs under UNIX, you can find out which platform and which version of UNIX.

> **CAUTION**
>
> `NPN_Version()` and `NPN_UserAgent()` enable you to tailor your plug-in's behavior. Use this capability as little as possible. When you start providing custom features for every platform and version, the plug-in begins to consume maintenance time. If you run out of time and fall behind, your plug-in gives the impression that it's out-of-date.
>
> When possible, dynamically link to existing code and let the platform help you keep up-to-date. If you dynamically link MFC on a Windows machine, for example, you'll always get the latest version of a control. As long as the calling interface stays the same, you get the look and feel of the new version without changing a line of code.

Accessing the *NPN_PostURL()*

The Hypertext Transport Protocol (HTTP), the protocol of the Web, allows several request methods. The two most-commonly used methods in servers are GET and POST.

You can use NPN_GetURL() to make a request to any of several different kinds of server. If your URL begins with http, Navigator interprets the request as an HTTP request and uses the GET method.

You can use an HTTP URL with NPN_PostURL() to send data via the POST method. The following code shows the syntax for NPN_PostURL():

```
NPError NPN_PostURL(NPP instance, const char *url, const char *window,
➥uint32 len, const char *buf, NPBool file);
```

Here url contains the URL to which the POST request should be sent and window points to the destination for the output—just as it did when used with NPN_GetURL().

Sending a File of Data

You can use NPN_PostURL() to send a buffer of data or a file. To send a file, set the Boolean parameter file to true and put the path to the file into buf. Set len to strlen(buf) + 1. (Remember to leave room for the terminating NULL.) You optionally may prepend file:// to the path.

N O T E If you use NPN_PostURL() to send a file, specify the path with *forward* slashes, even if you are sending from a Windows machine. ■

 T I P NPN_PostURL() expects files to conform to the UNIX line-break style—each line should be terminated with a newline ('\n') character. On Windows machines the usual line termination is a carriage return-linefeed ('\r"\n'), so you need to strip out the return before transmitting the file.

On the Mac, lines usually are terminated with a carriage return alone. You should read through the file and substitute linefeeds for returns before sending the file.

The exception to these rules is FTP. If you are using a URL that begins with ftp://, leave the line termination set to whatever makes sense for this transfer—often the native style of the machine.

Sending a Buffer

You can post a buffer of data by setting `file` to false. Set `len` to the length of the buffer and point `buf` to the data itself.

Some protocols, like HTTP, need an empty line between the headers and the content. If you want to leave the headers set at default values, you still must send a blank line before the content.

`NPN_PostURL()` doesn't accept blank lines between the headers and the content if the data is coming from a buffer. You must either send the data from a file or use `NPN_PostURLNotify()`.

Special Considerations for Older Versions of Navigator

Because Netscape releases new versions of Navigator so often and seems always to have two or three beta releases in common use, your plug-in may be loaded into browsers that are newer or older than the ones with which you test. Chapter 16, "Spanning the Windows World," includes a list of known problems when using plug-ins with the Windows versions of Navigator.

When Netscape releases beta versions of the Navigator Plug-Ins Software Development Kit (SDK) they typically put a list of known problems on their Web site. Check this list and test with as many versions of Navigator as possible. Then use `NPN_Version()` and `NPN_UserAgent()` to steer your user around unreliable combinations.

CAUTION

Calling `NPN_PostURL()` with a non-HTTP URL can cause the Windows version of Navigator to crash with a GPF. Although the Netscape documentation says that `NPN_PostURL()` works with `mailto`, `news`, and `FTP` URLs (in addition to `http`), these combinations are known to fail on older versions of Navigator.

If you allow the user to specify the URL, check to ensure that it begins with `http` before submitting the request to Navigator. If it doesn't, check the user's version of Navigator and warn the user before sending `NPN_PostURL()`.

If you are building plug-ins for an intranet, you have a good idea of which browsers your users have. If you are writing plug-ins for an existing site, use the server logs to find out how people access your site.

ON THE WEB

If you're building a new site, you can get an idea of which browsers and which versions of Navigator are in common use by visiting the listings of BrowserWatch at **http://www. browserwatch.com/**. BrowserWatch maintains statistics on the relative popularity of each browser, at **http://browserwatch.iworld.com/report-table-browsers.html**.

Part

II

Ch

9

Figure 9.4 shows typical figures for Mozilla, the internal name for Navigator (in this case, 75.7 percent). This topic also is discussed regularly in the mailing lists of the HTML Writers Guild (described further at **http://www.hwg.org/**) and on the **comp.infosystems.www.*** newsgroups.

FIG. 9.4
Use BrowserWatch to estimate which versions of Navigator are currently popular on the Web.

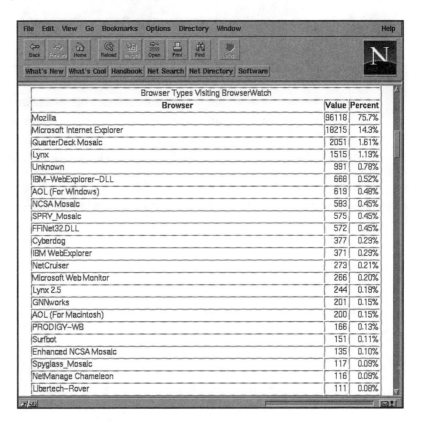

Browser Types Visiting BrowserWatch

Browser	Value	Percent
Mozilla	96118	75.7%
Microsoft Internet Explorer	18215	14.3%
QuarterDeck Mosaic	2051	1.61%
Lynx	1515	1.19%
Unknown	991	0.78%
IBM-WebExplorer-DLL	668	0.52%
AOL (For Windows)	619	0.48%
NCSA Mosaic	583	0.45%
SPRY_Mosaic	575	0.45%
FFINet32.DLL	572	0.45%
Cyberdog	377	0.29%
IBM WebExplorer	371	0.29%
NetCruiser	273	0.21%
Microsoft Web Monitor	266	0.20%
Lynx 2.5	244	0.19%
GNNworks	201	0.15%
AOL (For Macintosh)	200	0.15%
PRODIGY-WB	166	0.13%
Surfbot	151	0.11%
Enhanced NCSA Mosaic	135	0.10%
Spyglass_Mosaic	117	0.09%
NetManage Chameleon	116	0.09%
Libertech-Rover	111	0.08%

T I P For more information about how to analyze your server logs, see Chapter 42, "Processing Logs and Analyzing Site Use," of *Webmaster Expert Solutions* (Que, 1996).

Setting up a Distributed System

You can set up a powerful distributed application by combining one or more plug-ins with static HTML pages and scripts that produce dynamic content. Figure 9.5 revisits the system with multiple MIME media types originally introduced in Chapter 1, "Bridging the Gap from CGI and Helper Applications to Netscape Plug-Ins."

FIG. 9.5

By using Navigator as a starting point, the programmer can set up a distributed warehouse application quickly.

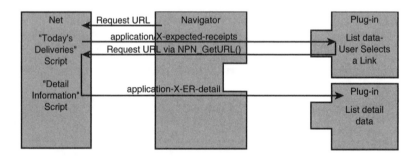

The system starts when the warehouse manager opens a page that includes an embedded plug-in listing all the receipts that are due in (sorted by date). On the newer Windows platforms, the plug-in can display this data in a tree view, so that the items on a given purchase order (PO) can be shown in a hierarchical fashion.

Design Tradeoff: How to Transmit the File One tradeoff the designer of this application must make is whether to download all the expected receipts at once or to send them on demand. In many warehouses this problem is compounded because material may arrive earlier or later than its expected arrival date, and POs with backordered material may remain open long after their expected arrival date has passed.

If the warehouse has, for example, 1,000 POs open and due in within the next week and an average of 20 items on each PO, a request for all of these POs would take about 195K (assuming each PO and each line item have a 10-character identifier). On the Internet, a file of this size may take too long to download because many users have a relatively slow dial-up connection.

On a corporate intranet, however, a file of 195K may transmit in just a second or two, so it's probably all right to send the whole file to the client. Figure 9.6 illustrates this aspect of the design.

FIG. 9.6
For many distributed applications, an entire file can be downloaded through an intranet in just a second or two

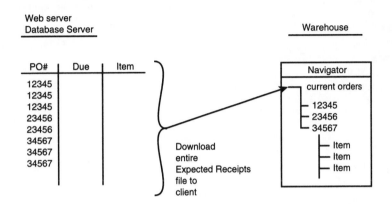

Design Tradeoff: File Updates from the Server   Another consideration for the designer is update frequency. In many organizations, buyers may make changes to the file of expected receipts right up to the time the truck arrives.

If a warehouse manager pulls down the file from the server at 6 a.m., the file may be missing important updates when a truck pulls in at 9 a.m. To solve this problem the designer may want to set a timer in the plug-in.

Every few minutes, as long as the plug-in is in existence, the plug-in re-requests its data. One approach is to specify _self as the target, so that the old plug-in is replaced with a new copy of itself.

Use the NPSavedData parameter of NPP_Destroy() to keep a bookmark of the warehouse manager's current PO. When the data is restored, position the window so that the bookmark is again visible. Figure 9.7 illustrates this technique.

If the plug-in allows the user to change the local copy of the expected receipts file, set the window parameter of NPN_GetURL() to NULL and read the data back into the plug-in. Use an associative container such as those available in the standard template library (STL) or one of the map classes from MFC to match records from the old file with records from the new one.

Figure 9.8 shows how this technique works.

FIG. 9.7
Before the file is refreshed, the warehouse manager has some items expanded, others collapsed, and one selected. After the new copy is downloaded, the plug-in sets each item back to its original state.

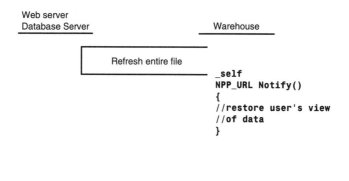

FIG. 9.8
In this design, the plug-in handles the data and deals explicitly with items that are added, deleted, or changed.

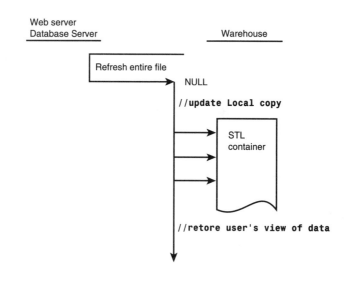

Design Tradeoff: Downloading Additional Files   As the warehouse manager reviews the expected receipts, he or she may need additional information about the items that are due in. The tree view enables the manager to get summary information quickly.

For more detail the manager can select an item (or a PO) and get a detail file. This file is handled in a different MIME media type and is sent to a different plug-in.

One design is to set up two frames—one for the tree view and one for the detail information. The second frame has a name, such as Details. This way NPN_GetURL() or better still, NPN_GetURLNotify(), can direct the results of the request right to that frame.

If the warehouse manager needs to see a lot of information or if the screen is cramped, the designer can send the output of NPN_GetURL() to_new so that Navigator starts a new browser window. In either case, the new plug-in should be designed as a full-page plug-in.

Interacting with the User   As the warehouse workers receive material, they can check the material off of printed lists or scan bar codes by using portable terminals. Eventually, this information is returned to the desktop machine on which Navigator is running. You want to allow local editing on the PC, even if the bulk of the data is uploaded through a serial port.

Local editing can be easily handled through edit fields in a dialog box. For example, a typical function may list all the items on a PO for which the quantity received doesn't match the quantity due in.

The warehouse manager can print this list and go through the receiving area looking for missing items. When found, the manager then can return to the PC, double-click the item in the list, and enter the corrected quantity in the dialog box.

Figure 9.9 shows such an arrangement.

FIG. 9.9
Use a dialog box to make local edits in the file.

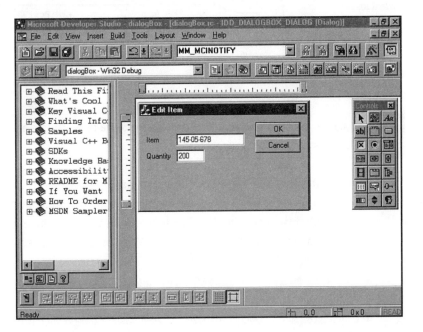

Keeping the Data Safe Often the user wants to edit and re-edit the data until satisfied. It makes no sense to post the data back to the server until all the edits are complete. In this case, loss of power or a crash on the client computer can result in catastrophic loss of data.

The solution is to back up the data. If the data can be kept on the user's hard drive, just use file I/O or MFC serialization to save the updated version of the data.

If this approach is inconvenient (perhaps the warehouse machine is a diskless workstation), use NPN_PostURL() to periodically post the data back to the server in a temporary storage area. (You can even use FTP to save the file, and then restore it if the data is lost from the PC's memory.)

Figure 9.10 illustrates this part of the design.

FIG. 9.10
Whether the data is on the local hard drive or on the server, be sure to save it periodically to prevent loss.

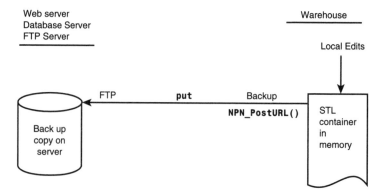

TIP If you use this approach, make sure that you delete the temporary file after the updated file is posted to the server application.

Final Update When the warehouse manager is satisfied that a PO is fully received, he or she can direct the plug-in to send the data back to the server. This time, rather than sending the data to a temporary file, send each record to a server application such as a CGI script or LiveWire program. The server application typically uses the data to update a database.

TIP For more information on coupling CGI and relational databases on the server, see Chapter 18, "How to Query Databases," of *Webmaster Expert Solutions* (Que, 1996).

Coupling with CGI or LiveWire

There are two big advantages to developing applications by using plug-ins. First, the application can be developed quickly because much of the networking and user interface portions are supplied by Navigator. Second, the design of Web servers and browsers makes it easy to extend the application across many machines and sites.

For example, one company with a headquarters on the U.S. East Coast manages its accounts on a large mainframe. Staff in their sales districts call operators on the East Coast to check on the status of their orders. The staff have local terminals that give them access to the database on the mainframe.

The company's largest single sales district is in southern California. Due to the time difference, employees in California have to check on their orders before mid-day, before the East Coast office has closed.

This restriction, as well as the frustrations of passing detailed numerical information over the phone, causes problems for the southern California sales staff. Sales representatives might promise delivery of material that is due in, only to find out that it wasn't yet received in the warehouse.

When material is received, the East Coast office might be closed, causing a delay of a day or more before the material is posted as being available for sale. Figure 9.11 illustrates this situation.

FIG. 9.11
West Coast staff are frustrated by having to check on their orders by phone.

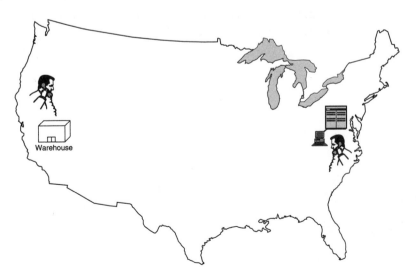

Warehouse

The solution is to "Webify" the mainframe application and to distribute portions of the application to desktop computers in southern California. The mainframe application is integrated with a Web server, which has a firewall to protect it from intruders.

The West Coast users get a local server and a high-speed connection to the Internet. They can use forms to query their order status. The HTML forms are connected to the mainframe's relational database manager, a program that understands the Structured Query Language (SQL). A Common Gateway Interface (CGI) script connects the database manager to the Web. When the user submits the form, the CGI script translates the request into SQL and sends it to the database manager. The same script then takes the results of the query from the database manager and formats them in HTML to build a reply page.

 TIP

For more information about connecting an HTML form to a database manager through a CGI script, see Chapter 18, "How to Query Databases," in *Webmaster Expert Solutions* (Que, 1996).

If you use a Netscape Web server, you can use server-side JavaScript to access a database manager. Server-side JavaScript has access to a library of SQL calls, so those scripts tend to be simpler and easier to implement than CGI scripts. For more information on using server-side JavaScript to access a database, see Chapter 12, "Using the Database," in *Special Edition Using Netscape LiveWire* (Que, 1996).

As material is received in the warehouse, this information is posted back to the mainframe. An account representative can find out instantly that the material he or she is looking for has arrived in the warehouse and is available for sale.

Figure 9.12 shows this new design.

FIG. 9.12
Using the Internet, a distributed version of the application is available 24 hours a day and is updated in realtime so material received is available for immediate sale.

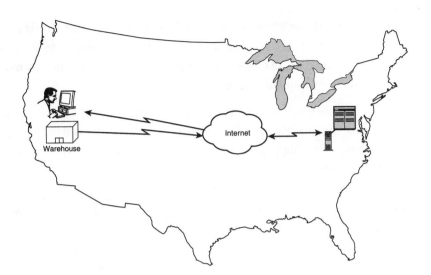

NPN_RequestRead()

Recall from Chapter 6, "NPP Methods: Starting the Plug-In," that the programmer has the option of setting the stream's stype parameter to NP_SEEK. This change takes the stream out of *server push* mode and sets it to *client pull*. The plug-in pulls data from the stream using the NPN_RequestRead() method.

Understanding Seekable Streams

The first Web servers used the GET and POST methods already described in this chapter. If a client sent a GET request for a file, the server responded with the entire file. Some newer servers use a byte-range request—the client can request certain parts of the file, and only these parts of the file in the specified ranges are sent.

If a server uses byte-range requests, Navigator sets seekable to true in the NPP_NewStream() call. Navigator also sets seekable to true if the source of the data is a local file. If seekable is true, you can set the stream's stype to NP_SEEK with no penalty.

If `seekable` isn't true and you set the stream to `NP_SEEK`, Navigator copies the entire stream to the local hard drive. The plug-in then can do seeks on the local file. This operation, of course, can be time-consuming and undoes most of the benefits offered by seekable streams.

Seekable streams make the most sense when a well-defined structure exists to the data. Suppose that the data consists of 1,000,000 records of 80 characters each. Even over a high-speed connection, the file would need between 10 and 15 *minutes* to transfer.

 TIP   Even if you are designing a plug-in for a high-speed intranet, remember that most companies have a few employees who access the Net from dial-up connections. This category may include outside sales staff, field maintenance staff, or traveling executives. If these employees will access your plug-in, you need to ensure its performance is acceptable over a 28,800-bps or even a 14,400-bps connection.

If the data is stored as a binary tree, the average number of reads to find a given record is as follows:

$$\frac{\log_2 n}{2}$$

Here, *n* is the number of records in the file. With 1,000,000 records, the average number of reads is 10 and the worst-case number of reads is 20.

The overhead of HTTP needs around 0.5 to 0.75 seconds to set up a connection, so 10 independent reads need between 5 and 8 seconds of overhead (and a negligible amount of actual transfer time).

Reducing the time to find the data from several minutes to a few seconds is dramatic, but even better methods are available. The server can be programmed to keep an index of the data, giving an approximate starting location for each record.

This technique is known as the *indexed sequential access method* (ISAM).

Suppose that the key field needs 32 bits (which gives enough room for over 4 billion records) and the offset needs another 32 bits (which gives room for a 4-gigabyte file). Then suppose that each cluster consists of 1,000 records.

There are 1,000,000 √ 1,000, or 1,000 clusters. Each cluster takes 64 bits in the index—32 bits for the key and 32 bits for the offset. Sixty-four bits can be packed into 8 characters, so the index is 8 × 1,000 or 8,000 bytes long.

Figure 9.13 illustrates this index. This file can be downloaded over a high-speed connection in less than a second, even considering overhead. Even a dial-up user can retrieve the index in 5 to 8 seconds.

FIG. 9.13

Pack the index as tight as possible to minimize download time.

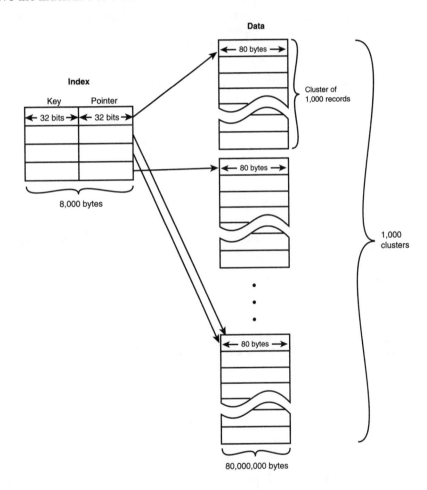

When the plug-in has the index, it can keep it for multiple searches of the database. Because the index is small and is stored in memory, searches are very fast.

When the byte offset of the correct cluster is identified, the plug-in can download the 80,000-byte cluster in about a second on a high-speed link or under 30 seconds on a 28,800bps dial-up link.

How to Use *NPN_RequestRead()*

The syntax for `NPN_RequestRead()` is as follows:

```
NPError NPN_RequestRead((NPStream *stream, NPByteRange *rangeList);
```

where `NPByteRange` is a structure with the following layout:

```
typedef struct _NPByteRange
{
  int32      offset;           /* negative offset means from the end */
  uint32     length;
  struct _NPByteRange* next;
} NPByteRange;
```

Note that `NPByteRange` includes a pointer to the "next" `NPByteRange`, so you can string these structures together to request multiple byte ranges in one request.

Each request needs a few hundred milliseconds of overhead. If you can design your application so that it requests more than one byte range in a single request, your plug-in incurs less overhead.

Occasionally, you get a big performance boost by taking advantage of the way people work. For example, in the warehouse application, if the warehouse manager requests one item from PO 12345, he or she is likely to request other items as well. You may want to retrieve all the items associated with a purchase order at once and store them locally in case the manager requests them.

Using *NPN_NewStream()*

So far, all the examples have involved processing additional streams from the Net. Your plug-in also can generate a stream that is sent to Navigator. To open a stream to Navigator, use `NPN_NewStream()`. `NPN_NewStream()`'s specification is as follows:

```
NPError NPN_NewStream(NPP instance, NPMIMEType type,
➥const char *target, NPStream **stream);
```

Here, each of these parameters has the same meaning it does in the other plug-in APIs. The `target` parameter is identical to the `window` parameter in `NPN_GetURL()` and `NPN_PostURL()`.

Streaming into Navigator

The NPMIMEType type is a typedef for char*; you specify the MIME type, followed by a forward slash, followed by the subtype. For example, an HTML page has the text/html type.

Because you can specify the MIME media type with the type parameter, you can force Navigator to start additional copies of your plug-in, a different plug-in, or a helper application. If the type parameter is for a type that is native to Navigator, then, of course, Navigator handles the actual stream.

For example, you could use NPN_NewStream() to write an HTML page on-the-fly and send it back to Navigator.

Part

II

Ch

9

> **CAUTION**
>
> Think through the implications of your choice of target. Just as we saw with NPN_GetURL(), you can destroy your current plug-in instance by specifying _self or _current as the target. There's nothing wrong with doing this, as long as it is what you intended.

When NPN_NewStream() returns, the parameter stream holds a handle to an NPStream. You use this stream in your calls to NPN_Write().

NPN_Write()

Write to your new stream using NPN_Write(), which is specified by the following:

```
int32 NPN_Write(NPP instance, NPStream *stream,
➥int32 offset, int32 len, void *buf);
```

There is no NPN_WriteReady()function that corresponds to NPP_WriteReady(). Instead, send as much data as you have ready to Navigator with NPN_Write().

If Navigator cannot handle all the data, it returns a number that is less than len. Just move the buf pointer to the point in the buffer where Navigator stopped, update len and offset, and call NPN_Write() again. When the return value equals len, Navigator has consumed all of your data.

If Navigator encounters an error while processing your stream, it returns a value less than zero. If this occurs, call NPN_DestroyStream() to free up the buffers associated with the stream. Of course, you should also call NPN_DestroyStream() when Navigator is finished with your data.

NPN_DestroyStream()

Your plug-in should call `NPN_DestroyStream()` when it is done with a stream it allocated by using `NPN_NewStream()`. The following line shows the syntax for `NPN_DestroyStream()`:

```
NPError NPN_DestroyStream(NPP instance, NPStream *stream, NPError
reason);
```

The `reason` parameter takes the same values as the `reason` parameter does in `NPP_URLNotify()`: `NPPRES_NETWORK_ERR`, `NPPRES_USER_BREAK`, and `NPPRES_DONE`. You usually return `NPPRES_DONE`.

The usual sequence for writing back to Netscape resembles the following code:

```
NPStream stream;
char* theData = "<HTML><B>This is a message from my plug-in!</B></
➥HTML>";
int32 theLength = strlen(myData) + 1;
err = NPN_NewStream(instance, "text/html", "_blank", &stream);
int32 theOffset = 0;
do
{
  err = NPN_Write(instance, stream, theOffset, theLength, theData);
  theOffset = err;
  theLength -= err;
  theData += err;
} while (err >= 0 && err != theLength);
if (err >= 0)
  err = NPN_DestroyStream(instance, stream, NPRES_DONE);
else
  err = NPN_DestroyStream(instance, stream, NPRES_USER_BREAK);
```

If your plug-in does anything between the call to `NPN_NewStream()` and the call to `NPN_DestroyStream()` that raises an exception, be sure to include a call to `NPN_DestroyStream()` in the exception handler and set the reason code to `NPRES_NETWORK_ERR`. Failure to destroy the stream will lead to a memory leak.

Using *NPN_Status()*

Under "Using NPN_GetURL()" in this chapter, we mentioned the `NPN_Status()` method, which enables your plug-in to duplicate the Netscape look and feel by putting up its own progress indicator. This section shows how to use `NPN_Status()`.

The specification for `NPN_Status()` is as follows:

```
void NPN_Status((NPP instance, const char *message);
```

You can use `NPN_Status()` to write any message into the Navigator status line. Remember that experienced Navigator users have certain expectations about what will appear in the status line. Your plug-in will be received more favorably if you stay close to the Navigator look and feel.

A Progress Indicator

One good use for the status line is to mimic the progress reports that Navigator gives while it is downloading a file. Recall that Navigator calls your `NPP_Write()` method and passes a `stream` parameter.

`NPStream` includes an `end` field that gives the location of the end of the stream, in bytes. If Navigator cannot determine the length of the stream, it puts a zero into this field.

If the field is nonzero, you can use `NPN_Status()` to report your plug-in's progress in reading the stream:

```
int32 NPP_Write(NPP instance, NPStream *stream, int32 offset,
➡int32 len, void *buf);
{
.
.
.
  CString theOutput;
  if (0 != stream->end)
  {
    int thePercentComplete = (int) ((float) 100 *
      (stream->end - offset) / stream->end);
    theOutput.Format("%d%% of %dK received",
      thePercentComplete,
      stream->end / 1024);
  }
  else
    theOutput.Format("%d bytes received",
      stream->end - offset);

  NPN_Status (instance, theOutput.GetBuffer(theOutput.GetLength()));
}
```

Reporting Time Remaining

Netscape itself reports more than just the percentage complete. It tries to estimate the download rate and the time remaining.

On the CD

The following program shows how to provide this additional information. This code appears on the CD-ROM as /source/chap 09/progress.cpp. Note that this example uses a Windows worker thread. Chapter 13, "Getting Back on the Network," provides more information on multithreaded plug-ins under Windows.

```
//
// ShowProgress
//
// Note: Be sure to add a DWORD member to this class called
// dwLastTickCount.
// Initialize that member to zero. Reset it to zero in
// NPP_DestroyStream().
void CWorker::ShowProgress (NPP instance,
                            uint32 FileSize,
                            int32 Offset,
                            int32 length)
{
  DWORD dwCurrentTick = GetTickCount();

  if (0 != this->dwLastTickCount)
  {
    float BytesPerSecond = (float) length /
       ((float) (dwCurrentTick - this->dwLastTickCount) /
       (float) (dwCurrentTick - this->dwLastTickCount) / (float)
1000.0);
        int SecondsRemaining = (int) ((FileSize - Offset) /
    ➥BytesPerSecond);
    int MinutesRemaining = SecondsRemaining / 60;
    SecondsRemaining -= MinutesRemaining * 60;
    CString OutPut;
    int PercentComplete;

    // Sometimes FileSize is zero. Handle that case properly.
    if (0 != FileSize)
    {
        PercentComplete = (int)((float)(100.0*Offset) /
    ➥(float)FileSize);

      OutPut.Format ("%d%% of %dK (at%8.0f Kbps, %2d:%02d remaining)",
        PercentComplete,
        FileSize / 1024,
        BytesPerSecond / 1024.0,
        MinutesRemaining,
        SecondsRemaining);
```

```
    }
    else
      OutPut.Format ("%8.0f kbps)",
        BytesPerSecond / 1024);
    NPN_Status (instance, OutPut.GetBuffer(OutPut.GetLength()));
  }

    this->dwLastTickCount = dwCurrentTick;
  }
```

Call ShowProgress by adding a line in NPP_Write() like the following:

```
    data->pWorker->ShowProgress(instance, stream->end, offset, len);
```

Note that this version of the status bar shows kilobytes per second, just like Navigator. Some designers prefer to see the speed in bits per second to enable the user to better compare his or her modem's rated speed with the transfer rate. If you want to change the status line to show bits per second, find the two lines which read

```
    BytesPerSecond / 1024);
```

and change them to

```
    BytesPerSecond * 8);
```

CAUTION

In any version of a progress indicator that you build, make sure that you handle the case in which FileSize is zero. If Navigator cannot determine the file size (which happens, for example, when the stream is coming from a CGI script), it sets stream->end to zero. If you attempt to compute the following line when FileSize is zero, you get a divide-by-zero error, and your plug-in causes Navigator to exit unexpectedly:

```
    PercentComplete = (int)((float)(100.0*Offset) / (float)FileSize);
```

Understanding *NPN_MemAlloc()* and *NPN_MemFree()*

Navigator provides NPN_MemAlloc() as a substitute for malloc or the built-in new. NPN_MemAlloc() allocates memory inside Navigator.

By allowing Navigator to manage the memory, your plug-in is more likely to *get* the memory it requests (because Navigator can free up memory it no longer needs). Navigator also preserves blocks of memory in NPSavedData as much as possible, so that two instances of your plug-in for the same URL can talk to each other.

In C++, the easiest way to use NPN_MemAlloc() and its corresponding method, NPN_MemFree(), is to put these methods into the new and delete operators. You can make one top-level class with plug-in-friendly new and delete, and derive all your other classes from that top-level class.

Chapter 6, "NPP Methods: Starting the Plug-In," shows how to perform this use under "Launching the Plug-In." That section also shows how to use NPN_MemFlush() to free up as much memory as possible on the Macintosh.

From Here...

Much of the work of a plug-in is done by Navigator. You use Navigator to read data from the Net, post data, and put up new Navigator windows with content generated by your plug-in.

Navigator also can display status in the status line on behalf of your plug-in, and report various version and user agent information.

- If you're new to C++ and object-oriented programming, review "A C++ Primer" in Chapter 2.

- To get started with plug-ins, see Chapter 4, "Building a Simple Plug-In," which shows the "Hello, world!" of plug-ins.

- Learn about NPP_ functions in Chapter 6, "NPP Methods: Starting the Plug-In."

- Learn more about NPP_ functions in Chapter 7, "NPP Methods: Handling Interaction."

- Chapter 8, "NPP Methods: Other Tasks," concludes this discussion of NPP_ functions by looking at printing and plug-in shutdown.

- The following chapter, "Example: Simple Plug-In," shows how to handle a plug-in's primary task; interpreting content that isn't native to Navigator.

CHAPTER 10

Example: Simple Plug-In

Despite its name, the "Simple Plug-In" that Netscape supplies with the Plug-in Software Development Kit (SDK) is far from simple. It includes a full implementation of the major methods, including LiveConnect. LiveConnect (described in more detail in Chapter 18, "Plug-Ins as a Programming Resource") is Netscape's integration technology that allows your plug-in to communicate with Java and JavaScript. ■

How to read a plug-in's source

By tracing the flow of control between Navigator and the plug-in, you can get a good idea of what the plug-in does and when it does it.

How to take advantage of Java and C++

Sophisticated plug-ins have at least two interfaces. One looks toward Navigator, the other talks to the user.

How JavaScript can send a message to a plug-in

"Officially," JavaScript can only talk to Java, but Netscape has made it almost trivial to set up a Java "peer" object for the plug-in.

How Java "native" classes are implemented in C and C++

This chapter covers these native classes, which are the key to letting Java call the plug-in's methods.

"Simple" in Action

To get an idea of what Simple does, start by compiling the plug-in and running it. This chapter uses the Windows version of the plug-in, but Netscape supplies a version for the Mac as well.

Compiling the Plug-In

Netscape uses Microsoft's Visual C++ on Windows, and MetroWorks' Code Warrior on the Macintosh. You can simplify the installation process if you use the same environment they do.

In Visual C++'s Developer Studio, choose File, Open Workspace and open Simple32.mdp in the Examples\Simple\Windows subdirectory of the Plugins SDK directory. After the project opens, choose Build, Build NPSimp32.dll. The project should compile and link with no errors or warnings.

Moving the Files into Position

Copy the Java class file Simple.class to the Navigator plug-ins directory.

 You may want to skim Chapter 18, "Plug-Ins as a Programming Resource," for a bigger picture of Java and LiveConnect. In Chapter 18 you learn how to use javac and javah to make your own class, header, and stub files.

Copy the NPSimp32.dll file, which you just built, to the plug-ins directory, and restart Navigator. Make sure that you are using a version of Navigator that is at least at v3.0b5 or you won't see all the features of this plug-in working.

Running the Plug-In

When Navigator restarts, it examines the files in the plug-ins directory and registers plug-ins based on their MIME media type. Chapter 19, "Installing the Plug-In," describes this process in more detail.

After Navigator is up, use File, Open File to open Examples\Simple\Testing\SimpleExample.html. You probably will want to bookmark this page while you learn about plug-ins.

Choose Options, Show Java Console and make sure that this item is checked. The Java Console is a small window to which your Java classes can send messages. When it opens you will see that your Simple plug-in has already been busy. If you have enough room on-screen, try to position your windows so that you can see both the Java Console and the plug-in's part of the Navigator window. Figure 10.1 shows the SimpleExample.html and the Java Console.

FIG. 10.1
Simple writes to both the Java Console and the Navigator window.

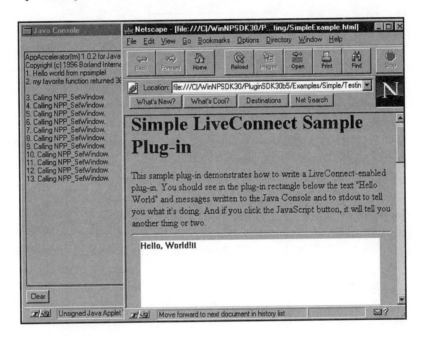

Notice that Simple wrote "Hello, World!" to its Navigator window. To see that Simple is listening to JavaScript as well, click the "Click Me" button a few times while watching the Java Console.

Understanding Flow of Control

Although you may not want to ship Simple as a finished product, Simple is rich enough to have hooks for many of the actions that you may perform with a more sophisticated plug-in.

Follow Navigator

As you saw when you ran Simple, a plug-in has two interfaces—one to Navigator and another to the user. Because the plug-in cannot do anything with the user until most of its Navigator functions are called, you start by tracing the flow of control between Navigator and Simple. Follow along on Figure 10.2.

FIG. 10.2
Navigator make a series of calls to the plug-in to get things started.

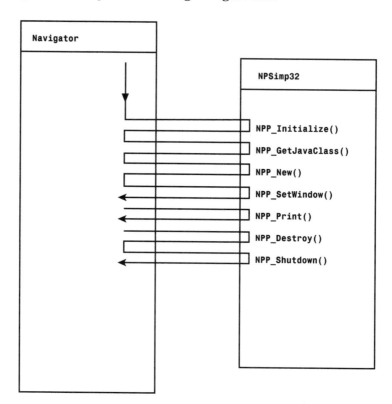

How Simple is Called   Return to Microsoft Developer Studio and use it to open SimpleExample.html. This file isn't part of the project—you need to use File, Open to open it. The plug-in is loaded because of the following line:

```
<EMBED type=application/x-simple-plugin name=simple1 width=400 height=300>
```

This line tells us that Simple doesn't read a stream from the Net. The TYPE attribute forces Navigator to load this plug-in by specifying the MIME media type.

Notice also that the plug-in has a name—Simple1. This name gets used by JavaScript later, in the section that reads as follows:

```
<form>
<input type=button value="Click Me"
  onclick='document.simple1.doit("Hello from JavaScript!")'>
</form>
```

NP_Initialize() When Navigator sees the `<EMBED>` tag it looks up the plug-in that registered to handle MIME type `application/x-simple-plugin`. Nzavigator finds npSimp32 and loads this library into its address space. Then it exchanges entry points, as Chapter 6, "NPP Methods: Starting the Plug-In," described. The first method it calls is `NP_Initialize()`—a function written by Netscape to get the plug-in started. Use Microsoft Developer Studio's ClassView to open this function. (It's in the Globals folder because it's not part of any class. The implementation is in the npwin.cpp file in the Common directory of the SDK.) Here's `NP_Initialize()`:

```
// NP_Initialize
//
// called immediately after the plugin DLL is loaded
//
NPError WINAPI NP_EXPORT
NP_Initialize(NPNetscapeFuncs* pFuncs)
{
  // trap a NULL ptr
  if(pFuncs == NULL)
    return NPERR_INVALID_FUNCTABLE_ERROR;
  g_pNavigatorFuncs = pFuncs; // save it for future reference

  // if the plugin's major ver level is lower than the Navigator's,
  // then they are incompatible, and should return an error
  if(HIBYTE(pFuncs->version) > NP_VERSION_MAJOR)
    return NPERR_INCOMPATIBLE_VERSION_ERROR;

  // We have to defer these assignments until g_pNavigatorFuncs is set
  int navMinorVers = g_pNavigatorFuncs->version & 0xFF;
  if( navMinorVers >= NPVERS_HAS_NOTIFICATION ) {
    g_pluginFuncs->urlnotify = NPP_URLNotify;
  }

  if( navMinorVers >= NPVERS_HAS_LIVECONNECT ) {
    g_pluginFuncs->javaClass = Private_GetJavaClass();
  }

  // NPP_Initialize is a standard (cross-platform) initialize function.
  return NPP_Initialize();
}
```

Most of NP_Initialize() is standard stuff you saw in Chapter 6, "NPP Methods: Starting the Plug-In." All implementations of NP_Initialize() should check their incoming parameters to make sure that Navigator has done its job.

Before exiting, NP_Initialize() checks to make sure that your version of Navigator is new enough to include notification and LiveConnect. If so, the function fills these slots in the function table.

NPP_GetJavaClass() Chapter 6, "NPP Methods: Starting the Plug-In," didn't mention NPP_GetJavaClass(). If your plug-in isn't using LiveConnect, you don't need to do much with it—just return NULL.

If you want to support LiveConnect, you may want to include an NPP_GetJavaClass() function similar to the one in Simple, as follows:

```
/*
** NPP_GetJavaClass is called during initialization to ask your plugin
** what its associated Java class is. If you don't have one, just return
** NULL. Otherwise, use the javah-generated "use_" function to both
** initialize the class and return it. If you can't find your class, an
** error will be signaled by "use_" and will cause the Navigator to
** complain to the user.
*/
jref NPP_GetJavaClass(void)
{
#ifdef __MC68K__
    return NULL;
#else
    struct java_lang_Class* myClass;
    env = NPN_GetJavaEnv();
    if (env == NULL)
      return NULL;               /* Java disabled */
    myClass = use_Simple(env);
    if (myClass == NULL) {
      /*
      ** If our class doesn't exist (the user hasn't installed it)
      ** then don't allow any of the Java stuff to happen.
      */
      env = NULL;
    }
    return myClass;
#endif
}
```

N O T E If you're writing a plug-in for the Macintosh, make sure that you include the
following lines:

```
#ifdef __MC68K__
    return NULL;
#else
    .
    .
    .
```

Netscape doesn't support LiveConnect on the 680x0 Macintosh—they do support it on
the Power Macintosh. ▪

Chapter 18, "Plug-Ins as a Programming Resource," goes into depth on
LiveConnect. This chapter shows why Navigator is calling this function, and why
you might want a Java class. For now, just note that NPP_GetJavaClass() calls
NPN_GetJavaEnv(), to put a pointer to the Java runtime environment into env. If
this step succeeds, the plug-in calls a function named use_Simple().
use_Simple() is a function written by an automated tool (javah) based on our Java
class, Simple. use_Simple() performs certain initializations and connections in
the Java Runtime Interface. As a plug-in programmer, you don't have to be familiar
with too many Java details yet. Figure 10.3 illustrates the flow of control between
the Java runtime and the plug-in during NPP_GetJavaClass().

Part
II

Ch
10

FIG. 10.3
The plug-in and
the Java runtime
interface work
together closely to
initialize the peer
object.

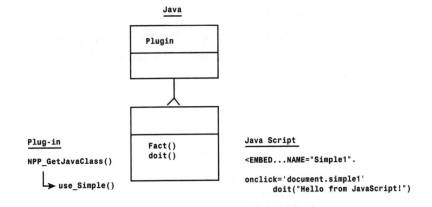

NPP_New() Now Navigator is ready to make the plug-in instance. Open
NPP_New() with ClassWizard. Note the following line:

```
instance->pdata = NPN_MemAlloc(sizeof(PluginInstance));
```

This line is a "heads-up" that the designer chose to associate a `PluginInstance` with the instance's `pdata`. Recall that `pdata` points to a block of Navigator memory that will be passed back to your plug-in on every NPP call. Inside the function the programmer uses `This` to point to this instance.

Simple and most other Netscape sample plug-ins uses the structure `PluginInstance` to hold the data passed through `pdata`. Netscape defines `PluginInstance` in npsimple.c:

```
typedef struct _PluginInstance
{
  NPWindow* fWindow;
  uint16    fMode;

/* Windows data members */
#ifdef _WINDOWS
  HWND       fhWnd;
  WNDPROC    fDefaultWindowProc;
#endif /* _WINDOWS */

/* UNIX data members */
#ifdef XP_UNIX
  Window     window;
  Display    *display;
  uint32     x, y;
  uint32     width, height;
#endif /* XP_UNIX */
} PluginInstance;
```

Although Simple doesn't store anything special in `PluginInstance`, this structure is custom in each plug-in because most plug-ins *will* store instance-specific data in the structure.

Here's Simple's version of `NPP_New()`:

```
/*
** NPP_New is called when your plugin is instantiated (i.e. when an EMBED
** tag appears on a page).
*/
NPError   NP_LOADDS
NPP_New(NPMIMEType pluginType,
  NPP instance,
  uint16 mode,
  int16 argc,
  char* argn[],
  char* argv[],
  NPSavedData* saved)
{
```

```
    NPError result = NPERR_NO_ERROR;
    PluginInstance* This;
    char factString[60];

    if (instance == NULL)
      return NPERR_INVALID_INSTANCE_ERROR;
    instance->pdata = NPN_MemAlloc(sizeof(PluginInstance));
    This = (PluginInstance*) instance->pdata;
    if (This == NULL)
      return NPERR_OUT_OF_MEMORY_ERROR;
    {
      /* mode is NP_EMBED, NP_FULL, or NP_BACKGROUND (see npapi.h) */
      This->fWindow = NULL;
      This->fMode = mode;

#ifdef XP_UNIX
      This->window = (Window) 0;
#endif /* XP_UNIX */
#ifdef _WINDOWS
      This->fhWnd = NULL;
      This->fDefaultWindowProc = NULL;
#endif /* _WIDOWS */

      /* PLUGIN DEVELOPERS:
       *     Initialize fields of your plugin
       *     instance data here.  If the NPSavedData is non-
       *     NULL, you can use that data (returned by you from
       *     NPP_Destroy to set up the new plugin instance).
       */
    }

    if (env) {
      jint v;

      /*
      ** Call the DisplayJavaMessage utility function to cause Java to
      ** write to the console and to stdout:
      */
      DisplayJavaMessage(instance, "Hello world from npsimple!", -1);

      /*
      ** Also test out that fancy factorial method. It's a static
      ** method, so we need to use the class object in order to call
      ** it:
      */
      v = Simple_fact(env, class_Simple(env), 10);
      sprintf(factString, "my favorite function returned %d\n", v);
      DisplayJavaMessage( instance, factString, -1 );
    }
    return result;
}
```

Part
II

Ch
10

After you define `PluginInstance` for your plug-in, the following lines provide a formula to open nearly every plug-in:

```
instance->pdata = NPN_MemAlloc(sizeof(PluginInstance));
This = (PluginInstance*) instance->pdata;
if (This == NULL)
   return NPERR_OUT_OF_MEMORY_ERROR;
```

In the following line from `NPP_New()`, env is a global pointer to a `JRIEnv`:

```
if (env)
```

If all went well in `NPP_GetJavaClass()`, env points to the Java runtime environment. To show that all this works, the Simple Plug-in makes a series of gratuitous calls to Java, writing its results to the Java Console. You'll see these calls to the Java Console scattered around the plug-in, in much the same way as you used calls to `MessageBox()` in Chapter 6, "NPP Methods: Starting the Plug-In."

Note that if the Java runtime is successfully set up, the plug-in goes on to call a Java method on class `Simple` (`Simple_fact()`). The return value of that function is a Java int—a jint. Chapter 18, "Plug-Ins as a Programming Resource," shows an entire table of these C/C++ names for Java native types.

DisplayJavaMessage()   DisplayJavaMessage() is one of the larger and more interesting functions in this plug-in. Its parameters include a char pointer and an int (for length), as follows:

```
/*
** This function is a utility routine that calls back into Java to print
** messages to the Java Console and to stdout (via the native method,
** native_Simple_printToStdout, defined below).  Sure, it's not a very
** interesting use of Java, but it gets the point across.
*/
void DisplayJavaMessage(NPP instance, char* msg, int len)
{
  jref str, javaPeer;
  if (!env) {
    /* Java failed to initialize, so do nothing. */
    return;
  }

  if (len == -1)
    len = strlen(msg);
```

```
/*
** Use the JRI (see jri.h) to create a Java string from the input
** message:
*/
str = JRI_NewStringUTF(env, msg, len);

/*
** Use the NPN_GetJavaPeer operation to get the Java instance that
** corresponds to our plug-in (an instance of the Simple class):
*/
javaPeer = NPN_GetJavaPeer(instance);

/*
** Finally, call our plug-in's big "feature" — the 'doit' method,
** passing the execution environment, the object, and the java
** string:
*/
Simple_doit(env, javaPeer, str);
}
```

The function calls the Java Runtime Interface (JRI) to allocate a string in Java:

```
jref str;
str = JRI_NewStringUTF(env, msg, len);
```

Then the function calls `NPN_GetJavaPeer()` to get a Java reference (`jref`) to its own peer object. Because the peer is known to be an instance of Java class `Simple`, the plug-in calls the C stub of its peer class and runs `Simple_doit()`. In following sections of this chapter, you read about Java class `Simple` and its `doit()` method.

Figure 10.4 traces the flow of control between the plug-in and the Java runtime.

FIG. 10.4
Netscape illustrates how the plug-in calls Java, with `DisplayJava-Message()`.

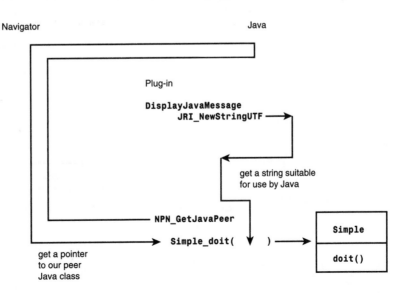

NPP_SetWindow()   Because there's no stream associated with this plug-in, you don't have to worry about `NPP_NewStream()`, `NPP_WriteReady()`, or `NPP_Write()`. These functions are available in this plug-in, but they do nothing useful.

The next call the plug-in expects is `NPP_SetWindow()`. Find the place in `NPP_SetWindow()` that reads as follows:

```
This->fDefaultWindowProc =
   (WNDPROC)SetWindowLong( (HWND)window->window, GWI_WNDPROC,
   (LONG)PluginWindowProc);
This->fhWnd = (HWND) window->window;
SetProp( This->fhWnd, gInstanceLookupString, (HANDLE)This);

InvalidateRect( This->fhWnd, NULL, TRUE );
UpdateWindow( This->fhWnd );
```

This code does the work of saving off the old `WindowProc` (into `This->fDefault-WindowProc`) and installing the new `PluginWindowProc`. Now that `PluginWindowProc` is installed as the `WindowProc`, any messages sent to our window by Windows are passed to your plug-in (and directed to `PluginWindowProc`). Figure 10.5 shows how subclassed windows work.

FIG. 10.5
After a window is subclassed, the new `WindowProc` has first shot at reading any messages.

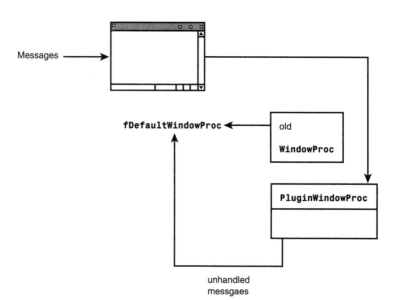

SetProp() is a Windows API call that adds a new entry to the property list of the window. This call puts a link in your Navigator-supplied hwnd back to your pdata. Recall that there can be more than one copy of our plug-in running at a time. By tying your instance data to the window, you can always find your own windowProc and your own data.

PluginWindowProc()   Lower down in the same file (npsimple.c) is PluginWindowProc(), which is the callback function the programmer defined to handle messages to our window. In this simple plug-in, the only message handled in PluginWindowProc() is WM_PAINT. All other messages are routed back to the default windowProc.

The WM_PAINT handler consists of just five lines as follows:

```
PAINTSTRUCT paintStruct;
HDC hdc;

hdc = BeginPaint( hWnd, &paintStruct );
TextOut(hdc, 0, 0, "Hello, World!", 15);

EndPaint( hWnd, &paintStruct);
```

When a WM_PAINT message comes to this plug-in, it sets up a device context (so it has someplace to draw), draws the string "Hello, World!", deallocates the device context, and exits.

> **N O T E**   Did you spot the defect in the TextOut? The programmer passes in the string "Hello, World!", which has 13 characters, not counting the terminating NULL. He has told Windows to display 15 characters. The last two characters are garbage characters. (cbString, the last parameter in TextOut, should be the number of printable characters, and doesn't need to take the trailing NULL into account.)
>
> Fix the bug while you're here—change the 15 to a 13 in this line. ■

NPP_Print()

What will happen if the user selects <u>P</u>rint? Because the plug-in is embedded, NPP_Print() gets called only once—when printInfo->mode is NP_EMBED. In this case the plug-in runs the following code and returns:

```
NPWindow* printWindow =
  &(printInfo->print.embedPrint.window);
void* platformPrint =
  printInfo->print.embedPrint.platformPrint;
```

Part
II

Ch
10

These lines retrieve the window into which the plug-in is to draw and the device context of the printer, but they don't do anything with them! If you want to complete the task, use `TextOut` to send "Hello, World!" to the printer's device context. You can use the `WM_PAINT` handler in `PluginWindowProc` as a starting point.

LiveConnect Details

Because Simple doesn't get a stream, there's not much else for it to do as far as Navigator is concerned. If the user resizes the window, Navigator obligingly sends another `NPP_SetWindow()`—you can watch this happen in the Java Console. All the user interaction, such as it is, comes through LiveConnect. Recall from Figure 10.3 the interaction between JavaScript, Java, and the plug-in.

Examining the Java Code

Recall that to install Simple, you copied a file named simple.class into the plug-in directory. The Java compiler, javac, turns Java classes (in .java files) that are human-readable into .class files, which contain bytecodes for the Java Virtual Machine. If there's a simple.class, you should look for a human-readable simple.java—and you find it in the source subdirectory:

```
import netscape.plugin.Plugin;

class Simple extends Plugin {
  /*
   ** A plug-in can consist of code written in java as well as
   ** natively. Here's a dummy method.
   */
  public static int fact(int n) {
    if (n == 1)
      return 1;
    else
      return n * fact(n-1);
  }
  /*
   ** This instance variable is used to keep track of the number of
   ** times we've called into this plug-in.
   */
  int count;
```

```
/*
** This native method gives us a way to print to stdout from java
** instead of just the java console.
*/
native void printToStdout(String msg);

/*
** This is a publicly callable new feature that our plug-in is
** providing. We can call it from JavaScript, Java, or from native
** code.
*/
public void doit(String text) {
  /* construct a message */
  String msg = "" + (++count) + ". " + text + "\n";
  /* write it to the console */
  System.out.print(msg);
  /* and also write it to stdout */
  printToStdout(msg);
}
}
```

Part

II

Ch

10

N O T E   Chapter 18, "Plug-Ins as a Programming Resource," describes the structure of a Java class file, and shows what each line means. This section concentrates on the methods and data members defined inside class `Simple`. ∎

Although you may not be a Java programmer, you can read the definition of the Java function `fact()` from this file. It's a simple function of the sort commonly used to teach recursion in freshman programming classes. You also will recognize `doit()`, the star of the show on the Java console.

fact()   `fact()` is a simple (and not very efficient) implementation of the factorial function. It's function here is to show how to call a native Java function.

count   Remember back on the Java Console that each line had a number? This little `int` here is responsible for that task. `count` gets managed by `doit()`, which will be described a bit further on in this chapter.

printToStdout()   On a Windows machine we don't think much about standard out, and it's difficult to actually see that this function is running. Still, this function shows how Java can call native (C/C++) code which is back in the plug-in.

Note the word `native` in the following function definition:

```
native void printToStdout(String msg);
```

This keyword tells Java to look for the definition of this function in a C or C++ function. Now go back over to the ClassView tool and search through the Globals section. Here, you find a function `native_Simple_printToStdout()`. The header for this function was produced by the Java Runtime Interface of javah. The programmer added the following two-line implementation:

```
const char* chars = JRI_GetStringUTFChars(env, s);
printf(chars);
```

Here, `env` is the Java runtime environment, and `s` is the Java string to be printed. Both variables are passed in as parameters from Java.

doit()   Simple's "big feature" is `doit()`. This function is called when the user clicks the button on the HTML page. The next section shows how messages get from JavaScript to this Java class. This section shows how `doit()` does its work:

```
public void doit(String text) {
String msg = "" + (++count) + "   " + text + "\n";
System.out.print(msg);
printToStdout(msg);
}
```

The first line of the function uses the plus operator to concatenate a series of strings. The sequence starts with an empty string, so that the finished result is a string. After the message is built, it is sent to the console by using the `print` method of the System's `out` class. Finally, the program sends a copy of the message to standard out (for what it's worth). Figure 10.7 illustrates this process.

How the JavaScript and HTML are Connected

Recall that the HTML file contained the following tiny form:

```
<form>
<input type=button value="Click Me"
  onclick='document.simple1.doit("Hello from JavaScript!")'>
</form>
```

FIG. 10.7
The doit() function, such as it is, is one of the few pieces of complexity in Simple.

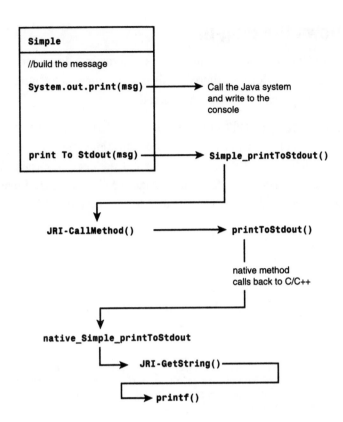

```
Simple

//build the message

System.out.print(msg) ─────────▶  Call the Java system
                                   and write to the
                                   console


print To Stdout(msg) ──────────▶  Simple_printToStdout()
```

JRI-CallMethod() ─────────────▶ printToStdout()

                                   │
                                   native method
                                   calls back to C/C++

native_Simple_printToStdout
            └──▶ JRI-GetString()─────
            └──▶ printf()

This form directs a function call, doit(), to the named plug-in. LiveConnect does not allow direct communication between a plug-in and JavaScript. But because Simple, the plug-in, has an associated Java class (also known as Simple), all is well. The JavaScript handler onClick calls doit() on the named plug-in Simple1. That method gets picked up by Java, which calls the Java method doit(). Java, in turn, handles the message construction and the write to the system console internally, but calls the native method printToStdout back in the plug-in. Figure 10.3, shown previously in this chapter, traces the flow of control between JavaScript, the Java peer object, and the plug-in.

Closing Down the Plug-In

When the interaction is over and the user is ready to leave Simple, Navigator calls NPP_Destroy(). Because there is only one instance, NPP_Shutdown() is called immediately after the instance is deleted.

NPP_Destroy() Recall from Chapter 8, "NPP Methods: Other Tasks," that NPP_Destroy() is the place to undo the allocations made in NPP_New(). Simple's implementation of NPP_Destroy() calls NPN_MemFree(), passing it the pdata pointer it's been carrying from one function call to the next. Finally it displays a message through Java to the Java console, and then exits. Here's Simple's version of NPP_Destroy():

```
NPError  NP_LOADDS
NPP_Destroy(NPP instance, NPSavedData** save)
{
  PluginInstance* This;
  if (instance == NULL)
    return NPERR_INVALID_INSTANCE_ERROR;
  This = (PluginInstance*) instance->pdata;

  /* PLUGIN DEVELOPERS:
   *       If desired, call NP_MemAlloc to create a
   *       NPSavedDate structure containing any state information
   *       that you want restored if this plugin instance is later
   *       recreated.
   */

  if (This != NULL) {
    NPN_MemFree(instance->pdata);
    instance->pdata = NULL;
  }
  DisplayJavaMessage(instance, "Calling NPP_Destroy.", -1);
  return NPERR_NO_ERROR;
}
```

CAUTION

Always remember to free pdata in NPP_Destroy(). If you don't, you'll leak memory out of Navigator and eventually crash the browser. Detecting the cause of such leaks can be time-consuming, and is frustrating to the end user (who naturally will blame Netscape for the supposedly buggy browser).

NPP_Shutdown()   Just as `NPP_Destroy()` undoes the work of `NPP_New()`, so `NPP_Shutdown()` is the counterpart of `NPP_Initialize()`. `NPP_Shutdown()` verifies that this plug-in has been running with a Java environment. Because it has, it severs the link between Java class `Simple` and the plug-in. Here's how simple it is to disconnect from the JRI:

```
/*
** NPP_Shutdown is called when your DLL is being unloaded to do any
** DLL-specific shut-down. You should be a good citizen and declare that
** you're not using your java class any more. This allows java to unload
** it, freeing up memory.
*/
void NPP_Shutdown(void)
{
  if (env)
    unuse_Simple(env);
}
```

N O T E   The plug-in actually connected to the Java class as part of `NPP_GetJavaClass()`, but because this function is called just after `NPP_Initialize()`, it's reasonable to use `NPP_Shutdown()` to undo `NPP_GetJavaClass`'s actions. ▪

From Here...

In this chapter you built a complete Windows plug-in, using Visual C++'s AppWizard. Although the plug-in doesn't "do" much, it's quite complete in terms of functionality, including support for LiveConnect.

- Chapter 6, "NPP Methods: Starting the Plug-In," provides an in-depth trace of the stream of control from the time the plug-in is invoked to the time it finishes displaying its data.

- Chapter 7, "NPP Methods: Handing Interaction," shows how the plug-in is notified of user actions, including both actions that take place in Navigator and actions that occur within the plug-in window.

- Chapter 8, "NPP Methods: Other Tasks," shows how to print the plug-in contents. It also shows what happens when the user closes the plug-in window.

Part
II

Ch
10

- Chapter 9, "Understanding NPN Methods," describes in detail the calls a plug-in programmer can make back to Navigator.

- The next chapter, "Example: CharFlipper Plug-In," looks at a complete plug-in that reads its content from a stream.

Example: CharFlipper Plug-In

The CharFlipper plug-in is considerably more complex than the Simple plug-in you looked at in Chapter 10. ■

How to read characters from a stream

CharFlipper is one of Netscape's principle stream-reading example plug-ins.

About the Netscape class library

Netscape has written a small set of "helper classes" to get you started programming plug-ins.

See how to tap MFC's message pump

Avoid long, tedious `WindowsProcs` by using MFC's message map.

See how to set a timer so your plug-in gets periodic events

The speed of the CharFlipper plug-in reading from its stream is far faster than a human can keep up with. Here, a timer is used to slow down the demonstration.

Introduction to CharFlipper in Action

To get an idea of what CharFlipper does, start by compiling and running the plug-in. This chapter uses the Windows version of the plug-in, but Netscape also supplies a version for the Mac.

Compiling the Plug-In

Netscape uses Microsoft's Visual C++ on Windows and MetroWorks' Code Warrior on the Macintosh. You can simplify the installation if you use the same environment they do.

In Visual C++'s Developer Studio, choose File, Open Workspace and open CharFlipper.mdp in the \Examples\CharFlipper\Windows subdirectory of the Plugins SDK directory. After the project opens, choose Build, Build NPFlip.dll.

This project has a few problems—it should compile without errors, but six warnings are issued. These warnings don't affect the running of the plug-in, but they are troublesome. If you choose to build one of your plug-ins around CharFlipper, start by fixing these warnings.

Moving the Files into Position

Copy the Java class file TimeMediaPlugin.class to the Navigator plug-ins directory.

 You may want to skim Chapter 18, "Plug-Ins as a Programming Resource," to get the bigger picture of Java and LiveConnect. In that chapter you learn how to use javac and javah to make your own class, header, and stub files.

Copy the NPFlip.dll file, which you just built, to the plug-ins directory and restart Navigator. Make sure that you are using a version of Navigator that is at least at 3.0b5, or you won't see all the features of this plug-in working.

Running the Plug-In

When Navigator restarts, it examines the files in the plug-ins directory and registers plug-ins based on their MIME media type. Chapter 19, "Installing the Plug-In," describes this process in more detail.

After Navigator is up, use File, Open File to open
\Examples\CharFlipper\Testing\CharFlipperExample.html. You probably will want
to bookmark this page while you learn about plug-ins.

As soon as it opens, CharFlipper goes to work. Figure 11.1 shows the
CharFlipper.html user interface.

FIG. 11.1
CharFlipper reads
from a stream and
writes to the window.
It's also listening to
JavaScript, waiting for
a user to press a
button.

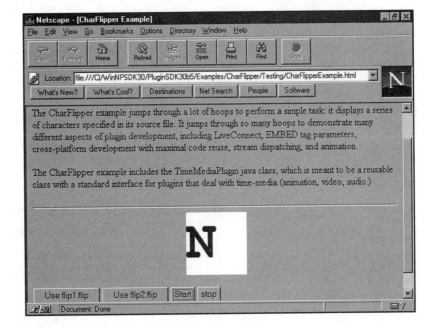

CharFlipper begins to display its data right way. You can use the controls to stop
and restart the display or to change the plug-in from one data file to another.

Flow of Control

CharFlipper is rich enough to have hooks for many of the things you might do with
a more sophisticated plug-in.

 If you're new to plug-ins, go back and read Chapter 10, "Example: Simple Plug-In." Simple
is much smaller than CharFlipper, so some of its interaction is a bit easier to follow. Then
come back here.

Follow Navigator

As you saw when you ran Simple, a plug-in has two interfaces—one to Navigator and another to the user. Because the plug-in can do nothing with the user until most of its Navigator functions are called, start by tracing the flow of control between Navigator and CharFlipper. Follow along on Figure 11.2.

FIG. 11.2
Navigator makes a series of calls to the plug-in to get things started.

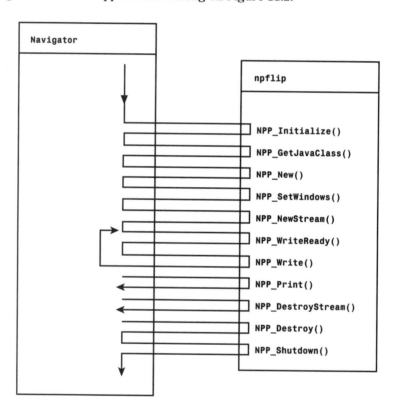

```
Navigator

                                                    npflip

                                            NPP_Initialize()
                                            NPP_GetJavaClass()
                                            NPP_New()
                                            NPP_SetWindows()
                                            NPP_NewStream()
                                            NPP_WriteReady()
                                            NPP_Write()
                                            NPP_Print()
                                            NPP_DestroyStream()
                                            NPP_Destroy()
                                            NPP_Shutdown()
```

How CharFlipper Is Called   Return to Microsoft Developer Studio and use it to open CharFlipper.html. That file isn't part of the project—you'll need to use File, Open to open it. The plug-in is loaded because of the line

```
<EMBED SRC="flip1.flip" ALIGN=CENTER WIDTH=100 HEIGHT=100
 speed=60 autostart=true loop=true name ="flipper">
```

Unlike Simple in Chapter 10, "Example: Simple Plug-In," CharFlipper reads a stream. The stream (in this case, a file) has the series of characters that will be displayed.

Because this stream is a local file, no server is needed to translate the file extension into a MIME type. Instead, Navigator looks at the file extensions registered by each plug-in and determines that files with suffix .flip get handled by CharFlipper.

Like Simple in the last chapter, this plug-in has a name: `flipper`. This name gets used by JavaScript later in this section of code:

```
<form>
<input    type=button
          onclick="document.flipper.SetSource('flip1.flip');"
          value="Use flip1.flip">
<input    type=button
          onclick="document.flipper.SetSource('flip2.flip');"
          value="Use flip2.flip">
<input    type=button
          onclick="document.flipper.Start();"
          value=Start>
<input    type=button
          onclick="document.flipper.Stop();"
          value=stop>
</form>
```

Note, too, the private parameters that are passed through <EMBED>. The plug-in reads these parameters back out in `NPP_New()`.

NPP_Initialize() When Navigator sees the <EMBED> tag, it looks up the plug-in that registered to handle files with the .flip suffix. It finds npFlip and loads this library into its address space. Then it exchanges entry points, as shown in Chapter 6, "NPP Methods: Starting the Plug-In."

The first method it calls that you, as the programmer, are responsible for is `NPP_Initialize()`. Use Microsoft Developer Studio's ClassView to open this function. (It's in the Globals folder because it's not part of any class.)

If you're not using Microsoft Visual C++ you may find it difficult to find `NPP_Initialize()` and the other standard plug-in functions. This is because CharFlipper is built with Netscape's plug-in framework. Look in the Examples/ FrameWork directory of the Plug-In SDK. The file that holds the implementation of the class `CNetscapePlugin`, CNetscapePlugin.cpp, also holds tiny implementations of the standard plug-in entry points. For example, here is the definition of `NPP_Initialize()`:

```
//-----------------------------------------------------------------
// NPP_Initialize:
//-----------------------------------------------------------------
```

```
NPError NPP_Initialize(void)
{
        NPError error = InitializeNetscapePlugin();
        return error;
}
```

Notice that `NPP_Initialize()` is simple—it merely uses a call to the `InitializeNetscapePlugin()` function. This function in turn calls the static method `Initialize()` for the class `CCharFlipper()`. Unlike Simple, CharFlipper takes advantage of object technology.

Find `CCharFlipper` toward the top of ClassView. Double-click the tag (not the button to the left) to open the class definition. As shown in the following section, `CCharFlipper` is derived from Netscape's class library class, `CNetscapePlugin`.

Expand the `CCharFlipper` class and find the `Initialize()` member. This member, too, is simple because it calls Netscape's framework member, `CNetscapePlugin::Initialize()`. Here's the definition of `CCharFlipper::Initialize()`:

```
//-----------------------------------------------------------------
// CCharFlipper::Initialize
//-----------------------------------------------------------------
NPError

CCharFlipper::Initialize( void )

{
    return CNetscapePlugin::Initialize();

}
```

So this plug-in initializes itself by calling the default `Initialize()` routine in the framework. This method is defined in CNetscapePlugin.h, also in the Framework directory:

```
class CNetscapePlugin : public CNetscapeMemObject {
        public:
            static NPError Initialize( void ) { return
    ➥NPERR_NO_ERROR; };


        .


        .


        .


}
```

NPP_GetJavaClass() Just as `NPP_Initialize()` ends up back at
`CNetscapePlugin::Initialize()`, so `NPP_GetJavaClass()` ends up having its
work done by a global function, `InitializeJavaClass()`, shown in the following
code. This function calls the `use` members for the two Java classes employed in
this plug-in (`TimeMediaPlugin` and `netscape.plugin.Plugin`), and then returns
the Java reference for TimeMediaPlugin. (Chapter 18, "Plug-Ins as a Programming
Resource," explains why this sequence is necessary.)

```
jref InitializeJavaClass(void)
{
    jref theRef = NULL;
    JRIEnv* env = NPN_GetJavaEnv();
    theRef = TimeMediaPlugin::_use( env );
    netscape_plugin_Plugin::_use( env );
    TimeMediaPlugin::_register(env);
    return theRef;
}
```

Figure 11.3 shows the hierarchy of classes that control startup.

NPP_New() Now Navigator is ready to make the plug-in instance. Open
`NPP_New()` with ClassWizard. (If you're not using Visual C++, you can find it in at
Examples/Framework/CNetscapePlugin.cpp.) In this case, you find that the work
is done by `CreateNetscapePlugin()`, which is simply a convenient wrapper for the
real plug-in: `CCharFlipper()`. Here's the framework's definition of `NPP_New()`:

```
//-------------------------------------------------------------
// NPP_New:
//-------------------------------------------------------------
NPError NP_LOADDS
NPP_New(NPMIMEType pluginType,
        NPP instance,
        uint16 mode,
        int16 argc,
        char* argn[],
        char* argv[],
        NPSavedData* saved)
{
  if (instance == NULL)
    return NPERR_INVALID_INSTANCE_ERROR;

  // Had to perform the (const char *[]) casts MSVC++ is retarded.
  CPluginArguments* theArgs = new CPluginArguments( argc,
                              (const char **)argn,
                              (const char **)argv );
```

```
            CNetscapePlugin* thePlugin = CreateNetscapePlugin( instance,
                                                               mode,
                                                               theArgs,
                                                               saved );
        if( thePlugin == 0 )
          return NPERR_OUT_OF_MEMORY_ERROR;
        return NPERR_NO_ERROR;
    }
```

FIG. 11.3

Very little of the work of the Netscape functions actually gets done in these functions.

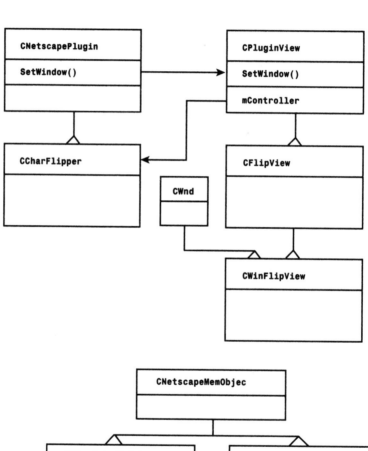

`CreateNetscapePlugin()` is defined in `CharFlipperFactory.cpp`:

```
CNetscapePlugin* CreateNetscapePlugin( NPP instance,
                                       uint16 mode,
                                       CPluginArguments* adoptedArgs,
                                       NPSavedData* saved )
{
    return new CCharFlipper( instance, mode, adoptedArgs );
}
```

So indirectly, `NPP_New()` calls the `CCharFlipper()` constructor, which initializes the class to the proper values:

```
CCharFlipper::CCharFlipper( NPP instance,
                            uint16 mode,
                            CPluginArguments* adoptedArgs )
    : CNetscapePlugin( instance, mode, adoptedArgs ),
        mCurrentChar(' '),
        mText( 0 ),
        mTextLength( 0 ),
        mTextIndex( 0 ),
        mTimeLastFlipped( 0 )
{
    SetSpeed( mArgs->ArgumentValueAsInt( kCharFlipperArgs_Speed,
    ➥ kDefaultSpeed ) );
    SetRunning( mArgs->ArgumentValueAsBool(
    ➥kCharFlipperArgs_Autostart kDefaultAutostart ));
    SetLooping( mArgs->ArgumentValueAsBool(
    ➥kCharFlipperArgs_Looping, kDefaultLooping ));
}
```

There is considerable delegation in this design, allowing the arguments to be decoded easily. Class `CCharFlipper` has a data member, `mArgs`, which is an instance of class `CPluginArguments` (another Netscape-supplied class from the class library). `CPluginArguments`, in turn, has members such as `AcceptArgumentValueAsInt()` and `AcceptArgumentValueAsBool()`, which parse the parameters into a form understandable by `CCharFlipper`.

NPP_SetWindow() `NPP_SetWindow()` quickly gets through to `CNetscapePlugin::SetWindow()`. `CNetscapePlugin`'s `mView` member is initialized here. `mView` is a pointer to a `CPluginView`, which has the following definition:

Part
II

Ch

11

```
class CPluginView {
  public:
    CPluginView( CNetscapePlugin* controller );
    virtual ~CPluginView();
    virtual NPError SetWindow( NPWindow* window )
      { return NPERR_NO_ERROR; };
    virtual void Paint() {};
    CNetscapePlugin* GetController();
  protected:
    CNetscapePlugin* mController;
};
```

Chapter 17, "Using Class Libraries and Frameworks," describes the Document/
View architecture as well as the Model, View, Presenter (MVP) architecture recommended by Taligent. Netscape's model is based on the View/Controller model,
like the MVP architecture used at Taligent. The Netscape CPluginView class is a
useful thing—it encapsulates the Paint routines from MS-Windows.

Figure 11.4 illustrates how the components of NPP_SetWindow() communicate.

Both CFlipView and CWinFlipView are derived from CPluginView:

```
class CFlipView : public CPluginView
{
  public:
    CFlipView( CCharFlipper* inController );
    virtual ~CFlipView();

    // CFlipView methods
    virtual void   SetChar( char inChar );
    CCharFlipper*  GetFlipper();

  protected:
    char mCurrentChar;
};
class CWinFlipView : public CWnd, public CPluginView {
  public:
    CWinFlipView( CCharFlipper* inController );
    ~CWinFlipView();
    virtual WNDPROC* GetSuperWndProcAddr();

    //{{AFX_MSG( CMainWindow )
    afx_msg void OnPaint();
    afx_msg void OnPaletteChanged(CWnd* pWnd);
    afx_msg void OnLButtonDown(UINT flags, CPoint point);
    afx_msg void OnRButtonDown(UINT flags, CPoint point);
    afx_msg void OnPlay();
```

```
        afx_msg void OnStop();
        afx_msg void OnRewind();
        afx_msg void OnForward();
        afx_msg void OnFrameBack();
        afx_msg void OnFrameForward();
    //}}AFX_MSG
    DECLARE_MESSAGE_MAP()
  protected:
    char mLastCharacter;
};
```

Note that CWinFlipView is derived not only from CPluginView but also from CWnd:

```
    public CWnd, public CPluginView
```

This class's primary role is to serve as a "gateway" into the Windows message system.

FIG. 11.4
NPP_SetWindow() is part of a complex hierarchy of structures and classes.

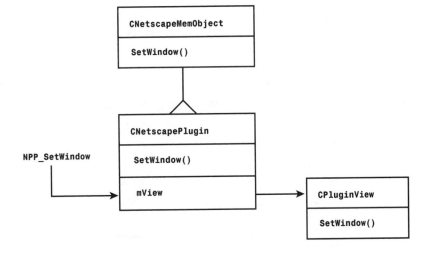

NPP_NewStream(), NPP_WriteReady(), and NPP_Write()   Netscape's class CNetscapeStream fully encapsulates Netscape's concept of a stream. In NPP_NewStream() the designer builds a new stream based on the CNetscapePlugin pointer controller.

```
//-------------------------------------------------------------
// NPP_NewStream:
//-------------------------------------------------------------
NPError NP_LOADDS
NPP_NewStream(NPP instance,
              NPMIMEType type,
              NPStream *stream,
              NPBool seekable,
              uint16 *stype)
{
  if (instance == NULL)
    return NPERR_INVALID_INSTANCE_ERROR;
  CNetscapePlugin* controller = (CNetscapePlugin*) instance->pdata;
  CNetscapeStream* theStream = controller->CreateStream(type,
                                                        stream,
                                                        seekable,
                                                        *stype );

  if( theStream == 0 )
    return NPERR_OUT_OF_MEMORY_ERROR;
  *stype = theStream->GetStreamType();
  return NPERR_NO_ERROR;
}
```

The stream is left at its default stype (NP_NORMAL). NPP_WriteReady() and NPP_Write() just call their underlying CNetscapeStream counterparts.

```
//-------------------------------------------------------------
// NPP_WriteReady:
//-------------------------------------------------------------
int32 NP_LOADDS
NPP_WriteReady(NPP instance, NPStream *stream)
{
  if (instance == NULL)
    return -1;
  CNetscapeStream* theStream = CNetscapeStream::EvolveStream( stream
➥);
  if( theStream == 0 )
    return -1;
  return theStream->WriteReady();
}

//-------------------------------------------------------------
// NPP_Write:
//-------------------------------------------------------------
int32 NP_LOADDS
NPP_Write(NPP instance,
          NPStream *stream,
          int32 offset,
          int32 len,
          void *buffer)
{
```

```
        if (instance == NULL)
          return -1;
        CNetscapeStream* theStream = CNetscapeStream::EvolveStream( stream
        ➥);
        if( theStream == 0 )
          return -1;
        return theStream->Write( offset, len, buffer );
     }
```

This approach is a bit naive, but considering that the application only reads a short file and the buffer size is 256M, the designer need not be too aggressive in looking for buffer overflow.

NPP_Print()   Like Simple, NPP_Print() is not fully hooked up. There is, however, a tantalizing set of hooks for a future programmer to use:

```
//-----------------------------------------------------------------
// NPP_Print:
//-----------------------------------------------------------------
void NP_LOADDS
NPP_Print(NPP instance, NPPrint* printInfo)
{
  if(printInfo == NULL)    // trap invalid parm
    return;
  if (instance != NULL)
  {
    CNetscapePlugin* This = (CNetscapePlugin*) instance->pdata;
    This->Print( printInfo );
  }
}

//-----------------------------------------------------------------
// CNetscapePlugin::Print
//-----------------------------------------------------------------
void
CNetscapePlugin::Print( NPPrint* printInfo )
{
  if(printInfo == NULL)    // trap invalid parm
    return;
  if (printInfo->mode == NP_FULL)
  {
    NPBool printResult = PrintFull( printInfo->print.fullPrint );
    printInfo->print.fullPrint.pluginPrinted = printResult;
    ➥// Do the default
  }
  else     // If not fullscreen, we must be embedded
  {
    PrintEmbeded( printInfo->print.embedPrint );
  }
}
```

Part
II

Ch
11

LiveConnect Details

So far you have seen a lot of encapsulation but nothing written to the screen. CharFlipper, even more so than Simple, is a creature of LiveConnect. Figure 11.5 shows the interaction between JavaScript, Java, and the plug-in.

Examining the Java Code

Netscape intends the Java class `TimeMediaPlugin` to become a general-purpose tool for use with time-based content. A look at the Java code reveals that all of the real work is done in native methods:

```
class TimeMediaPlugin extends Plugin {
  public void SetSource(java.net.URL inSourceURL) {
    SetSourceNative( inSourceURL.toString() );
  }
  public void SetSource(java.lang.String inSourceString) {
    SetSourceNative( inSourceString );
  }
  public native void SetSourceNative( java.lang.String inSourceString
  ➥);
  public native void Start();
  public native void Stop();
  public native boolean IsRunning();
  public native void Loop( boolean inLoop );
  public native boolean IsLooping();

  // speed is in 60ths of a second
  public native void SetSpeed( int inSpeed );.
  public native int GetSpeed();
}
```

"Native" Java methods are the methods implemented outside of Java, usually in a language like C or C++. Netscape supplies a tool, javah, which reads Java files and writes function stubs. (The use of the javah tool is described in more detail in Chapter 18, "Plug-Ins as a Programming Resource.") When javah reads the following line

```
public native void Start();
```

in class `TimeMediaPlugin`, it writes a series of function definitions in _gen/ TimeMediaPlugin.h, including the following:

```
extern JRI_PUBLIC_API(void)
native_TimeMediaPlugin_Start(JRIEnv* env, struct TimeMediaPlugin*
➥self);
```

FIG. 11.5
Although the plug-in
and JavaScript
cannot talk directly,
the Java peer object
is quick and easy to
set up.

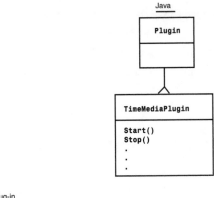

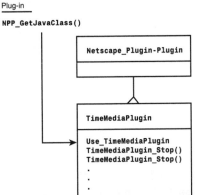

The plug-in programmer then writes an implementation of the native functions.
The Netscape programmer has put these implementations in the file
TimeMediaNatives.cpp. For example, `native_TimeMediaPlugin_Start()` is
implemented as follows:

```
extern JRI_PUBLIC_API(void)
native_TimeMediaPlugin_Start(JRIEnv* env, struct TimeMediaPlugin*
self)
{
  NPP instance = (NPP) (self->getPeer(env));
  CCharFlipper* flipper = (CCharFlipper*) instance->pdata;
  flipper->StartAtFrame( 0 );
}
```

This function calls `CCharFlipper::StartAtFrame()` with `inFrame` set to zero. If
that function passes its internal tests, `CCharFlipper::SetRunning()` is set to TRUE,
and the flipper begins to flip.

When tracing through large amounts of code, particularly in an object-oriented system where so many small functions call other small functions, it's good to be able to tell the system, "Show me where this function is used," or "Show me who defines this function." To get this kind of information from Microsoft, C++ rebuild the project with "browse into" turned on.

Triggering the Plug-in with Periodic Events

Your desktop computer can read streams, even those coming in through a dial-up connection, quickly. If the plug-in displayed each character and immediately "flipped" to the next, you'd see only a blur as characters passed from the stream to the screen. To solve this problem, CharFlipper keeps each character on the screen until a timer tells the program to move on to the next character.

Examine `CCharFlipper::HandleTimePassed()`. As long as `isRunning` remains true, this function looks at the time and the current speed, and decides whether or not it's time to read another character. If so, the character is received from the (`GetNextChar()`) buffer and displayed in the (`SetChar()`) view.

Finally `Paint()` is called. `Paint()` simply invalidates the rectangle and waits while Windows comes back through to dispatch the `WM_PAINT` message.

```
CCharFlipper::HandleTimePassed()
{
  NPBool isRunning = GetRunning( );
  if( isRunning ) {
    unsigned long currentTicks = GetNormalSysTime();
    long speed = GetSpeed();
    if( mTimeLastFlipped <= ( currentTicks - speed ) ) {
      mTimeLastFlipped = currentTicks;
      mCurrentChar = GetNextChar();
      ((CFlipView*)mView)->SetChar( mCurrentChar );
      mView->Paint();
    }
  }
}
```

Note also that CharFlipper handles mouse-down messages. The generic `HandleMouseClick()` simply toggles the running state:

```
void
CCharFlipper::HandleMouseClick()
{
```

```
    NPBool isRunning = GetRunning();
    SetRunning( ! isRunning );
}
```

What triggers `HandleTimePassed()`? If you compiled the project with "Build browse info file" turned on in the Build Settings, you can right-click the mouse on `HandleTimePassed()` and find that this function is triggered by a timer.

A similar inquiry on `SetTimer()` reveals that the timer is set in `CWinFlipView::SetWindow()`. Every 10 milliseconds this timer sends a `WM_TIMER` message.

Figure 11.6 illustrates the process of producing and consuming timer messages.

FIG. 11.6

Use a periodic timer if you are looking for something that can happen at any time.

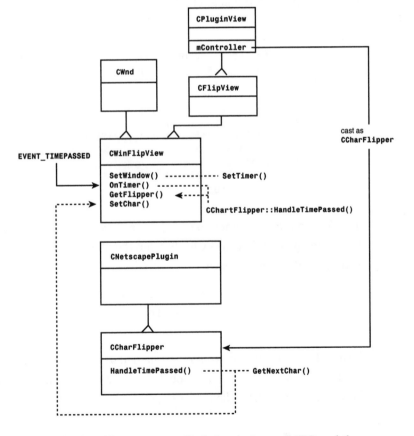

Part
II

Ch
11

`CharFlipper` also is the first Netscape-supplied plug-in to use MFC and the message map. Examine the message maps in `WinFlipView.cpp` and `CWinFlipView.cpp`.

CWinFlipView::OnTimer(), in turn, calls CharFlipper::HandleTimePassed(), as follows:

```
void CWinFlipView::OnTimer(UINT nIDEvent)
{
    // TODO: Add your message handler code here and/or call default
    if( nIDEvent == EVENT_TIMEPASSED ) {
        GetFlipper()->HandleTimePassed();
    }
    CWnd::OnTimer(nIDEvent);
}
```

How the JavaScript and HTML Are Connected

Recall that the HTML file held a form:

```
<form>
<input    type=button
          onclick="document.flipper.SetSource('flip1.flip');"
          value="Use flip1.flip">
<input    type=button
          onclick="document.flipper.SetSource('flip2.flip');"
          value="Use flip2.flip">
<input    type=button
          onclick="document.flipper.Start();"
          value=Start>
<input    type=button
          onclick="document.flipper.Stop();"
          value=stop>
</form>
```

This form directs the function calls such as start(), stop(), and setSource() to the named plug-in. Because CharFlipper, the plug-in, has an associated Java class (TimeMediaPlugin), all is well.

The JavaScript handler onClick calls start or one of the other functions on the named plug-in flipper. This method gets picked up by Java, which calls the Java method start().

Java, in turn, calls the native method named start, which is back in the plug-in. Figure 11.5, which appears previously in this chapter, traces the flow of control between JavaScript, the Java peer object, and the plug-in.

Closing Down the Plug-In

When the interaction is over and the user is ready to leave CharFlipper, Navigator calls NPP_Destroy(). Because there is only one instance, NPP_Shutdown() is called immediately after the instance is deleted.

NPP_Destroy() is in Examples/Framework/CNetscapePlugin.cpp:

```
//-----------------------------------------------------------------
// NPP_Destroy:
//-----------------------------------------------------------------
NPError NP_LOADDS
NPP_Destroy(NPP instance, NPSavedData** save)
{
  if (instance == NULL)
    return NPERR_INVALID_INSTANCE_ERROR;
  CNetscapePlugin* thePlugin = (CNetscapePlugin*) instance->pdata;
  if (thePlugin == 0)
    return NPERR_INVALID_PLUGIN_ERROR;
  NPError result = thePlugin->SaveData( save );
  delete thePlugin;
  return result;
}
```

Note that because CharFlipper is designed with Netscape's class library, the code has hooks for all the usual plug-in features, such as the use of NPSavedData. Although the function isn't used here, it could be hooked up easily in CCharFlipper::SaveData().

From Here...

This chapter showed how to build a complete Windows plug-in, using Visual C++'s AppWizard. Although the plug-in doesn't "do" much, it is quite complete in terms of functionality, including support for LiveConnect.

- The next chapter, " Example: npAVI Plug-In," looks at a complete plug-in that approaches commercial grade.
- Chapter 6, "NPP Methods: Starting the Plug-In," provides an in-depth trace of the stream of control from the time the plug-in is invoked to the time it finishes displaying its data.

Part
II

Ch
11

- Chapter 7, "NPP Methods: Handling Interaction," shows how the plug-in is notified of user actions, including both actions that take place in Navigator and actions in the plug-in window.

- Chapter 8, "NPP Methods: Other Tasks," shows how to print the plug-in contents. It also shows what happens when the user closes the plug-in window.

- Chapter 9, "Understanding NPN Methods," describes in detail the calls a plug-in programmer can make back to Navigator.

CHAPTER 12

Example: npAVI Plug-In

The "npAVI" plug-in is easily the most complex plug-in in this book. It includes full LiveConnect integration, and exercises nearly all of the NPP methods. This plug-in also uses Microsoft Foundation Classes (MFC) to put up a custom pop-up menu. npAVI has some of the same capabilities as Netscape's LiveVideo plug-in—one of the major features that distinguishes Navigator 3.0 from Navigator 2.0.

The plug-ins described in Chapter 10, "Example: Simple Plug-In," and Chapter 11, "Example: CharFlipper Plug-In," were intended purely for illustrative purposes. In contrast, npAVI could be released as a commercial product, and few users would question it. ■

How to build npAVI

Unlike other examples supplied by Netscape, npAVI is built by using nmake and a makefile.

How Netscape's special version of javah builds stub interface classes

Be sure to use the "JRI" version of javah.

How to use Microsoft Foundation Classes to implement user controls

npAVI displays a pop-up menu when the user presses the right mouse button.

About adding resources (from .rc files) to your plug-in

Separately compiled resources such as strings are the key to internationalizing your plug-in.

How to use "dummy commands" to help communications between Java and the plug-in

npAVI uses MM_MCINOTIFY to tell the AVI to stop.

npAVI in Action

npAVI displays a video (in AVI format) inside the Navigator window. (It's intended for use as an embedded plug-in.)

For an idea of how npAVI looks, start by compiling and then running the plug-in. Because this plug-in uses a Windows-specific AVI engine, Netscape provides a version only for Windows.

Installing the Sun JDK

Chapter 10, "Example: Simple Plug-In," and Chapter 11, "Example: CharFlipper Plug-In," described plug-ins in which the Java classes already had been hooked into the plug-in. This transformation is an essential step in using LiveConnect, Netscape's client-side integration technology. (LiveConnect is described in greater detail in Chapter 18, "Plug-Ins as a Programming Resource.")

In the npAVI project you, as the programmer, are expected to build your own header and interface files from the Java `.class` files. You need the Java compiler, javac, and Netscape's special version of the Java utility javah.

ON THE WEB

Install the Java Developers Kit (JDK) that comes from JavaSoft. You can find the Kit at **http://www.javasoft.com/**.

The readme file supplied by Netscape suggests that you install the JDK into a directory named C:\java. Instead, install it in C:\jdk. That way, you can use the makefile's default definition of JDK_ROOT, saving a step (and an opportunity to make a mistake) when building the plug-in with nmake.

Compiling the Plug-In

Unlike the Netscape sample plug-ins in Chapter 10, "Example: Simple Plug-In," and Chapter 11, "Example: CharFlipper Plug-In," npAVI is built from a makefile. Use Microsoft Developer Studio to open Examples\npavi\Source\makefile. Note the message in the file header: you must either set SDK_ROOT and JDK_ROOT in the environment or in your command line. (`SDK_ROOT` is the directory that contains `bin\win32\javah.exe`; `JDK_ROOT` contains `bin\javac.exe`.) The fastest way to build npAVI is to specify these directories in the command line. For example, you can type the following:

```
nmake -f makefile JDK_ROOT=\jdk
```

 If you leave `SDK_ROOT` and `JDK_ROOT` undefined, the makefile has definitions it uses. It defines `SDK_ROOT` as `..\..\..`, which is perfect if you are building in, say, C:\PluginSDK30b5\Examples\npavi\Source\.

If you leave `JDK_ROOT` undefined, the makefile sets it to `c:\jdk\`.

 If you turn on DEBUG, javah builds type-safe functions rather than macros. Opt for safety, even when you're not building a debug version. Leave `DEBUG=1` in the command line *all* the time.

Building *all* If you previously used any member of the `make` family (including `nmake`) you probably know that, by default, `make` makes the first target it finds in the file. In the Netscape-supplied makefile, that target is specified in the following line:

```
all : java .\objs\$(TARGET).dll
```

Here, `$(TARGET)` was previously specified by the following:

```
TARGET = npavi32
```

Building *java* The target `java` includes `dirs`, `$(CLASSES)`, `$(ZIP)`, `$(GEN)`, and `$(STUBS)`. The target `dirs` calls the MS-DOS command `mkdir` for each of the three subdirectories: `_gen`, `_stubs`, and `objs`. These directories are used to hold the results of the builds of the remaining targets.

The target `CLASSES` resolves to the two targets `.\AviPlayer.class` and `.\AviObserver.class`. Toward the bottom of the file is a set of implicit rules. One of these rules, shown on the following lines, says that to make a file of type `.class` from a file of type `.java`, run the Java compiler (javac) on the `.java` file, using the switches given in `JAVA_CLASSES`:

```
java.class:
  $(JAVAC) $(JAVA_CLASSES) $<
```

These switches resolve to `-classpath ..\..\..\classes\moz3_0.zip`.

Part
II

Ch
12

T I P You can change JAVA_CLASSES if you need to keep your Netscape classes someplace else. Remember, however, that Netscape has a reputation for bringing out a new release of Navigator every few months. You may find it easier to leave the makefile alone and just install the file of the SDK in their default locations.

> **CAUTION**
>
> The file moz3_0.zip is used by Netscape as a convenient package for their Java classes. Under no circumstances should you use WinZip, PKUNZIP, or similar tools to unzip moz3_0.zip.

The target ZIP resolves to three files:

- ._gen\java_lang_Object.h
- ._gen\netscape_plugin_Plugin.h
- ._stubs\netscape_plugin_Plugin.c

These three files are rebuilt with explicit rules every time moz3_0.zip changes. They are built by using a special "Java Runtime Interface" (JRI) version of the utility javah. The JRI version is produced by Netscape—it builds .h and .c files based on the contents of Java source files.

N O T E The -jri switch must be on for the Netscape-enhanced version of javah to work correctly.

Javah's real work is to produce header files (which go in the _gen directory) and stub C files (which go in the stub directory). The make targets GEN and STUBS resolve to the header and stub files for the two Java classes AviObserver and AviPlayer. When you build your plug-in, use this makefile as a starting point and change GEN and STUBS to name your own Java classes. The "Implicit Rules" section of the makefile contains rules for transforming .class files to .h and .c files, using javah.

Building .\objs\$(TARGET).dll The final target associated with all is .\objs\$(TARGET).dll. (By substituting your project name into TARGET, you can easily customize this makefile to generate your own plug-in.) This target depends (via an explicit rule) on $(TARGET).def, $(OBJS), and $(RES). The .def file, of course, is handwritten, and identifies the following three entry points required of every plug-in:

- NP_GetEntryPoints
- NP_Initialize
- NP_Shutdown

Except for changing the name of the library, you seldom need to edit your plug-in's .def file.

OBJS, of course, lists the object files, which are generated (via implicit rule) from the C++ source files of your plug-in.

Note that npAVI includes a resource file, npAVI32.res. The final implicit rule in the makefile describes how to run the resource compiler to transform a .rc file into the .res file.

Moving the Files into Position

After you've built the plug-in using nmake, your Source directory will contain the files AviObserver.class and AviPlayer.class, and the objs subdirectory contains npavi32.dll.

Copy the two Java class files and the .dll file to the Navigator plug-ins directory.

 TIP You may want to skim Chapter 18, "Plug-Ins as a Programming Resource," to get the bigger picture of Java and LiveConnect. In Chapter 18 you learn how to use javac and javah to make your own class, header, and stub files.

Part
II

Ch
12

You must now restart Navigator. Make sure that you are using a version of Navigator that is at least at v3.0b5, or you won't see all the features of this plug-in working.

Running the Plug-In

When Navigator restarts, it examines the files in the plug-ins directory and registers plug-ins based on their MIME media type. Chapter 19, "Installing the Plug-In," describes this process in more detail.

After Navigator is up, use File, Open File to open Examples\npAVI\Testing\npAVIExample.html. You probably want to bookmark this page while you learn about plug-ins.

As soon as it opens, npAVI downloads its stream and displays the first frame of the movie. Figure 12.1 shows the npAVIExample.html user interface. The plug-in is now waiting for commands that you enter through the buttons via JavaScript.

FIG. 12.1

npAVI reads from a stream and writes to the window. It's also listening to Java-Script, waiting for a user to press a button.

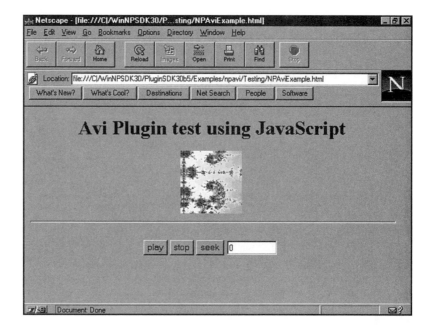

npAVI displays its first frame immediately, and then pauses the movie. You can use the controls to stop and resume the movie, or to seek directly to a specific frame. (The default movie, "seahorse.avi," has 199 frames.)

Use Navigator's View, Document Source to see how the buttons are hooked up. The start and stop buttons call `document.avi.play(false)` and `document.avi.stop(false)`, respectively. The seek button picks up the value of the frame field through JavaScript:

```
onclick="document.avi.seek(false, parseInt(form.editSeek.value))"
```

Putting npAVI into a Project

In its default configuration you can't use Microsoft Developer Studio's ClassView to open that function because Netscape has not built npAVI into a project.

You can take advantage of ClassView by choosing File, New, Project Workspace. Select "Makefile" from the list of possible project types, and give the project a new name and path.

Microsoft Developer Studio offers to take you to the Project Settings dialog box, where you can specify the path to the makefile. (See Figure 12.2.) Answer "Yes" to this offer.

FIG. 12.2
When you build a new project from a makefile, Microsoft Developer Studio offers to hook up the makefile for you.

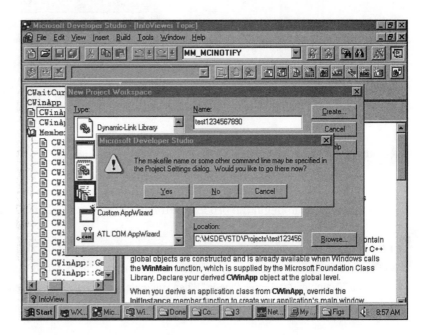

If you want to use this project to build the plug-in, as well as the way to examine classes, fill in the command line field in the Project Settings dialog with your real nmake command line, including **DEBUG=1**, if you are using it. Make sure that you specify the path of the makefile relative to the project directory. (If you are copying the files into the project directory and have set up the SDK and JDK following the recommended values, use **nmake -f makefile DEBUG=1**.) Figure 12.3 shows this dialog.

If you just want to examine the npAVI files, use Insert, Files into Project… to make the npAVI .cpp and .rc files in the Examples\npavi\Source directory a part of the new project. To use npavi as a starting point for your plug-in, copy the npavi files to the new project directory, and then add them into the project. In this way, all changes you make become part of the new project, and you won't inadvertently change npAVI.

FIG. 12.3
By building a project
around the makefile,
you get the benefits
of Microsoft
Developer Studio
without the com-
plexity of a custom
build.

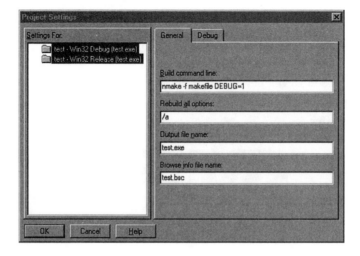

Flow of Control

npAVI is a sophisticated plug-in that uses nearly all the NPP methods. Open
npshell.cpp to begin the process of tracing this plug-in's flow of control.

If you're new to plug-ins, read Chapter 10, "Example: Simple Plug-In." Simple is far
smaller than npAVI, so some of its interaction is easier to follow. Then move to Chapter
11, "Example: CharFlipper Plug-In." When you understand these plug-ins, come back here
to npAVI, the most sophisticated of the bunch.

Follow Navigator

As you saw when you ran Simple and CharFlipper, a plug-in has two interfaces—
one to Navigator and another to the user. Because the plug-in can't do anything
with the user until most of its Navigator functions are called, this section starts
by tracing the flow of control between Navigator and npAVI. Follow along on
Figure 12.4.

FIG. 12.4
Navigator makes a
series of calls to the
plug-in to get things
started.

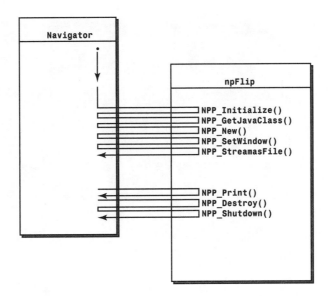

How npAVI is Called   Unlike Simple (but like CharFlipper) npAVI reads a
stream—in this case, an AVI movie. Because this stream is a local file, there is no
server to translate the file extension into a MIME type. Rather, Navigator looks at
the file extensions registered by each plug-in and determines that files with suffix
.avi get handled by npAVI.

> **CAUTION**
>
> Because the file extension `.avi` and the MIME media types `video/msvideo` and `video/x-msvideo` are so common, you already may have a plug-in configured to handle these types. In Navigator, select Help, About Plug-ins to display the list of configured plug-ins. Figure 12.5 shows the table that describes npAVI.
>
> If NPAVI32 isn't listed as handling Video for Windows, temporarily remove the conflicting plug-in from the plug-ins subdirectory (the one named "plugins"), restart Navigator, and check Help, About Plug-ins again.

FIG. 12.5
Be sure that
about:plugins
shows npAVI
handling the Video
for Windows types.

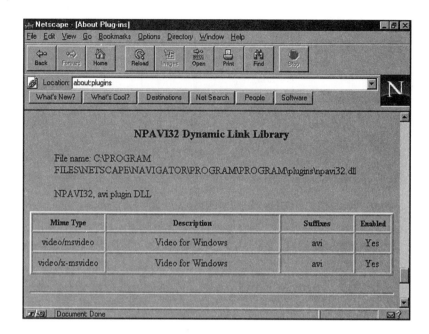

NPP_Initialize( )   When Navigator sees the <EMBED> tag, it looks up the plug-in that registered to handle files with suffix ".avi". Navigator finds npAVI32 and loads this library into its address space. Then it exchanges entry points, as Chapter 6, "NPP Methods: Starting the Plug-In," described. The first method it calls for which you, the programmer, are responsible is NPP_Initialize().

If you built npAVI into a project as previously described, you can use Microsoft Developer Studio's ClassView to open this function. (It's in the Globals folder because it isn't part of any class.)

You will see that NPP_Initialize() is less than trivial: it simply returns NPERROR_NO_ERROR.

NPP_GetJavaClass( )   NPP_GetJavaClass() follows a classic design: npAVI gets a pointer to the Java runtime environment through NPN_GetJavaEnv(). Then it calls the use... function for each of the Java classes: netscape.plugin.Plugin, AviObserver, and AviPlayer. The function returns the reference from use_AviPlayer(). (Chapter 18, "Plug-Ins as a Programming Resource," explains why this sequence is necessary.) Here's the implementation of NPP_GetJavaClass().

```
jref NPP_GetJavaClass(void)
{
  JRIEnv* env = NPN_GetJavaEnv();
  use_netscape_plugin_Plugin(env);
  use_AviObserver(env);
  return use_AviPlayer(env);
}
```

The use... functions like use_netscape_plugin_Plugin() and use_AviObserver()
are written by javah. (See Chapter 18, "Plug-Ins as a Programming Resource" for
more information on javah.)

NPP_New()   Now Navigator is ready to make the plug-in instance. Open
NPP_New() with ClassWizard. Note that the new instance parses out the autostart
and loop parameters from argv. Then it builds a CPluginWindow, which is used as
the basis for instance data.

```
// NPP_New
//
//   create a new plugin instance
//   handle any instance specific code initialization here
//
NPError NP_LOADDS
NPP_New(NPMIMEType pluginType,
        NPP instance,
        uint16 mode,
        int16 argc,
        char* argn[],
        char* argv[],
        NPSavedData* saved)
{
  BOOL bAutoStart, bLoop;

  // CPluginWindow is the main plugin object. Keep state information
  // about the specific instance to be created
  CPluginWindow* pluginData;

  // trap a NULL ptr
  if (instance == NULL)
    return NPERR_INVALID_INSTANCE_ERROR;

  // extract the pseudo command line arguments which were passed as
  // attributes in the embed tag of the document

  // for this example the plugin takes a true/false value for both
  // autostart and loop to determine the plugin style characteristics
  bAutoStart = FALSE;
  bLoop = FALSE;
  for (int idx =0; idx<argc; idx++) {
```

Part
II

Ch
12

```
       if (!strcmpi(argn[idx],"autostart")) {
         if (!strcmpi(argv[idx],"true")) {
           bAutoStart = TRUE;
         }
       }
       if (!strcmpi(argn[idx],"loop")) {
         if (!strcmpi(argv[idx],"true")) {
           bLoop = TRUE;
         }
       }
     }

     // create a data pointer to pass around with the instance
     pluginData = new CPluginWindow (bAutoStart, bLoop, mode, instance);

     // save my data pointer in the instance pdata pointer
     instance->pdata = pluginData;
     // this will be passed back to me in all calls so that I
     // can extract it later
     return NPERR_NO_ERROR;
   }
```

Because you encapsulated npAVI in a project, you can read the definition of
CPluginWindow by using ClassView. Double-click the class name at the top of the
ClassView pane. (You can view the implementation by expanding that branch of
the tree and double-clicking the member name.) Figure 12.6 shows CPluginWindow
as viewed through ClassView.

FIG. 12.6
Use ClassView to
examine the classes
of npAVI.

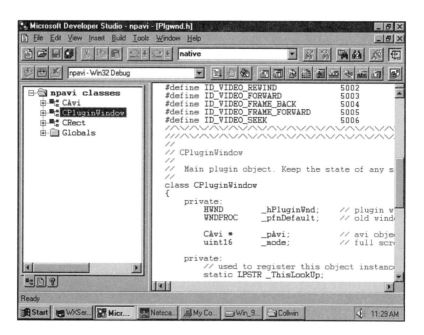

NPP_SetWindow()   `NPP_SetWindow()` quickly gets through to
`CPluginWindow::SetWindow()`. It lets the work be done by this class member, and
then calls `InvalidateRect()` and `UpdateWindow()` so that the plug-in gets a new
`WM_PAINT` message and redraws the window's contents. Here's the implementation
of `NPP_SetWindow()`, from npshell.cpp:

```
// NPP_SetWindow
//
// Associates a platform specific window handle with a plug-in instance.
//     Called multiple times while, e.g., scrolling. Can be called for
//     three reasons:
//
//          1.  A new window has been created
//          2.  A window has been moved or resized
//          3.  A window has been destroyed
//
// There's also the degenerate case; that it was called spuriously, and
// the window handle and or coords may have or have not changed, or
// the window handle and or coords may be ZERO. State information
// must be maintained by the plug-in to correctly handle the degenerate
// case.
//
NPError NP_LOADDS
NPP_SetWindow(NPP instance, NPWindow* window)
{
  // strange...
  if (!window)
    return NPERR_GENERIC_ERROR;

  // strange...
  if (!instance)
    return  NPERR_INVALID_INSTANCE_ERROR;

  // get back the plugin instance object
  CPluginWindow * pluginData = (CPluginWindow *)instance->pdata;
  if (pluginData) {
    if (!window->window) {

      // watch out this case.
      // window went away
      //delete pluginData; (?????)
      return NPERR_NO_ERROR;
    }
    if (!pluginData->GetWndProc()) {
```

```
        //\\// First time in //\\//
        // grab the handle so we can control the messages flow
        pluginData->SetWindow((HWND)window->window);
    }

    // resize or moved window (or newly created)
    InvalidateRect(*pluginData, NULL, TRUE);
    UpdateWindow(*pluginData);
    return NPERR_NO_ERROR;
}

// return an error if no object defined
return NPERR_GENERIC_ERROR;
}
```

CPluginWindow::SetWindow() is quite short: it simply subclasses the Netscape-supplied window with our own CPluginWindow::PluginWndProc:

```
// SetWindow
//
//   store the window handle and subclass the window proc
//   Associate "this" with the window handle so we can redirect window
//   messages to the proper instance
//
void
CPluginWindow::SetWindow(HWND hWnd)
{
  hPluginWnd = hWnd;

  // subclass
  pfnDefault = (WNDPROC)::SetWindowLong(hWnd,
                                        GWL_WNDPROC,
                                        (LONG)CPluginWindow::
                                          PluginWndProc);

  // register "this" with the window structure
  ::SetProp(hWnd, CPluginWindow::ThisLookUp, (HANDLE)this);
}
```

Figure 12.7 illustrates how the components of NPP_SetWindow() communicate.

FIG. 12.7
As a result of calling NPP_SetWindow(), CPluginWindow:: PluginWndProc is installed as the new WindowProc for the plug-in's window.

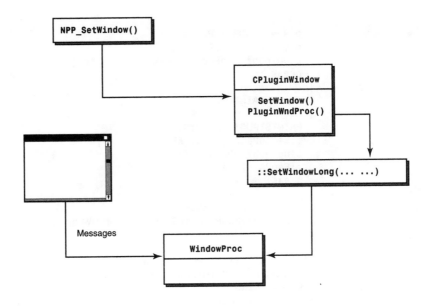

`CPluginWindow::PluginWndProc()` is defined in plgwnd.cpp, as follows:

```
// PluginWndProc
//
//   static member function of CPluginWindow
//   this is the window proc used to subclass the plugin window the
//   navigator created and passed in NPP_SetWindow (npshell.c)
//
LRESULT CALLBACK
CPluginWindow::PluginWndProc(HWND hWnd,
                             UINT Msg,
                             WPARAM WParam,
                             LPARAM lParam)
{
  // pull out the instance object receiving the message
  CPluginWindow* pluginObj =
    (CPluginWindow*)GetProp(hWnd,
                            CPluginWindow::ThisLookUp);
  // message switch
  switch (Msg) {
    case WM_LBUTTONDOWN:
    {
      POINT p;
      p.x = LOWORD(lParam);
      p.y = HIWORD(lParam);
      pluginObj->OnLButtonDown(WParam, &p);
      break;
    }
    case WM_RBUTTONDOWN:
    {
```

```
      POINT p;
      p.x = LOWORD(lParam);
      p.y = HIWORD(lParam);
      pluginObj->OnRButtonDown(WParam, &p);
      break;
}
case WM_PAINT:
{
  PAINTSTRUCT  PaintStruct;
  ::BeginPaint(hWnd, &PaintStruct);
  pluginObj->OnPaint();
  ::EndPaint(hWnd, &PaintStruct);
  break;
}
case WM_PALETTECHANGED:
  pluginObj->OnPaletteChanged((HWND)WParam);
break;

// the following two messages are used from the CAvi class
// MM_MCINOTIFY informs about a stop event
case MM_MCINOTIFY:
  pluginObj->GetAviStream().OnStop();
break;

// WM_TIMER is used to update the position status
case WM_TIMER:
  pluginObj->GetAviStream().OnPositionChange();
break;

// menu handling
// pass to CPluginWindow instance? (too much work...)
//
// WARNING
// those ids are also used from native functions (avijava.cpp)
// when the flag isAsync is setted to TRUE (see avijava.cpp
// and AviPlayer.java)
case WM_COMMAND:
  if (!HIWORD(WParam)) {
    switch LOWORD(WParam) {
      case ID_VIDEO_PLAY:
        pluginObj->OnLButtonDown(0, 0);
        return 0;
      case ID_VIDEO_STOP:
        pluginObj->GetAviStream().Stop();
        return 0;
      case ID_VIDEO_REWIND:
        pluginObj->GetAviStream().Rewind();
        return 0;
      case ID_VIDEO_FORWARD:
        pluginObj->GetAviStream().Forward();
        return 0;
```

```
          case ID_VIDEO_FRAME_BACK:
            pluginObj->GetAviStream().FrameBack();
            return 0;
          case ID_VIDEO_FRAME_FORWARD:
            pluginObj->GetAviStream().FrameForward();
            return 0;

          // this is hidden to the menu but it's used from
          // the java class in asynchronous mode (see AviPlayer.java
          // and avijava.cpp)
          case ID_VIDEO_SEEK:
            pluginObj->GetAviStream().Seek(lParam);
            return 0;
          }
        }
        default:
          return CallWindowProc(pluginObj->GetWndProc(), hWnd, Msg,
          ➥WParam,lParam);
      };
      return 0;
  }
```

Notice that `CPluginWindow::PluginWndProc()` includes handlers for `WM_LBUTTONDOWN`, `WM_RBUTTONDOWN`, and `WM_COMMAND`, and also the now-expected `WM_PAINT`. When the user clicks the left mouse button, `CPluginWindow::OnLButtonDown()` gets called—this method toggles the run state of the AVI movie.

When the user right-clicks the mouse, the plug-in calls the Windows global function `::CreatePopupMenu()` and reads strings from the string table in the resource file to populate the menu.

Here's the implementation of `OnRButtonDown()`:

```
// OnRButtonDown
//
//   bring up a menu with avi commands
//
void
CPluginWindow::OnRButtonDown(UINT uFlags, LPPOINT pPoint)
{
  UINT uState;
  char szMenuString[128];

  //  Create the popup.
  HMENU hPopup = ::CreatePopupMenu();
  if(hPopup == 0)  {
    return;
```

```
        }
        if(_pAvi->isPlaying())
          uState = MF_GRAYED;
        else
          uState = MF_ENABLED;

        //"Play..."
        ::LoadString(g_hDllInstance, MENU_PLAY, szMenuString, 128);
        ::AppendMenu(hPopup, uState, ID_VIDEO_PLAY, szMenuString);

        //"Pause..."
        ::LoadString(g_hDllInstance, MENU_PAUSE, szMenuString, 128);
        ::AppendMenu(hPopup, !uState, ID_VIDEO_STOP, szMenuString);

        // Separator
        ::AppendMenu(hPopup, MF_SEPARATOR, 0, 0);
        uState = MF_ENABLED;

        //"Rewind (Start of movie)..."
        ::LoadString(g_hDllInstance, MENU_REWIND, szMenuString, 128);
        ::AppendMenu(hPopup, uState, ID_VIDEO_REWIND, szMenuString);

        //"Forward (End of movie)..."
        ::LoadString(g_hDllInstance, MENU_FORWARD, szMenuString, 128);
        ::AppendMenu(hPopup, uState, ID_VIDEO_FORWARD, szMenuString);

        // Separator
        ::AppendMenu(hPopup, MF_SEPARATOR, 0, 0);

        //"Frame Back..."
        ::LoadString(g_hDllInstance, MENU_FRAME_BACK, szMenuString, 128);
        ::AppendMenu(hPopup, uState, ID_VIDEO_FRAME_BACK, szMenuString);

        //"Frame Forward..."
        ::LoadString(g_hDllInstance, MENU_FRAME_FORWARD, szMenuString, 128);
        ::AppendMenu(hPopup, uState, ID_VIDEO_FRAME_FORWARD, szMenuString);
        ::ClientToScreen(_hPluginWnd, pPoint);
        ::TrackPopupMenu(hPopup,
                         TPM_LEFTALIGN | TPM_RIGHTBUTTON,
                         pPoint->x,
                         pPoint->y,
                         0,
                         hPluginWnd,
                         NULL);
    }
```

TIP To add new commands to the menu, just add a string for the menu item in the string table, and add the string to the menu in `CPluginWindow::OnRButtonDown()`. Then add the handler for the new command in the `WM_COMMAND` section of `CPluginWindow::PluginWndProc`.

NPP_NewStream( ), NPP_StreamAsFile( )   Movies (AVI and also other formats) take too much bandwidth to play in realtime. npAVI specifies `*stype=NP_ASFILE` so that the entire movie is downloaded to the cache. Here's the implementation of `NPP_NewStream()`:

```
// NPP_NewStream
//
//   Notifies the plugin of a new data stream.
//   The data type of the stream (a MIME name) is provided.
//   The stream object indicates whether it is seekable.
//   The plugin specifies how it wants to handle the stream.
//
//   In this case, I set the streamtype to be NPAsFile. This tells the
//   Navigator the plugin doesn't handle streaming and can only deal with
//   the object as a complete disk file.  It will still call the write
//   functions but it will also pass the filename of the cached file in
//   a later NPE_StreamAsFile call when it's done transfering the file.
//
//   If a plugin handles the data in a streaming manner, it should set
//   streamtype to NPNormal  (e.g. *streamtype = NPNormal)...the NPE_
//   StreamAsFile function will never be called in this case
//
NPError NP_LOADDS
NPP_NewStream(NPP instance,
              NPMIMEType type,
              NPStream *stream,
              NPBool seekable,
              uint16 *stype)
{
  if(!instance)
    return NPERR_INVALID_INSTANCE_ERROR;

  // save the plugin instance object in the stream instance
  stream->pdata = instance->pdata;
  *stype = NP_ASFILE;
  return NPERR_NO_ERROR;
}
```

Part
II

Ch
12

Then `NPP_StreamAsFile()` is called so that the player can play the movie from the hard drive. Here's how this function is implemented:

```
// NPP_StreamAsFile
//
//   The stream is done transferring and here is a pointer to the file
//   in the cache. This function is only called if the streamtype was
//   set to NPAsFile.
//
void NP_LOADDS
NPP_StreamAsFile(NPP instance, NPStream *stream, const char* fname)
{
  if(fname == NULL || fname[0] == NULL)
    return;

  // get back the plugin instance object
  CPluginWindow * pluginData = (CPluginWindow *)instance->pdata;

  // get the avi object controller
  CAvi& aviPlayer = pluginData->GetAviStream();

  // open the avi driver with the specified name
  aviPlayer.Open(*pluginData, fname);
  aviPlayer.Update();

  // The AVI window Update() paint doesn't work in Win95.
  // It works fine in NT and Win3.1, but Win95 is doing something
  // hostile.  So, I have a hack here that steps the frame forward
  // to paint the window;  barf ...

  // figure out whether to hack for Win 95
  DWORD dwVer = GetVersion();
  int iVer = (LOBYTE(LOWORD(dwVer))*100)+HIBYTE(LOWORD(dwVer));
  if(iVer > 394) {
    // Win 95
    aviPlayer.FrameForward();
  }
}
```

`NPP_StreamAsFile()` gets the `aviPlayer` object (`_pAvi`) built into `CPluginWindow`, directs it to open on the Netscape-supplied filename, and calls the player's `Update` method. These Java-based methods are described in following sections of this chapter.

NPP_Print() `NPP_Print()` is hooked up, drawing a rectangle onto the print window's device context. Here's the implementation of `NPP_Print()`:

```
// NPP_Print
//
```

```
//  Printing the plugin (to be continued...)
//
void NP_LOADDS
NPP_Print(NPP instance, NPPrint* printInfo)
{
  if(printInfo == NULL)    // trap invalid parm
    return;
  if (instance != NULL) {
    CPluginWindow* pluginData = (CPluginWindow*) instance->pdata;
    pluginData->Print(printInfo);
  }
}
```

The work is done in CPluginWindow::Print(), shown here:

```
// Print
//
void
CPluginWindow::Print(NPPrint* printInfo) const
{
  if (printInfo->mode == NP_FULL) {
    //
    // *Developers*: If your plugin would like to take over
    // printing completely when it is in full-screen mode,
    // set printInfo->pluginPrinted to TRUE and print your
    // plugin as you see fit.  If your plugin wants Netscape
    // to handle printing in this case, set printInfo->pluginPrinted
    // to FALSE (the default) and do nothing.  If you do want
    // to handle printing yourself, printOne is true if the
    // print button (as opposed to the print menu) was clicked.
    // On the Macintosh, platformPrint is a THPrint; on Windows,
    // platformPrint is a structure (defined in npapi.h) containing
    // the printer name, port, etc.
    //
    void* platformPrint = printInfo->print.fullPrint.platformPrint;
    NPBool printOne = printInfo->print.fullPrint.printOne;
    printInfo->print.fullPrint.pluginPrinted = FALSE; // Do the default
  }
  else {
    // If not fullscreen, we must be embedded
    //
    // *Developers*: If your plugin is embedded, or is full-screen
    // but you returned false in pluginPrinted above, NPP_Print
    // will be called with mode == NP_EMBED.  The NPWindow
    // in the printInfo gives the location and dimensions of
    // the embedded plugin on the printed page.  On the Macintosh,
    // platformPrint is the printer port; on Windows, platformPrint
    // is the handle to the printing device context.
    //
    NPWindow* printWindow = &(printInfo->print.embedPrint.window);
    void* platformPrint = printInfo->print.embedPrint.platformPrint;
    HPEN hPen, hPenOld;
```

```
#ifdef WIN32
    /* Initialize the pen's "brush" */
    LOGBRUSH lb;
    lb.lbStyle = BS_SOLID;
    lb.lbColor = RGB(128, 128, 128);
    lb.lbHatch = 0;
    hPen = ::ExtCreatePen(PS_COSMETIC | PS_SOLID, 1, &lb, 0, NULL);
#else
    COLORREF cref = RGB(128, 128, 128);
    hPen = ::CreatePen(PS_SOLID, 32, cref);
#endif
    HDC hDC = (HDC)(DWORD)platformPrint;
    hPenOld = (HPEN)::SelectObject(hDC, hPen);
    BOOL result = ::Rectangle(hDC,
                            (int)(printWindow->x),
                            (int)(printWindow->y),
                            (int)(printWindow->x + printWindow->width),
                            (int)(printWindow->y + printWindow->height));
    ::SelectObject(hDC, hPenOld);
    ::DeleteObject(hPen);
  }
}
```

Although this Print() function doesn't attempt to print the *contents* of the plug-in window, it at least prints a rectangle as a place-holder on the page with an embedded plug-in. You can use this routine as a starting point for the implementation of NPP_Print() in your plug-in, and then replace the call to ::Rectangle() with something more meaningful for your plug-in's content.

LiveConnect Details

The real work of npAVI is done through the Java classes. Much of this work, in turn, is implemented back in the plug-in through native methods Figure 12.8 shows the interaction between JavaScript, Java, and the plug-in.

FIG. 12.8
Although the plug-in and JavaScript cannot talk directly, the Java peer object is quick and easy to set up.

Java

Plugin

Avi Observer

Avi Player

Get Observer
Advise
Set Time Out

Play()
Stop()
Seek()
Rewind()
•
•
•

Plug-in

NPP_GetJavaClass()

→ Use_AviObserver()
→ Use_AviPlayer()

Native_AviPlayer_SetTimeOut()

→ CPluginWindow:GetAviStream (),
SetFrequency()

Native_Avi Player_Play()
→ :: PostMessage(...,WM_Command,
...,ID_Video_Play,...)
Native_AviPlayer_Stop()
→ ::PostMessage(...,WM_Command,
..., ID_Video_Stop,...)
Native_Avi Player_Seek()
→ ::PostMessage(..., WM_Command,
...,ID_Video_Seek,...)
•
•
•

Java Script

<EMBED...NAME=qvi>
onclick="Document.Avi.Play
False)"
onclick="Document.Avi.Stop(
false)"
onclick="Document.Avi.Seek
(False, Parse Int(
Form.EditSeek.Value)

Examining the Java Code

Open the file AviPlayer.java. (You have to use File, Open; .java files are not part of the project.) Note that class AviPlayer includes a private member, AviObserver. This section looks at the implementation of both classes.

> **TIP** Make sure that you turn on the browser information to make it easier to trace from one class and method to the next.

Java Class *AviPlayer* Most of the methods in class AviPlayer are native. Follow the thread of control out of class AviPlayer and back to AviPlayer.c, in the _stubs directory. Pick one function, such as SetTimeOut(). SetTimeOut() is specified as native in AviPlayer.java, so it appears in the stub file AviPlayer.c. Here's the native declaration, in AviPlayer.java:

```
public class AviPlayer extends Plugin {
    .
    .
    .
    // set the timeout for the position checking timer
    public native void setTimeOut(int timeout);
    .
    .
    .
}
```

Note, also, that by specifying DEBUG you get the typesafe C function
`AviPlayer_setTimeOut()` rather than the macro. `AviPlayer_setTimeOut()` relies on
`use_AviPlayer_setTimeOut()` being called as part of `use_AviPlayer`. (Recall that
`use_AviPlayer()` was called by `NPP_GetJavaClass()`.)

The programmer's implementations for native methods such as `SetTimeOut()` are
in the file avijava.cpp. There, you learn that `native AviPlayer setTimeOut()` calls
`CAvi::SetFrequency()`, which, in turn, calls the Window API `::SetTimer()`:

```
extern "C" JRI_PUBLIC_API(void)
native_AviPlayer_setTimeOut(JRIEnv* env, struct AviPlayer* self,
    ➥jint timeout)
{
  NPP instance = (NPP)self->getPeer(env);
  CPluginWindow* pPluginData = (CPluginWindow*)instance->pdata;
  pPluginData->GetAviStream().SetFrequency(timeout);
}
```

N O T E The timer in npAVI is used in much the same way as the timer in CharFlipper is
used—it sets the pace for the playback, so that each frame pauses on-screen
long enough for the user to see it. The timer in an AVI movie, of course, runs on a much
shorter interval than the timer in CharFlipper. ■

Java Interface AviObserver Recall that the Java class `AviPlayer` includes a private
member of type AviObserver. To understand AviObserver, start from a plug-in
member such as `CAvi::OnStop()`. When Windows sends the `MM_MCINOTIFY`
message, the `WindowsProc` dispatches `CAvi::OnStop()`. This method is
implemented by getting the Java peer object (with `NPN_GetJavaPeer()`), and then
retrieving a pointer to its observer. Finally, `CAvi::OnStop()` calls the observer's
`onStop()` method.

How the JavaScript and HTML are Connected

The connection between JavaScript and the Java class follows the pattern described in Chapter 11, "Example: CharFlipper Plug-in." The buttons of the form directly call methods of the Java applet.

This form directs the function calls such as play() to the named plug-in. Refer to Figure 12.8 to see the flow of control between JavaScript, the Java peer object, and the plug-in.

Closing Down the Plug-In

When the interaction is over and the user is ready to leave npAVI, Navigator calls NPP_Destroy(). Because there is only one instance, NPP_Shutdown() is called immediately after the instance is deleted. The implementation of NPP_Destroy() follows the standard pattern—it deletes pdata and resets that pointer to NULL:

```
// NPP_Destroy
//
// Deletes a plug-in instance and releases all of its resources.
//
NPError NP_LOADDS
NPP_Destroy(NPP instance, NPSavedData** save)
{
  CPluginWindow * pluginData = (CPluginWindow *)instance->pdata;
  delete pluginData;
  instance->pdata = 0;
  return NPERR_NO_ERROR;
}
```

Note that NPP_Destroy has hooks for all the usual plug-in features, including NPSavedData. Although the function isn't used here, it can be hooked up easily.

From Here...

This chapter showed how to build a complete Windows plug-in, including Java headers and stubs, through a makefile. The plug-in is full-featured, including support for LiveConnect.

■ The next chapter, "Getting Back on the Network," looks at multitasking in plug-ins.

Part
II

Ch
12

- Chapter 6, "NPP Methods: Starting the Plug-In," provides an in-depth trace of the stream of control from the time the plug-in is invoked to the time it finishes displaying its data.

- Chapter 7, "NPP Methods: Handing Interaction," shows how the plug-in is notified of user actions, including both actions that take place in Navigator and actions that occur within the plug-in window.

- Chapter 8, "NPP Methods: Other Tasks," shows how to print the plug-in contents. It also shows what happens when the user closes the plug-in window.

- Chapter 9, "Understanding NPN Methods," describes in detail the calls a plug-in programmer can make back to Navigator.

Plug-In Compatibility

13   Getting Back on the Network   337

14   If All the World Used Microsoft…   363

15   ActiveX and Plug-Ins in Other Browsers   391

16   Spanning the Windows World   411

CHAPTER 13

Getting Back on the Network

Many developers whose early experience was with MS-DOS tend to think of computers and programs as sequential beasts. First we do this, then we do that, and then we wait while the real world catches up. In fact, all modern operating systems support some form of multitasking. Programs benefit from multitasking when they must wait for some real-world event.

In a plug-in, many real-world events have to do with waiting for the Net. If our plug-in calls, say, NPN_GetURLNotify(), there may be a delay of many milliseconds, or even seconds, before the Navigator calls NPP_URLNotify() to report that the data is available.

The difference between the various forms of multitasking

Examine your task to decide which method is best for your plug-in.

How each of the three major Navigator platforms handles multitasking

Match your multitasking requirements with each platform's capabilities.

How to implement multitasking quickly and easily on Windows

The latest version of Microsoft Foundation Classes (MFC) makes it easier than ever to use the Win 32 multithreading model.

How to use timers

Connect back to the real world by triggering periodic events.

How to write reentrant code

When you have the computer multiprocessing, your plug-in may meet itself in mid-thread.

Sometimes, the plug-in itself needs to take some time. If you want to sort data as it arrives, for example, you may want to call a sort-and-merge routine from inside `NPP_Write()`. Sorts and merges are computationally expensive, and Navigator is waiting for us to finish up and turn control back over to the browser. You may want to start a separate process or thread and leave it up to this task to finish the job, while the main thread returns control to Navigator. ▪

Introduction to Multitasking

Many compute-intensive programs benefit from getting the CPU and hanging onto it, but most programs aren't so CPU-intensive. They do some computing, and then wait for the user. Next, they may do some file I/O or some socket I/O to the network, and then they wait for the user again. These programs benefit from *multitasking*, a system by which a single processor works on more than one task. This situation is quite common in plug-ins that open more than one stream to (or from) the Net. The program spends a great deal of time waiting for network I/O to complete. You can make your plug-ins more efficient by allowing the operating system to take advantage of free time on the processor while your plug-in waits for data. This section introduces the concept of multitasking and shows how to start multiple tasks on Windows, the Macintosh, and under UNIX.

Understanding Processes and Threads

Modern operating systems support a variety of ways to keep the processor busy. Older operating systems, such as UNIX, originally had multiple users. (Many UNIX installations still do.) These systems were *multiuser*—each user had his or her own set of *processes* that were well-isolated from all other processes. When MS-DOS arrived, the processors were so tiny that no one could conceive of running more than one process. The 8088 was usually hard-pressed to keep up with one user!

With newer, faster processors came the opportunity for multitasking. A user might have one window open, doing a recalculation on a large spreadsheet. The same user could have another window running a communications program and downloading a file through a modem. The same user could have yet another window open on a graphic, sending it to the printer. Finally, the user might be focused on still another window, using a word processor.

Although the computer still has only one processor, each of the windows in this example benefits from running a separate process, just as the users of a UNIX system benefit from having their own set of processes. A system that can run independent processes in this way is known as a *multiprocessing* system.

Early multiprocessing systems for desktop computers (such as Windows 3.*x* and Macintosh System 7) were based on the *cooperative multitasking* model. Each process ran through its main event loop. When the main event loop was done, it called a "yield" function to tell the operating system that the operating system could give control to another process. Figure 13.1 illustrates this design. This system is known as "cooperative" because one ill-behaved process could mess up the works, as shown in Figure 13.2.

FIG. 13.1
Cooperative multitasking is based on the "yield" function.

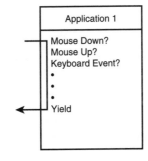 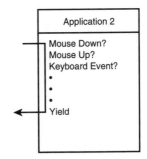

NOTE Cooperative multitasking was introduced on the Macintosh with System 7.0. At the bottom of the main event loop, the application calls `WaitNextEvent()`, a native routine that yields control back to the Mac OS until another event is available for processing.

Don't bother looking for the "yield" function in Windows—it's implicit in the operating system. The operating system keeps sending messages to your program as long as they're in the queue. When the queue runs empty, Windows just stops calling you. You have "yielded" without even knowing it. ∎

The alternative to cooperative multitasking is *preemptive multitasking*. In a preemptive scheme, the operating system keeps track of which application gets to run when (usually through some timer-based mechanism). When it's time for process A to run, process B is summarily suspended, and control passes to process A. The operating system resumes process B when it's that process's turn again. In a pre-emptive system, the application doesn't even need to know that it was suspended. Unless it looks at the clock, it thinks it just ran to completion.

FIG. 13.2
In a cooperative multitasking system, one process can hog the system.

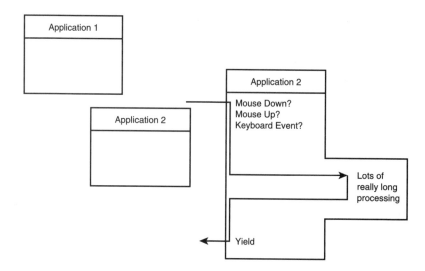

Preemptive multitasking offers the following three advantages over cooperative multitasking:

- The programmer doesn't have to worry about yielding, so the program is simpler to write.
- A program that *doesn't* yield cannot lock up the machine.
- The programmer can easily build powerful background processes (known as *daemons* in some operating systems).

Processes

UNIX, with its heritage as a multiuser system, places a great deal of emphasis on processes. Most programs are written as a single thread of execution—you could put your finger on the program listing and follow it down the page. At any one time, your finger would show the one step on which the computer was working.

Some advanced programs have more than one process. In the UNIX vocabulary the function fork() starts a new process by first making a copy of the existing process's address space. Then the child process follows one path of execution, and the parent process follows another. If all goes well, the child finishes before the parent (or the parent ends up waiting patiently for the child), and then both processes exit. Forking is illustrated in Figure 13.3.

FIG. 13.3
In a multiprocessing system like UNIX, each process can fork, copying its address space and resuming execution on a different path.

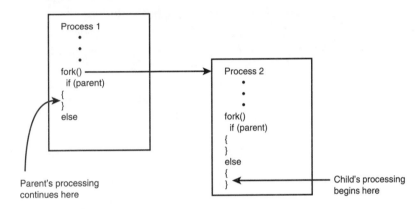

In a multiprocessing system, you need more than one finger to keep track of program execution—you need one finger for the parent process and one finger for every child process forked. Because the child process can itself fork new processes, you may quickly run out of fingers.

Some of the newest computers have more than one physical processor. These machines, known as Symmetric Multiprocessors or SMPs, can perform true multiprocessing—assigning a process to its own CPU.

Threads

The advantage of a multiprocessing system based on fork() is that each process has its own address space. A programming error in one process cannot affect any other process. To communicate between processes, a variety of Interprocess Communications (IPC) methods have been invented, including pipes, semaphores, shared memory, and sockets.

Part

III

Ch

13

The disadvantage of fork() is that copying a whole address space is computationally expensive. On many UNIX systems with sophisticated multiprocessing applications, a large percentage of the system's time is taken up by the overhead of forking.

In the late 1980s a newer multitasking design, based on *threads*, become popular. Threads are "lightweight processes." They behave like processes in that they support an additional path of execution, but they share the same address space as their parent. Because there is only one address space, there is little need to think about IPC. It also means that a programming error in one thread can ruin data in the other thread.

Today most versions of UNIX (and Windows 95 and Windows NT) support threads. The latest version of the Mac OS, System 8, also supports threads.

Multithreading is not appropriate for some applications. As was pointed out previously, a compute-intensive task gains little by being multithreaded. Many I/O-bound programs get a degree of multitasking from the operating system. The system often initiates a large data transfer and then frees the processor to work on other jobs.

Even when multithreading is the right attack, it can add complexity to the design, implementation, and debugging of the application. The threads share memory, so a value in a variable may change unexpectedly. Slight differences in the way the threads are scheduled can make defects intermittent and difficult to reproduce and pin down. When the program exits, extra pains must be taken to ensure that each thread has finished and has deallocated all its resources before the application itself is allowed to exit.

Synchronization and Critical Sections

All the multithreaded and multiprocessing operating systems provide mechanisms to ensure that two tasks do not compete for the same memory at the same time. These mechanisms aren't automatic—they must be carefully programmed. This section shows an example of one such mechanism, called the *semaphore*.

N O T E If you were formally trained in computer science, you will recognize the semaphore described in this section as the *p-v semaphore*. There are several other semaphore designs, including the resource counter, which ensures that no more than *n* tasks are allowed into the critical section.

For simplicity, this chapter describes only the p-v semaphore. ■

Suppose that two threads share access to a resource, such as a printer or a sound card. Because there is only one resource, only one thread can use the resource at a time. What is needed is a mechanism by which the first task that needs the resource can seize it, locking out the other task. Only when the first task gives up the resource can the second task access it. The mechanism that allows the two tasks to coordinate their use of the shared resource is referred to as a *synchronization mechanism*. The piece of code that accesses the shared resource is a *critical section*. One type of synchronization mechanism is the semaphore.

A semaphore is a special flag that is shared between two tasks. The operating system guarantees that the read-and-set operation is *atomic* (a task can read the semaphore, see that it's clear, and set it without fear that some other task will read it at the same time and see that the semaphore is clear). Figure 13.4 illustrates the difference between an atomic and a non-atomic read-and-set operation.

FIG. 13.4
Only the operating system can provide an atomic read-and-set operation on a semaphore.

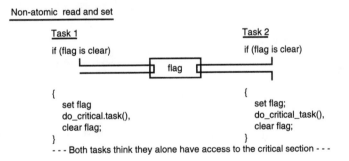

> **CAUTION**
>
> Non-atomic semaphore operations can lead to subtle errors in multithreaded applications. Don't try to build your own semaphores out of shared memory. Use the operators provided by the operating system.

Deadlocks

When designing multitasking code with critical sections and synchronization mechanisms, be careful to avoid a condition referred to as *deadlock* (also known as the "deadly embrace"). Figure 13.5 illustrates a deadlock. Task A seizes Resource 1, and then attempts to seize Resource 2. Task B already has Resource 2, and now attempts to seize Resource 1. Neither task can proceed. Unless someone (or something) intervenes, both tasks remain blocked indefinitely.

FIG. 13.5
A deadlock occurs when a circular chain of resource requests exists.

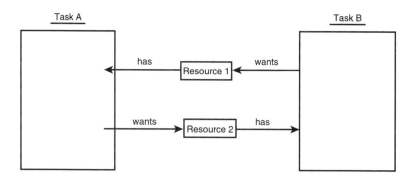

There are various automated techniques for dealing with deadlock. None of them works perfectly. The best defense against deadlock is careful design. Many designers carefully draw resource graphs to show which task waits for which resource, in order to satisfy themselves that no opportunity exists for a circular wait condition.

In general there are four ways to deal with the problem of deadlock:

- Ignore the problem, and hope it doesn't happen in your application.
- Detect the problem when it occurs and recover from it.
- Prevent the problem by careful design.
- Avoid the problem at run-time by careful resource allocation.

Under some conditions the "ostrich approach"—ignoring deadlock and hoping it doesn't happen—is a perfectly acceptable solution. On some systems a deadlock is theoretically possible, but actually occurs so infrequently and with so little impact that the problem cannot be solved in a cost-effective manner. When the cost of a deadlock is low, and the price of detecting or preventing deadlocks is high, consider imitating the ostrich.

An operating system can maintain a resource graph or just look for tasks that remain blocked for an extended period. Then the operating system can arbitrarily kill one of the processes to clear the deadlock. This approach is simple and effective, if occasionally you can live with one of your tasks being killed. If this solution is unacceptable, you may need to design deadlocks out of the system.

One simple (although tedious) way to prevent deadlocks is to sequentially number all resources. Then design (or even code) with a rule that says that requests must be made in numerical order. A task that holds Resource 3 cannot request Resource 1 or 2 without first relinquishing 3. After Resource 1 is allocated, the task can ask for 2. If this request is met, the task then can ask for Resource 3 back.

The resource-numbering technique works well for most applications, although it can break down in an environment such as an operating system in which the number of resources and the number of requestors is large. In this kind of environment the time required to check the allocation sequence, deallocate, and reallocate resources may become so large that the solution becomes unfeasible.

There is an algorithm that can always avoid deadlock by making the right allocation all the time, if you have the right information available. This algorithm, known as the *banker's algorithm*, was proposed by Dijkstra in his paper "Co-operating Sequential Processes," which appeared in *Programming Languages* (Academic Press, 1965). A simple version of the banker's algorithm is described in the sidebar in this section, "The Banker's Algorithm Unlocked."

The Banker's Algorithm Unlocked

If your multitasking program shares critical hardware or other resources (such as records in a data file) consider using the banker's algorithm to prevent deadlock.

The name "banker's algorithm" comes from the fact that this algorithm could be used by a small-town banker to manage loans. Suppose that a bank has four customers, A, B, C,

continues

continued

and D, and $100 million to loan. In this analogy the banker is an operating system or other "master program" responsible for allocating resources. The customers are tasks, and the money is a critical resource, such as a set of buffers. Each "customer" in the banker's algorithm has an assigned "credit limit," beyond which they cannot request resources. Table 13.1 shows the credit line available to each customer. The credit line corresponds to the maximum amount of the critical resource the task will ever need.

Table 13.1   Customer Credit Limits

Customer	Credit Limit
A	$60,000,000
B	50,000,000
C	40,000,000
D	70,000,000

If all the customers asked to borrow up to their credit limit at the same time, the bank would run out of money. The banker knows that this occurrence is unlikely, and he or she wants to be as fair to the customers as possible. On the other hand, the banker knows that these customers are using the loans for commercial projects. If the banker is forced to defer a loan indefinitely, the project never completes, and the original loans can never be repaid. (This condition corresponds to deadlock.) The banker uses the following rule in deciding whether or not to grant a loan request:

The banker considers each request for a resource as it occurs. If granting the request leads to a "safe state" the request is approved. A state is "safe" if the banker first checks to see if he or she has enough resources to satisfy the customer who is closest to his or her maximum. If so, the banker assumes that these loans are repaid, and then performs the same check on the customer next closest to his or her maximum. This process continues until the banker has computed a way that all customers could reach their maximum and repay their loans. If all loans eventually can be repaid, the state is considered safe and the initial request is granted.

Suppose that the banker has made the loans shown in Table 13.2, and receives a request from Customer B for an additional $10,000,000.

Table 13.2 Bank Status After a Few Loans

Customer Remaining	Credit Limit	Current Loan Balance	Credit
A	$60,000,000	$10,000,000	$50,000,000
B	50,000,000	10,000,000	40,000,000
C	40,000,000	20,000,000	20,000,000
D	70,000,000	40,000,000	30,000,000
		$80,000,000	Remaining funds: $20,000,000

If the banker grants the loan, the bank will have only $10,000,000 left. Customer C is $20,000,000 from her credit limit—if the banker satisfies B, and then C needs the remaining $20,000,000 to finish her project, the banker will be unable to satisfy that loan. C's project will fail, and none of the loans can ever be repaid. This situation corresponds to deadlock.

But if Customer C asks for $20,000,000, the banker can grant it, even if it brings the available funds to zero. This state is safe because, after the $20,000,000 is loaned, C's project completes and the customer can pay off the loan. See Table 13.3. After C pays off her loan, the bank has enough funds to satisfy the full demands of the next-closest customer.

Table 13.3 C Pays Off the Loan

Customer Remaining	Credit Limit	Current Loan Balance	Credit
A	$60,000,000	$10,000,000	$50,000,000
B	50,000,000	10,000,000	40,000,000
C	40,000,000	0	40,000,000
D	70,000,000	40,000,000	30,000,000
		$60,000,000	Remaining funds: $40,000,000

Part
III

Ch
13

continues

continued

After C's loan is repaid, the banker has $40,000,000 available, and can satisfy other requests. The customer next closest to the limit is B. If B requests the full $40,000,000, the request can be granted. When it is repaid, the bank has $50,000,000 available—more then enough to satisfy Customer D. Finally, after D's loan is repaid, the banker can clearly satisfy Customer A, which means that although B's request for $10,000,000 leads to an unsafe state, C's request for $20,000,000 leads to a safe state, and C's request is approved.

More elaborate versions of the banker's algorithm exist, and more efficient algorithms are available (although they tend to be more complex). The two principal weaknesses of the banker's algorithm are as follows:

- Tasks rarely know the total resources they need—their "credit limit."

- In many real-world applications, the number of tasks varies over time.

Regardless, for specific applications such as those associated with many plug-ins, these weaknesses can be overcome, and the relatively simple banker's algorithm can keep the system out of deadlock.

If your application reads and writes records from a shared file, you may want to consider a technique known as *two-phase locking* as an approach to preventing deadlock. Two-phase locking is important in preserving data integrity. Many transactions require that either all the changes be made or none of them be made. With two-phase locking, a task is blocked until it can get all the resources it needs. If all the tasks competing for a file follow the algorithm, a deadlock is impossible.

The two-phase locking algorithm requires an atomic lock such as semaphore on each record. A task first goes through the file, requesting every lock that it needs for a given transaction. If it gets all the locks, it proceeds with the update, and then releases all its locks. If *any* locks fail, it releases all locks, waits, and then tries to reacquire all locks.

Platform Capabilities and Limitations

Each of the three major Navigator platforms offers multitasking in various forms. The ins and outs of multitasking with each platform are discussed in the following sections.

UNIX

If your application can stand the overhead of forking, UNIX makes multitasking easy. Just fork a new process, and use one of the UNIX IPC mechanisms to pass information between parent and child processes.

To avoid the overhead of forking, use threads. Although every major version of UNIX now supports threads, their API varies somewhat. Solaris, from Sun Microsystems, is representative—it supports mutual exclusion locks (mutexes), condition variables, semaphores, and read/write locks for synchronization.

UNIX makes it easy to start a *daemon* process—a process that is not connected to any user and is running in the background, waiting to satisfy user requests. Print spoolers, Web servers, and the Network File System are all associated with daemons. If you run the UNIX command to list the processes (ps -ef on some versions of UNIX, ps -aux on others), you can recognize a daemon process because it has process 1 as its parent. You also may recognize daemons by their name—by convention, the last character in a daemon's name is 'd'. Figure 13.6 shows a ps -ef and highlights several daemon processes. Notice that the Web server, httpd, has one process that is a true daemon (process ID 13460). The other copies of the Web server were forked by process 13460.

Macintosh

The Mac OS has provided cooperative multitasking since 1991. The "Process Manager" provides a variety of options for initiating and scheduling processes. The "Program-to-Program Communications Toolbox," part of the native OS, supports IPC and synchronization.

The Macintosh supports one *foreground process* and zero or more *background processes*. The foreground process is the one currently interacting with the user—it has its menu bar up and its windows are in front of the windows of all other applications. If you're writing a plug-in, expect Navigator to be the foreground process.

An application can be designed without windows, corresponding to a UNIX daemon process. (Apple refers to them as *background-only applications*.)

A Macintosh application can launch other applications, corresponding to forking in UNIX. Use LaunchApplication() to launch another application. If you want your

Part
III

Ch
13

application to continue to run, sharing the CPU with the launched application, set the `launchContinue` flag in the `launchControlFlags` field of the launch parameter block. If you want your application to be notified when an application it has launched terminates, set the `acceptAppDiedEvents` flag in your `SIZE` resource. Your application receives an "Application Died" Apple Event ('aevt' 'obit') when the launched application terminates.

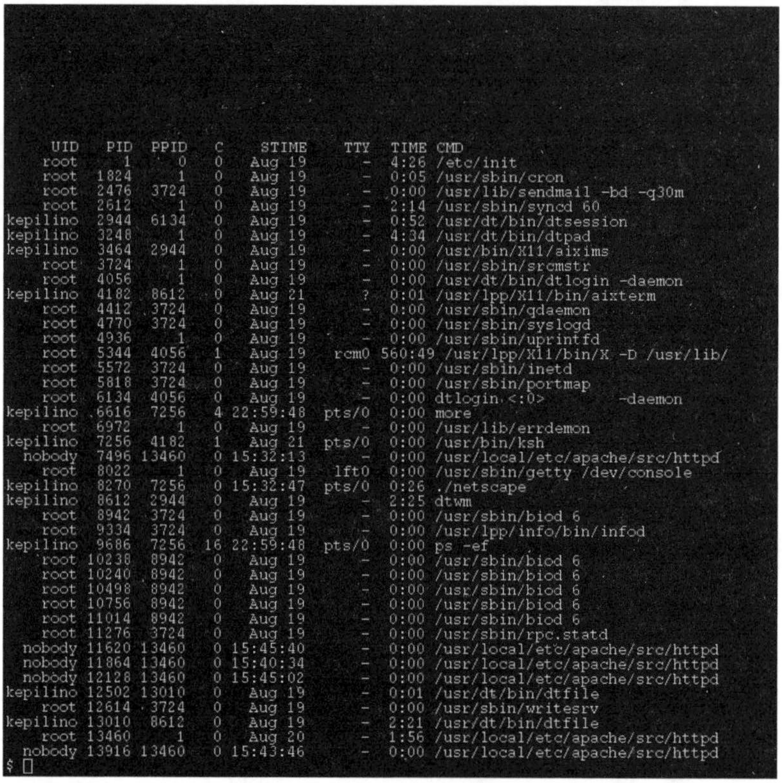

FIG. 13.6

Daemons have a Parent Process ID (PPID) of 1, and usually have a name that ends in a 'd'.

```
     UID   PID  PPID   C    STIME  TTY   TIME CMD
    root     1     0   0    Aug 19   -   4:26 /etc/init
    root  1824     1   0    Aug 19   -   0:05 /usr/sbin/cron
    root  2476  3724   0    Aug 19   -   0:00 /usr/lib/sendmail -bd -q30m
    root  2612     1   0    Aug 19   -   2:14 /usr/sbin/syncd 60
 kepilino 2944  6134   0    Aug 19   -   0:52 /usr/dt/bin/dtsession
 kepilino 3248     1   0    Aug 19   -   4:34 /usr/dt/bin/dtpad
 kepilino 3464  2944   0    Aug 19   -   0:00 /usr/bin/X11/aixims
    root  3724     1   0    Aug 19   -   0:00 /usr/sbin/srcmstr
    root  4056     1   0    Aug 19   -   0:00 /usr/dt/bin/dtlogin -daemon
 kepilino 4182  8612   0    Aug 21   ?   0:01 /usr/lpp/X11/bin/aixterm
    root  4412  3724   0    Aug 19   -   0:00 /usr/sbin/qdaemon
    root  4770  3724   0    Aug 19   -   0:00 /usr/sbin/syslogd
    root  4936     1   0    Aug 19   -   0:00 /usr/sbin/uprintfd
    root  5344  4056   1    Aug 19  rcm0 560:49 /usr/lpp/X11/bin/X -D /usr/lib/
    root  5572  3724   0    Aug 19   -   0:00 /usr/sbin/inetd
    root  5818  3724   0    Aug 19   -   0:00 /usr/sbin/portmap
    root  6134  4056   0    Aug 19   -   0:00 dtlogin <:0>       -daemon
 kepilino 6616  7256   4 22:59:48 pts/0  0:00 more
    root  6972     1   0    Aug 19   -   0:00 /usr/lib/errdemon
 kepilino 7256  4182   1    Aug 21 pts/0  0:00 /usr/bin/ksh
  nobody  7496 13460   0 15:32:13   -   0:00 /usr/local/etc/apache/src/httpd
    root  8022     1   0    Aug 19  lft0  0:00 /usr/sbin/getty /dev/console
 kepilino 8270  7256   0 15:32:47 pts/0  0:26 ./netscape
 kepilino 8612  2944   0    Aug 19   -   2:25 dtwm
    root  8942  3724   0    Aug 19   -   0:00 /usr/sbin/biod 6
    root  9334  3724   0    Aug 19   -   0:00 /usr/lpp/info/bin/infod
 kepilino 9686  7256  16 22:59:48 pts/0  0:00 ps -ef
    root 10238  8942   0    Aug 19   -   0:00 /usr/sbin/biod 6
    root 10240  8942   0    Aug 19   -   0:00 /usr/sbin/biod 6
    root 10498  8942   0    Aug 19   -   0:00 /usr/sbin/biod 6
    root 10756  8942   0    Aug 19   -   0:00 /usr/sbin/biod 6
    root 11014  8942   0    Aug 19   -   0:00 /usr/sbin/biod 6
    root 11276  3724   0    Aug 19   -   0:00 /usr/sbin/rpc.statd
  nobody 11620 13460   0 15:45:40   -   0:00 /usr/local/etc/apache/src/httpd
  nobody 11864 13460   0 15:40:34   -   0:00 /usr/local/etc/apache/src/httpd
  nobody 12128 13460   0 15:45:02   -   0:00 /usr/local/etc/apache/src/httpd
 kepilino 12502 13010  0    Aug 19   -   0:01 /usr/dt/bin/dtfile
    root 12614  3724   0    Aug 19   -   0:00 /usr/sbin/writesrv
 kepilino 13010  8612   0    Aug 19   -   2:21 /usr/dt/bin/dtfile
    root 13460     1   0    Aug 20   -   1:56 /usr/local/etc/apache/src/httpd
  nobody 13916 13460   0 15:43:46   -   0:00 /usr/local/etc/apache/src/httpd
$ []
```

The Pascal prototype for `LaunchApplication()` is as follows:

```
FUNCTION LaunchApplication(LaunchParams: LaunchPBPtr) : OSErr;
```

For more details on `LaunchApplication()` and related functions, see *Inside Macintosh* (Addison-Wesley, 1994).

N O T E Although Macintosh programmers have to wait for System 8 to get threads and preemptive multitasking, many toolbox routines have been asynchronous since the introduction of System 7.0 in 1991. For example, all of the low-level routines in the Data Access Manager, and some of the high-level routines, are asynchronous. To call one of these routines asynchronously, prepare a parameter block called an *asynchronous parameter block* and pass it to the routine. The database extension of the Data Access Manager turns control over to the device driver and returns control to your application.

As your application runs, it periodically calls `WaitNextEvent()`, which allows other tasks (including the database device driver) to run. The `DBState()` function tells you when the database device driver completes its task. When `DBState()` reports that the transaction completes, your plug-in calls `DBGetItem()` repeated to read out the database's response. ▓

System 8 will support both threads and processes. Early versions have been available to developers since mid-1996. *MacUser* magazine (October, 1996) has a cover story on Apple's Future—they spend two pages on Apple's plans for rolling out new versions of Mac OS, including the OpenDoc extensions, Harmony (the interim release of Mac OS based on System 7.5,) and Gershwin (the *next* big release after System 8).

ON THE WEB

For more information on System 8 (including the latest estimate of the release date), see Apple's Web site **http://www.macos.apple.com/macos8/**.

Windows

Microsoft introduced cooperative multitasking (which Microsoft refers to as *process multitasking*) in Windows 3.0. The newest versions of Windows (Windows NT and Windows 95) include preemptive multitasking (but only between the threads of a given process).

N O T E   Although most of the topics in this book that mention Windows 95 and Windows NT also pertain to Windows 3.1 (when 3.1 runs Win32s), thread-based multitasking is an exception. Windows 3.1 is essentially a process that runs on top of MS-DOS; as such, it supports only cooperative multitasking. ▓

With most operating systems, it's natural to think of the user "starting" the application, which then makes calls to the operating system. When thinking about the multitasking aspects of Windows, it's better to imagine the operating system as calling various entry points into the application. `WinMain` is one such entry point, but so are the `WindowsProcs` associated with each window. Messages arrive at the operating system and are dispatched to the appropriate handlers. Figures 13.7 and 13.8 show this difference.

FIG. 13.7
With most operating systems, it's natural think of the application running "above" and independent of the operating system.

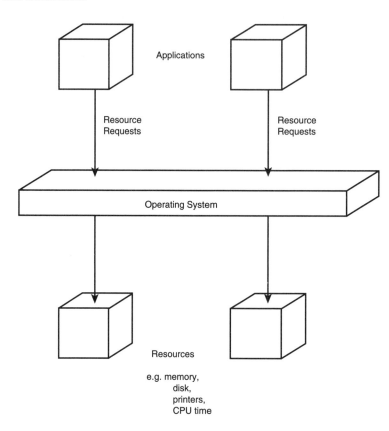

Applications

Resource Requests

Resource Requests

Operating System

Resources

e.g. memory,
disk,
printers,
CPU time

When an application finishes handling a message, it returns control to Windows. Additionally, many of the application's functions are Windows calls, so Windows has many opportunities to take control. If the application has no messages in its queue, it has implicitly yielded to the operating system.

FIG. 13.8
With Windows, it's more natural (and more correct) to regard the operating system as always being in control, making calls to the application as necessary.

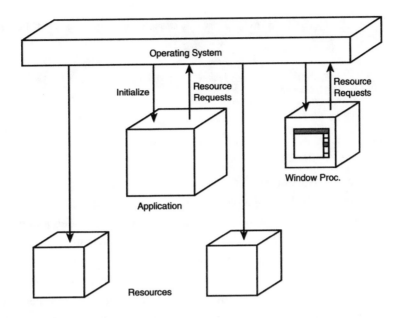

Because Win32 includes thread-based multitasking, there is a new emphasis on synchronization mechanisms. The Win32 API has a complete subsystem devoted to synchronization. Microsoft Foundation Classes (MFC) fully encapsulates this subsystem.

The remainder of this chapter uses Win32 to illustrate multitasking in plug-ins. Similar code can be written for UNIX, or for Mac OS System 8.

Multitasking on the Cheap

An HTML programmer can easily start two or more instances of your plug-in. Consider the following HTML page:

```
<HTML>
<HEAD>
.
.
.
</HEAD>
<BODY>
.
.
.
```

Part
III
Ch
13

```
<EMBED SRC="http://www.somemachine.com/file1.tst HEIGHT=100 WIDTH=50>
.
.
.
<EMBED SRC="http://www.someothermachine.com/file2.tst HEIGHT=200
WIDTH=100>
.
.
.
</BODY>
</HTML>
```

When Navigator reaches the first `<EMBED>` tag, it contacts the remote server and gets the MIME media type of the stream. Assume that this type is the one that causes your plug-in to be invoked. Your plug-in is loaded into memory, and Navigator calls its `NPP_Initialize()` method. Then Navigator makes the first instance and calls `NPP_New()`. Next, Navigator makes the window and calls `NPP_SetWindow()`. Finally, Navigator calls `NPP_NewStream()` and gives the plug-in a chance to tell Navigator how it wants to receive the data. This example assumes that your plug-in sets the stream's `stype` to `NP_NORMAL`. Navigator begins sending you the data with a series of `NPP_WriteReady()` and `NPP_Write()` calls.

The first instance of your plug-in is now active, responding to calls from Navigator as well as mouse messages, keyboard messages, timer messages, and other messages sent by Windows to your window's `WindowProc`. Navigator moves on to the second `<EMBED>` tag.

Assuming that file2.tst is mapped to the same MIME media type as file1.tst, Navigator recognizes the need to start a second instance of your plug-in. It can bypass `NPP_Initialize()` because your plug-in is already loaded. Instead it goes right to `NPP_New()` and continues just as it did with the first file. After the second file is loaded, you have one process (Navigator) with one thread of control: the main thread in Navigator runs through each of your plug-in instances. Because the two instances share any plug-in-global data, there is a potential for conflict between the instances.

Recall that when Navigator calls `NPP_New()`, it sends you an `NPP` named `instance`. The `pData` member of `instance` provides a convenient place to keep instance-specific data. If *all* your data is instance-specific, you don't need to think too much about multitasking. But what should happen if you have plug-in-global data? Figure 13.9 illustrates this situation.

FIG. 13.9
When two copies of a plug-in instance are loaded, there is a potential for conflict on the plug-in-global data.

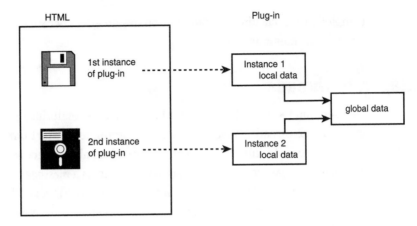

Returning to the Net

If your plug-in initiates any network transfers through NPN_GetURL(), NPN_PostURL(), or their ...Notify() counterparts, you can expect significant delays while the network I/O is in progress. Moreover, when the content comes back, it may trigger yet another instance of your plug-in. Chances are good that your user will be mostly idle while waiting for the transfer.

If you have background processing to do, start a thread and do it. You can afford to do a lot of work between the time of the request and the time the data comes back. To ensure reliability, use the ...Notify() version of the call, so you get a positive confirmation that the request was completed.

You also can use a thread to put up a progress control or status message. Chapter 9, "Understanding NPN Methods," in the section, "A Progress Indicator," shows how to use NPN_Status() to put up a status message similar to Netscape's.

Lack of a "Yield" Function

Another issue to consider is that there is no "yield" function between your plug-in and Navigator (or the rest of the system). Suppose that your plug-in renders a complex graphic—a compute-intensive task. Rather than hold up Navigator during the rendering, you would prefer to start the task, and then periodically yield to Navigator to let it tend to the user interface. However, if you keep the rendering task in the main thread, all of Navigator must wait for the rendering task to

Part
III

Ch
13

complete. Even clicking the Stop button has no effect because Navigator isn't listening to its messages.

Separate Threads

One solution to the problem of long tasks (such as rendering) is to split them off into separate threads. Win32 allows the programmer to start *interface threads* and *worker threads*. An interface thread is a thread capable of receiving and processing messages—it has what MFC's designers refer to as a *message pump*. Worker threads are simply threads without a message pump. Most applications have only one interface thread—the main thread that was started by Windows. All other threads are usually worker threads.

To start a thread, call `AfxBeginThread()`. The prototype for `AfxBeginThread()` is as follows:

```
CWinThread* AfxBeginThread(AFX_THREADPROC ThreadFunc,
                           LPVOID Param,
                           int InitPriority = THREAD_PRIORITY_NORMAL,
                           UINT StackSize = 0,
                           DWORD dwFlags = 0,
                           LPSECURITY_ATTRIBUTES Security = NULL);
```

The parameter *ThreadFunc* is started in its own thread. The thread continues asynchronously until *ThreadFunc* returns. All *ThreadFuncs* have the following prototype:

```
UINT ThreadFunc(LPVOID TFParam);
```

The parameter *Param* is a 32-bit value passed to *ThreadFunc*. For type safety, your *ThreadFunc* should cast *Param* to the proper type as soon as it receives it. If your compiler supports Runtime Type Identification (RTTI), you may even want to consider passing a pointer to an object, and using RTTI in *ThreadFunc* to ensure that *ThreadFunc* was called correctly.

TIP The parameter *StackSize* defaults to zero. You should leave it at this value. If `AfxBeginThread()` sees *StackSize* at zero, it starts the new thread's stack out at the same size as the calling application (in the case of a plug-in, the same size as Navigator's stack). As the thread function runs, Windows adjusts the stack size dynamically to ensure that the thread always has enough room on the stack.

Similarly, leave *dwFlags* and *Security* at their default values. The default for *dwFlags* is for the thread to begin execution immediately. The alternative is to suspend the new thread and wait for a call to CWinThread::ResumeThread(). The default value for *Security* causes the new thread to inherit its security attributes from the calling thread (again, in the case of a plug-in, from Navigator).

Be careful about changing the thread's priority. If you set the priority too high, the thread can hog the CPU, and Navigator becomes sluggish. If you set the thread's priority too low, it may take a long time to do its work, giving the appearance that your plug-in performs poorly. The priorities, from highest to lowest, are as follows:

```
THREAD_PRIORITY_TIME_CRITICAL

THREAD_PRIORITY_HIGHEST

THREAD_PRIORITY_ABOVE_NORMAL

THREAD_PRIORITY_NORMAL

THREAD_PRIORITY_BELOW_NORMAL

THREAD_PRIORITY_LOWEST

THREAD_PRIORITY_IDLE
```

By default, your thread runs at THREAD_PRIORITY_NORMAL. If you set *InitPriority* to zero, the new thread takes the same priority as the calling thread (Navigator's).

Synchronization of Access to Global Data with a Semaphore

The previous section of this chapter, "Multiple Simultaneous Streams," introduced the concept of the semaphore. Windows provides semaphores, as well as the following other synchronization mechanisms:

- Critical sections
- Event objects
- Mutex semaphores

This section uses semaphores to illustrate synchronization.

Make a new semaphore by calling new on the class CSemaphore. The CSemaphore constructor is specified by the following:

Part
III

Ch
13

```
CSemaphore(LONG InitialCount = 1,
          LONG MaxCount = 1,
          LPSTR lpszName = NULL,
          LPSECURITY_ATTRIBUTES Security = NULL);
```

With its default values, CSemaphore behaves like a conventional p-v semaphore. You can control access to a CSemaphore object by using a CSingleLock or CMultiLock object. The constructor for CSingleLock is simple:

```
CSingleLock(CSyncObject* SyncOb, BOOL InitialState = FALSE);
```

Here, *SyncOb* points to a CSyncObject (the parent class of CSemaphore). If *InitialState* is TRUE, the newly constructed CSingleLock object attempts to get a lock on the CSyncObject specified by *SyncOb*.

After you have a CSingleLock, you can use its member functions to control access to the semaphore. Call its methods Lock() and Unlock() to set and clear the semaphore. These functions have prototypes:

```
BOOL CSingleLock::Lock(DWORD dwDelay = INFINITE);
BOOL CSingleLock::Unlock();
```

and

```
BOOL CSingleLock::Unlock(LONG Count, LONG* Previous = NULL);
```

> **CAUTION**
>
> CSemaphore is a kind of CSyncObject. Microsoft provides methods
> CSyncObject::Lock() and CSyncObject::Unlock(), but recommends the use of
> CSingleLock or CMultiLock objects instead. The example in this chapter illustrates the
> use of CSingleLock.

Lock() and Unlock() return TRUE if successful and FALSE if they fail.

dwDelay specifies a time to wait in milliseconds. If the time-out expires, the Lock() function returns a time-out error. For a simple p-v semaphore, only the first version of Unlock() is used.

To restrict access to a resource such as plug-in-global data by using a p-v semaphore, follow these steps:

1. Construct a new semaphore like so:

```
CSemaphore* theSemaphore = new CSemaphore();
```

2. Construct a new `CSingleLock` object that encapsulates the semaphore:

   ```
   CSingleLock* theLock = new CSingleLock(theSemaphore);
   ```

3. Request a lock; block until it is available, as follows:

   ```
   theLock->Lock();
   ```

4. Access the resource;

5. Release the lock, as follows:

   ```
   theLock->Unlock();
   ```

You could put step 1 into `NPP_Initialize()`, and construct a `CSingleLock` object on this class variable in each instance. To use the lock in a method such as `NPP_Write()`, request the lock, access the global data, and release the lock.

Remember to delete the lock in `NPP_Destroy()` and the semaphore in `NPP_Shutdown()`.

Managing Thread Termination Through Events

When Navigator calls `NPP_Destroy()` to shut down your instance, your plug-in must painstakingly notify all threads it has started to stop. Win32 doesn't allow a parent thread to force a child thread to terminate. Rather, you must either wait for the child to exit on its own, or you must notify it that you want it to terminate and wait for it to exit or call `AfxEndThread()`.

This section shows how to use a Boolean flag to notify a thread that it should terminate. This section shows how to use the MFC `CEvent` class to force the parent to wait until the child has terminated. In general, you can use `CEvent` to notify any thread or process that an event has occurred. The constructor for `CEvent` is as follows:

```
CEvent(BOOL InitialState = FALSE,
       BOOL Manual = FALSE,
       LPSTR lpszName = NULL,
       LPSECURITY_ATTRIUBUTES Security = NULL);
```

With its default parameters, the `CEvent` is constructed in such a way that the event hasn't yet occurred, but that when it occurs, it will automatically be reset by the first thread to gain access. These defaults usually are acceptable for plug-ins.

To wait on an event, a thread constructs a `CSingleLock` object, just as was done for semaphores.

To signal an event, a thread calls the CEvent method SetEvent().

A typical sequence that allows the plug-in to do some work asynchronously follows:

1. In NPP_New(), construct a new CEvent that is used to notify the child thread that it's time to terminate. Save the CEvent in this instance's pData so the child thread can reach it.

2. In NPP_New() construct a CSingleLock and save it in the pData.

3. When the new thread is started, have it construct its own CSingleLock on the instance's CEvent.

4. Place a Boolean "kill flag" in the instance's pData, where it can be written by the parent and read by the child thread. Initialize this flag to FALSE in NPP_New().

5. In NPP_Destroy(), set the kill flag to TRUE and attempt to acquire a lock on the CSingleLock. The main thread will block until the event is signaled.

6. Have the main loop of the child thread read the kill flag. If the kill flag is FALSE, the child goes about its business. If the kill flag is TRUE, the child thread cleans up, and then calls SetEvent() on the shared event.

7. When NPP_Destroy() sees the event occur, it acquires the lock and proceeds. Delete all dynamically allocated objects (including the lock) and exit.

Figure 13.10 illustrates this process.

FIG. 13.10
Use a Boolean flag and a CEvent object to coordinate the shutdown of child threads during NPP_Destroy().

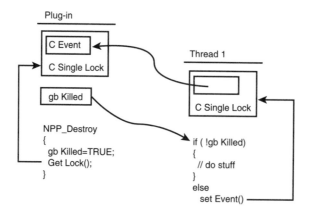

Timers

Occasionally, you may not need the power of a separate thread, but just want a periodic "ping" to trigger your plug-in to perform some chore. In NPP_New() you can set up a timer to send your timer messages. The start a timer, call SetTimer(), which is a member of CWnd. SetTimer() is specified by the following:

```
UINT CWnd::SetTimer(UINT ID,
                    UINT Length,
                    void (CALLBACK EXPORT *TFunc)(HWND, UINT, UINT,
                                                  DWORD));
```

ID specifies a numeric identifier to the timer, so your code can tell which timer is going off. Length is the period of the timer, in milliseconds. When the timer goes off, it calls your callback function, TFunc.

For ease of use, set TFunc to NULL. Then the timer sends WM_TIMER messages to your main window. Subclass the window and put WM_TIMER in your message map to have these messages sent to your plug-in.

The handler for WM_TIMER messages is named OnTimer(), and is specified by the following

```
afx_msg void OnTimer(UINT ID);
```

Windows will pass the ID of the timer in ID; double-check that the ID matches the ID of the timer you set before taking action based on this message.

If you set a timer in NPP_New(), make sure that you turn it off in NPP_Destroy(). The call to disable a timer is as follows:

```
BOOL CWnd::KillTimer(int ID);
```

Here, ID is once again the ID of the timer.

Reentrant Calls

After you allow control to leave your plug-in asynchronously, you are open to reentrant calls from Navigator. Remember that MFC classes are reentrant, but individual objects are not. You should endeavor to store any objects you generate in NPP_New() as part of the pData structure. Anything you generate in NPP_Initialize(), of course, belongs to the plug-in as a whole. You should protect it by a semaphore or a similar synchronization object so that multiple instances can successfully read and write that data.

From Here...

Multitasking is an essential part of modern operating systems such as Windows. You can start a thread to run large background tasks, or to put up a status bar or a progress indicator during file transfers. When you start running multiple instances and multiple threads, you need to think about synchronization and deadlock.

- Review the basics of plug-ins in Chapter 6, "NPP Methods: Starting the Plug-In," Chapter 7, "NPP Methods: Handling Interaction," Chapter 8, "NPP Methods: Other Tasks," and Chapter 9, "Understanding NPN Methods."

- Continue to learn about advanced programming topics and their impact on plug-ins in the next chapter, "If All the World Used Microsoft... ."

- Learn about the limitations and capabilities of Windows 3.x—a system that will be with us for years to come—in Chapter 16, "Spanning the Windows World."

- Chapter 17, "Using Class Libraries and Frameworks," reviews the Microsoft Foundation Classes library, and contrasts it with Borland's OWL and with Symantec's Class Library for the Macintosh.

- Learn about the integration of Java, JavaScript, and plug-ins in Chapter 18, "Plug-Ins as a Programming Resource."

CHAPTER 14

If All the World Used Microsoft...

Microsoft is in an awkward position. Their Microsoft Internet Explorer (MSIE) is the leading competitor to Netscape Navigator. Their Internet product line matches Netscape's product for product, niche for niche.

If Bill Gates had his way, all Internet users would run MSIE on Windows 95, and all Web sites would be on Windows NT servers.

Netscape is working hard to make sure that Mr. Gates doesn't have his way.

Despite this Netscape effort, Microsoft's operating systems *do* have the dominant share of the desktop computer market. More often than not, Navigator is running on a Windows machine.

About OLE 2

Use Microsoft's leading integration technology to fit your plug-in into the larger Microsoft world.

How to use OLE-based clipboard functions

Copy data from your plug-in to the clipboard so the data can be used by other Windows applications.

About OLE-based, drag-and-drop programming

Design your plug-in so that content can be dragged out of Navigator and into other applications.

How to use ODBC to access local databases

Many distributed applications benefit by having a simple database management system (DBMS) on the client machine to supplement a more powerful DBMS on the server.

How ActiveX, Microsoft's answer to plug-ins, can be used in your plug-ins

ActiveX technology is built on Microsoft's OLE controls and provides a ready-made solution to many common programming needs.

The tools and technology that Microsoft made available to help applications pro-grammers are available for plug-in programmers. When the platform is Windows 95 or Windows NT (or, to a lesser extent, Windows 3.11), you can take advantage of Microsoft's advanced technology to add more power to your plug-ins. ∎

It's Not Just Object Linking and Embedding Anymore

In 1991 Microsoft introduced "Object Linking and Embedding" or OLE. OLE 1 was intended to start Microsoft down the road toward *compound documents*.

Simple documents include one form of content. A paint program produces docu-ments with a bitmapped "painting." A word processor's document contains, well, words.

By the late 1980s, it was clear that users wanted more. They wanted to be able to embed a painting into a word-processing document.

Apple introduced this technology way back in 1984 and had added dynamic links with System 7 in 1991. Microsoft wasn't about to let Apple have this technology to itself. OLE 2 is Microsoft's entry into the "compound document" race.

What Are Compound Documents?

A compound document includes objects from other documents in one of two ways. Figure 14.1 illustrates an *embedded* object—the bitmap was cut (or copied) from the paint document and embedded (via pasting) in the word-processing document.

Figure 14.2 shows a *linked* object. Here, the bitmap never moved. A pointer to the bitmap was added to the word-processing document.

FIG. 14.1

An embedded object is actually copied into the document.

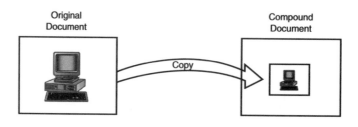

FIG. 14.2
When an object is linked to a document, the document has only a pointer to the original.

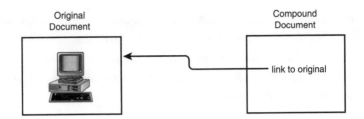

Both approaches have their advantages. If an object is embedded in a document, it cannot get lost. The new document is not dependent on the document that originally held the object.

An embedded object, however, is static. If the original author of the object updates it, the embedded copy is now out-of-date.

For example, suppose that Jane prepares a spreadsheet that shows this quarter's sales projections. John embeds her projections into his presentation to management.

A day before John presents, Jane discovers that the company has won a big account and updates her figures. John makes the presentation to management with outdated numbers and is embarrassed.

If John had linked Jane's spreadsheet rather than embedding it, the presentation would have presented the latest figures automatically. Of course, if Jane had deleted her spreadsheet, John would have had no data at all! There's a downside to everything.

Introducing OLE 2

OLE 1 was not a success. It was slow and difficult to use. Most developers decided that OLE's learning curve was too steep to justify the benefits it offered.

In response to these problems, Microsoft reinvented OLE. OLE 2 is a whole new product, with new capabilities and a faster implementation. The learning curve is still about as steep as with OLE 1, but with end users demanding more functionality, OLE 2 is being accepted more widely than OLE 1. Because OLE 2 is now the standard, we call it simply *OLE* in this chapter.

This section describes the major capabilities offered by OLE in addition to basic object linking and embedding.

Part
III

Ch
14

The Component Object Model   The component object model forms the basis for OLE. This model defines the standard interfaces that every OLE application must have. After these interfaces are in place, the component object model specifies how the applications interact—how they communicate, how they manage memory, and how they load the needed objects.

The component object model defines two types of applications—*containers* and *servers*. Servers provide data and containers use data.

When an OLE container needs to interact with a server, the container first negotiates a common interface. OLE interfaces, illustrated in Figure 14.3, are a way for applications to disclose a table of pointers to their functions.

FIG. 14.3
An OLE interface is a set of functions the container can call in a server.

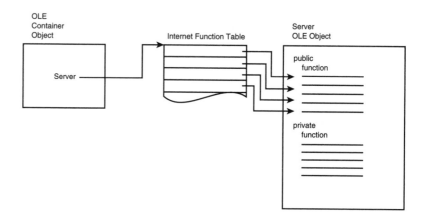

OLE interfaces are conceptually similar to a plug-in's NP_GetEntryPoints(), although the mechanisms are completely different and plug-ins do not use OLE interfaces to communicate with Navigator.

To get the negotiations started, all OLE-compliant applications must use an interface named IUnknown. The container uses the QueryInterface() function of the IUnknown interface to find out what other interfaces are available.

Clipboard Transfers

One of the simplest operations two applications can do together is to share data via the clipboard. Windows doesn't need you to use OLE to use the clipboard, but if you're using OLE anyway, you can make your clipboard transfers OLE-compliant.

When the user of an OLE-compliant application tells the application to paste, the application reviews the contents of the clipboard, examining the various formats available. A spreadsheet, for example, may be available as text (with tabs and returns separating the data), as a bitmap (a screen shot of the window), and as a native format that is understandable by the spreadsheet application.

Frequently, the data itself is not on the clipboard. The clipboard lists the formats and has information about where to get the data for each format.

This technique is known as *delayed rendering* and is conceptually similar to OLE linking. Unlike linking, however, delayed rendering works from a snapshot of the data. The clipboard is "linked" to a static copy of the data in a source data object and not to the live content.

When the application and the clipboard find a compatible format, the application transfers the data and places it into the current document.

To transfer data using the clipboard with OLE, the programmer uses the following objects (illustrated in Figure 14.4).

FIG. 14.4
Transferring data by using the clipboard requires many steps in OLE but adds functionality when the destination is OLE-compliant.

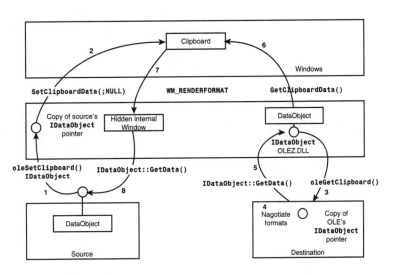

- An `IDataObject` in the source application, set up by the source application programmer. `IDataObject` is one of the OLE interfaces that can be found through `IUnknown`.

■ An enumerator for the list of formats associated with the data, set up by the source application programmer.

■ A hidden window inside OLE2.DLL. The `WindowProc` for this window handles the `WM_RENDERFORMAT` message when the destination application calls `GetClipboardData()` for one of the formats. This window is set up by OLE when your plug-in calls `OleInitialize()`.

■ An `IDataObject` generated and owned by OLE, which gets a copy of the source application's data.

■ The clipboard itself—a piece of global memory maintained by Windows itself.

The sequence for transferring data via the clipboard, using the objects is shown in the following list:

1. When the user of the source application requests a Cut or Copy operation, the source application makes a new data object and format enumerator, and calls `OleSetClipboard()`.

2. OLE itself calls `OpenClipboard`, `IDataObject::AddRef()`, and `IDataObject::EnumFormatEtc()`. For each enumerator format OLE calls `SetClipboardData(formatetc.cfFormat, NULL)`. Specifying `NULL` for the data handle—the second parameter in `SetClipboardData()`—marks the data as available upon request—the heart of delayed rendering.

3. The destination application calls `OleGetClipboard()`. OLE returns a pointer to *OLE's* data object, not the data object in the source application. This mechanism ensures that OLE-compliant applications can always read the clipboard, without worrying about whether the data on the clipboard comes from an OLE-compliant application or a non-OLE-compliant application.

4. When the destination application has a pointer to the `IDataObject`, it can call `IDataObject::EnumFormatEtc()` to get the enumerator that shows which formats are available. If the destination application allows only a small number of formats, it may want to call `IDataObject::QueryGetData()`, which reports whether or not the specified format is available.

5. When the destination application has selected an appropriate format, it enables the Paste menu item. When the user selects Paste, the application calls `IDataObject::GetData()`. When Windows sees this request, it sends a `WM_RENDERFORMAT` message to the hidden window in OLE2.DLL.

The `WindowProc` for this hidden window handles `WM_RENDERFORMAT` by calling `IDataObject::QueryGetData()` to double-check that the format is available. Then it calls `IDataObject::GetData()` to transfer the data.

If you are using Microsoft foundation classes (MFCs), the preceding steps are fully encapsulated by the classes `COleDataSource` (in the source application) and `COleDataObject` (in the destination). The following list shows how to implement Cut and Paste by using MFC.

1. When the user of the source application requests Cut or Copy, the application instantiates a new object of a class you derive from `COleDataSource`.

2. The source application moves data into the `COleDataSource`-derived object by calling `COleDataSource::DelayRenderData()` for each format allowed.

3. In the `OleDataSource`-derived object, override `COleDataSource::OnRenderData()`, providing code that is specific to your data formats.

4. The destination application instantiates a `COleDataObject` and a `FORMATETC` structure.

5. The destination application calls the data object's `AttachClipboard()` member, which associates the data object with the data on the clipboard.

6. If the destination application only allows one or two formats, it can check for its formats by calling the data object's `IsDataAvailable()` method. Otherwise, the application calls the data object's `BeginEnumFormats()`, then repeatedly calls `GetNextFormat()` until it finds the format it wants to use.

   When you request a format, you also can specify how the data will transfer. Your choices are global memory (`HGLOBAL`), a file (`CFile`), or a `STGMEDIUM` structure (`IStorage`).

7. When the application has confirmed that the data on the clipboard is available in a format that it can use, the application enables the Paste menu item.

8. When the user chooses Paste, you transfer the data by using the selected medium. If you opted to transfer through global memory, for example, call `COleDataObject::GetGlobalData()`.

   The data now is in the destination application and can be inserted into the document.

T I P If your plug-in handles many data formats, you may want to provide a Paste Special...
menu item and put up a dialog box listing the available formats so the user can choose
how to paste the data.

Drag-and-Drop Transfers

Drag-and-drop is conceptually similar to cut and paste, although drag-and-drop
doesn't go through the clipboard. If you have used a paste function, you can easily
add a drop function to your plug-in. Figure 14.5 shows the interfaces in drag-and-
drop.

FIG. 14.5
To use drag-and-drop,
the source applica-
tion must allow the
IDataObject and
IDropSource
interfaces, and the
destination must
allow IDropTarget.

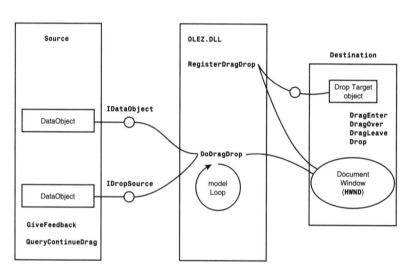

IDropSource has two member functions. You can override either or both of these
functions to use the behavior specific to your plug-in. The functions are

- QueryContinueDrag()—Lists the conditions under which the drag completes
  (and turns into either a drop or a cancellation).

- GiveFeedback()—Sets the cursor to show what will happen if the data is
  dropped at the current location.

The destination application builds an IDropTarget interface and informs OLE that
the interface is available by calling RegisterDragDrop(). If you want your plug-in to
stop being a drag-and-drop target, call RevokeDragDrop() on the same HWND.

IDropTarget has four member functions. To provide feedback and behavior specific to your plug-in, override these functions. The functions are as follows

- DragEnter()—Informs the application that the cursor has entered the window and is dragging data. The application should provide visual feedback of what would happen on a drop.
- DragOver()—Called when the mouse moves or if the keyboard state changes. Use this function to update the feedback if needed.
- DragLeave()—When the cursor has left the window. The destination application cleans up anything that was set up in DragEnter() or DragOver(), such as a special cursor.
- Drop()—Means that the source's IDropSource::QueryContinueDrag() said "drop." The destination application should paste the data into the document and clean up.

 The IDropTarget member functions have a POINTL parameter that gives the current mouse position. This position is reported in screen coordinates. Make sure that you call ScreenToClient() before hit-testing the cursor position.

With these interface objects instantiated and the IDropTarget registered, drag-and-drop can begin. Typically, a drag is initiated when the user positions the cursor over an on-screen representation of some data and left-clicks the mouse. The source application calls the OLE function DoDragDrop(), passing pointers to its IDropSource and IDataObject interfaces.

When OLE gets a DoDragDrop() call, it watches the cursor and calls the destination's IDropTarget::DragEnter() function when the cursor reaches the destination window. DragEnter() is a good place for the destination to negotiate formats.

If no common formats exist, IDropTarget::DragEnter() should set the pdwEffect parameter to DROPEFFECT_NONE, indicating that the destination cannot accept this data. Otherwise, set pdwEffect to DROPEFFECT_COPY, DROPEFFECT_MOVE, DROPEFFECT_LINK, or DROPEFFECT_SCROLL, depending on how your plug-in handles this data.

Part
III

Ch
14

DoDragDrop() calls IDropSource::GiveFeedback(), which changes the cursor to reflect the pwdEffect and gives additional feedback (such as moving an outline of the dragged object).

As the cursor moves around in the destination window, DoDragDrop() repeatedly calls IDropTarget::DragOver(). DragOver() sets pdwEffect just as DragEnter() does. DragOver()also checks its grfKeyState parameter—by convention, if the control key is down, the operation should change from a move to a copy.

DoDragDrop() calls IDropSource::QueryContinueDrag()if the keyboard or mouse state changes. QueryContinueDrag() tells OLE whether or not to drop or terminate. If the user presses the Esc key, the operation is usually terminated. If WM_LBUTTONUP occurs, QueryContinueDrag() typically calls for a drop.

If QueryContinueDrag() calls for a drop, DoDragDrop() calls IDropTarget::Drop(). Your object can call the same code it used for the clipboard operation OnPaste().

DoDragDrop() now returns in the source application. It sets the effect parameter to the last effect in the destination. If the effect is DROPEFFECT_MOVE, the source should cut the selected data from the document.

As with clipboard operations, MFC fully encapsulates the Windows drag-and-drop API with the COleDataSource and COleDataObject classes.

N O T E If you are using your plug-in as a drag-and-drop target, you don't need to instantiate a COleDataObject. OLE makes a COleDataObject and provides a pointer to it in OnDrop(). Copy the data from this object and into your document—OLE owns the data object and will delete it. ■

In-Place Activation

In the early- to mid-1990s, the computer industry began a move from application-centered interfaces to document-centered interfaces. Here's an example of what this means.

At one time, if you had some spreadsheet data and some presentation graphics, you could put them together in a presentation tool by using cut (or copy) and paste. If you needed to change the spreadsheet, data you launched the spreadsheet application, opened the document that contained the data, made the changes, and then copied the data from the spreadsheet application to the presentation tool.

This technique is at the heart of embedded data. Figure 14.6 illustrates this technique.

FIG. 14.6
Embedded objects have to be changed by using the application that produced them.

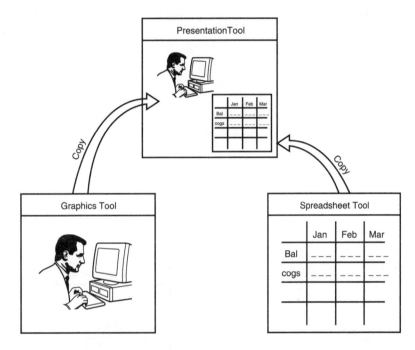

More recently, you could build a link from the presentation tool back to the spreadsheet tool and the graphics tool. If you updated a graphic or the spreadsheet data, the presentation tool changed dynamically to reflect the new content. Figure 14.7 shows how this change works.

With compound documents, the user no longer has to think in terms of spreadsheet applications and graphics tools. To edit data in a compound document, the user just double-clicks on the data, as shown in Figure 14.8.

Figure 14.9 shows an example of a compound document. You can use the tools you probably have on your Windows machine to build a similar document. To make this document, open a paint program such as Paint and draw an image. Now copy the image to WordPad.

Part
III

Ch
14

FIG. 14.7
Linked objects are updated dynamically but still must be changed by using the application that produces them.

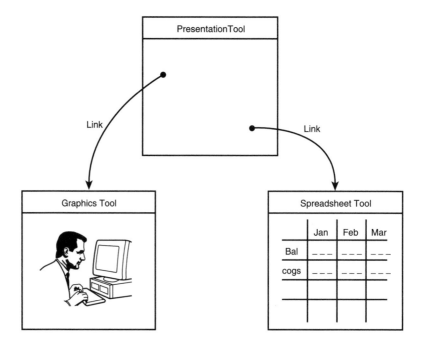

FIG. 14.8
With in-place activation, the user focuses on the document, not on the application.

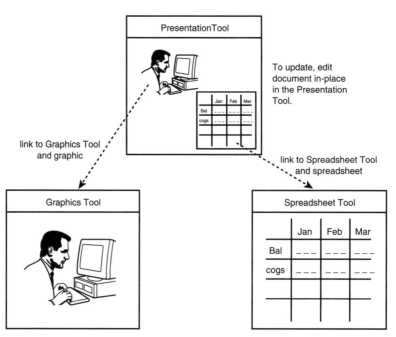

FIG. 14.9
Drag or copy an object into an OLE-compliant application such as WordPad to produce a new compound document.

You can continue putting objects into the compound document. If you need to edit one of the objects, just double-click it. The native application opens the object in place. To return to the document view, click anywhere outside the object's window.

> **CAUTION**
>
> If you choose to include nonnative objects in your plug-in content, remember that not everyone has the same set of applications. If you embed a Microsoft Word document in your plug-in window, a user who uses WordPerfect cannot open the Word object.

OLE Automation

One sophisticated aspect of OLE programming is *OLE automation*. Using OLE automation, one application can take control of another application's objects. To understand why automation is useful, look at the UNIX operating system.

Why Is Automation Useful?   By today's standards, UNIX is an arcane operating system with an obsolete user interface. It also is wildly successful, particularly with technically sophisticated users.

Part
III

Ch
14

One big reason for this success is UNIX's philosophy: build a lot of small tools, and make sure that each tool does a few related jobs really well. Then, make it easy to connect these tools together to build a sophisticated application.

Modern graphical user interfaces are a boon to users, but they were never intended for the kind of "hook-it-all-together" tool-crafting popular with UNIX. UNIX has command interpreters known as *shells* to integrate its tools. The Macintosh has AppleScript and Apple Events. Windows has… OLE.

Calling an Automated Object from Your Plug-In   The OLE automation capabilities are not an integral part of OLE. Rather, these capabilities form a separate technology that you can use or ignore, depending on your plug-in's needs.

Suppose that you work on an intranet and you know that many users in your company have the spreadsheet application, Microsoft Excel. If you want to display financial data from the Net, you can write a plug-in that reads in the data, calls Excel, loads a spreadsheet with a specific set of formulas, and then reads back the results and reports it (or even graphs it) in your window.

Automation objects expose a set of commands and functions by using the OLE interface mechanism. Typically, these functions resemble user-level commands such as File, Open or Format, Character.

Applications (or plug-ins) that call other applications are known as *automation clients*. OLE uses the following two kinds of automation clients:

- If you know which application(s) you want your client to use and you know the properties and operations that server uses, you can compile this information into your client statically.

- If you want to give the user more flexibility, you can program your client to find information about the server at runtime, and build a list of properties and operations dynamically.

Statically bound clients can use the MFC class `COleDispatchDriver`, which encapsulates the `IDispatch` interface.

T I P   If you use Microsoft's Visual C++ development environment, use the ClassWizard to set up `COleDispatchDriver` for you.

To set up a COleDispatchDriver using ClassWizard, follow this procedure:

1. Open the ClassWizard and click the Add Class button.
2. Choose From an OLE TypeLib, as shown in Figure 14.10.
3. Select the server application's .TLB file (which contains the type library).
4. Click the OK button, then edit the file names in the Confirm Classes dialog and click OK.

FIG. 14.10
If you use Microsoft Visual C++, you can use ClassWizard to build a COleDispatch Driver-derived class from another application's type library.

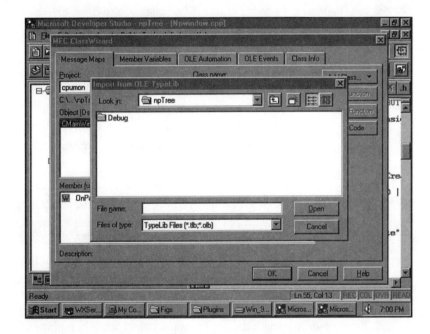

ClassWizard builds a dispatch class that serves as a proxy for the real application. Your application binds statically to the dispatch class. At runtime, when your application calls the functions in the proxy class, OLE forwards these requests to the server application.

Dynamically bound clients can call the IDispatch interface directly.

NOTE OLE automation servers can expose their properties and functions through IDispatch, through the *virtual function table* (VTBL) interface, or both. Microsoft strongly recommends that server programmers use both IDispatch and the VTBL interface, which means that if your client queries a server's IUnknown interface looking for an IDispatch interface, your client probably will find one. ■

Part
III

Ch
14

If you want your plug-in to bind to functions dynamically, call the server's
IUnknown::QueryInterface() method to get the server's IDispatch interface. Then
call IDispatch::GetIDsOfNames(). GetIDsOfNames() returns an array of Dispatch
IDs (DISPIDs) that match the names you pass in. Use the DISPID with the
IDispatch::Invoke() function to call the server's function.

TIP   Dynamic binding, also known as *late binding*, takes two calls to IDispatch:
GetIDsOfNames() and Invoke(). Static binding, also called *ID binding*, takes only one
runtime call. In general, static binding may double the performance of the interface. If you
can statically bind to the application, you should do so.

Allowing Your Plug-In to Be Called   In some applications you may want to write a
standalone application (or use a macro language in an existing application) that
looks for Navigator and takes control of your plug-in. Applications that expose a list
of commands and functions for use by automation clients are *automation servers*.

TIP   If your plug-in can be called as an automation server, you can save a sequence of
function calls into a local file and play it back as a macro. You also can store these kinds
of files on a remote server and have your plug-in read them as a remote command file.

Setting up an automation server is more complex than building an automation
client, but ClassWizard can help.

Your top-level exposed object is the Application object. Have a few high-level functions associated with the Application object, and then place other commands below Application in the hierarchy. Figure 14.11 shows a portion of the hierarchy for
Microsoft Excel.

Note that Excel and most other automation servers provide a way for the client to
make a new, blank document or to open a document from a file. You probably don't
want to accept these kinds of requests in your plug-in.

Rather, you may want to build your interface around something such as Excel's
ActiveSheet function, which gives the client access to the current active document. Remember to deal with the reality that the HTML coder may have more
than one copy of your plug-in instantiated. You need to decide whether a client can
call up any of several instances or whether all clients connect to a specific window.

FIG. 14.11
Starting from the
`Application`
object at the root,
Microsoft exposes a
range of properties
and functions.

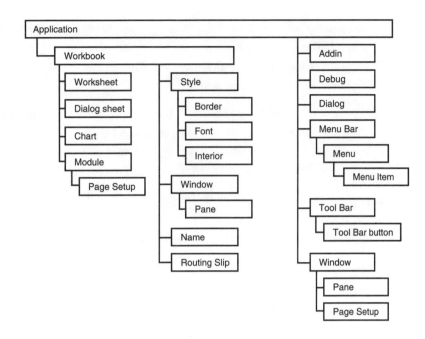

 TIP If you make your plug-in an OLE automation server, provide a type library so that client programmers can easily access your functions. To make a type library, write a description of your object in the Object Description Language (ODL), and then run the ODL file through Microsoft's MkTypLib tool.

ODL and the MkTypLib are described in the Win32 SDK, available as part of Microsoft's InfoView CD-ROM that comes with their compilers.

TIP You can expose your interface either through the IDispatch interface class, or through the VTBL, or both. Microsoft strongly recommends that you use both.

If you provide both interfaces (and a type library), client programmers who want to link to your server statically can do so through the type library and the VTBL. Programmers who prefer dynamic linking usually prefer the IDispatch interface.

During your plug-in's initialization, you should register the active object with OLE. This step allows an OLE client to find the object.

Part
III

Ch
14

You usually will want to use the `CLSCTX_LOCAL_SERVER` and `REGCLS_SINGLEUSE` constants in the registration routines. The first constant says that the client runs in a separate process space from the server. The second constant says that the server supports only one client at a time.

If your plug-in will be used in more than one instance in a single copy of Navigator (for example, with two `<EMBED>` tags on the same page), think carefully about how you register the active object. Usually, you want only one copy of the plug-in so no ambiguity arises about which window to use to display the results requested.

As your plug-in shuts down, make sure that you call `CoRevokeClassObject()` and `RevokeActiveObject()` to cancel connections from clients. Finally, call `OleUninitialize()` to free up resources allocated by OLE.

N O T E   Windows uses the system registration database to track all the OLE objects in the system. When a client informs OLE that it is looking for a server, OLE looks in this database to learn if the server is available.

As a plug-in, your server is available only when the user has Navigator running and has a page open that loads your plug-in. You may decide that you don't want your plug-in permanently listed in the registration database.

Instead, you can register your plug-in during `NPP_Initialization()` and remove it from the registry (with `RegDeleteKey()`) during `NPP_Shutdown()`. ▨

N O T E   Using a plug-in as an OLE automation server creates the possibility that Navigator might shut down your plug-in (if, for example, the user changes to a new Web page) while an automation client is using the plug-in. As a minimum you may want to include a call to `MessageBox()` in `NPP_Shutdown()` that warns the user that the plug-in is no longer available.

A more robust design might include using a separate server process statically linked to the client, (see Figure 14.12.). With this design, a client can start up the server, which then checks to see if the plug-in is available. If it is not, the server refuses the request.

As long as the plug-in is active, the server forwards requests from the client to the plug-in. When the plug-in exits—on `NPP_Shutdown()`—it informs the server.

The server continues to run after the plug-in exits (and continues to run until the last client detaches from it). If a client makes a request, the server can again refuse the request, based on the fact that the plug-in isn't open in Navigator. ▨

FIG. 14.12
One way to ensure that the server doesn't disappear from under the client is to use a stand-alone server that provides reliable communications with the plug-in.

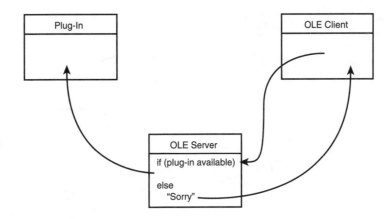

Integration the Microsoft Way

So far, this chapter concentrates on OLE as Microsoft's leading way to exchange data between applications. Not all of Microsoft's technology, however, revolves around OLE.

If your plug-in needs to read or write data to a database, you should look into open database connectivity (ODBC). ODBC enables you to access data managed by database management systems (DBMSs) that are running on the local PC or on servers around the network.

Figure 14.13 illustrates several possible ODBC-plug-in configurations.

N O T E ODBC is based on the *client/server* architecture. Typically, this architecture has a database on a central machine, with desktop computers running clients. You also can use ODBC with PC databases such as Access, Paradox, and dBase, with both client and server running on the same machine. ■

Using ODBC

The first step to access a database through ODBC is to set up the data sources. Use the ODBC Administrator program (available with many Microsoft products, including Visual C++ and Visual FoxPro) to specify the data source and the ODBC driver. Figure 14.14 shows ODBC Administrator in action.

Part
III

Ch
14

FIG. 14.13
ODBC can access
data on the local
machine or over
the network.

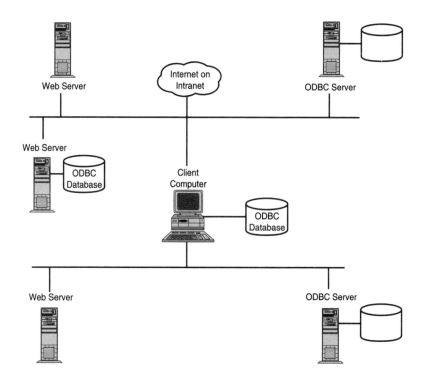

FIG. 14.14
Use the ODBC
Administrator pro-
gram to configure the
data source.

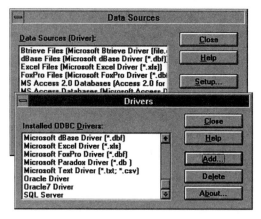

If you want your plug-in to query a database through ODBC, follow these steps:

1. Connect to a data source.
2. Select the records (and do something with them).
3. Shut down the connection.

Your code size will be smaller and your plug-in more understandable if you use the MFC classes that encapsulate ODBC. This section shows how to access ODBC from a plug-in by using MFC.

CAUTION

If you use MFC with ODBC on a Win32 platform such as Windows 95, the client machine must have a 32-bit ODBC driver. Visual C++ comes with ODBC drivers for

- SQL Server
- Microsoft Access
- Microsoft FoxPro
- Microsoft Excel
- dBASE
- Paradox
- Text files

Microsoft has other drivers available. Contact Microsoft customer service at **1-800-426-9400** and ask about the ODBC driver pack. Outside the U.S. you need to contact your local Microsoft subsidiary.

Connecting to a Data Source   Data source connections are managed by the MFC class `CDatabase`. Instantiate a new `CDatabase` object and call `CDatabase::Open()` to establish the connection.

If you don't give enough information in your program to make the call, the ODBC driver opens a dialog box and prompts the user. `Open()` expects the `lpszConnect` parameter to have all the information the server needs, including a user ID and password.

If you prefer not to store the password in the program, you can allow the driver to prompt the user at runtime. You also may decide that *you* want to handle the interaction—just open a dialog box before calling `Open()` and get the information you need from the user.

TIP For many plug-ins, you will want to have one connection shared across all instances. This approach is efficient and, if the DBMS is licensed by the number of simultaneous connections, cost-effective.

To share one connection across all instances, make the connection in `NPP_Initialize()` and store the `CDatabase` object as a class variable of the class that you attach to `Instance->pData`. Remember to shut down the connection and delete the object in `NPP_Shutdown()`.

CAUTION

`CDatabase::Open()` can throw two kinds of exceptions: `CDBException` and `CMemoryException`. Make sure that you catch these errors in the same function that calls `Open()` so your plug-in doesn't crash.

`CDBException` is thrown if the requested connection is unavailable, or if it times out. Check the `m_nRetCode` for the exact reason for the failure.

`CMemoryException` is thrown when the application is out of memory. (For more information about exceptions, see Chapter 2, "A C++ Primer.")

If you decide to associate different connections with different URLs, you may want to store `Open()`'s `lpszConnect` parameter in `NPSavedData`. Get the string by calling `CDatabase::GetConnect()`. If it remembers the string between calls, the plug-in doesn't have to prompt the user for connection information each time it is instantiated on the same URL.

Selecting Records   The principal language used when communicating with databases is SQL (pronounced "see-quel"), the Structured Query Language. SQL queries return a collection of records—each record has columns specified by the database's schema.

As an ODBC programmer, you must derive a plug-in-specific class from `CRecordSet`. Your `CRecordSet`-derived class specifies a data source, a SQL table, and the columns of this table.

TIP In Microsoft Visual C++, you can use AppWizard or ClassWizard to set up your `CRecordSet`-derived class. Figure 14.15 shows AppWizard in the process of setting up an application with database support.

To use ClassWizard to set up a CRecordSet-derived class, click the Add Class button in ClassWizard and specify CRecordSet as the base class. Figure 14.16 shows the resulting dialog.

You specify the CRecordSet-derived class to have a data member that corresponds to every column in the query. As you move through the recordset, the contents of the recordset fields are updated to reflect the "current record."

Make sure that you check IsBOF() or IsEOF() before moving forward or backward respectively. These functions let you check to make sure that more data is available at each end of the recordset.

When developing ODBC classes for use with plug-ins, ClassWizard is more convenient than AppWizard. Both Wizards produce similar results but AppWizard adds database support only to new MFC applications, not to DLLs, so you have to copy the database-related classes to your plug-in or change the application to a DLL after it is built.

FIG. 14.15
Use AppWizard to build database support into an MFC application.

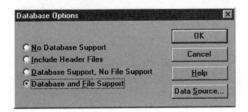

After your plug-in has a CRecordSet, it can call (or customize) any of this class's members. Some of the more important members include the following:

- Open()—Retrieves the first record of the data specified by the current recordset definition.
- m_strFilter—Has a SQL WHERE clause to filter the data.
- AddNew() and Update()—Together, provide the mechanism for adding a new record.
- Edit() and Update()—Together, change the contents of a record.
- Delete()—Removes a record.
- Move(), MoveFirst(), MoveLast(), MoveNext(), and MovePrev()—Collectively, serve to select a new current record.
- IsBOF() and IsEOF()—Together, tell the programmer if the current record is at the beginning or end of the table.

Part
III

Ch
14

- ■ `OnWaitForDataSource()`—Yields processing time to other applications.

- ■ `Close()`—closes the record set and deallocates the supporting memory. Call `Close()` before deleting a dynamically allocated `CRecordSet`.

FIG. 14.16

ClassWizard can add a new CRecordSet-derived class to an existing application or plug-in.

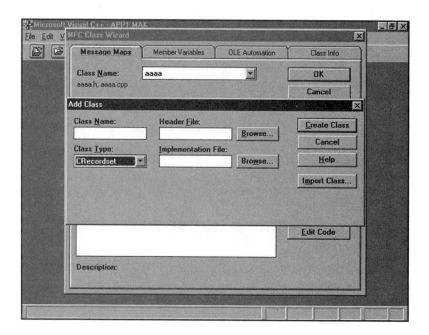

N O T E   When you use AppWizard or ClassWizard to set up a record set, Visual C++ includes code to use the record field exchange (RFX). RFX simplifies the transfer of data between the data source and your record set. ■

In a plug-in, you may want to read the data out of the record set and display it in your window. Alternatively, you may decide to put up a form by using MFC's `CRecordView` class. You use a dialog editor to design the form. If you use Microsoft Visual C++, you can use the `ClassWizard` to derive a class from `CRecordView`.

ClassWizard uses dialog data exchange (DDX) in the recordview. DDX is Windows' standard mechanism for mapping fields in a dialog to variables in the program. You also can use `ClassWizard` to associate buttons with the various `Move...` members to easily click forward or backward through the data.

Shutting Down the Connection   After you are done with the database—for example, in `NPP_Destroy()` or `NPP_Shutdown()`—complete all calls to `AddNew()` or

Edit() that were not yet applied and commit all open transactions (if your DBMS allows transactions). Then close and delete any record sets. Finally, close the connection and delete the CDatabase object.

Custom Controls with Active X

Part of the promise of object-oriented programming is that much of what you do as a programmer isn't original. If one programmer has written a good component, other programmers may be able to reuse it.

One of the best examples of the success of this approach is in *OLE controls*. Until they were subsumed by *ActiveX* controls, OLE controls (also referred to as *.OCXx*) were among the most popular code resources on the Net.

OLE controls were reusable software components with broad applicability. They were implemented by using OLE control classes, including the following:

- CConnectionPoint—An implementation of a simple outgoing interfaces, useful for sending event notifications.
- CFontHolder—An encapsulation of the OLE IFont interface and related font objects.
- CPictureHolder—A class to manage picture properties.
- COleControl—The principal base class of OLE controls.
- COleControlModule—A class that corresponds with CWinApp in an application. Each module uses one or more controls.
- COlePropertyPage—Used to put up a graphical interface that shows the properties of the control.
- CPropExchange—A class that makes it easy to save a control's properties to the disk and retrieve them again.

ON THE WEB

Although you can still build OLE controls, the latest version of the technology is ActiveX, described on-line at **http://www.microsoft.com/activex/activex-contents1.htm**. ActiveX is a set of technologies that extend OLE controls to the Internet.

Chapter 15, "ActiveX and Plug-Ins in Other Browsers," explores ActiveX technology in more detail.

What about OpenDoc?

The introduction to this chapter makes the point that if Bill Gates has his way, all the world will use Microsoft products.

For better or for worse, all the world does *not* use Microsoft products—at least not exclusively. The biggest competitor to OLE is an open technology sponsored by IBM, Apple, and Adobe (among others) called *OpenDoc*. These organizations formed Component Integrations Laboratories (CI Labs) to advance component technology.

Not only is OpenDoc different, some reviewers consider it *better*. The industry journal *InfoWorld* in their January 29, 1996, edition named its Best of 1995 and awarded OpenDoc the Landmark Technology Award.

They write, "OpenDoc has become easily the more flexible, powerful, extensible, and forward-looking object model when compared with its closest business competitor, Microsoft Corp.'s OLE."

OpenDoc works seamlessly with OLE in that OLE objects can be served from OpenDoc servers, and OpenDoc containers can retrieve objects from OLE servers.

ON THE WEB

Download **ftp://opendoc.apple.com/opendoc/docs/ODinfo/OD-OLE.pdf** or visit **http://web.xplain.com/mactech.com/Articles/Vol.10/10.08/OpenDoc-vs-OLE/ text.html** for a comparison between OLE and OpenDoc. You can get IBM's implementation of OpenDoc for Windows 95 and Windows NT at **http://www.software.ibm.com/ clubopendoc/**.

The Macintosh version is available at **http://www.opendoc.apple.com/users/ getod.html**. CI Labs is working with UNIX vendors to develop implementations of OpenDoc on UNIX. (IBM is already shipping an implementation for their UNIX operating system, AIX.)

OpenDoc is standard in the latest versions of the Mac OS and is endorsed by both Netscape and Sun (ensuring compatibility with the plug-in shell and with Java applets). Apple developed a set of OpenDoc components, collectively known as

CyberDog, to extend Internet capabilities into OpenDoc-compatible applications, such as ClarisWorks.

This design means that a user working on a ClarisWorks document can seamlessly access the Web, pull down some information, and embed it or link it into the ClarisWorks document.

ON THE WEB

At least one article (**http://www.macweek.com/mw_1027/opinion_otr.html**) reports that Navigator 4.0 will be built by using OpenDoc (making it compatible with OLE as well). If this report proves correct, Navigator plug-ins based on OpenDoc may be a more natural fit and offer higher functionality than plug-ins based on OLE.

At least one reviewer gives OpenDoc higher marks than OLE for the quality of user interface. (Not a surprise, considering the role Apple played in developing OpenDoc.)

MacWeek also reported (at **http://www.macweek.com/mw_1026/news_nav4.html**) that Navigator 4.0 for the Mac may be bundled with CyberDog by Apple.

If you develop plug-ins principally for Windows, you can choose between OLE and OpenDoc. If you develop plug-ins for all major platforms, evaluate OpenDoc to see if your cross-platform workload will be less by developing in OpenDoc.

From Here...

"If all the world used Microsoft...," you could write plug-ins exclusively for Windows and use OLE to integrate the plug-in with the rest of the software on the desktop computer. Everyone could access local or remote databases with ODBC. Rather than plug-ins, we would be writing ActiveX controls.

Of course, if all the world used Microsoft, you'd be writing for Microsoft Internet Explorer instead of Netscape Navigator, but this subject is for the next chapter.

- Learn about Microsoft's approach to plug-ins in the next chapter, "ActiveX and Plug-Ins in Other Browsers."
- Review the basics of plug-ins in Chapter 6, "NPP Methods: Starting the Plug-In," Chapter 7, "NPP Methods: Handling Interaction," Chapter 8, "NPP Methods: Other Tasks," and Chapter 9, "Understanding NPN Methods."

Part
III

Ch
14

■ Learn about the limitations and capabilities of Windows 3.x—a system that will be with us for years to come—in Chapter 16, "Spanning the Windows World."

■ Chapter 17, "Using Class Libraries and Frameworks," reviews the MFCs library, and contrasts it with Borland's OWL and with Symantec's Class Library for the Macintosh.

■ Learn about the integration of Java, JavaScript, and plug-ins in Chapter 18, "Plug-Ins as a Programming Resource."

CHAPTER 15

ActiveX and Plug-Ins in Other Browsers

If you want to present a nonnative MIME media type to a user with a Web browser, you have three choices: use a Navigator plug-in, use ActiveX technology with Microsoft Internet Explorer (or, to some extent, NCSA Mosaic), or use a helper application (with nearly any browser).

Helper applications are described in Chapter 1, "Bridging the Gap from CGI and Helper Applications to Netscape Plug-Ins." This chapter explores Microsoft's alternative to Navigator plug-ins—not just ActiveX but the whole integrated solution, including JScript, VBScript, and ISAPI.

Of course, Netscape also has an integrated solution, which it calls *LiveConnect*. You can read about the topic of LiveConnect in Chapter 18, "Plug-Ins as a Programming Resource." ■

About ActiveX controls

These interactive objects can download faster than a plug-in, and can make your site interactive.

How ActiveX documents compare with Navigator plug-ins

Microsoft uses ActiveX documents to give Web users access to non-native MIME types, such as Microsoft Excel or Word files.

How ActiveX scripting compares with LiveConnect

Microsoft enables you to integrate the behavior of ActiveX controls and Java applets from the client or the server.

How Microsoft's VBScript and JScript compare to mainstream solutions such as CGI scripts in Perl

Given their deep pockets, Microsoft's solutions *may soon be* the mainstream solutions.

About the ActiveX server framework

Microsoft has integrated Web server functions in a way that is like Netscape's second-generation servers and LiveWire.

ActiveX Controls

Chapter 14, "If All the World Used Microsoft…," observes that Microsoft has been developing component solutions with OLE (Object Linking and Embedding) technology since 1991. When the World Wide Web ballooned in 1995, Microsoft was out of position—concentrating on a proprietary Microsoft network that would have competed with CompuServe and Prodigy.

To their credit, Microsoft bounced back quickly with a Web browser that rivals Navigator, a credible Web server, and a set of tools for authoring sophisticated, high-quality pages.

In 1996 Netscape led a revolution away from purely static HTML pages. Netscape introduced JavaScript, a scripting language for client browsers. Then they introduced server-side JavaScript, a key component of LiveWire.

LiveWire offers an integrated environment for developing Web applications, which combine static HTML with server-side JavaScript and even offer access to relational databases (in LiveWire Pro). Table 15.1 shows corresponding Netscape and Microsoft technologies. Microsoft is offering products in nearly every Internet niche.

Table 15.1   Microsoft Products for Internet Niches

Category	Netscape Product	Microsoft Product
Web Browser	Navigator	Microsoft Internet Explorer
Web Server	Fast Track, Enterprise	Internet Information Server
Other Servers	Many	None
Application Tool	LiveWire	VBScript, FrontPage
Client Extensions	Plug-Ins, Java, JavaScript	ActiveX, Java, VBScript, Jscript

Microsoft has met Netscape product for product. Although the jury is still out regarding which company will win the Internet market (or whether there will be any winner), clearly Netscape has only one serious competitor.

One way Microsoft was able to get into position so quickly was by changing some of their existing technology. Recall that Chapter 14, "If All the World Used Microsoft…," introduces OLE technology. One member of the OLE family is the OLE control (often referred to as *OCXs*, after the name of their file extension).

OLE controls are reusable components such as hierarchical listers or file viewers that can be controlled by a container object. Many Microsoft development environments, including Visual Basic, Visual FoxPro, and Visual C++ allow a programmer or even a sophisticated end-user to build containers and embed OLE controls.

ActiveX controls are a Web-based solution that use OLE controls. The easiest way to write OLE controls is to use Microsoft foundation classes (MFC). Likewise, ActiveX controls benefit if they are written using MFC.

The downside is that such ActiveX controls work only if they are installed on a machine with the MFC library. The MFC library is an encapsulation of the Windows API, but Microsoft offers a cross-platform version of the library that works on the Macintosh.

Microsoft also has licensed MFC and the Win32 interface to Mainsoft and Bristol Software. These companies are reportedly working on a version of MFC for UNIX. Note that the MFC library isn't installed on all Windows machines—a user must download the MFC library once before any of the MFC-based ActiveX controls will work.

N O T E Microsoft has announced their commitment to making ActiveX run on all major platforms. They are working with Metroworks (a leading tool vendor for Macintosh), and Bristol and Mainsoft (leading UNIX developers) to port ActiveX to these platforms.

Some industry observers speculate that Microsoft might use Java as a language for writing ActiveX controls. Because Java is platform-independent, such controls would run on the Mac or a UNIX machine.

The drawback is that programmers write plug-ins precisely because they need to reach native calls to the operating system. Java programmers are isolated from the OS. The *Java Virtual Machine* offers only a fraction of the API of Win32 or the Macintosh Toolbox. ■

One advantage ActiveX controls have over Navigator plug-ins is that Microsoft has a track record by which controls vendors get paid for their work, while most plug-ins are distributed for free. While it's not yet clear that this business model can be extended to the Internet, if Microsoft is successful they will provide a powerful incentive for software developers to write for the ActiveX market rather than for Navigator.

Another advantage ActiveX offers is that the ActiveX controls are true OLE controls—they can be used with many containers, not just Microsoft Internet Explorer (MSIE). You can use an ActiveX control to embed a new MIME media type in Microsoft PowerPoint or Microsoft Word, just as you do in MSIE. Therefore, there is a large market for ActiveX controls, even if MSIE never gets the same market share as Navigator.

Critics point out that ActiveX is a proprietary technology and is focused on Windows (even if Microsoft is ultimately successful in porting ActiveX to other platforms). Microsoft countered that ActiveX began its life as an industry standard, with input from thousands of developers. Microsoft also announced that they will transition ActiveX to a new industry standards body in the near future.

ON THE WEB

To get a quick feel for ActiveX controls while staying in Navigator, download the ActiveX plug-in from Ncompass Labs. The Windows plug-in, available at **http://www.ncompasslabs.com/binaries/download_plugin.htm**, allows Navigator to use ActiveX controls.

Installing ActiveX Controls

For HTML authors, Navigator plug-ins are almost transparent. The author specifies content to download (in an <EMBED> tag) or link to (for a full-page plug-in) and Navigator takes care of loading the plug-in at the right time.

ActiveX controls are more akin to Java applets than Navigator plug-ins. Unlike their counterpart, ActiveX documents, controls aren't associated with a MIME media type. To put a control on a page, the HTML author uses the <OBJECT> tag as shown in Listing 15.1 (found on this book's companion disk, in the \source\Chap 15 directory):

Listing 15.1 *objecttg.htm*—Using the *<OBJECT>* Tag to Install an ActiveX Control

```
<HTML>
<HEAD>
<TITLE>Demo of an ActiveX Installation</TITLE>
<SCRIPT LANGUAGE="VBScript">
Sub HelloWorld_Click(ByVal x)
  Select Case x
    Case 1
      MsgBox "Hello, World!"
    Case 2
      MsgBox "2nd menu item"
  End Select
End Sub
Sub theButton_OnClick
  call HelloWorld.PopUP
EndSub
</HEAD>
<BODY>
<H1>Popup Menu</H1>
<OBJECT id=HelloWorld CODEBASE="http://www.microsoft.com/workshop/
➥iemenu.ocx#Version=4,70,0,1086"
classid="clsid:7823A620-9DD9-11CF-A662-00AA00C066D2">
<param NAME="Menuitem[0]" value="Say 'Hello'">
<param NAME="Menuitem[1]" value="2nd menu item">
</OBJECT>
<FORM>
<INPUT TYPE="button" NAME="theButton" VALUE="Click Here" ALIGH=RIGHT>
</FORM>
</BODY>
</HTML>
```

Note that the <OBJECT> tag includes an assigned ID, the URL where the control is stored on the Web, and the class ID (CLSID) for the system registry. Note also that, whereas JavaScript and VBScript benefit by being inserted in the <HEAD> section, the <OBJECT> belongs in the <BODY>.

Note, too, the CODEBASE attribute, which tells MSIE where to find the control. Before going to the Net, MSIE first checks its cache—if it finds the control already on the hard drive, it skips the download.

If MSIE needs to download the control, it first alerts the user and asks for permission to download. If permission is granted, the control is copied from the Net to the user's hard drive.

Some users are hesitant to accept software downloaded from the Net, fearing that it may have a virus. Microsoft uses *code signing*—when the control is downloaded, the user can check the electronic signature to verify the software vendor and to confirm that the copy that was downloaded has not been changed since it was signed. Microsoft hopes that these mechanisms will give most users the confidence to accept downloaded controls.

> **CAUTION**
>
> When you build ActiveX controls, be sure to set the version correctly. MSIE uses this version information to decide whether or not to download a new copy.

 T I P If you want to get a feel for ActiveX controls without programming your own, download MSIE 3.0 or later. MSIE 3.0 comes with a few simple controls, including Chart, Label, New Item, Preloader, and Timer.

 ON THE WEB

The ActiveX Gallery, online at **http://www.microsoft.com/activex/gallery/default.htm**, contains detailed descriptions and <OBJECT> and <param> syntax for each control.

In developing plug-ins, Netscape has striven to support all three major platforms: Windows, Macintosh, and UNIX. Although plug-ins are written in native code, the best plug-ins make few assumptions about the destination machine. (For example, plug-in developers are encouraged to statically link the MFC library to make sure that it is available on the client computer.)

In Navigator 3.0, the end-user works with Navigator to download the plug-in. Navigator 4.0 uses auto-downloading but only if the plug-in developer, the HTML author, and the end-user cooperate.

Netscape's non-plug-in technologies, Java, client-side JavaScript, and server-side JavaScript, are careful not to write to the client's hard drive. Therefore, a page with 4K of client-side JavaScript downloads this script each time the page is requested (unless, of course, the page is already in the cache).

By contrast, ActiveX controls are automatically downloaded and install themselves on the hard drive by default. If a user downloads a page that includes an ActiveX control, the browser first checks to see if that control is already available on the local disk.

If so, the browser skips the download and immediately invokes the local copy. This technique dramatically decreases the time needed to start the interactive page.

Moreover, when the ActiveX control is dynamically linked to MFC, it's smaller than a plug-in with a statically linked copy of MFC. By encouraging programmers to assume that MFC is available on the destination machine, Microsoft makes the average size of an ActiveX control smaller than a comparable plug-in.

N O T E   Statically linking the MFC library to a DLL or control can swell the size of the file anywhere from 50K to 1M, depending on which pieces of the MFC are used. At 14.4Kbps, a 1M file takes about 10 minutes to download. If your controls and plug-ins link MFC dynamically, this penalty is paid only once on each user's machine.

If you choose to link MFC statically, edit your MFC precompiled header, stdafx.h, so that you only use the pieces of MFC that you really need. Define VC_EXTRALEAN to get the preprocessor to drop some seldom-used classes. ▪

T I P   When you build an ActiveX control, you can choose whether or not to include runtime licensing. If you include the licensing classes, a copy of the control can be set to have either a *developers license* or a *runtime license*.

A developer's license allows you to place the control in a tool or on a Web page. When visitors to your site download your page, they also download a copy of the ActiveX control.

The copy only has a runtime license. With a runtime license, visitors can use the control on their hard disk but cannot put it into a tool or copy it to their own Web page.

If you want to be paid by people who use your ActiveX control on their Web site, turn on the licensing feature.

Native Support for Network Protocols

Microsoft has built Internet protocols such as TCP/IP, PPP, and FTP directly into the newer releases of the Windows operating system (for example, Windows 95,

Windows NT 3.51, and Windows NT 4.0). They call the new interfaces Win32 Internet or WinInet for short.

These new interfaces mean that native applications such as plug-ins and ActiveX controls can call Win32 APIs to access the Net. This capability is of less importance to plug-in authors, who can get this functionality from Navigator.

But to ActiveX authors whose components may run in a non-MSIE container, these enhancements are crucial. For applications programmers, the new interfaces offer a way to get their applications "on the Net" without writing plug-ins and using the functionality of the browser.

The "Active" in ActiveX

Most Web pages consist of files of HTML tags and attributes. Regardless of when the file is downloaded or by whom, the file is the same and the resulting Web page looks the same.

Navigator users can embed client-side JavaScript on the page to give it dynamic behavior. They also can download Java applets or use server-side techniques, such as CGI scripts and server-side JavaScript.

Developers targeting the MSIE browser can use VBScript rather than JavaScript to put client-side interaction on the page. VBScript is the scripting edition of Visual Basic. The language is a slimmed-down Visual Basic version and is upwardly compatible with that language. VBScript is included with Internet Explorer 3.0.

How to Write an ActiveX Control

An upcoming version of Visual Basic allows the developer to write ActiveX controls. Meanwhile, however, a developer can write an ActiveX control in one of three ways:

- Use the OLE Control development facilities in Visual C++
- Use the ActiveX SDK as an example
- Use the ActiveX Template Library (ATL)

Each of these options is explored in the next three sections.

Visual C++   Chapter 14, "If All the World Used Microsoft...," describes OLE controls. A Visual C++ programmer can use MFC and the OLE control development facilities to build an ActiveX control.

Visual C++ AppWizard supports an OLE ControlWizard that builds a basic control in just two steps, as shown in Figure 15.1. make sure that you link the control with MFC dynamically to avoid the download time associated with MFC.

FIG. 15.1
Use the Visual C++
OLE ControlWizard to
quickly set up an OLE
control.

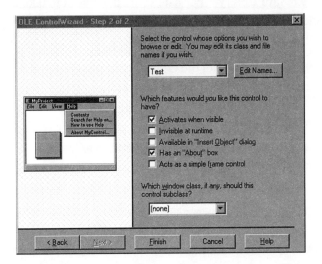

ActiveX SDK   You can find the ActiveX SDK online. In this kit, Microsoft includes a sample named BaseCtl, which includes FrameWrk, ToDoSvr, and WebImage examples. You can use these examples as a basis for writing your own plug-in.

ON THE WEB

You can fine the ActiveX SDK online at **http://www.microsoft.com/intdev/sdk/**.

CAUTION

Microsoft's sample code in the ActiveX SDK needs intimate knowledge of the OLE Component Object Model (COM) and the ActiveX control architecture. If you haven't written OLE controls before, take plenty of time to climb the learning curve.

To start, you will want to review much of Kraig Brockschmidt's book, *Inside OLE 2* (Microsoft Press, 1994).

CAUTION

The Microsoft ActiveX SDK is over 13M *compressed*. Even if you're prepared to handle the learning curve, make sure that you're prepared to handle the download time and the disk space!

ActiveX Template Library   For users who don't want to take on the full details of COM and the ActiveX control architecture, there's the ActiveX Template Library, or ATL. The ATL comes with two examples—Beeper and Labrador.

These templates do some of the OLE work, but you still need to be familiar with COM and the ActiveX control architecture.

ON THE WEB

The ATL is available online at **http://www.microsoft.com/visualc/v42/atl/ default.htm**.

N O T E   The Windows 95/Windows NT 4.0 version of the ATL only takes up 590K compressed—and that's with all of the documentation and sample code. The Windows NT 3.51 version is zipped and is even smaller. If you're looking for a kinder, gentler introduction to ActiveX, you may want to start with the ATL. ▄

Recall from Chapter 14, "If All the World Used Microsoft…," that Microsoft recommends that OLE automation servers provide two interfaces—both the IDispatch interface for dynamic linking and the VTBL interface (with a type library) for static linking. Starting with version 1.1, the ATL includes a custom AppWizard that builds COM objects with these dual interfaces.

Find the file named Atlwiz.awx in the Template subdirectory of the ATL directory. Copy it into the Template subdirectory of your Visual C++ 4.x directory.

Now choose File, New in Microsoft Developer Studio and open a new Project Workspace. You should see a new custom AppWizard named ATL COM AppWizard. Name your project and you see a screen similar to the one shown in Figure 15.2.

FIG. 15.2
Use the custom
AppWizard in the ATL
to build small, highly
optimized ActiveX
controls.

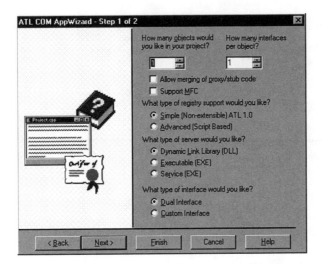

Listing 15.2 shows the exports from a minimal ActiveX control generated by the
AppWizard (see the companion CD-ROM in the \source\Chap 15 directory).

Listing 15.2   *baz.def*—The Definition File of a Skeleton ActiveX Control

```
; baz.def : Declares the module parameters.
LIBRARY        BAZ.DLL
EXPORTS
       DllCanUnloadNow         @1 PRIVATE
       DllGetClassObject       @2 PRIVATE
       DllRegisterServer       @3 PRIVATE
       DllUnregisterServer     @4 PRIVATE
```

Note how compact this interface is. Listing 15.3 shows the complete implementation of the minimal ActiveX control.

**Listing 15.3   *baz.cpp*—A Complete Implementation of the Skeleton
ActiveX Control**

```
// baz.cpp : Implementation of DLL Exports.

// You will need the NT SUR Beta 2 SDK or VC 4.2 in order to build this
// project. This is because you will need MIDL 3.00.15 or higher and new
```

continues

Listing 15.3   Continued

```
// headers and libs. If you have VC 4.2 installed, then everything should
// already be configured correctly.

// Note: Proxy/Stub Information
//          To build a separate proxy/stub DLL,
//          run nmake -f bazps.mak in the project directory.

#include "stdafx.h"
#include "resource.h"
#include "initguid.h"
#include "baz.h"
#include "Baz1.h"

#define IID_DEFINED
#include "baz_i.c"

CComModule _Module;

BEGIN_OBJECT_MAP(ObjectMap)
    OBJECT_ENTRY(CLSID_CBaz1, CBaz1)
END_OBJECT_MAP()

class CbazApp : public CWinApp
{
public:
    virtual BOOL InitInstance();
    virtual int ExitInstance();
};

CbazApp theApp;

BOOL CbazApp::InitInstance()
{
    _Module.Init(ObjectMap, m_hInstance);
    return CWinApp::InitInstance();
}

int CbazApp::ExitInstance()
{
    _Module.Term();
    return CWinApp::ExitInstance();
}

/////////////////////////////////////////////////////////////////////////
// Used to determine whether the DLL can be unloaded by OLE

STDAPI DllCanUnloadNow(void)
```

```
{
    AFX_MANAGE_STATE(AfxGetStaticModuleState());
    return (AfxDllCanUnloadNow()==S_OK && _
        Module.GetLockCount()==0) ? S_OK : S_FALSE;
}

/////////////////////////////////////////////////////////////////////
// Returns a class factory to create an object of the requested type

STDAPI DllGetClassObject(REFCLSID rclsid, REFIID riid, LPVOID* ppv)
{
    return _Module.GetClassObject(rclsid, riid, ppv);
}

/////////////////////////////////////////////////////////////////////
// DllRegisterServer - Adds entries to the system registry

STDAPI DllRegisterServer(void)
{
    // registers object, typelib and all interfaces in typelib
    return _Module.RegisterServer(TRUE);
}

/////////////////////////////////////////////////////////////////////
// DllUnregisterServer - Removes entries from the system registry

STDAPI DllUnregisterServer(void)
{
    _Module.UnregisterServer();
    return S_OK;
}
```

Even this tiny program can register and unregister itself with Windows. It also maintains a simple reference counter. Every time a container uses it, the counter is incremented. The control is not unloaded until the last container releases it.

CAUTION

Remember that ATL is designed to build small ActiveX or OLE controls. What it does, it does well; but if you find yourself spending a lot of time adding interfaces and functions, chances are you could do better using the ActiveX SDK.

N O T E Version 1.1 and higher of the ATL use some of the newest features in Visual
C++, such as the MIDL compiler (which replaces MkTypLib). If you have Visual
C++ 4.0, you can upgrade to the latest version. ■

ActiveX Documents

If you're a long-time MSIE watcher, you may recall Microsoft talking about *document objects*. These objects were intended to give MSIE users a way of viewing nonnative MIME media types in an MSIE window.

Sound familiar? By the time they got to implementation, these document objects had been renamed. The direct competitor to Navigator plug-ins is now named *ActiveX documents*.

Recall that OLE allows an object from one application to be embedded in a document from another application. Chapter 14, "If All the World Used Microsoft…," showed how to build such a compound document by copying a Paint bitmap to a WordPad document.

The container (in this case, WordPad) is responsible for maintaining and displaying the compound document. If the user clicks the bitmap, the container calls Paint's interface. Paint, the server, puts up its own menus and controls, and becomes the active application.

A document-aware browser such as MSIE (known as the *host*) uses OLE interfaces to contain objects from servers.

N O T E The real situation is just a little more complex than presented here. In OLE, the
container handles document-level issues such as pagination. Browsers
typically don't know much about pagination or printing, so the server must provide this
functionality. ■

ActiveX Scripting

Netscape's LiveConnect technology allows a JavaScript programmer to integrate Java and plug-ins with JavaScript. Similarly, ActiveX scripting allows the VBScript programmer to communicate with Java applets and with ActiveX controls.

Listing 15.4 shows an example of VBScript on a Web page. Note the resemblance to JavaScript. Like JavaScript, this example comments out the actual script. If the browser isn't VBScript-aware, it ignores everything in the comments. MSIE recognizes the `<SCRIPT LANGUAGE="VBScript"...>` tag and reads the script in the comments (see \source\Chap 15 directory on the companion CD-ROM).

Listing 15.4   *script.htm*—A Small VBScript Example

```
<HTML>
<HEAD>
<TITLE>VBScript Demo</TITLE>
<SCRIPT LANGUAGE="VBScript">
<!--
Sub theButton_OnClick
  MsgBox "Hello, World!"
End Sub
-->
</SCRIPT>
</HEAD>
<BODY>
<H1>Demonstration of VBScript</H1>
<FORM>
<INPUT NAME="theButton" TYPE="Button" VALUE="Click Me">
</FORM>
</BODY>
</HTML>
```

Like Navigator, MSIE also recognizes JavaScript. Listing 15.5 shows a JavaScript example that does the same work as the VBScript demo.

Listing 15.5   *javascri.htm*—A Small JavaScript Example

```
<HTML>
<HEAD>
<TITLE>JavaScript Demo</TITLE>
<SCRIPT LANGUAGE="JavaScript">
<!--
```

continues

Listing 15.5 Continued

```
  function handleClick()
  {
    alert("Hello, World!");
  }
//-->
</SCRIPT>
</HEAD>
<BODY>
<H1>Demonstration of JavaScript</H1>
<FORM>
<INPUT TYPE="Button" VALUE="Click Me" OnClick="handleClick()">
</FORM>
</BODY>
</HTML>
```

Both JavaScript and VBScript give similar results. If a developer is familiar with Visual Basic, VBScript may be a bit easier to learn, but the good news is that both languages work.

In general, a programmer can write a script in any language for which a scripting engine is available (such as VBScript, JavaScript, or even Perl) and run the script on any compatible host. MSIE is the most popular client-side host. Microsoft's client-side project is codenamed Sweeper.

The examples given in this section so far show how ActiveX scripts interact with a simple form. Much of the power of ActiveX scripting, like the power of Netscape's LiveConnect, comes from the capability to integrate control objects and Java applets.

Recall that an HTML author can install an object on a Web page simply by adding an <OBJECT> tag and a series of <PARAM> tags. The following code fragment adds an ActiveX control named Label to the page.

If you've used Visual Basic and OCX controls you'll recognize the <PARAM>s as the property settings of the control, which you might use on a form in Visual Basic.

```
<OBJECT
    classid="clsid:99B42120-6EC7-11CF-A6C7-00AA00A47DD2"
    id=lblActiveLbl
    width=250
    height=250
    align=left
    hspace=20
    vspace=0
```

```
        >
        <PARAM NAME="Angle" VALUE="90">
        <PARAM NAME="Alignment" VALUE="2">
        <PARAM NAME="BackStyle" VALUE="0">
        <PARAM NAME="Caption" VALUE="A Default Caption">
        <PARAM NAME="FontName" VALUE="Arial">
        <PARAM NAME="FontSize" VALUE="20">
        <PARAM NAME="FontBold" VALUE="1">
        <PARAM NAME="FrColor" VALUE="0">
    </OBJECT>
```

Figure 15.3 shows how this label appears on the page.

FIG. 15.3

The <PARAM> tags define the properties of the associated control object.

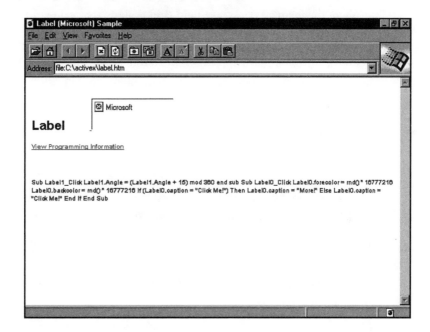

After a control object is loaded onto the page, you can take control of it with a script:

```
<FORM NAME="LabelControls">
    <INPUT TYPE="TEXT" NAME="txtNewText" SIZE=25>
    <INPUT TYPE="BUTTON" NAME="cmdChangeIt" VALUE="Change Text">
    <INPUT TYPE="BUTTON" NAME="cmdRotate" VALUE="Rotate Label">
</FORM>
```

Now link the form control to the ActiveX control object with a bit of VBScript, which should be put in the <HEAD> section of the HTML page.

```
<SCRIPT LANGUAGE="VBScript">
<!--
     Sub cmdChangeIt_onClick
          Dim TheForm
          Set TheForm = Document.LabelControls
          lblActiveLbl.Caption = TheForm.txtNewText.Value
     End Sub
-->
</SCRIPT>
```

When the user clicks the cmdChangeIt button, the cmdChangeIt_OnClick()
procedure is run. This script grabs the form named LabelControls, pulls in the
Value of the form's txtNewText field, and assigns that value to lblActiveLbl.
Caption.

Taking control of a Java applet is reported to be just as simple. Microsoft has announced that Java applet control will be implemented in a future release of MSIE.

The ActiveX Server Framework

The Internet is gradually moving away from freeware servers such as NCSA and
Apache, and is moving toward commercial servers such as those from Netscape.
Microsoft is pursing this market aggressively.

Just as Netscape offers a Netscape Server Application Programming Interface
(NSAPI), Microsoft offers their Internet Server Application Programming Interface (ISAPI), now named *server-side ActiveX*. Netscape offers LiveWire and with it,
server-side JavaScript.

Microsoft offers ActiveX server scripting. Server-based ActiveX scripting is being
developed as part of Microsoft's Tarantula and Gibraltar projects.

Many servers provide additional functionality by using Common Gateway Interface (CGI) scripts, most often written in Perl. Microsoft's server supports CGI, and
the Windows platform supports Perl, but Microsoft servers are more often
scripted in a language such as VBScript (a subset of Visual Basic).

Microsoft maintains, with some reason, that many more people can learn Visual
Basic than will ever learn Perl, so their servers can be configured by a broader
range of users.

From Here...

In early 1995, Mosaic was the clear winner of the browser wars. By the end of that year Netscape Navigator had taken the lead. Now, one year later, Navigator's lead is being challenged by Microsoft Internet Explorer. Which browser will dominate the market in years to come? Navigator? MSIE? Or a new browser that hasn't even been introduced yet? Or will the question become moot as browser technology disappears into components such as Apple's Cyberdog, integrated throughout every application?

ON THE WEB

Microsoft does a nice job of providing documentation, software, and (of course) press releases online. For the latest in ActiveX, visit **http://www.microsoft.com/activex/**.

- Review the basics of plug-ins in Chapter 6, "NPP Methods: Starting the Plug-In," Chapter 7, "NPP Methods: Handling Interaction," Chapter 8, "NPP Methods: Other Tasks," and Chapter 9, "Understanding NPN Methods."

- Learn about advanced techniques suitable for the newest versions of Windows in Chapter 14, "If All the World Used Microsoft...." Learn about the limitations and capabilities of Windows 3.x, a system that will be with us for years to come, in the following chapter, "Spanning the Windows World."

- Chapter 17, "Using Class Libraries and Frameworks," reviews the MFCs library, and contrasts it with Borland's OWL and with Symantec's Class Library for the Macintosh.

- Learn about the integration of Java, JavaScript, and plug-ins in Chapter 18, "Plug-Ins as a Programming Resource."

CHAPTER 16

Spanning the Windows World

Although users still have millions of copies of Windows 3.x installed, Microsoft has estimated that less than two percent of Visual C++ development is being targeted for Windows 3.x. Much of this chapter addresses the special techniques you need so that you can write for Windows 3.x. If you're developing for an intranet that still uses Windows 3.x or if you want to be sure that all Windows users (even users with older versions of Windows) can use your plug-in, be sure to read this chapter. ■

A few reasons why faithful users cling to classic Windows

Like it or not, Windows 3.x is here to stay. This chapter explains why many users are reluctant to move to Windows 95/NT.

Special considerations when targeting older versions of Windows

Your plug-in should flourish on both older and newer machines.

How MS-DOS and classic Windows manage memory

Understanding the segmented memory model that underlies these systems can help you avoid problems in your plug-in.

About differences between Win32s and true Win32

A simple check in your plug-in allows you to run the same code on Windows 3.1, NT, and 95, without sacrificing the advanced capabilities of the newer operating systems.

Some of the defects that were reported in connection with plug-ins

Some defects were corrected, others need a workaround in your plug-in, which this chapter covers.

Special Considerations for Classic Windows

Modern software development is an imperfect art. Lest we forget, the users remind us of our imperfections every time we roll out a new software product.

MS-DOS was, in its day, functional but uninspiring. Windows was initially regarded as a toy, but it grew in functionality and acceptance. So much so that users began to grumble about its limitations. Windows 3.*x* was, after all, really only a sophisticated wrapper around DOS. Users couldn't get true multitasking, and programmers had to put up with the idiosyncrasies of DOS (such as the 8+3 limit on file names, and the 640K barrier). Figure 16.1 shows the Windows family of products.

FIG. 16.1
Microsoft has many products named "Windows"—the big dividing line, however, was the transition between Win16 and Win32.

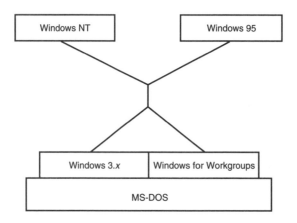

Windows 3.*x* was based up the assumption that most quantities and addresses are 16-bits wide. In the early 1990's Microsoft announced a new set of Windows calls (known as an Application Programming Interface, or API) based on entities 32-bits wide. The new interface, Win32, served as the basis for Windows NT and, later, Windows 95. Microsoft also offered a "simulator" that allowed developers to write Win32 code that ran on a Windows 3.*x* machine. The simulator wasn't perfect, and small inconsistencies existed between the various versions of Win32 but eventually, it all came together.

On August 24, 1995, Microsoft released its long-awaited Windows 4.0, also known as Windows 95. While the band played and the crowds cheered out front, the tech support lines at Microsoft handled an unprecedented number of trouble calls. Users bought Windows 95 in droves, but many uninstalled it a few days later. More than a year later, Windows 95 is being called the most successful software product in history, but many users have clung faithfully to their old copies of Windows 3.*x*.

This section looks at Windows *before* Win32—a collection of products known to the user as Windows 3.*x*, which this section calls "classic Windows." You will look at the reasons why many users are sticking with classic Windows, and explore how you must program in order to succeed in this difficult environment.

Why Do They Spell it "Windoze?"

More than a year after Microsoft's much-ballyhooed release of Windows 95, many users continue to run classic Windows. One memo that is circulating anonymously on the Internet summarizes the reasons that many individuals and many companies have elected not to move to Windows 95 right away.

WINDOWS 95 update - Jan 96

The purpose of this article is to update XYZ staff on the issue of installing the Windows 95 operating system. As yet there is no necessity to upgrade to Windows 95. Indeed there are substantial reasons not to do so. Note that:

* There is no software essential to our operations that requires Windows 95 to run.

* Unless your machine is very recent there are many costs in ensuring your system can operate optimally under Windows 95. For example, if your machine has only 8M of RAM it is highly likely you will need to add another 4-8M to run efficiently. Note that where laptop memory is required it will be quite expensive. This extra cost factor, together with the cost of the upgrade, effectively nullifies any cost advantage offered by purchasing Office 95.

continues

---

continued

* Setup is complicated and time consuming and prone to failure if non-standard hardware or configurations are encountered. It is especially troublesome when installed over a pre-existing setup.

* Retraining for the new interface will be necessary as it is very unlike previous versions of Windows.

* Compatibility issues abound, e.g. between 16 and 32-bit versions of Windows software such as Word for Windows and Excel, and some software may not even work, or will work more slowly.

Thus significant human and material resources will be required to implement Windows 95 across the Division. In these days of diminishing research budgets this will not be welcome news.

Be assured that IT Section staff are exploring the use and implementation of Windows 95, particularly in connection with the Vines network. Windows 95 is being installed on an IT Section machine at each centre where you are welcome to trial it.

Thus our existing strategy (as outlined previously by (deleted) in this newsletter) remains. That is, in the absence of identifiable productivity gains, the implementation of Windows 95 across the Division is neither necessary or desirable. In this context we note that Information Management Branch (IMB) has adopted an identical policy for the Department as a whole. Clearly the most cost-effective implementation of Windows 95 would be on a whole of Department basis in cooperation with IMB.

In counterpoint, many programmers point to the essential limitations of classic Windows—it's a 16-bit application that runs on top of DOS. Even users have been frustrated by classic Windows. The following list of areas where users have problems with Windows 3.*x* is derived from *Platinum Edition Using Windows 95* (Que, 1996):

■ Overlapping windows caused confusion due to visual clutter. Windows that filled the screen hid other programs that were open.

- Windows seemed to disappear when minimized.

- The hierarchical display of directory structures in the File Manager was intimidating and not intuitive to non-technical users.

- The File Manager and Program Manager shared some functionality, such as starting applications, but they used different metaphors and appearance.

- Switching between running applications and knowing which applications were running was not obvious. Many users started multiple instances of the same application, thereby using up system resources and increasing the potential for an application failure.

- Double-clicking and many keystrokes, such as Alt+Tab, although important, were not obvious.

- File names were limited to eight characters with a three-letter extension.

Frustration with classic Windows was not limited to novice users only. *Platinum Edition Using Windows 95* goes on to list some problems that power users had with the older systems:

- Resources and utilities needed for customizing and fine-tuning were scattered all over the Windows system in different groups, such as Control Panel, Print Manager, Setup, File Manager, and Program Manager.

- Information such as IRQ and I/O address settings were difficult to find.

- Many graphical elements could not be customized.

- Networking with non-Microsoft networks required a great deal of study, work, and workarounds.

- Hardware was difficult to install and could easily cause conflicts with existing hardware. The conflicts were difficult to resolve.

Microsoft has gambled that Windows 95 will be wildly successful. Although the product got off to a rocky start, there are indications that the PC community eventually will adopt the product (or its new cousin, Windows NT 4.0 Workstation). Still, there are many reasons for end users to hesitate before adopting Windows 95. Look for Windows 3.*x* to remain on many desktops for years to come.

The Burden of 16-Bit-Hood

As programmers, the use of 16-bit words as the default data width had far-reaching consequences. For example, messages in classic Windows were passed with a 16-bit-wide wParam and a 32-bit-wide lParam. Figure 16.2 illustrates how classic Windows allocated these two parameters for the WM_COMMAND message.

FIG. 16.2

Classic Windows packed the cmd and the hwnd into one 32-bit quantity.

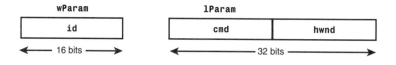

In Win32, all quantities are, by default, 32-bits-wide. In particular, handles have grown to 32 bits, so no room exists for both the hwnd and the cmd in the lParam. Fortunately, the move to 32 bits gives more room in the wParam. Microsoft kept the id at 16 bits, so there is room in the wParam for both the id and the cmd. The Win32 design of WM_COMMAND is illustrated in Figure 16.3.

FIG. 16.3

Win32 packed the cmd and the id into one 32-bit quantity—in wParam.

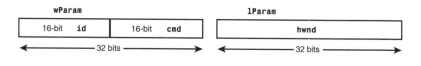

When a programmer writes a WM_COMMAND message handler for a Windows application, he or she must take care to use the correct interface. Today many Windows applications are loaded with sequences like the following:

```
#ifdef _WIN32
    .
    .
    .
#else
    .
    .
    .
#endif
```

CAUTION

Never use the specifier int in a Windows program. To do so puts you at the mercy of the compiler. Sometimes a compiler interprets int as 16 bits, under different circumstances it reserves 32 bits.

For best results, use native C types sparingly. Microsoft provides macros such as BYTE, BOOL, DWORD, and LONG, which will resolve during compilation to the proper specifiers.

Memory Models

One dramatic shortcoming for the programmer in classic Windows is the memory model. By default, MS-DOS and classic Windows quantities are 16-bits-wide. These "quantities" include pointers. Because a 16-bit-wide pointer can access only 64 kilobytes (64K), memory in classic Windows is broken into 64K chunks known as *segments*. This design fits well with the Intel processors on which classic Windows runs, but can turn a clean software design into a "maze of twisty passages, all alike."

C and C++ programs need two blocks of memory—space for code and space for the data. Because real-world programs nearly all require more than 64K for code, and more than 64K for data, MS-DOS (which is sitting underneath classic Windows, doing the dirty work) has to allocate more than two segments to the program. DOS (and Intel's) solution is to use the 80x86 CS register to hold the base for the code segment, and the 80x86 DS register to hold the base for the data segment.

The Small Memory Model   When you write a program for classic Windows, by default the compiler allocates 16-bit pointers (called near pointers). Each of these pointers can point anywhere within its segment. When the program is loaded, the CS and DS registers are set by DOS to the actual segments where the code and data are placed. (See Figure 16.4.) This memory model is called "small," and is characterized by using near pointers for both code and data.

FIG. 16.4

In the small memory model, one segment (called _TEXT) is allocated for code, and one (called _DATA) for data.

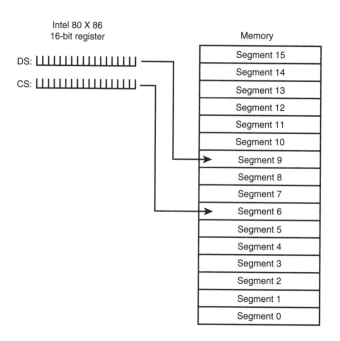

N O T E   There is also a "tiny" memory model, in which both code and data are squeezed into a single segment. The tiny model was used to produce .COM files, which were popular at one time under MS-DOS. The tiny model does not run under Windows, only under DOS. ▮

Far Pointers   Most programs need more than one segment for code, or more than one segment for data, or both. MS-DOS provides 32-bit pointers, called "far pointers," which can point anywhere in memory. These far pointers are bigger (obviously) which means they use up more memory. They are also slower to use because each use of the pointer requires two 16-bit quantities to be combined.

N O T E   Far pointers are often written with a two-part notation, such as `0000:0FFF`. This notation means that the address is in base segment 0000_{16}, at an offset of 0FFF_{16}. The physical address is computed by shifting the base segment left four bits, and then adding the 16-bit offset.

One problem with this approach is that a single physical location can have more than one *segment:offset* notation. For example, 1231:0052, 1232:0042, 1233:0032, 1234:0022, 1235:0012, and 1236:0002 both point to physical location 12362_{16}, which means that a program cannot compare two logical addresses without doing the math to turn them into physical addresses. Figure 16.5 illustrates this math.

To translate from this kind of notation to a true pointer, the DOS programmer calls MK_FP (found on the companion CD_Rom in the /source/ chap. 16 directory), as shown in Listing 16.1. ■

FIG. 16.5
To convert a logical address to a physical address, shift the segment base left four bits and add the offset.

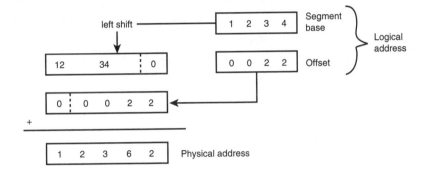

Listing 16.1   *mkfp.c*—Use *MK_FP* to Transform a Segment and an Offset into a Far Pointer

```
#include <dos.h>
#include <stdio.h>
#include <stdlib.h>
int main()
{
  char far *p;
  unsigned int segment = 0xb800, offset = 0;

  p = MK_FP(segment, offset);
  printf("The CGI video buffer is at %lp\n", p);
  return EXIT_SUCCESS;
}
```

Another consequence of the Intel processors' segmented memory is the fact that only 20 bits are available for addresses. Although this limitation was relaxed in later versions of the 80x86 family, DOS (and consequently, classic Windows) was built to use only 2^{20} memory locations—1 megabyte (1M). Because DOS itself uses 6 segments, the application is limited to the remaining 10 segments, spanning 640 kilobytes (640K).

T I P   To facilitate the reuse of code between different versions of Windows, don't use near and far specifiers. Rather, use the Microsoft-defined macros NEAR and FAR. When the platform doesn't need this distinction, the C preprocessor turns these macros to the empty string.

Extended and Expanded Memory   MS-DOS programs long ago ran off the top of the 640K limit. Clever programmers came up with the Expanded Memory Specification (EMS)—a hardware-software solution that allows programs to access up to 32M. The software used to access expanded memory is known as the Expanded Memory Manager, or EMM. The EMM is an MS-DOS device driver supplied with the expanded memory hardware or software product. The EMM is installed by adding a line to the config.sys file, such as the following:

```
DEVICE=C:\DOS\EMM386.EXE
```

An older, software-only solution, emulated expanded memory in the 16M address space of 80286 processors. (This scheme was known as extended memory.) If you see a line like the following in config.sys, your computer is using the Extended Memory Standard, XMS:

```
DEVICE=C:\DOS\HIMEM.SYS
```

Other solutions, such as Quarterdeck's QEMM and MS-DOS's EMM386, use the memory-mapping capabilities of the 80386/I486 chip to manage expanded memory. Regardless of the details of the mechanism, expanded memory works by temporarily replacing a region of conventional memory (known as a *page frame*) with a block of expanded memory. Figure 16.6 shows expanded memory in action.

The page frame is divided into 16K blocks, known as physical pages. The hardware and/or software maps logical pages in expanded memory into physical pages in the 1M address space of the processor. Figure 16.7 shows the MS-DOS memory map, with a typical EMS installation.

FIG. 16.6

When a programmer needs to access data in expanded memory, the underlying hardware and software work together to swap a page of conventional memory with the page of expanded memory.

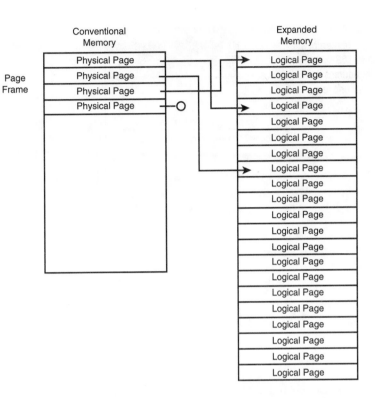

Suppose that an expanded memory board is installed in a DOS computer, with a 64K page frame starting at 1E00:0000. The application can ask the EMM to map the first logical page of expanded memory to the first physical page in the page frame (1E00:0000 through 1E00:3FFF). If the program later asks the EMM to remap the page frame, bringing the second logical page into the first physical page, the data from the first logical page is safe, but inaccessible, out in expanded memory.

With a 64K page frame the computer could have up to 4 logical pages at a time mapped into conventional memory. The EMM tracks which logical pages are in the page frame in a data structure known as the *mapping context*.

FIG. 16.7

The "top" of memory, between 768K and the 1M address limit, is usually unused.

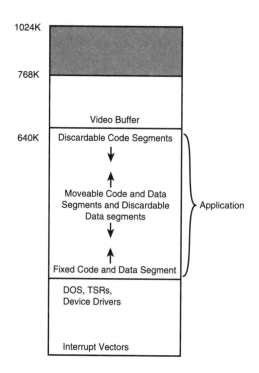

To use expanded memory, take the following general steps:

1. Test to see if an Expanded Memory Manager is installed.

2. Determine whether enough expanded memory pages are available to meet the application's needs.

3. Ask the EMM to allocate the required number of logical pages. The EMM returns a handle to the allocated pages.

4. Ask the EMM to translate the EMM handle into the base address of the physical pages.

5. The EMM maps one or more of the logical pages into the page frame.

6. The application interacts with the memory at the physical address, within the 1M conventional address space.

7. The application and the program loop through steps 5 and 6 as often as necessary.

8. When the application is done with expanded memory, the application tells the EMM to deallocate its pages.

Part

III

Ch

16

DOS Protected Mode Interface   With the newer processors came the capability to shift more of the memory management function into the processor. DOS programs are said to run in *real* mode—they can access only the first megabyte of memory. Starting with the 80386, Intel processors have a *protected mode* in which the processor and Windows work together to give each application access to all available memory in a flat (unsegmented) 2G (2 gigabytes) address space. This special mode is known as *enhanced mode*. The Windows memory management system is named the DOS Protected Mode Interface, or DPMI. Beginning with Windows 3.1, Windows always runs in protected mode.

In protected mode, the segment address is replaced by a *selector*—a hardware register that allows the processor to manage the segments. The processor is responsible for updating the selector, so the application always has access to the proper segment. On an 80386 processor or above, Intel replaced the 16-bit segment registers with 32-bit registers. If your plug-in is running on a 386 or above (generally a safe assumption), you can access data objects larger than 64K, although these larger objects go beyond the bounds of one segment.

Microsoft's WINMEM32.DLL library is the standard method for implementing a flat model in your program.

N O T E   Although Windows gives the *application* access to a flat address space, classic Windows still uses segmented memory. DOS and Windows still use much of the special first megabyte of memory. Moreover, when your plug-in interacts with classic Windows, you are restricted to a single, non-discardable 16-bit code segment. This 16-bit code segment is known as the *helper segment*.

Because Windows is a segmented program, you cannot pass a 32-bit offset through the Win16 API. To call Windows, put the code that actually talks to Windows in the helper segment. Code in the helper segment must convert 16:32 far pointers to 16:16 far pointers before passing them to Windows.

Windows applications also need to set their stack pointer to either a 16:32 far pointer or a 16:16 far pointer, depending on whether the code is running from a 16:32 segment or from a 16:16 segment. Some programmers prefer to maintain two stacks, and then copy data from one stack to the other when the application switches from one code segment to the next.

Classic Windows supports two kinds of memory—global and local. *Local memory* is memory that has been allocated to the data segment of a Windows application. *Global memory* is all the memory that wasn't allocated by an application or the system. Because Windows 3.1 allocates all memory from a single global heap, one runaway program can gobble up all of memory. Moreover, all of the applications run in the same address space. A malicious or poorly designed program can construct a pointer that points into another application's code or data space and do all kinds of damage. This design is one reason that a misbehaving program that triggers a General Protection Fault (GPF) brings down the entire system.

 Although classic Windows isolates you from the 1M memory limit, you still should not forget about this limit. Your Windows plug-ins run on machines where users also run MS-DOS programs in real mode. If you are porting old (Windows 3.0) code, you may see references to GMEM_LOWER or GMEM_NOT_BANKED, which were used to allocate memory in the first megabyte. These flags are ignored in Windows 3.1—all requests for global memory are satisfied from memory above the 1M limit. If you must get memory in the first megabyte, use GlobalDosAlloc().

Avoid using low memory as much as possible because this memory is a scarce resource that is in demand by MS-DOS programs.

Running Win32 and Win16 Programs Side By Side   If you develop plug-ins exclusively for Win32 you may think you don't have to worry about the arcane memory management issues of Win16. Think again. You may be in for an unpleasant surprise. Win32 applications that run on Windows 3.1 (which is using Win32s) coexist in the same shared global memory heap as other Win32 and Win16 applications. One consequence of a global shared heap and not being able to use selectors for dereferencing addresses is that multiple instances of Win32 applications don't share code. When classic Windows loads a Win32 application, the loader fixes up all 32-bit linear addresses. If the user requests a second copy of the application, Windows has no segment registers to allow it to change context. Consequently, it copies the whole application into memory and fixes it up again.

Multitasking in Classic Windows

Recall from Chapter 13, "Getting Back on the Network," that classic Windows doesn't support preemptive multitasking. When Win32 and Win16 applications share a classic Windows machine, the Win32 applications operate under the same scheduling algorithm as the Win16 applications. When an application has pending messages in its message queue, Windows schedules it to run. If the application fails to check its messages, it continues to get processor time and "locks out" any other processes. To keep Windows 3.1 looking responsive to the user, be sure to check your messages promptly.

Part
III

Ch
16

> **CAUTION**
>
> Even if your plug-in is a good citizen, reading its messages and completing its work quickly, there's no guarantee that the rest of the applications will be as well behaved. Prepare for the possibility that one slow application can bring the rest of the processes on classic Windows to a crawl, or even a halt.
>
> Remember, too, that your application can "get away" with some misbehavior on Windows NT or Windows 95 because these systems support preemptive multitasking. If you plan to deliver a version for classic Windows, make sure that you test your plug-in on a heavily loaded system under Win32s.

Deciding Whether to Use Win32s

You can write a classic Windows plug-in in Win32 (using Win32s) or in Win16. As time passes, vendors such as Microsoft offer less support for the older platforms. If your application makes big data transfers (`bitblt`) or has computational or image-manipulation operations that benefit from being done 32 bits at a time, you almost certainly want to move to Win32s.

If your application doesn't need the Win32 API, the overhead of converting back and forth from 16 bits to 32 may decrease performance. You may want to experiment with building a 16-bit version of your plug-in to see whether your performance moves up or down. (Test programs that use the Win32 API heavily take about 10 percent longer than comparable programs that run Win16.)

To wring every erg of performance possible out of Win32s, use the `PolyLine()` function rather than the more common `MoveTo()`/`LineTo()` sequence. Remember, too, that pointers going in and out of Windows have to be translated between 32 and 16 bits. Pointers to local variables are translated fastest because they are on the application's stack, and Win32s optimizes translation of the stack pointer.

The Best of Both Worlds

Ideally, you can write one body of code for Win32 and have it run on Windows NT, Windows 95, *and* Win32s. This isn't quite possible because some calls supported in Win32 are not present in Win32s. If you call for a new thread, for example, Win32s returns `ERROR_CALL_NOT_IMPLEMENTED`.

Don't rely on the `ERROR_CALL_NOT_IMPLEMENTED` return code. Rather, call `GetVersion()` before trying to call any functions that aren't part of Win32s. If your application is running on classic Windows, the high-order bit of the `DWORD` that is returned from `GetVersion()` is 1. Check this bit in `NPP_Initialize()`. If you find that you are on Win32s, record this in a class variable and "steer around" code that cannot run on Win32s. This technique allows you to compile one version of your plug-in that works correctly on any 32-bit Windows platform.

The following Win32 features are not supported on Win32s:

- Console APIs
- Unicode APIs
- Security APIs
- Comm APIs
- Asynchronous file I/O
- Threads
- Paths (graphics object)
- Enhanced metafiles
- Bezier curves

Some Known Problems with Windows Plug-Ins

With all of the differences between Win16, Win32s, and Win32, it isn't surprising that Netscape has had difficulty getting its plug-in SDK to run smoothly on all Windows platforms. This section lists some problems that were reported with Windows plug-ins. When designing your plug-in, try to steer around these problems. Many of these problems were discovered in beta versions and were since fixed, or soon will be fixed, in a future release of the SDK or of Navigator. Still, avoiding a known trouble spot is generally a good idea, and is highly recommended.

Some of these problems are an integral part of the design of the SDK. For example, Navigator provides no mechanism by which a full-page plug-in can get parameters. It is, therefore, not surprising that it is an error for a full-page plug-in to attempt to dereference the parameter pointers.

Problems with the 16-Bit Version of Navigator

For some of the reasons given previously in this chapter, the Win16 version of any product faces special challenges. This section describes the known defects in the 16-bit version of Navigator for Windows.

NPN_UserAgent() Call GPFs Navigator   On the 16-bit version of Navigator, the NPN_UserAgent() function has been reported to crash Navigator. If you need to call NPN_UserAgent() in this environment, test the plug-in thoroughly with older versions of Navigator to see how far back you can safely go.

Win32 Navigator Loads Win16 Plug-Ins   Recall that each copy of Navigator on a hard disk has its own Plug-Ins subdirectory. The 32-bit version of Navigator should have 32-bit plug-ins *only* in its Plug-Ins subdirectory, and the 16-bit version should have *only* 16-bit plug-ins. Navigator, however, doesn't check the plug-in before loading. If the user becomes confused and puts a plug-in in the wrong folder, Navigator loads the plug-in and attempts to execute it, resulting in a GPF.

Part
III

Ch
16

The best solution to this problem is to prevent the plug-ins from getting mixed up in the first place. Chapter 19, "Installing the Plug-In," provides information on how to have Navigator download and install a plug-in.

As a safeguard, call GetVersion() during NPP_Initialize(). If you find that a 16-bit plug-in is running under Win32, put up a message box that describes the problem, and then return NPERR_INVALID_PLUGIN_ERROR from NPP_Initialize().

 TIP You may be tempted to write an install program that makes sure that your plug-in gets put away in the correct directory. Nothing is wrong with this approach. In fact, it's such a good idea that Netscape is already ahead of you. One major change in dealing with plug-ins with Navigator 4.0 has to do with how plug-ins are installed.

Check the latest on-line information on Navigator 4.0 or read Chapter 19, "Installing the Plug-In," for more information on this subject.

Problems with an Easy Workaround

Some "defects" are triggered because the plug-in programmer made a mistake. Although future versions of Navigator may handle this problem better, these problems are easy to avoid by fixing the plug-in.

Plug-In Requires FileOpenName Resource   If you forget to specify the FileOpenName field in the VERSIONINFO resource the pull-down list box is wrong. Add this item to your checklist of things to look at before you release your plug-in.

Failed Plug-In Loads Don't Unregister   When Navigator starts, it scans the files in the plug-in subdirectory and reads each one for the proper VERSIONINFO resource. If the VERSIONINFO appears to be correct, Navigator registers the plug-in. You can see this information by looking at the URL **about:plugins**.

When the plug-in is loaded, it may return an error code from NPP_Initialize() or NPP_New(). If so, Netscape doesn't unregister the plug-in, so future calls for the plug-in will just load the failing plug-in again.

The best solution is to find and fix the problem that causes the plug-in to fail. If the problem is a defect in the plug-in, fix it. If the problem is an inherent run-time error, you may want to consider putting up a message box that gives the user as much information as possible before returning the error.

Problems with Full-Page Plug-Ins

Full-page plug-ins take on more autonomy than their embedded cousins. With the power, comes more opportunity for failure.

NPP_New() argn and argv Pointers Invalid When your plug-in is called from an `<EMBED>` tag, Navigator sets `pluginType` to `NP_EMBED` and fills in `argn` and `argv` with information about the parameters in the `<EMBED>` tag. If the HTML author calls your plug-in through a link, however, Navigator sets `pluginType` to `NP_FULL`. Under these conditions, `argn` and `argv` are meaningless.

Make sure that you check `pluginType` before using `argn` and `argv`. Even if you don't expect your plug-in to be called as a full-page plug-in, practice safe programming—check the parameter.

NPP_Print() Doesn't Pass Default Printer When a full-page plug-in's `NPP_Print()` method is called, Navigator sometimes sends NULL rather than a pointer to the currently selected printer. Navigator needs to fix this problem. Always check the value of this pointer, as you should check any pointer you receive from Navigator.

NPSavedData Doesn't Work During `NPP_Destroy()`, you have an opportunity to save data with Navigator. If all goes well, this data is returned to the next instance of this plug-in to visit this URL, during `NPP_New()`. Netscape has reports that this mechanism doesn't work for full-page plug-ins (although it appears to be reliable for embedded plug-ins).

If this behavior is important to you, check and see if the problem was fixed in a recent version of Navigator.

General Problems with the Windows Navigator

Some problems seem rooted in Navigator's core code. They show up regardless of the type of plug-in or the version of Windows. Much of Navigator's code is common across all three major platforms—also watch for these problems on Windows or UNIX implementations.

NPP_StreamAsFile() Intermittently Returns a *NULL* Filename   If the cache is smaller than the incoming stream, NPP_StreamAsFile() may report a NULL filename. The best solution, of course, is to use NP_NORMAL as the stream's stype.

If you choose to use NPP_StreamAsFile(), check for the NULL filename before dereferencing it. If the filename is NULL, return with no further processing. (You cannot return an error message because NPP_StreamAsFile() returns void.)

Calling *NPN_PostURL()* Can Cause a GPF   With some versions of the SDK, calling NPN_PostURL() with a non-HTTP URL or a non-NULL window causes a GPF. Netscape intends to fix this problem. Double-check on the versions of Navigator and the version of SDK you use. If the problem was not fixed on the versions popular with your users, add a check in the code to prohibit the fatal operation.

Returning an Error from *NPP_New()* GPFs Navigator   Netscape needs to fix this problem. Double-check with your version of the SDK and your versions of Navigator to see if the problem was cleared up. As a workaround, trap as many errors as possible in NPP_Initialize().

Various Errors When the Window Is Resized   Netscape has reports that NPP_SetWindow() is not called when only the vertical dimension of a frame is resized. They also have reports that the plug-in is destroyed and recreated when the page is resized. These problems seem to have been fixed, or are difficult to reproduce. Check your versions of Navigator and your SDK to see if these problems occur for your plug-in.

NPN_GetURL() with *NULL* Window Can Fail   Recall that if window is set to NULL in NPN_GetURL(), the stream associated with the URL is supposed to be directed back to the plug-in with NPP_NewStream(). If the URL has a file extent other than .html the stream is not produced or returned to the plug-in.

If you need this behavior, check to see if Netscape has fixed it in the current version. If you need a workaround, put the data into a small HTML file. For example, if you want to send **http://some.machine.com/myData.tst** back to the plug-in, build a file with content like the one shown in Listing 16.2. You find this listing on the companion CD-ROM in the /source/chap. 16 directory.

Listing 16.2 *noExtent.htm*—**A Workaround to the Extent Defect**

```
<HTML>
<HEAD>
<TITLE>Proxy</TITLE>
</HEAD>
<BODY>
<EMBED SRC="http://some.machine.com/myData.tst">
</BODY>
</HTML>
```

Part

III

Ch

16

Then call NPN_GetURL() on this page. When NPN_GetURL() succeeds, it may set the MIME media type of the stream to the type of the plug-in's original NPP NewStream() stream. Check the latest version—Netscape is working on this problem.

Interrupted "Reason" Is Wrong   Following NPP_NewStream(), if the user presses Navigator's Stop button, Navigator correctly stops the transfer and calls NPP_DestroyStream(). The reason code, however, is not reliably set, and the upper word of the reason is uninitialized.

When you read the reason, mask out the upper word. Then use a switch statement, and include a default case to handle the possibility that the reason doesn't match one of the known reason codes. In this case, your plug-in should assume a "generic reason" and proceed as best it can.

Navigator Doesn't Handle Two Duplicate Instances on the Same Page   Suppose that an HTML author writes a page like the one in Listing 16.3. You find this in the companion CD-ROM in the /source/chap. 16 directory.

Listing 16.3 *twoInst.htm*—**Two Instances of the Same URL**

```
<HTML>
<HEAD>
<TITLE>Two Instances</TITLE>
</HEAD>
<BODY>
<H1>Two Instances</H1>
<H2>First Instance</H2>
<EMBED SRC="http://www.somemachine.com/myFile.tst" HEIGHT=200 WIDTH=200>
<H2>Second Instance</H2>
<EMBED SRC="http://www.somemachine.com/myFile.tst" HEIGHT=100 WIDTH=100>
</BODY>
</HTML>
```

Navigator should start two instances of the plug-in. Instead it only starts the first one. As a workaround, make two copies of the target page, and call it with two different URLs.

> **N O T E** Navigator has a similar problem if the two instances are on two different pages, except in this case Navigator GPFs. Until Netscape fixes the defect, the workaround is the same. ◼

NPN_RequestRead() Is Sometimes Lost If the plug-in calls NPN_RequestRead() while Navigator is calling NPP_Write(), Navigator may fail to return any data to the NPN_RequestRead(). Retry the NPN_RequestRead()—the second attempt usually will succeed.

From Here...

Microsoft Windows is easily the most successful software product in the industry, but by providing backward compatibility with older versions of Windows, and with MS-DOS, it is plagued with being "bug-for-bug compatible" with its predecessors. Classic Windows, with its roots in the segmented and expanded memory models of MS-DOS, presents special challenges for the programmer. The boundary between 16-bit software and the new 32-bit software can prove troublesome.

Newer versions of Windows, including Windows NT and Windows 95, solve many of the problems of classic Windows, but by continuing to support Win16 and even MS-DOS software, they cannot completely escape some of the ugliness of these older products.

Consequently, both Netscape and you, as the plug-in programmer, face special challenges when writing Windows software. Netscape's implementation of the portions of Navigator that handle plug-ins isn't perfect. During beta testing many defects were discovered—most of which are closed in the finished version.

■ The next chapter, "Using Class Libraries and Frameworks," reviews the Microsoft Foundation Classes library, and contrasts it with Borland's OWL and with Symantec's Class Library for the Macintosh.

■ Review the basics of plug-ins in Chapter 6, "NPP Methods: Starting the Plug-In," Chapter 7, "NPP Methods: Handling Interaction," Chapter 8, "NPP Methods: Other Tasks," and Chapter 9, "Understanding NPN Methods."

■ Learn about advanced techniques suitable for the newest versions of Windows in Chapter 14, "If All the World Used Microsoft…"

■ Learn about the integration of Java, JavaScript, and plug-ins in Chapter 18, "Plug-Ins as a Programming Resource."

Part
III

Ch
16

Plug-In Foundations

17 Using Class Libraries and Frameworks   437

18 Plug-Ins as a Programming Resource   455

19 Installing the Plug-In   479

CHAPTER 17

Using Class Libraries and Frameworks

The original Windows API had about 350 functions. Win32 has over 1,000. Although a given programmer may only use a fraction of these calls, the learning curve is substantial. Whose great idea was it to make DeleteObject() the opposite of CreateBrush()?

Some class libraries, such as Microsoft Foundation Classes (MFC), encapsulate the operating system's interfaces. Rather than dealing with hundreds of individual functions, the programmer learns about a few dozen integrated classes.

Advanced class libraries, like CommonPoint from Taligent (now a part of IBM) go farther—they constitute a simple application right out of the box. The programmer can arrange the pieces and derive from the classes to make a custom application in a fraction of the time it takes to build one from scratch. ■

About the difference between class libraries and frameworks

Choosing a framework may cut your development time by more than half.

About the most important class library in the world: Microsoft Foundation Classes

By using the advanced features of MFC you can build sophisticated plug-ins in just two classes.

How class libraries such as Borland's OWL or Rogue Wave's product line supplement operating system-level libraries

Many vendors offer cross-platform class libraries that allow you to write more portable code.

How to use an application framework

Apple's MacApp and Taligent's CommonPoint supply many of the pieces of an application, ready to be put into final form.

Class Libraries

Class libraries are collections of classes (typically, C++ classes) that provide the programmer with a model. A model is, of course, a simplified way of looking at the world. When the programmer puts the pieces of the model together in a way that form an application (or a plug-in), the complexity hidden by the model comes together, and the application works. (Well, that's how it's supposed to work!)

 This chapter assumes that the classes in the class libraries and frameworks are implemented in C++. If you need to brush up on C++ or object-oriented methodology, go back and skim Chapter 2, "A C++ Primer."

Go ahead. We'll wait!

This section shows two ways to use a class library—you want to use both methods on most projects. This section then takes a detailed look at the Microsoft Foundation Classes library, as well as some of its cousins and competitors.

Using a Class Library

As mentioned in the introduction, one common use for a class library is to place some order around the operating system interface. For example, the MFC class CDialog encapsulates the Windows interfaces to a dialog box. Rather than having to hunt through the Windows API documentation looking for things related to dialog boxes, the programmer looks at the pages that describe CDialog.

A class in a class library offers five features that interest the programmer:

- A place in the inheritance hierarchy
- One or more constructors
- A destructor
- Public members, for manipulating the object
- Public and protected members, which can be overridden by derived classes

Introducing *CDialog*   As shown in Figure 17.1, CDialog is derived from CWnd. This statement means that any public or protected member of CWnd is automatically a part of CDialog. In fact, Microsoft's documentation shows that CWnd is derived from CCmdTarget, which in turn is derived from CObject, so just the act of saying the following says a great deal:

```
class CDialog : public CWnd
{
};
```

> **N O T E** Recall that, usually, data members are kept private or protected. If they are exposed at all, it is through access methods. You *can* make a data member public, which is sometimes done for efficiency. You can be almost as efficient and still preserve the interface by making the access methods in-line. ■

FIG. 17.1
CDialog is derived from CWnd, so all public and protected members of CWnd are part of CDialog.

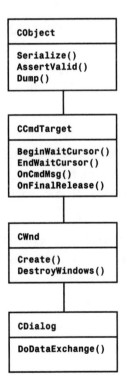

CObject Let's start at the top of the hierarchy. The ultimate ancestor of CDialog is CObject. This class provides four basic services:

■ *Serialization*—The object can be read or written from a medium such as the hard drive.

■ *Run-time class information*—Allows run-time access to the class name (useful in debugging).

■ *Object diagnostic output*—Supports debugging.

■ *Compatibility with collection classes*—So that you can put a CObject into a collection, such as a list or an array.

Some objects, such as CObject, are too abstract to instantiate. For example, what does it mean to call AssertValid() on an instance of CObject? What do you write when someone calls Serialize()? Abstract objects such as CObject serve as base classes—they are used by deriving concrete classes that actually implement these functions.

CCmdTarget   CCmdTarget is derived from CObject. It has all the functionality of CObject, and it adds the capability to interface with the MFC MESSAGE_MAP architecture. CCmdTarget also supports dispatch maps, which are used with the IDispatch OLE interface described in Chapter 14, "If All the World Used Microsoft...."

Because most delay at the user interface is associated with message processing, Microsoft elected to include the functions that handle the familiar hourglass cursor here in CCmdTarget. If you want to replace the hourglass with, say, a wristwatch, change the implementation of CCmdTarget::BeginWaitCursor(), and then relink the applications.

CWnd   Despite the name, class CWnd isn't the same as a window, but it's close. Class CWnd has a member function, Create(), which instantiates a Windows window (see Figure 17.2). Here's the usual sequence:

1. The application instantiates a new CWnd, using the new operator.
2. The application calls CWnd::Create(), which makes a new window and attaches it to the CWnd instance.
3. The application interacts with the window, using methods on CWnd.
4. When the application is done with the window, it calls CWnd::DestroyWindow().
5. Immediately after calling DestroyWindow(), the application deletes the CWnd.

FIG. 17.2
A Windows window attaches to a CWnd through its HWND member, m_hWnd.

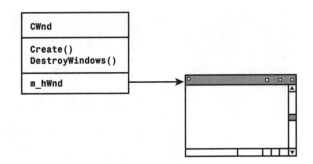

CWnd is a big class. As you might suppose in a system named "Windows", the CWnd class has member functions that allow the program to manage the windows on-screen appearance such as BringWindowToTop(), its content such as OnPaint(), and its controls such as ScrollWindow().

What's surprising is that much of the functionality of a dialog box is actually part of CWnd. For example, CWnd::GetNextDlgGroupItem() allows you to step through a group of controls. CWnd::GetNextDlgTabItem() has a similar function, but follows the window's defined tab order.

And Back to *CDialog* Most of the functionality added by CDialog has to do with notification. If you use Microsoft Visual C++, you can quickly see what this statement means. Open a new MFC-based DLL project and use the resource editor to add a new dialog to the project (see Figure 17.3). Now use ClassWizard to add a new class derived from CDialog. (ClassWizard will recognize the new dialog resource and suggest that deriving from CDialog is a reasonable step to take.)

After ClassWizard is open and the new class is in place, select the new class in the Object IDs field. The field on the right, Messages, fills with all the methods and messages a dialog might reasonably be expected to handle. This screen is shown in Figure 17.4. You will recognizes some of these methods from the parent classes. There's Serialize() from CObject, OnCmdMsg and OnFinalRelease from CCmdTarget, and Create() and DestroyWindow() from CWnd. Usually you only want to override a small number of these methods—often, just DoDataExchange().

If you wanted to override one of the methods of CDialog and provide your own implementation, you can just click on the message name, and then click the Edit Code button. Figure 17.5 shows the default code provided by ClassWizard for DoDataExchange().

Part
IV

Ch
17

FIG. 17.3
Before ClassWizard can derive a class from `CDialog`, it expects to see a dialog resource in the project.

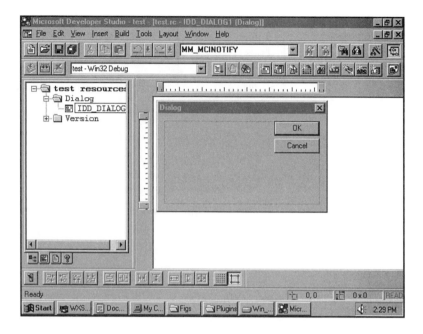

FIG. 17.4
Your new `CDialog`-derived class could handle over 60 methods and messages.

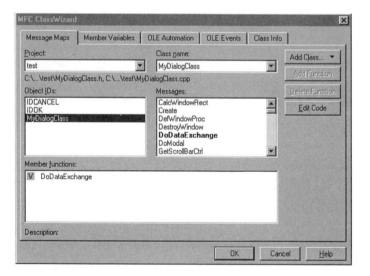

Deriving New Classes If you look at the ClassView in Visual C++, you see that this new DLL has nothing in it but an application (derived from `CWinApp`) and the new dialog class that you added (see Figure 17.6). Yet this project is complete, in the sense that you can compile it and link it without errors.

FIG. 17.5
ClassWizard is smart enough to set up skeleton code and get you into position to write your implementation.

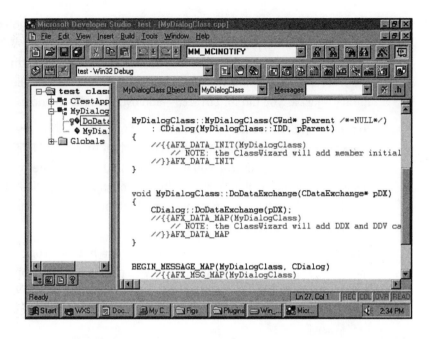

FIG. 17.6
AppWizard built a skeleton DLL with a CApp and your dialog box.

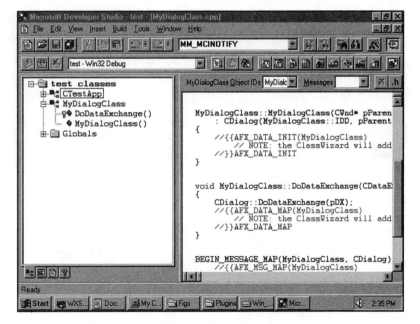

When you use a class library half of the work is in deciding which classes to use. To use a class as-is, just instantiate a new instance. Often, you will be happy with nearly everything the class does for you, but you will want to add one or two minor changes. In this case, derive your own class from the one supplied by the class library—just as you did for CDialog—and override the methods.

Rearranging the Pieces   The other half of using a class library is to make sure that your classes' methods get called at the right times. If you trace an MFC application's flow of control, you usually will find an object derived from CWinApp being built on the stack. Then this object's constructor is called, the main window is built, the menu bars go up, and the application sits there waiting for a message (WM_COMMAND).

In a plug-in the flow of control is a little different, but the programmer's tasks are the same. Typically in a plug-in you derive a plug-in window from CWnd. In NPP_New() you instantiate your window (but not display it), and then save the window in your plug-in's instance data. For this example call your CWnd-derived class CPluginWnd.

When Navigator calls NPP_SetWindow() your plug-in usually calls CPluginWnd::SubclassWindow. Now your window's WindowProc gets called when messages are received by the plug-in's window. You handle interactions just like a full-blown application, as well as handling incoming stream data and other requests from Navigator.

TIP If you're unfamiliar with Navigator's plug-in methods, review Chapter 6, "NPP Methods: Starting the Plug-In," Chapter 7 "NPP Methods: Handling Interaction," Chapter 8, "NPP Methods: Other Tasks," and Chapter 9, "Understanding NPN Methods."

If you want to drive this example to its logical conclusion, build a class CPluginWnd and hook it into npshell.cpp as described. In CPluginWnd's constructor, put up the dialog box and call DoModal(). You probably will want to add more controls to the dialog box by using the dialog editor. You should add code into DoDataExchange() to copy the data out of these controls and into the plug-in. You could call NPN_PostURL() to send this data off to the Net or, for simplicity, just post the results in a message box to show that you succeeded.

See this book's companion CD-ROM (source/chap17/dialog/) for a developed example of the above plug-in.

Accessing Microsoft Foundation Classes

On Windows machines, the most important class library is Microsoft Foundation Classes. Taken together with the AppWizards and the ClassWizard, MFC qualifies as a framework—a skeleton application that can be used as a starting point for the programmer.

Although you can use MFC to write many kinds of applications and DLLs, one of the more powerful architectures is the *document/view model*.

So far, the MFC examples you've seen have had an application class (derived from CWinApp) and a window class (derived from CWnd). Although the AppWizard builds an application class, you don't use it in the plug-in. Windows applications need to have exactly one CWinApp, and the one you use is inside Navigator.

> **NOTE** If you look up CWinApp in the MFC documentation, you see that it is derived from CWinThread, which in turn is derived from CCmdTarget. The combination of a command target and a thread gives a message pump. Remember from Chapter 13, "Getting Back on the Network," that most applications only need a message pump in their main thread. ■

The Document Classes   The plug-ins seen so far in this chapter are based on the application/window model. Because Netscape provides the application, all of the work is done by the window. Typically, the WindowProc of the window handles the messages, CPluginWindow::OnPaint() handles the display of the data (possibly by copying a virtual window into place with bitblt()), and the derived class from CWnd contains the data members (which are riding along in the instance's pData member).

For simple plug-ins this design may be acceptable but for complex plug-ins, the window class becomes quite busy. If, for example, you need more than one way to display the data, OnPaint() becomes complex. In most plug-ins, you want to paint the data onto the screen *and* onto the printer, and you may want to have separate methods for these two tasks.

In the document/view model, you still have a window class (for a frame) and an application class, but you add a document class that stores the data, and one or more view classes, which manage how the data is presented.

In a plug-in, Navigator provides a window and an application. You can derive a document from CDocument and attach it to pData. The document is responsible for serialization of the data. If you want to allow the user to save the contents of the plug-in window to the local hard drive, to post the data back to the Net, or even to load the data *from* the net (in NPP_Write()), override CDocument's Serialize method (inherited from CObject::Serialize()).

N O T E Don't attach too much significance to the term "document." Although the name makes you think of a file with text in it, the term is used in this model to mean anything with content in it. A document can hold a WAV file, a bitmapped image, or data in some proprietary format. Of course, a document also can hold text. ▮

The View Classes A *view* (derived in MFC from class CView) is a presentation of your data. You may want to have one view for the screen and a different view for the printer. You may want to allow the user to choose the view. A clock plug-in, for example, might store the current time in the document, then have views that display an analog clock, a digital 12-hour clock, or a digital 24-hour clock.

N O T E Don't bother looking for OnPaint() in the view class. Your plug-in should override OnDraw(). Windows will pass a device context instance into OnDraw()—call your painting functions on that CDC. ▮

Using Symantec's ObjectWindows Library

If you're not using a Microsoft compiler, you still may be able to use MFC. MFC comes with the Symantec C++ compiler, for example. You also can purchase and install the low-end Visual C++ (named the Standard Edition), and then delete everything except the MFC library. Borland provides a procedure that allows you to compile MFC under Borland C++ 5 and use MFC in your Borland-compiled programs.

T I P To find out more about using MFC under Borland C++ 5, read Appendix C of *Special Edition Using Borland C++ 5* (Que, 1996).

Borland also offers their own class library—the ObjectWindows Library, or OWL. Like MFC, OWL encapsulates the Windows API. Because Borland is at a natural disadvantage in this task (compared to Microsoft), they had to go beyond Microsoft to stay competitive. OWL, for example, not only includes the new Windows 95 common controls, it also provides 16-bit emulations of these controls and a Windows NT 3.51 implementation. Using OWL, your plug-in can offer the look and feel of Windows 95 on all Windows platforms.

 TIP For information on the differences between Win16, Win32s, and Win32, see Chapter 16, "Spanning the Windows World."

OWL also includes new controls that go beyond those offered in MFC. For example, OWL supports a class `TGauge`, which physically resembles the Windows 95 progress control, `CProgressCtrl`. `CProgressCtrl` offers the following seven member functions:

- Construction
    - `CProgressCtrl()`—The class constructor
    - `Create()`—The method that actually instantiates the control and attaches it to the `CProgressCtrl`
- Attributes
    - `SetRange()`—Sets the minimum and maximum positions
    - `SetPos()`—Sets the current position of the progress bar
    - `OffsetPos()`—Makes relative changes in the position
    - `SetStep()`—Sets a default step increment for use by `StepIt()`
- Operations
    - `StepIt()`—Advances the current position by the default step increment—set by `SetStep()`

By contrast, OWL's `TGauge` offers almost twice as many public functions, and has even slimmed down the construction interface by one function.

- Construction
    - `TGauge()`—The class constructor, which includes the functionality of `CProgressCtrl::Create()`

■ Attributes

- SetRange()—Sets the minimum and maximum positions
- SetValue()—Sets the current position of the progress bar
- DeltaValue()—Makes relative changes in the position
- SetStep()—Sets a default step increment for use by StepIt()
- GetRange()—Returns the current range
- GetStep()—Returns the current default step increment
- GetValue()—Returns the current position of the bar
- SetLed()—Manages the thickness and spacing of the elements of the progress bar
- SetColor()—Sets the color of the progress bar
- SetNativeUse()—Determines whether the native (such as Windows 95) class is built, or the enhanced Borland class

■ Operations

- StepIt()—Advances the current position by the default step increment (set by SetStep())
- operator++()—Provides a shorthand access to StepIt()

If your plug-ins need to span the Windows universe and you like the idea of enhanced controls and classes, consider switching to the Borland compiler. If you prefer Microsoft's classes for access to the Win API, by all means compile MFC under Borland C++ 5, and get the best of both worlds.

TIP Just as Microsoft includes the Standard Template Library (STL) with their compiler, Borland includes not only STL but also BIDS, the Borland International Data Structures. Both STL and BIDS are class libraries that emphasize *container classes* such as lists, queues, and arrays.

If portability and long-term maintenance issues are important, you may want to use STL rather than BIDS or the container classes of MFC. STL now is part of the ANSI standard and is likely to be part of C++ for a long time.

If you want to get something up and running quickly with a shallow learning curve, look closely at BIDS. BIDS doesn't do as much as STL, but if it does what you want, BIDS may be easier to learn.

Class Libraries for UNIX

Although UNIX is too diverse an environment to have just one or two leading suppliers of class libraries, some clear standards are emerging. Rogue Wave enjoys a good reputation—it provides a variety of class libraries for use in statistics, math, and database access, and also standard collection classes. Figure 17.7 shows a portion of their product line, from their Web page.

ON THE WEB

You can find Rogue Wave on the Internet at **http://www.roguewave.com/**.

FIG. 17.7
Rogue Wave offers high-quality libraries that compile on most common UNIX platforms.

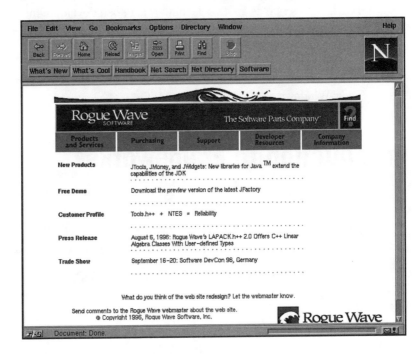

TIP Many of Rogue Wave's class libraries also are available for Windows. If you need to support both Windows and UNIX, increase your code portability by using a cross-platform library such as the ones offered by Rogue Wave.

One of the most exciting cross-platform class libraries to come along in years is CommonPoint, from Taligent (now a part of IBM). Learn more about CommonPoint later in this chapter, in the section, "Taligent's CommonPoint."

TCL from Symantec

One of the most venerable class libraries is the THINK Class Library (TCL) from Symantec. TCL started life under THINK Pascal and THINK C on the Macintosh, languages with some object-oriented extensions that come short of the current C++ standard. THINK C, for example, doesn't have constructors, so each class has an initialization method. For example, to make a new `CDataFile` object, you write the following:

```
CDataFile* theDataFile = new CDataFile;
theDataFile->IDataFile();
```

TCL is not as rich as another leading Macintosh development system, MacApp, but TCL has been used to develop a long list of successful commercial products.

In recent years Symantec extended their Symantec C++ product beyond the Macintosh, and it now also is a significant player in the Windows market as well. Their Windows product ships with MFC.

Introduction to Frameworks

The hottest topic in class libraries in recent years is frameworks. Frameworks differ from class libraries in that they offer an already-built program. As an applications programmer, you derive new classes to add functionality and rearrange the calls to the various methods to make the product do what you want.

Does this description sound a lot like class libraries? The distinction between class libraries and frameworks gets blurrier every day. Previously, this chapter made the point that, taken together with AppWizard and ClassWizard, MFC constitutes a framework. Borland C++ 5 includes a variety of tools, including AppExpert and ClassExpert, which do much the same thing as AppWizard and ClassWizard. Whether Microsoft's environment is a better match than Borland's is a matter of debate and some personal taste. Figure 17.8 shows a representative screen from Borland's AppExpert.

FIG. 17.8
Borland's AppExpert does the same kind of work as Microsoft's AppWizard, but offers additional options.

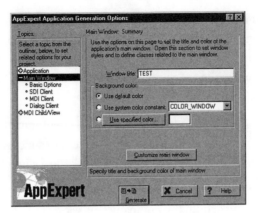

MacApp

For a decade, the leading framework for Macintosh developers was MacApp. The Macintosh was, of course, the first widespread graphical user interface (GUI). At a time when "the other guys" were writing for MS-DOS, Mac programmers came face-to-face with the Macintosh Toolbox, and a learning curve that resembled a vertical wall.

Apple developed MacApp in response to the difficulties early Mac programmers had learning to manage the GUI. (In fairness, Windows programmers went through the same learning process when the Windows SDK was released a few years later.) Right out of the box, the programmer could compile MacApp into a complete skeleton application. With this much done, he or she could begin to add functionality by deriving new classes to replace the application's existing objects. The programmer also could rearrange calls to objects and their methods. At one point Apple boasted that a new Macintosh application was being released every day—a large percentage of this success was due to the ease of use of MacApp.

Taligent's CommonPoint

The story goes that a team of engineers at Apple Computer was listing features for their next generations of operating system. Features planned to go in the next generation went on blue Post-It notes. Features planned to be implemented after that went on pink Post-It notes, and long-range ideas went on red Post-It notes. After they were done, the blue slips were collected and formed the basis of Macintosh's System 7.0, a complete rewrite of the Mac operating system. (Trivia buffs, take note: For a while the engineers working on System 7.0 were known as the "Blue Meanies." Now you know why!)

Apple assigned a different team to collect the pink Post-It notes—this team began work on a complete object-oriented operating system to succeed System 7.0. Along the way, IBM got interested, then Hewlett-Packard; the Taligent consortium was born.

Over the life of the consortium the company's mission shifted slightly. Taligent's investors determined that developers were less interested in a new operating system than they were an environment for rapid development.

In August 1995 at the Object World conference in San Francisco Taligent unveiled CommonPoint, their implementation of what had been the "Pink" project. Taligent boasted that CommonPoint had over 100 frameworks and over 1,000 discrete classes. Although Taligent uses the word "framework" in a way that isn't quite the same as it is used in the rest of this chapter, one thing is clear: CommonPoint is a large, rich development environment that offers cross-platform capability and many times the functionality of even as rich a library as MFC.

At the Object World conference several developers who had been seeded with the beta version of CommonPoint demonstrated sophisticated document-centric applications that was developed in a fraction of the time required in a traditional environment. Although the development environment was AIX (IBM's version of UNIX), Taligent demonstrated CommonPoint running on an HP UNIX machine, a Windows machine, and a Macintosh (using a pre-prerelease of Copland, Apple's next-generation operating system).

By the end of 1995 Taligent was reabsorbed into IBM, where development of CommonPoint continues. If CommonPoint survives the market and political pressures associated with its consortium heritage, it may become the cross-platform development environment of choice. Taligent also has cooperated with Addison-Wesley to bring out several books, including *Power of Frameworks*, *Inside Taligent Technology*, and *Taligent's Guide to Desiging Programs*.

ON THE WEB

For the latest information on CommonPoint, visit **http://www.taligent.com/**. This site has several white papers on CommonPoint and on object technology in general.

Figure 17.9 is a screen shot of **http://www.taligent.com/Technology/ Tech_Directions/MVP/mvp11.htm**, part of a Taligent presentation on their "Model-View-Presenter" architecture. This architecture is a logical extension of the document-view architecture described earlier in this chapter in connection with MFC. If you think that CommonPoint may be in your future as a plug-in programmer, you may want to begin to migrate today toward the document-view model.

FIG. 17.9
Taligent's Model-View-Presenter model may represent the next generation of software design.

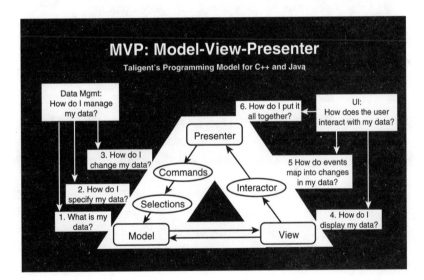

From Here...

Software developers are in a competitive environment. Developers who can quickly go from concept to product to marketplace have an advantage. Class libraries are now an essential part in helping programmers efficiently produce high-quality code. The even newer frameworks give the programmer a ready-to-compile starting point, taking over many repetitive tasks such as managing controls and tracking the cursor.

Among the most ambitious frameworks is CommonPoint, a product developed by Taligent, a consortium of engineers from IBM, Apple, and Hewlett-Packard. Now an IBM subsidiary, Taligent continues as a focal point of thinking about ways to apply object technology to software development.

■ Learn about the integration of Java, JavaScript, and plug-ins in the next chapter, "Plug-Ins as a Programming Resource."

■ Review C++ and the fundamentals of object technology in Chapter 2, "A C++ Primer."

■ Review the basics of plug-ins in Chapter 6, "NPP Methods: Starting the Plug-In," Chapter 7, "NPP Methods: Handling Interaction," Chapter 8, "NPP Methods: Other Tasks," and Chapter 9, "Understanding NPN Methods."

CHAPTER 18

Plug-Ins as a Programming Resource

As our civilization becomes increasingly dependent upon computers, many people foresee a shortage of programmers. Foresee? It's *here!* And those of us *in* the industry have to be the ones to do something about it.

One solution that seems to be firming up is the concept of *component architectures*. In this model programmers build sophisticated software components—small tools that do various jobs. Then end users or others who are not professional programmers put these components together into an application.

With LiveConnect, Netscape gives sophisticated end users a way to control complex components (plug-ins and Java applets) from a relatively simple language—JavaScript, bringing component architecture to the Web. ■

Why "small, sharp tools" that can be assembled into applications are more powerful than monolithic code

In the "UNIX-style" versus "Microsoft-style" design war, history favors the little guy.

How to pass parameters to a plug-in

Many applications don't require JavaScript; you can configure a plug-in from the <EMBED> tag.

Why LiveConnect is more than a multimedia control

LiveConnect is a key Netscape technology that promises to make plug-ins cost-effective (especially on intranets).

How Java classes talk to JavaScript

Java the central figure in LiveConnect, allows client-side JavaScript to communicate with plug-ins.

How Java classes talk to plug-ins

By completing the other side of the circuit, your Web pages can fully integrate Java, JavaScript, and plug-ins.

Compound Documents... Again

Recall from Chapter 14, "If All the World Used Microsoft...," that Microsoft's Object Linking and Embedding (OLE) technology is designed to allow users to build *compound documents*. With in-place activation (also known as *Visual Editing*) and OLE automation, the components of a compound document do more than just look good—they can be changed in place by the user or by other software. The distinction between "program" and "data" was never blurrier. This transition from a world in which end users have to think about which application they are using to one in which end users just manipulate their data (and let the system figure out which application to use) is known as *document-centric computing*.

Document-Centric Computing Meets the Web

This brings us back to the Web. Today, when a user wants to access the Web, he or she launches an application, Netscape. If they want to copy some content from a Web page to a word-processing document, they have to launch their word processor and copy (or drag) the contents from one window to the next. If Apple's Cyberdog is any indication, in the next generation of software the user may start by opening a document. They would put in text content by typing. They would put in graphics content by drawing. And they could put in Web content by...surfing?

In this scenario the embedded plug-in becomes an agent, controlled in part by the end user (through interaction) and in part by the page into which it is embedded. When copied or dragged into a compound document, the plug-in negotiates its content with this document, and either embeds its content or maintains a link through the browser back to the Net.

Although it may take a professional programmer to write a plug-in, the end user is fully able to assemble content into a compound document. So it is the end user who builds the solution (which was once called an application), using these professionally developed components.

The UNIX Way

There is adequate precedent for the success of this approach. The designers of
UNIX started with a vision of "small, sharp tools" that could be connected together
as needed. Do you need to see how many copies of the HTTP daemon are running
on your Web server? The UNIX command `ps -ef` lists all of the processes. The
command `grep httpd` scans its input (standard in) for the string "httpd," which is
the name of the HTTP daemon. The UNIX tool `wc` counts things—`wc -l` counts
lines. So the following line of code creates a one-time application where none existed before:

```
ps -ef ¦ grep httpd ¦ wc -l
```

Do you want to keep this little program around? Save this line in a file (named, say,
daemonCount.ksh). Make the file an executable program by typing the following:

```
chmod +x daemonCount.ksh
```

Also, make sure that daemonCount.ksh is in the path your computer searches
when you issue commands.

Now, when you type "daemonCount.ksh" this little application runs and returns
the number of server processes. Hey, presto!

Figure 18.1 illustrates a typical document-centric component-based environment.

The Microsoft Way

Contrast this approach with, say, Microsoft Word. The flagship application of the
world's largest software company has it all. Do you need an outline? It's right there
on the View menu. Ready to spell-check? It's at the top of the list under Tools.
Graphics? Spreadsheets? Databases? You can connect them all through Microsoft
Office. Microsoft has tried to anticipate your every need. But if they haven't, until
recently, you were out of luck.

But only "until recently." Microsoft has more to lose by encouraging component
architectures, because components can be written by smaller companies, potentially carving up part of Microsoft's pie. OLE 2 is a major step toward component
architecture, and so are compound documents, especially with in-place activation.
DLLs make it easier to add or change functionality after a product is fielded.

FIG. 18.1

In a component-based environment, the user's request is satisfied by small tools assembled for a specific purpose.

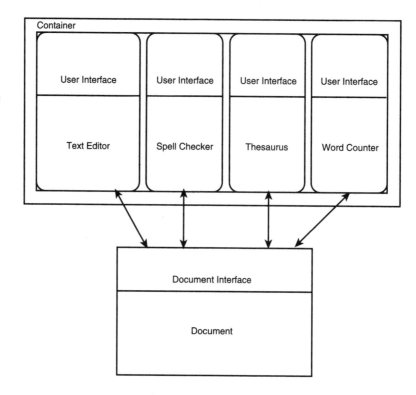

ActiveX seems to be a big step toward components. Over time, perhaps driven by market pressures from software initiatives like OpenDoc and CommonPoint (and yes, even Netscape plug-ins), Microsoft is moving in the direction of component architecture.

VBScript versus Radical Document-Centric Architectures

You can review some of the technologies that make component architectures possible right here in this book. Chapter 14, "If All the World Used Microsoft...," describes Microsoft's approach to compound documents—OLE. A section at the end of Chapter 14 describes OLE's biggest competitor: an open technology known as OpenDoc.

Chapter 15, "ActiveX and Plug-Ins for Other Browsers," is mostly about ActiveX, a Microsoft technology that allows small OLE automation objects to use in Microsoft Internet Explorer and other applications.

Chapter 17, "Using Class Libraries and Frameworks," describes how components (also known as objects) are used at the programming level. The last section in Chapter 17 describes CommonPoint, a huge collection of "small, sharp tools" in C++, ready to be used by the programmer.

These chapters didn't tell you that the people behind the non-Microsoft solutions are all the same folks. Taligent's CommonPoint supports OpenDoc. Apple, a key member of the OpenDoc consortium, may bundle Navigator in their next release of the Mac OS, right alongside Cyberdog. The next release of Navigator may support OpenDoc on all major platforms, including Windows. And Taligent, which was founded on Apple's vision of the "Pink" operating system, is now a subsidiary of IBM.

As we pull into the last years of this decade, lines are being drawn: Microsoft is promoting an all-Microsoft solution, with scripting done in VBScript and components added by using ActiveX controls. All of Microsoft's competitors, including IBM and Apple, are promoting radical document-centric architectures, with a lot of room for OpenDoc components written by the smaller players.

Keep watching. This looks like fun.

Integrating Plug-Ins with HTML

Although only experienced programmers are writing plug-ins and Java applets, almost anyone can learn to write JavaScript or HTML. As a programmer, you can give the user a certain amount of control over your plug-in by passing parameters through the <EMBED> tag. Recall from Chapter 6, "NPP Methods: Starting the Plug-In," that NPP_New() passes a description of the parameters in argc, argn, and argv. If the HTML author writes, for example, the following, your plug-in can read these parameters:

```
<EMBED SRC="http://www.somemachine.com/myFile.tst"
➥HEIGHT=100 WIDTH=100
  AUTOSTART=True LOOP=False AUTOSCALE=Often>
```

What it *does* with these parameters is, of course, determined by you as the programmer.

Figure 18.2 illustrates the mapping from <EMBED> attributes to argc, argn, and argv.

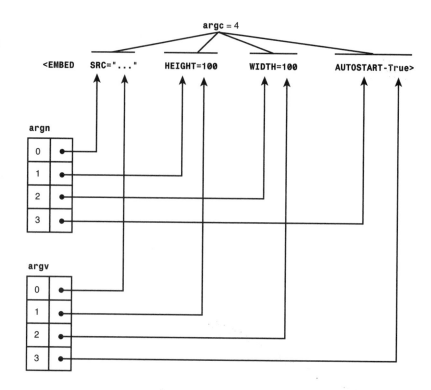

FIG. 18.2
The HTML author can control plug-in options through attributes of the <EMBED> tag.

Integrating Plug-Ins By Using LiveConnect

As you read Chapter 7, "NPP Methods: Handling Interaction," you may have thought, "There must be a simpler way to get messages into the plug-in." You're right. The techniques described in Chapter 7 hook platform-native controls such as menus and pushbuttons into your plug-in. This approach has the advantage of looking familiar to the user. It also gives you a great deal of control over the appearance of your plug-in. (For example, a pop-up menu that appears in response to the user right-clicking the mouse may offer a dozen or more menu items, yet it doesn't clutter the screen when not in use.)

Sometimes, however, you will be happy to have a little HTML form with some buttons that tell the plug-in to "Start" or "Stop." Netscape provides all this flexibility and more through a technology known as LiveConnect.

If you want the user to truly interact with the plug-in, your best approach is to add user controls, such as pop-up menus, to the plug-in and send messages to the plug-in, as described in Chapter 7. But if you only need control the plug-in, you may find LiveConnect sufficient.

The distinction between "interact" and "control" is a fine line. Here's an example. If your plug-in downloads a drawing from the Web, allows you to annotate it, and post it back to the Web, you need to use native controls. For example, you probably want a pop-up menu (perhaps triggered by the right mouse button) that allows you to zoom, save, and revert.

If your plug-in is simpler, such as a video player, and you want to allow the HTML author to add buttons to the page like "Start" and "Stop," LiveConnect may be faster and easier to implement. You can *do* more complex tasks with LiveConnect. The tradeoff is between portable code (with LiveConnect) and native look and feel (with native controls and messages).

Many plug-ins will want to use both native controls and LiveConnect. It's up to you to decide how to best design your plug-in.

Part
IV

Ch
18

What is LiveConnect?

LiveConnect, new with Navigator 3.0, integrates applets written in the platform-independent language Java (from Sun Microsystems) with Netscape's JavaScript and with your plug-ins. Figure 18.3 illustrates the communications paths between Java, JavaScript, and the plug-in.

FIG. 18.3
LiveConnect is Netscape's approach to integrating Java, JavaScript, and plug-ins.

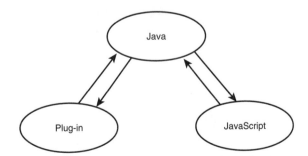

Note that LiveConnect doesn't allow your plug-in to communicate directly with a script written in JavaScript. All communications go through Java. This design isn't a problem, however, as you will read in a moment.

How Much Java Do I Need to Know?

Recall that LiveConnect doesn't give a JavaScript programmer direct access to the plug-in, or vice versa. If you're comfortable with C++ and object technology, you can write a proxy class in Java that sits between your plug-in and JavaScript, giving a JavaScript programmer access to your plug-in.

To get started in Java, see the sidebar in this section entitled "A Java Primer." To go further with Java, check out *Special Edition Using Java* (Que, 1996). Then read on in this section to learn about the Netscape-specific packages that you need to use to connect Java to JavaScript and to your plug-ins.

A Java Primer

To get started with Java, you need a Java development environment. The Java SDK from Sun is available on the CD-ROM that accompanies this book. To use LiveConnect with Java, you also need the java_30 file, which comes with Navigator 3.0.

Start by writing a Java "Hello, world!" program. The text file for this program is shown in Listing 18.1. This sidebar will describe how to put this applet into an HTML page. For now you can compile the applet from the command line with the following:

```
javac hello.java
```

The Java compiler, javac, produces a file with Java bytecodes that may be run in a browser like Hot Java or Navigator. This output file is called hello.class. You can run it by typing this line:

```
appletviewer hello.html
```

The file hello.html need have only a single line:

```
<APPLET CODE="hello.class" WIDTH=120 HEIGHT=120></APPLET>
```

Let's go through hello.java, line by line.

Just as you do in C++, you usually can find some Java class to serve as a starting point for your program, so that you don't have to write everything from scratch. Sun conveniently supplies class Applet, so we derive hello from Applet. (Note that Java, like C++, is case-sensitive.)

Java uses the following notation to access a specific method:

```
packageName.className.methodName
```

Therefore, to access the drawString() method of an instance of Java class Graphics, you import the class java.awt.Graphics, and then call drawString on the instance. You can get all methods on all of the classes in a package by placing * in the *className* position.

Start by telling the Java compiler that Applet is defined in another file, in the classes\java\Applet subdirectory, which is what the following line does:

```
import java.applet.*;
```

All your applets will start with this line.

Many applets do some kind of drawing to the window, so you want to use class Graphics. Graphics is defined in the java\awt\Graphics subdirectory. For convenience, you bring in all of these useful built-in classes.

```
import java.awt.*;
```

By default, Java classes are not public. Because you want to be able to access class hello from the outside world, declare it to be public. you also declare that it is derived from class Applet. Note that, when a class name is made public, the class must be defined in a file of the same name. Therefore, class hello must be saved to a file named hello.java, as follows:

```
public class hello extends Applet
```

Just like C++ classes in class libraries such as MFC, Java classes have methods that the outside world calls. When the class is constructed, its init() method is called. You define init() as a *stub*—anything that should be done by the class when it is constructed can go in here.

```
public void init()
{
}
```

Just as Windows sends the message WM_PAINT every time the windows need to be redrawn, and Navigator calls NPP_SetWindow(), so Java calls your class's method paint() when the window has to be displayed. paint() takes a Graphics object as its parameter, as follows:

```
public void paint(Graphics g)
{
  g.drawString("Hello, world!", 10, 50);
}
```

To access the applet from Navigator (rather than just from AppletViewer, copy the line from hello.html into the HTML file of your Web page. Now you have a (very simple) Java applet on your page.

Listing 18.1   hello.java—The Java "Hello, World!" Program

```
import java.applet.*;
import java.awt.*;
public class hello extends Applet
{
  public void init()
  {
  }
  public void paint (Graphics g)
  {
    g.drawString("Hello", 10, 50);
  }
}
```

 ON THE WEB

You can download the latest version of Sun's Java Developer's Kit (JDK), with Netscape modifications, as part of the Netscape Plug-ins SDK, at **http://home.netscape.com/ eng/mozilla/3.0/handbook/plugins/index.html**.

You also can use commercial packages such as Symantec's Cafe or Natural Intelligence's Roaster, but you need the classes from Netscape's version of the kit. You also need Netscape's special version of javah (also part of the kit).

Using LiveConnect to Talk to JavaScript

The first step in connecting a script in JavaScript to your plug-in is to connect Java-Script to Java. After that, you'll build a Java class that does its work by calling your plug-in. From the point of view of JavaScript, this Java class serves as a proxy for your plug-in.

Calling JavaScript from Java Methods   In order for a Java class to talk to JavaScript, you must import the Netscape `javascript` package in the Java file, as follows:

```
import netscape.javascript.*
```

The `netscape.javascript` package, described in a following section of this chapter, includes two important classes—`JSObject`, which represents the JavaScript object, and `JSException`, which is raised to pass JavaScript errors back to your Java class.

For a Java class to call JavaScript, the HTML author must explicitly set the MAYSCRIPT attribute in the APPLET tag. For example:

```
<APPLET NAME="hello" CODE="hello.class" WIDTH=100 HEIGHT=100 MAYSCRIPT>
```

Note that in this example, a name was assigned to the applet. You will use the name when we begin talking to the applet from JavaScript.

> **CAUTION**
>
> If a Java applet attempts to run a page's JavaScript and the HTML author hasn't set MAYSCRIPT, Navigator raises an exception. You should catch this exception and put up an appropriate message to the user.
>
> One good way to put up an error message is to use the *Java console* defined by Netscape. From inside Java, write the following:
>
> ```
> System.out.println("Error: Applet unable to access JavaScript.
>    Set the applet's MAYSCRIPT attribute and try again.");
> ```

To access JavaScript, your Java class must get a handle to the Navigator window, as shown in Figure 18.4. Your class's init() member is a good place to do this:

```
JSObject win;
public void init()
{
  win = JSObject.getWindow(this);
}
```

Part
IV
Ch
18

FIG. 18.4
Java gets a pointer to the JavaScript document in order to access its members.

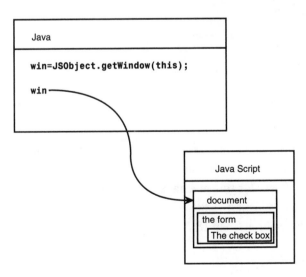

If the HTML page has a form named `theForm` which, in turn, has a check box named `theCheckbox`, you can access the status of this check box by following the membership hierarchy from the form to the check box, as follows:

```
JSObject win;
public void init()
{
  win = JSObject.getWindow(this);
  JSObject doc = (JSObject) win.getMember("document");
  JSObject theForm = (JSObject) doc.getMember("theForm");
  JSObject check = (JSObject) myForm.getMember("theCheckBox");
  Boolean isChecked = (Boolean) check.getMember("checked");
}
```

Just as `getMember()` gives you access to the components of the JavaScript form, `call()` and `eval()` give you access to the JavaScript methods. You can write the following:

```
public void init()
{
  win = JSObject.getWindow(this);
}

public boolean mouseUp(Event e, int x, int y)
{
  win.eval("alert(\"Hello, world!\");");
  return true;
}
```

or, equivalently,

```
public void init()
{
  win = JSObject.getWindow(this);
}

public boolean mouseUp(Event e, int x, int y)
{
  win.call("alert(\"Hello, world!\");");
  return true;
}
```

Calling Java Methods from JavaScript   You can communicate in the opposite direction, from JavaScript *to* the applet, by making sure that the applet has a name. Figure 18.5 illustrates this mechanism. Suppose that you had a Java class like count, shown in Listing 18.2. You find count.java on this book's companioon CD-ROM, in the \source\Chap 18\.

FIG. 18.5
The HTML author assigns the applet a name, so JavaScript can talk to it.

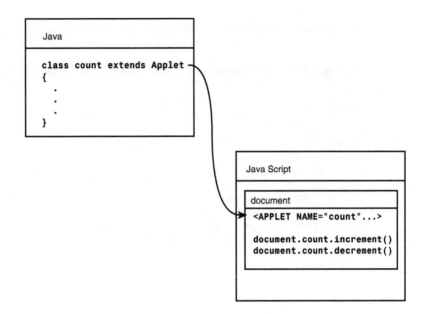

Listing 18.2 count.java—A Simple Java Class that Accepts Two Commands

```java
import java.applet.*;
import java.awt.*;
public class count extends Applet
{
  int i;
  public void init()
  {
    I = 0;
  }
  public void paint (Graphics g)
  {
    g.drawString("The count is" + i, 10, 50);
  }
  public void increment()
  {
    I++;
    repaint();
  }
  public void decrement()
  {
    I--;
    repaint();
  }
}
```

You can install `count` on your Web page, as is shown in Listing 18.3.

Listing 18.3 count.html—A Web Page with a Controllable Applet

```
<HTML>
<HEAD>
<TITLE>Test count/TITLE>
</HEAD>
<BODY>
<H1>Test the Count Applet</H1>
<APPLET NAME="count" CODE="count.class" WIDTH=100, HEIGHT=100></APPLET>
<FORM>
<INPUT TYPE="Button" VALUE="Increment" NAME="IncrementButton"
➥onClick="document.count.increment()">
<INPUT TYPE="Button" VALUE="Decrement" NAME="DecrementButton"
➥onClick="document.count.decrement()">
</FORM>
</BODY>
</HTML>
```

Now that you know how Java and JavaScript can talk, you just have to get the plug-in to talk to Java.

Talking to the Plug-In

When you add plug-ins to an HTML page, JavaScript puts them into an array named `embeds`. For example, if the following is the first `<EMBED>` tag on your page, JavaScript shows the associated plug-in in `document.embeds[0]`:

```
<EMBED SRC="http://www.somemachine.com/myFile.tst HEIGHT=100
WIDTH=100>
```

From JavaScript, you can access `document.embeds.length` to find out how many plug-ins are on the page.

N O T E Because full-page plug-ins are, by definition, on a page with no JavaScript (and no HTML!), it only makes sense to talk about controlling embedded plug-ins. ■

To make a plug-in visible from inside Java, your Java class must use `netscape.plugin.Plugin`. Netscape provides a file `java_30` with Netscape 3.0. This file contains three Java packages, `java`, `sun`, and `netscape`:

- java
- sun
- netscape.applet
- netscape.net
- netscape.javascript
- netscape.plugin

The java and sun packages are replacements to packages of the same name in the Sun 1.0.2 Java Development Kit (JDK). They include security enhancements necessary for LiveConnect. Netscape and Sun are working together to ensure that these new packages are included in a future release of the Sun JDK.

netscape.applet is Netscape's replacement to sun.applet. Similarly, netscape.net replaces sun.net.

netscape.javascript implements JSObject and JSException, described previously in this chapter.

netscape.plugin implements the Plugin class. As a Java programmer, you use methods on the Plugin class to communicate with the plug-in.

> **N O T E** To use the Netscape-supplied packages with the JDK compiler, add the path
> of the java_30 and classes.zip to the compiler's classpath. You can
> either specify a CLASSPATH environment variable or use the -classpath command
> line option when you run javac. ▪

T I P As a plug-in programmer, you have a C++ development environment such as Microsoft Visual C++ handy. Don't waste time running javac from the command line. Put your plug-in's Java proxy class in the makefile, and automatically call javac each time your plug-in is rebuilt. If you use Visual C++, just add the javac command line (with the -classpath option) to the Custom Build settings.

While setting up the makefile, add the call to javah described in the following section. It will save you time later.

Calling Java Methods from the Plug-In   The plug-in talks to Java through Netscape's Java Runtime Interface. Figure 18.6 illustrates the JRI.

FIG. 18.6
The plug-in connects to the Java Runtime Interface, which handles communications with Java.

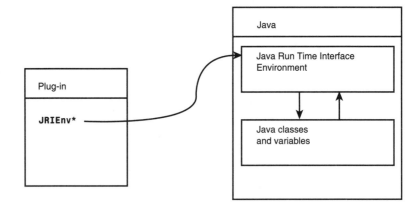

Netscape has defined the Java Runtime Interface to allow native code (such as a plug-in) to call Java methods.

ON THE WEB

The full specification of the Java Runtime Interface is available online as part of the Netscape Plug-in SDK (**http://home.netscape.com/eng/mozilla/3.0/handbook/plugins/index.html**).

Netscape also supplies a new version of javah, named the JRI (Java Runtime Interface) version, which writes a C/C++ header file from a Java class. To control the count class previously described from your plug-in, start by typing (or including in the makefile) the following:

```
javah -jri -classpath pathTojava_30Andclasses.zip count
```

The result of running javah is a header file for class count. Recall that count has one public data member, i. javah produces in-line accessor functions

```
jint i(JRIEnv* env);
```

and

```
void i(JRI* env, jint);
```

to get and set this data member.

Note that javah has transformed the Java `int` into a variable of type `jint`. Table 18.1 shows the JRI definitions of the Java primitive types. Netscape's version of javah transforms Java variables into C/C++ variables with a new Java-specific type.

Table 18.1   JRI Definitions of Java Primitive Types

Java Type	C/C++ Type	Size
boolean	jbool	1 byte
byte	jbyte	1 byte
char	jchar	2 bytes
short	jshort	2 bytes
int	jint	4 bytes
long	jlong	8 bytes
float	jfloat	4 bytes
double	jdouble	8 bytes

These sizes are defined through a series of `#ifdefs` in the file jri_md.h, which is included in the header file jri.h. Make sure that your compiler sets up the proper preprocessor symbols for your target machine, so your code gets the right size types.

Part IV

Ch 18

> **CAUTION**
>
> Make sure that you use the JRI types described in Table 18.1 when talking to Java methods. If you use the compiler's types (in other words, `int`), you run the risk of a size mismatch when you move to a new compiler or a new platform.

> **CAUTION**
>
> javah doesn't do a very good job of protecting the privacy of data members in Java classes. You will be able to access private members from inside your plug-in. Avoid this temptation, and use accessor methods and other public methods exclusively.
>
> By restricting yourself to public methods, your plug-in is less likely to need maintenance when the implementation of the Java class changes.

To call the `increment()` method of the Java class `count`, just write the following:

```
count->increment(env);
```

Here, `env` is the result of the function `NPN_GetJavaEnv()`. `NPN_GetJavaEnv()` has the following specification:

```
JavaEnv* NPN_GetJavaEnv(void);
```

Typically you call `NPN_GetJavaEnv()` once, in `NPP_Initialize()`.

 TIP Netscape starts the Java Runtime Interpreter when you first call `NPN_GetJavaEnv()`. This first call can impose a delay on your plug-in. If you're sure that your plug-in needs to call Java, call `NPN_GetJavaEnv()` in `NPP_Initialize()` and get it out of the way. The user expects to wait a few seconds when he or she accesses the plug-in content, anyway.

 TIP The pointer to the Java environment is thread-specific. If you call it in `NPP_Initialize()` you can use it in any instance, but if you spawn a new thread, you need to call `NPN_GetJavaEnv()` for this thread, and reserve the new `JavaEnv` pointer for use in this thread only.

Recall that most object-oriented languages, including both C++ and Java, support overloaded methods. That is, two more methods can have the same name, as long as they take different parameters. (Sets of parameters are called *signatures*.) In C++, the compiler performs *name mangling* to make sure that the internal names are unique. Netscape's javah appends an index to all but the first occurrence of a name. If you have three functions named `foo`, javah produces `foo`, `foo_1`, and `foo_2`. To find out which name to call for which signature, just check the header file output by javah. Without the use of an index on all but one of the names, the function name "foo" would be ambiguous. For this reason the index is sometimes known as a "disambiguating index."

 TIP If you have overloaded methods, first declare the one you plan to use most frequently from your plug-in. In this way, the declared version of the method will not have an index.

Similarly, if you have a Java-implemented version of a method and a native (such as C or C++) version of the same method, put the declaration of the native method first. In this way, you don't have to worry about index names when you write the native implementation.

> **TIP** Because javah uses the underscore followed by a number to disambiguate overloaded methods, it performs name-mangling on Java methods with an underscore in their name. Save yourself a headache—don't use underscores in Java method names.

Calling the Plug-In from Java Methods You can define *native methods* in Java that are implemented in C or C++. These methods give your Java applet access to low-level library routines in the operating system and also can be more efficient than Java alone. Figure 18.7 illustrates a Java class calling its native method.

FIG. 18.7
Java invokes a native method, allowing access to the operating system.

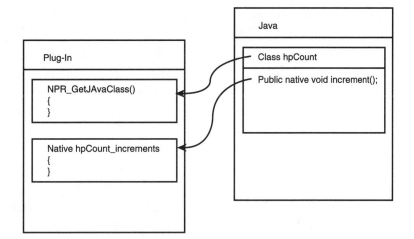

Just as calls by the plug-in to Java are made through the C or C++ header files produced by javah, Java methods call the plug-in by calling a Java peer of the plug-in. This peer is of type `netscape.plugin.Plugin`.

If you instantiate a Java object of type `Plugin`, your Java method will be able to refer to the plug-in, but will not be able to call any plug-in specific methods. If you derive a new Java class from `Plugin`, you can define native methods in the derived class that correspond to these plug-in methods you want to expose to Java.

Suppose that you want to write a plug-in that does the same work as `count`, the Java class shown previously. The new plug-in will be named npCount. For convenience, call the Java peer class npCount as well. Besides the `increment()` and `decrement()` methods defined for `count`, npCount has a new method, `post()`, which calls `NPN_PostURL()` and sends the current count back to a CGI script or LiveWire application on the Web site. The file shown in Listing 18.4 implements npCount.

Listing 18.4   npCount.java—A Java Peer Class for the *npCount* Plug-In

```
import netscape.plugin.Plugin;
class npCount extends Plugin
{
  public native void increment();
  public native void decrement();
  public native boolean post();
}
```

Compile npCount.java with javac, and run the JRI version of javah on it, as follows:

```
javah -jri -classpath pathTonpcount npCount
javah -jri -stubs -classpath pathTonpcount npCount
```

The second call to javah builds C stubs for the native methods. These stubs include a special initializer for each Java class. The initializer sets up the interface
between Java and your plug-in. Be sure to call the initializer before you use the
class! (If you have other Java classes with native methods outside of your plug-in,
call their initializers, too.)

For npCount, the initializer is specified by the following line:

```
extern java_lang_Class* init_npCount(JRIEnv* env);
```

You can add initialization code to this init_ method. You can add balancing code
to the Java peer's destroy() method. This method is called just before
NPP_Destroy() is called on the instance. You also can check (from Java) to see if
the native instance is still active by calling isActive(), which returns a boolean.

For Navigator to set up your Java peer class, it calls your plug-in's implementation
of NPP_GetJavaClass() NPP_GetJavaClass() is specified as follows:

```
jref NPP_GetJavaClass(void);
```

For npCount, a reasonable implementation of NPP_GetJavaClass() is:

```
jref NPP_GetJavaClass()
{
  return init_npCount(NPN_GetJavaEnv());
}
```

If your plug-in uses other Java classes that have native methods, call their
initializers before you return, to register their native methods with the JRI.

Make sure that you add the stub file (here, npCount.c) into your project, so that it
will be compiled and linked into the plug-in.

TIP You should always include an implementation of NPP_GetJavaClass() in your plug-in, even if you don't plan to use connect to Java. Just write a stub implementation that returns NULL.

Follow the javah naming conventions (rather than C++ name mangling) when implementing the native methods. Therefore, you might write the following:

```
jbool native_npCount_post(
  JRIEnv* env,
  npCount* self,
  JRIMethodThunk* methodThunk,
  other parameters...);
```

You can use the self parameter to access any other class members.

The *other parameters* in the last line are the parameters that you declared for this method in your Java class. The env parameter is supplied by the runtime in case you need to make calls back to Java. You can ignore the methodThunk parameter.

From the native method, you can access the plug-in instance by writing the following:

```
NPP npp = (NPP)self->getPeer(env);
```

From the plug-in, you can access the Java peer by calling NPN_GetJavaPeer(). The prototype of that function is:

```
jref NPN_GetJavaPeer(NPP instance);
```

If your plug-in is embedded on a page with JavaScript, the HTML author can activate the plug-in by calling it through the embeds interface. The first time JavaScript needs the Java peer object, Navigator makes an internal call to NPN_GetJavaPeer(), which instantiates the Java peer object. As part of NPN_GetJavaPeer(), Navigator calls the init_ method.

JavaScript then actually communicates to the Java peer object, which does its work through the native methods.

Part
IV

Ch

18

Putting It All Together

Figure 18.8 shows the flow of control from JavaScript through npCount and back again.

FIG. 18.8

The npCount plug-in communicates both to and from JavaScript.

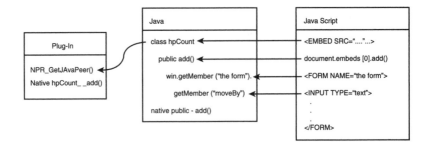

When the plug-in is loaded, it reads the current count from the Net—through NPP_Write()—and writes it to the window—through NPP_SetWindow(). When Navigator calls NPP_GetJavaPeer(), npCount returns its peer object, which is made available to JavaScript through embeds. When the user clicks a button, Navigator calls the method on the Java peer object pointed to by embeds[0]. If the method is add or decrease, the peer object talks to JavaScript to read the contents of the MoveBy field. All the remaining work of the Java class is done back in the plug-in. The plug-in runs the native method and calls InvalidateRect() to trigger an update of its window.

From Here...

After a plug-in and its peer Java object have been set up, they can be called by an HTML author, who doesn't have to be a professional programmer. By building a few well-written general-purpose plug-ins, programmers allow HTML authors and other users to access the Web in powerful and sophisticated ways. As the demand for quality software continues to outstrip the supply of talented programmers, the use of component architectures such as LiveConnect plug-ins will continue to be important.

■ After your plug-in is complete, use the techniques in the following chapter, "Installing the Plug-In," to make it easy for the end user to hook up and install.

■ Review C++ and the fundamentals of object technology in Chapter 2, "A C++ Primer."

■ Review the basics of plug-ins in Chapter 6, "NPP Methods: Starting the Plug-In," Chapter 7, "NPP Methods: Handling Interaction," Chapter 8, "NPP Methods: Other Tasks," and Chapter 9, "Understanding NPN Methods."

Part
IV

Ch
18

CHAPTER 19

Installing the Plug-In

Plug-ins are a good idea. Installing them is a pain in the neck! During the beta-testing period for Navigator 3.0, developers' biggest complaint was that the installation process was arbitrary, cumbersome, and error-prone. As plug-ins have moved into the marketplace, end users say the same thing.

Netscape got the message. Although an improved installation routine didn't make it into Navigator 3.0, Netscape has promised top priority to this issue in Navigator 4.0.

How to manually install a plug-in

If you write plug-ins for all three major platforms, you should be aware of subtle differences.

How Netscape loads plug-ins

You can use JavaScript to find out which plug-ins are on the client's machine.

How to write an HTML page that checks for your plug-in

Have your Web site initiate a download.

About the Assisted Installation process

Navigator will help your users find your site.

About MIME type conflict

If your plug-in conflicts with others, you may be able to walk users through a conflict-resolution process.

The Installation Process: A User Perspective

When a user visits a page that contains non-native content, Navigator looks at its list of installed plug-ins and their MIME media types. If Netscape finds a matching MIME media type, it loads the library, calls `NPP_Initialize()`, instantiates a copy of the plug-in, calls `NPP_New()`, and starts the process that the rest of this book describes in detail.

If no plug-ins on the list match, Navigator looks at the list of helper applications. If none of *these* match, Navigator starts the installation process.

Navigator 3.0 offers two kinds of installation—manual and assisted. You can use JavaScript to walk the user through the installation process, even offering some improvements over assisted installation.

Manual Installation

Although you won't often ask the user to install your plug-in manually, you will use this process many times while you develop the plug-in. Moreover, your installation pages and scripts automate this process, so you will want to know the details.

Generally, plug-ins must be installed in a special subdirectory, and they must be present when Navigator is started.

Windows   On Windows, the special plug-ins subdirectory must be named "plugins" and the plug-in files must have file names that begin with "np". Windows, of course, is not case-sensitive.

Macintosh   On the Macintosh, the special plug-ins subdirectory must be named "plug-ins" (note the hyphen). No special naming requirement is needed on the plug-in files.

OS/2 Warp   Under OS/2 Warp, the special plug-ins subdirectory must be named "plugins" but the plug-in files don't need special file names that begin with "np".

UNIX   UNIX uses a mechanism similar to the mechanism described for OS/2 Warp, Windows, and Macintosh. UNIX looks through the shared objects in the

Plug-ins directory for libraries that advertise Netscape plug-in functions. When UNIX finds these libraries, it looks up the MIME types they handle, and then links and loads the correct plug-in at run-time.

Assisted Installation

With Navigator 3.0, the best way to install a plug-in is to let Navigator help. If the plug-in is being loaded by using the <EMBED> tag, you can add the attribute PLUGINSPAGE=*url* to the tag. If a plug-in isn't found that can handle the MIME media type, Navigator puts up a dialog box that tells the user what is happening. Figure 19.1 shows this dialog box.

FIG. 19.1
If Navigator cannot find a plug-in to handle the MIME media type of the incoming stream, it prompts the user to download the plug-in.

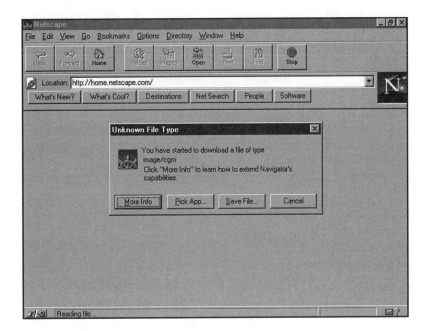

If the user chooses cancel, then of course the installation process is terminated. If the user chooses to continue, however, Navigator follows the URL given in the PLUGINSPAGE attribute. When the user arrives at your page, you are in control of the download process.

T I P Navigator offers the assisted installation process the first time a particular non-native MIME type is encountered. After that, it puts up the "missing plug-in" icon and proceeds. You may want to supply some JavaScript—to anyone who uses your MIME type—to supplement assisted plug-ins, with JavaScript. JavaScript, which will tell you if your plug-in is available on the client's machine, is coming up in the following section.

Adobe was among the first companies to use plug-ins—their current product, a version of the Acrobat Portable Document Format reader codenamed Amber, is one of the more advanced plug-ins available. Figure 19.2 shows the Web page on which Adobe begins the user download process.

 ON THE WEB

You can find Amber at **http://www.adobe.com/acrobat/readstep.html**.

FIG. 19.2
Adobe's plug-in download site opens by describing the product and offers to download. It shows the user a 4-step process, which includes registering the plug-in, choosing the right version, downloading the software, and configuring the browser.

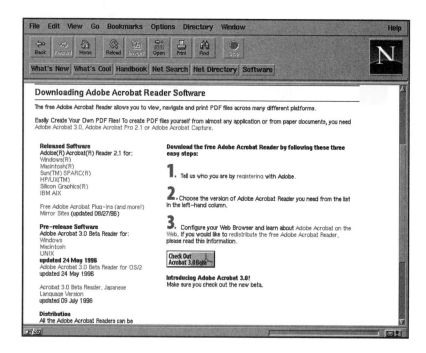

Note that Adobe takes advantage of the visit to capture registration information. Anything you can do to learn more about your client base can help you meet your organization's objectives.

N O T E At the Adobe site the registration step is optional. Although the site doesn't draw attention to this, it's entirely possible to download their software without registering.

You should decide whether your organization's objectives are best served by mandatory registration, or whether you want to allow visitors to bypass this step. ◼

Here are some thoughts that may help in the design of your download page:

- Because you can read the browser type and, consequently, the platform ID in a CGI script or LiveWire program, you can default to the correct platform.

- You should offer other versions of the plug-in. (For example, a Macintosh user shouldn't be prohibited from downloading the Windows version, though doing so may be unusual.)

- Because the plug-in is intended for Navigator, it's a safe bet that the visitor is using Navigator. You can enhance the page accordingly, including using JavaScript and Java, as desired.

- You can write your plug-in in a way so that it "phones home" from time to time. This section contains a procedure for having your plug-in keep itself up-to-date.

You can design your plug-in and your download page to keep your plug-in up to date by taking the following steps:

1. Design the download page with some JavaScript that checks to see if your plug-in is already on the user's machine. (You will find more information on this subject in the following section.) If your plug-in isn't loaded, proceed with the download in the usual way.

2. If the user already has a copy of your plug-in, use JavaScript to start your plug-in. Have your download page tell your plug-in (in a private MIME media type) its current version on this platform.

3. Your plug-in compares the version it gets from the download page with its major and minor version numbers, tells the user if the plug-in version you are using is out-of-date, and offers to download the latest version. You may want

Part
IV

Ch
19

to offer to take the user to a new page where you list the latest features. You can even make this feature list longer or shorter, depending upon how obsolete the user's copy of the plug-in is.

4. After the user has a chance to download the new version, write a record of the date and time to the user's hard drive. You can use a Netscape cookie, or you can write the information to a small file. In Windows 95, you might save the data in the system registry.

5. In your plug-in's `NPP_Initialize()`, check the date-time stamp to see how much time has passed since the user checked the download site. If too much time has elapsed, use `NPN_GetURL()` with `window` set to NULL to ask your site if a newer version exists.

6. If your plug-in discovers that it is obsolete, discreetly inform the user. You may want to enable a menu item in a pop-up menu, for example, that says `Download newer version`.

If you follow this procedure, make sure that you tell the user about it somewhere in the documentation, and consider giving them a way to turn off any auto-download of the newer version. Some users are quite uncomfortable with software writing to their hard drive or calling up Web sites without their permission.

It's a good idea to tell the user about the system requirements before they download the plug-in. On one of Adobe's Web pages, Adobe describes the minimum requirements a Windows machine needs to run version 2 of their product. (See Figure 19.3.)

 ON THE WEB

You can find the Windows minimum requirements at **http://www.adobe.com/acrobat/windows.html.**

Note also that Adobe's download page tells the user the size of the file they are about to download, and includes detailed instructions about how to run the installation program. If you require the user to read and accept a license agreement as part of the installation process, link to a copy of the agreement here.

FIG. 19.3
Tell the user the minimum system requirements so they can make an intelligent choice about downloading the plug-in.

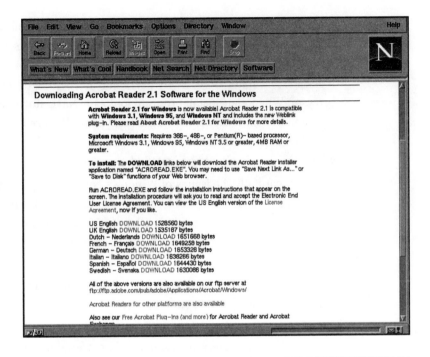

T I P All major platforms make it easy to internationalize your software. You can include help files, dialog text, and menu items in nearly any language. If your software is internationalized, provide a <SELECT> tag or other option on the download page to allow your users to request the right version.

If you're a really big firm, like Netscape, you may want to ask the user where they are physically located so that you can steer them to a server on their continent.

It is, after all, a *World Wide* Web.

Part
IV

Ch
19

Installation Scripts and Pages

In Navigator 3.0 you will often want to have the user download an installation script or executable. Give them instructions in the download page about how to run it. This section points out a few considerations you may want to remember:

■ Although Netscape discourages it, prepare for the possibility that the user may have more than one copy of Navigator installed. Netscape seems to always have at least one beta version active, not to mention versions of Netscape Navigator Gold. Many users may have three or four copies of the browser. When your install program looks for Navigator, consider allowing it to run until it finds *all* copies on the local drive. If more than one version already exists, put up a list that shows the path to each one, and ask the user where the plug-in should be installed.

■ Consider carefully the issues of Windows compatibility. Think about having your installation script check for the presence of Win32s (on classic Windows). Review the information in Chapter 16, "Spanning the Windows World," to see if you need to make special arrangements for older (or newer) versions of Windows.

■ On a Windows 95 machine, make sure that you take advantage of the Wizard control. Users are used to running a setup program and launching a Wizard.

■ On a Macintosh, offer native versions for both 68K and PowerPC Macintoshes. Mac users are used to being offered three choices: 68K, PowerPC, and "Fat Binaries," which work on either kind of machine (but take longer to download). Use Apple's single-button installer. If it's appropriate for your plug-in, offer a custom configuration option as well as the default "Easy Install."

■ Remember that UNIX is in many ways the least-restricted environment. UNIX comes in many flavors with subtle differences. Not all users will have the "standard" configuration. If you're not a UNIX expert, enlist the help of one. Remember that you may have to get more than one expert to span the UNIX world.

LiveConnect and Installation

New features in JavaScript make it easy to find out what plug-ins the user has on their machine. You can use this information to do the following:

■ Warn the user about potential MIME type conflicts

■ Direct the user to your download page from your content page

■ Offer the content in one of several formats, depending upon what MIME types the user's computer can read

How Navigator Loads Plug-Ins

When Navigator launches, it looks through the files in the plug-ins subdirectory. On Windows it looks for certain fields in the VERSIONINFO resource. On the Mac, Navigator looks at STR# 128. When Navigator finds a plug-in, it reads the MIME type information and registers the plug-in for use with that type.

MIME Type Conflict

If your plug-in reads a common MIME type, you will inevitably find your software competing for registration with another plug-in. Even if your MIME type is unique, you may find that you are competing with an older version of your own plug-in.

Macintosh and UNIX users can specify which plug-in gets to handle which MIME type, although few users may be aware of it. On those platforms, the user goes to Options, General Preferences and chooses the Helpers tab. The user then can specify which plug-in handles each MIME type, just as they specify a helper application. Figure 19.4 shows the Helpers screen.

Part
IV

Ch
19

FIG. 19.4
Macintosh and UNIX users can select which plug-in gets to handle each MIME type.

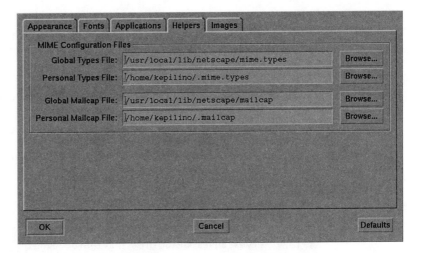

On Windows machines the Helpers tab under Options, General Preferences doesn't include a plug-in option. The *last* plug-in to load gets to handle the MIME type. If you want to make sure that *your* plug-in will handle the data, use JavaScript to discover the conflict and warn the user.

The *plugins* and *mimeTypes* Arrays

As each plug-in is registered, Navigator reads information from each plug-in into an array named `plugins`. You can read this array with client-side JavaScript. A JavaScript `plugins` object has the following four properties:

- `name`—The name of the plug-in
- `filename`—The name of the plug-in file on the disk
- `description`—The description of the plug-in, read from the plug-in's resources
- An array of MIME types that the plug-in can handle

Navigator also tracks how many plug-ins it has registered, so you can read the `length` property of the `plugins` array.

If your plug-in is named "npQuux," you can easily check to see if it is registered as follows:

```
var myPlugin = navigator.plugins["npQuux"];
if (myPlugin)
  --the plug-in is loaded
else
  --no quux here
```

Not only does Navigator track all registered plug-ins, it also maintains a list of which plug-in is assigned to handle which MIME type. (In a clever display of originality, Navigator's engineers chose to call this array `mimeTypes`.) Recall that this assignment is a function of load order (on Windows) or of the user's selection (on Macintosh and UNIX machines). To see if your plug-in has been selected to handle your MIME type, write the following:

```
var myMIMEtype = navigator.mimeTypes["application/x-quux"];
if (myMIMEtype)
  if (myMIMEtype.enabledPlugin == navigator.plugins["npQuux"])
    --all is well. We are in control, here
  else
```

```
        --this machine uses someone else's plug-in to handle _our_ type
else
    --oops. This machine can't handle our type at all. They need our
    ➥plug-in.
```

Depending on your organization's objectives, you have several options if you find that the user isn't using your plug-in:

- You can allow them to proceed. After all, they can read the content with *someone's* plug-in.

- You may display a warning; if they're on a Mac or UNIX machine, you can ask them to reconfigure. If they're on a Windows machine, you can suggest that they remove the offending plug-in (give them myMimetype. enabledPlugin.filename to give them the full path).

- If the user doesn't have a plug-in that can read your MIME type, you can negotiate content. Perhaps your plug-in can read several MIME types. Use client-side JavaScript to find a format the user's machine *can* read, and write an appropriate link or <EMBED> tag into the page.

- Put up a notice to the user that tells them they need your plug-in, and write a link to your download site into the document.

The *embeds* Array

After a page with embedded plug-ins is up, JavaScript can read the embeds array of the current page. Each element of embeds is a Plug-in object. Therefore, embeds[0] is associated with the plug-in that will handle the first <EMBED> tag on your page, embeds[1] is associated with the second <EMBED> tag, and so on. Chapter 18, "Plug-Ins as a Programming Resource," describes JavaScript you can write to communicate from JavaScript back to your plug-in. This code routes messages to a Java object associated with your plug-in, addressed by the embeds array.

N O T E The embeds array is read-only. You cannot override the registered plug-in assignment at run-time. ■

Navigator 4.0

One of the biggest objections to plug-ins has been the complexity of the process of finding the right plug-in and downloading it. Navigator 4.0 (codenamed Galileo) will largely automate this process—Netscape is working out the details of just how this auto-downloading will work.

Until Netscape announces the details, it's a safe bet that using the <EMBED> tag with the PLUGINSPAGE attribute will serve as a good starting point for auto-download. Use this attribute on any pages you write that include embedded data; check the Galileo documentation when it becomes available for additional details and examples.

From Here...

From the beginning, Netscape Navigator has supported helper applications that allow users to access data types other than the ones built into Navigator. The mechanism for describing these data types is the MIME-compliant media type.

Navigator 2.0 and 3.0 support in-line plug-ins, enabling programmers to write native code to read data and present it inside the Netscape window. Navigator 3.0 also includes LiveConnect, which integrates plug-ins, JavaScript, and Java. Now all programming techniques for the client can be brought together into an integrated solution.

Starting with Navigator 4.0, Netscape is supporting automated downloading and installation of plug-ins, making the use of plug-ins even more transparent to the end user.

You can write JavaScript on your content pages and in your download site, which ensures that users do not get a "Plug-in Not Present" message. Rather, your pages can negotiate with the user's machine to find a compatible format, or offer to take the user to your download site.

- Navigator plug-ins must be written in C++. Chapter 2, "A C++ Primer," lays a foundation of object-oriented methods, C++ syntax, and language-specific topics such as templates and the Standard Template Library (STL).

- Chapter 3, "Integrating Plug-Ins into Web Site Design," shows how plug-ins fit into the "grand scheme" of Web design, which includes client- and server-side JavaScript, Java, CGI scripts, and the integrating technology of LiveConnect.

- Chapter 18, "Plug-Ins as a Programming Resource," returns to the subject of LiveConnect, and describes the LiveConnect methods in detail.

Part
IV

Ch
19

Appendixes

A Glossary   495

B What's On the CD-ROM   507

Glossary

abstract class   A class that cannot be instantiated, because it has one or more *pure virtual* functions. See also *pure virtual*.

access method   A *method* that encapsulates data members.

AIFF   Audio Interchange File Format, developed by Apple Computer for storing high-quality sampled sound.

allocate   To grant a resource, such as memory, to a requesting program.

ANSI   American National Standards Institute, a major U.S. standards-setting organization.

API   Application Program Interface; a specification for functions, routines, and data available from a library or program shared or integrated with another program.

applet   A small Java program, designed to run in connection with a Web browser such as Netscape Navigator.

applications   Software designed and written to solve a problem or create a Web-based environment through dynamic page generation or system tasks.

associative class   A container class in which the position of each instance depends upon the contents of the instance. See *container class*. Contrast *sequence container*.

asynchronous   Used to describe the multitude of individual events that occurs simultaneously and without relation to other events except within a larger closed system.

back end   The system-level support that is unseen by the client user, but that provides the Web server, database, and external services to help create the interfaces available to the client user.

browser   A software application that enables a user to look up information on the Internet, primarily on the World Wide Web.

buffer   A temporary storage area for information, usually for a short period and in the order in which the information is received.

cache   To store a copy of something, usually for fast local access; also, the storage space used for caching.

CCITT   The international standards-setting organization for telephony and data communications.

CGI   Common Gateway Interface, a mechanism that allows Web users to access non-Web programs.

CGM   Computer Graphics Metafile, a file format that accommodates both vector and raster images in a single file.

class variables   Variables that are associated with the class as a whole, rather than any specific instance of the class.

client pull   Technology developed for the Web environment that enables a page to reload automatically when the client requests new pages. The client software must be capable of recognizing the special tags, which are added to HTML for this purpose.

CMM   Capability Maturity Model, a multiple-layer description of software engineering process maturity developed at the Software Engineering Institute.

concrete class   A class with no *pure virtual* functions, so it may be *instantiated*.

container class   A class, such as a vector or set, that holds instances of other classes.

copy constructor   In C++, a constructor that takes an instance of the class as its parameter and sets the data members to match the value of that instance.

daemon   A program that is left running in the background, waiting for a particular set of circumstances (such as a request) to trigger it into action.

database   A system of applications and data that stores information (retrievable by way of a query interface) in a persistent, stable, and organized fashion.

DBMS   Database Management System, a mechanism for storing data in files and accessing it with a high-level language. Also see *SQL* and *RDBMS*.

deallocate   To release control of memory that was previously allocated.

default constructor   In C++, the class constuctor that takes no parameters (and consequently, sets all data members to their default values).

DNS   Domain Name System, a system that translates between human-readable domain names and machine-usable IP addresses.

document root   The directory in the Web server's file system that is the beginning of the file tree of documents available from the Web server. In the URL **http://some.where.com/**, for example, the trailing slash (/) signifies the document root.

dynamically generated   Made at run-time by the invocation of scripts or programs that are ultimately requested by a user, or the programmed/scheduled events supported by the Web server. A feedback-acknowledgment page is dynamically generated. A sports-score page that updates after every new score, independently of the user, also is dynamically generated.

dynamic library   A code resource designed to be linked into an application on the end user's computer, at load time or run-time. See also *static library*.

environment variables   The shell data components of a process in the UNIX environment.

environments   Places within a Web site where the associations between pages lead to the belief that the pages have a common theme to explore or use for a specific purpose. A Web chat environment, for example, is a set of pages that supports the chat model.

EPS   Encapsulated PostScript, a self-contained PostScript program that draws an image; also known as EPSF.

EPSF   See *EPS*.

file system   The hardware and software components of an operating system that manages the access and management needs of electronic files.

filter   A hardware or software component that processes an input data stream into an output data stream in some well-defined way, and does no I/O to anywhere else except possibly on error conditions.

flat   Lacking any internal structure.

flat-ASCII   Said of a text file that contains only 7-bit ASCII characters and uses only ASCII-standard control characters. Also known as plain-ASCII.

flat file   A flattened representation of some database or tree or network structure as a single file from which the structure implicitly can be rebuilt, esp. one in flat-ASCII form.

flatten   To remove structural information, esp. to filter something with an implicit hierarchical structure into a simple sequence; also tends to imply mapping to flat-ASCII.

flush   To discard all remaining data in an input or output device. But in C and UNIX, the `fflush(3)` call forces buffered disk I/O to complete. These two meanings are logically opposite.

FTP   File Transfer Protocol, part of the TCP/IP family of protocols. *Anonymous FTP* is a common way of offering files to the public.

GET   An access method in HTTP.

handle   A pointer to a pointer to data.

helper application   An application invoked by a Web browser for MIME types that the browser cannot handle internally. Also see *plug-in*.

HTML form   An HTML construction that includes the <FORM> tag declaration with one or many <INPUT> tags, with the purpose of collecting data to be passed as input to a CGI program.

HTTP   HyperText Transport Protocol, the protocol of the World Wide Web.

httpd   The HTTP daemon, the UNIX name for the Web server.

IEEE   Institute of Electrical and Electronics Engineers, an international professional group and standards-setting organization.

IESG   Internet Engineering Steering Group. This committee was formed to help the IETF chair.

IETF   Internet Engineering Task Force. This group develops the specifications that become Internet standards.

imagemap   A graphic set up to allow a user's click to select different pages or programs, depending on where the click is on the graphic. It is customary to associate hot spots on the graphic with specific files or programs. Imagemaps can be implemented on the client or on the server.

instance variables   Data members that appear in every copy (instance) made from the class.

instantiate   To make an object from a class.

Internet   The world-wide interconnection of networks to form the network of networks. The Internet originally was a research project for the U.S. Department of Defense named the ARPANET; now, it is mostly organized for commercial and educational purposes.

IP   Internet Protocol, one of the communications protocols of the Internet. IP usually is specified as part of a family known as TCP/IP.

IP address   Four 8-bit numbers used to uniquely identify every machine on the Internet. An IP address usually is written with dots between the numbers, as in `127.0.0.1`.

IPC   Inter-Process Communication. The mechanisms by which software processes talk with one another. Typical UNIX IPC mechanisms include shared memory, pipes, semaphores, and message queues.

ISO   International Standards Organization, an international standards-setting organization.

ISOC   Internet Society, a professional society to facilitate, support, and promote the evolution and growth of the Internet as a global research communications infrastructure.

ISP   Internet Service Provider, an organization that provides access (usually dial-up) to the Internet.

JFIF   JPEG File Interchange Format (commonly referred to as *JPEG*), a popular image format for Web pages.

JPEG   Joint Photographic Experts Group; also, the common name for the JFIF image standard.

LAN   Local Area Network. A collection of computers at one physical location or campus that share resources, and their internetworking hardware and software. Also see *WAN*.

local guide   The manual or documentation, assembled for users, that describes the custom software and tools installed.

make   A utility used to generate an output file based on changes in a set of component files.

markup language   A syntax and procedure for embedding in text documents tags that control formatting when the documents are viewed by a special application. A Web browser interprets HTML (Hypertext Markup Language).

method   A function that is a member of a class.

MIME   Multimedia Internet Media Extensions, a mechanism used by e-mail and Web servers to tell a client what type of content is being sent, so that the client can interpret the data correctly.

mix-in classes   Classes that typically cannot be instantiated themselves, but that are added to an *abstract class* by multiple inheritance to add features to a new *concrete class*.

Mozilla   The internal name of the Netscape browser.

MPEG   Moving Pictures Experts Group; also, the audio and video compression standards developed by that group.

multitasking   Performing more than one task at the same time. Multitasking is a feature of some operating systems, such as UNIX.

navigation   The act of traversing a chain of hypertext links from a starting point to a final result.

NCSA   National Center for Supercomputer Applications, which developed the NCSA Server, a popular UNIX-based Web server. Visit NCSA's Web site at **http://hoohoo.ncsa.uiuc.edu/**.

Netscape Communications Corporation   Developer of a popular browser (Netscape Navigator) and several commercial servers.

Netscape Navigator   A popular Web browser by Netscape Communications Corporation.

NIST   U.S. National Institute of Standards and Technology, formerly known as the National Bureau of Standards.

operating system   A collection of software written to provide the fundamental instructions that a computer needs to manage resources such as memory, the file system, and processes.

overloading   In a programming language, the ability to have more than one function of the same name, which differ only in the number and type of parameters. See *signature*.

PATH   An environment variable used to list directories that should be searched for a given file.

PCL   Hewlett-Packard Printer Control Language. An HP-proprietary language used to render pages on Hewlett-Packard printers. See also *PDL*.

PDL   Page Description Language. A generic term, encompassing PostScript and Hewlett-Packard's PDL.

Perl   Practical Extraction and Report Language (also Pathologically Eclectic Rubbish Lister), a rich language developed by Larry Wall. Perl is often used to implement CGI scripts.

PERL   The interpreter for Perl, typically located on a UNIX system at `/usr/bin/perl`.

plug-in   A technology developed by Netscape and now adopted by some other Web browser vendors to handle certain *MIME* media types inside the browser environment, instead of with a helper application.

PNG   Portable Network Graphic, an alternative to GIF for Web graphics.

polymorphism   The ability in a programming language to use instances of subclass as though they were instances of the parent class.

POST   An access method in HTTP.

PostScript   A sophisticated *page description language* (PDL) that's used for high-quality printing on laser printers and other high-resolution printing devices.

process ID   A number associated with a process, which can be used to uniquely identify the process.

proof of concept   A prototype that's built to show that the technique, system design, or marketability of a proposed application or system is likely to be as good as expected.

pure virtual   As of a function, a virtual function that must be overridden by a derived class. See *virtual*.

PUT   An access method in HTTP.

QUERY_STRING   The environment variable that contains the information passed to a CGI script by means of GET.

QuickTime   Apple Computer's standard for time-based material, such as video, sound, and multimedia sequences. Available for Windows and UNIX computers as well as for Macintoshes.

RDBMS   Relational Database Management System, a database mechanism in which the user's logical view of the data is based on tables (also known as *relations*). Also see *SQL*.

real-time   Describes an application that requires a program to respond to stimuli within some small upper limit of response time (typically, milli- or microseconds).

reloading   The act of requesting a page from a Web server that is already visible in the Web browser. The purpose of reloading is mainly to verify changes in documents or to reinvoke certain actions (such as CGI scripts) on the Web server.

RFC   Request for Comment, the place where all of the official standards in the Internet community are published.

RIFF WAVE   An audio format, commonly known as WAV.

script   A program that runs on the Web server, written in an interpreted language such as Perl or Tcl.

SEI   Software Engineering Institute, a research center at Carnegie-Mellon University.

semaphore   A mechanism for restricting access to critical sections of code to a single user or process at a time.

sequence container   Container classes in which the order of the stored instances depends upon how and when the instance was added to the container, rather than the contents of the instance. See also *container class*. Contrast *associative container*.

server push   Technology developed for the Web environment that allows a page to reload automatically when the server generates new content. The MIME type used for server push is `multipart/x-mixed`.

SIGHUP   The hang-up signal. In UNIX, SIGHUP is commonly used to tell a daemon to reread its configuration files. Signals are sent in UNIX with the `kill` command.

signature   Of a function, the number and type of parameters.

skeleton   A program that contains the proper header and footer declarations, but lacks actual code to perform a task; also, a file stub that provides the framework for the details of the program to be inserted.

SLOC   Source Line of Code, one line in a computer program. In many languages, each SLOC ends with a semicolon. SLOC is used in COCOMO and PROBE as the basis for estimating software-development time.

SQL   (Pronounced "*see-quel*") Structured Query Language, an ANSI-standard language for accessing databases.

SSI   Server-side include, a method by which Web pages can include small pieces of information that are not directly stored in their file.

static HTML file   An HTML document that is represented and stored as a file under the Web server's document root. A static HTML file can be changed or updated only by editing the file. Also see *dynamic HTML*.

static library   A code resource designed to be linked into an application on the developer's machine, when the application is linked. See also *dynamic library*.

STDERR   Standard Error, a file handle open for output by default in many operating systems and languages; typically used for program error messages.

STDIN   Standard Input, a file handle open for input by default in many operating systems and languages; typically used for program input.

STDOUT   Standard Output, a file handle open for output by default in many operating systems and languages; typically used for program output.

TCP   Transmission Control Protocol, one of the communications protocols of the Internet. TCP usually is specified as part of a family known as TCP/IP. TCP connections are set up by using a three-way handshake to ensure the delivery of every packet.

text box   An area of a Web page, usually created with <INPUT> tags, that accepts a single line of input.

thread   A "lightweight process" that allows asynchronous work to be done within another process's address space.

TIFF   Tag Image File Format, a popular high-end file format for images.

time stamp   Time of day, encapsulated in an alphanumeric quantity for registering an event. When files are modified, their "last modified" time stamp is updated with a new time.

toolbar   A compact textual, or graphical region of a page that contains hypertext links to other parts of the site or the Web.

URL   Uniform Resource Locator, the address of an Internet resource, such as a Web page.

App
A

virtual As of a function. May be overridden by derived classes. See also *pure virtual*.

WAN Wide Area Network. A collection of computers that are geographically distributed but that share resources, and their internetworking hardware and software. See also *LAN*.

Web server A machine (or a set of machines) connected to the network that runs software that supports the HTTP requests for documents from client machines.

Webmaster The person who usually maintains the content and operational status of a Web server. Most Webmasters are involved with design and development issues for new content and also with business and marketing issues, network topology design, and any other issue related to the development and maintenance of the Web server.

World Wide Web A network of hosts on the Internet that share data and information with the public (or with private groups) through the transfer of documents via the HTTP protocol.

XBM X Bit Maps, a simple graphics standard used in the X Window system.

What's on the CD-ROM?

The CD-ROM included with this book is packed full of valuable programs and utilities. This appendix gives a brief overview of the contents of the CD. For a more detailed look at any of these parts, load the CD-ROM and browse the contents. ■

Browsing the Contents of the CD-ROM

The CD-ROM contains an easy-to-use HTML-based index that allows you to navigate the CD-ROM's files and select the software you want to install to your hard drive.

You need to open the file Index.htm in your favorite Web browser to load the master index, which is a file in the root directory of the CD-ROM. If your CD-ROM drive letter is D and you use Netscape Navigator as your browser, for example, follow these steps to access the file:

1. Start Netscape Navigator.
2. Click File, Open File.

    The Open File dialog box is displayed on-screen.

3. Type **d:\index.htm**. The index page loads in your browser.

Electronic Versions of other Que Publications

As an added bonus, this CD-ROM also contains electronic versions of other Que books that are related to building plug-ins. In these books, you will find a wealth of information that makes building plug-ins easier.

Here's the list of electronic books that you will find on this CD-ROM:

- *Special Edition Using JavaScript*
- *Special Edition Using CGI*
- *Special Edition Using JAVA*
- *Special Edition Using HTML*, 2nd Edition

Source Code

Here you'll find examples from the book. Simply click the chapter number of interest and either read the code or cut and paste as desired.

Plug-Ins

Plug-ins are great, but finding and downloading them from the Web can be a hassle and is definitely a time-consuming process. This book's companion CD-ROM supplies over a dozen of some of the hottest plug-ins available, including the following:

- Acrobat
- Corel CMX
- Envoy Reader
- Fig Leaf Inline
- INSO Word Viewer
- Intercap Inline
- Look@Me
- Scream
- Shockwave for Director
- Sizzler
- VDOLive

Helpers

The following sections cover several collections of helper applications to aid in the creation of multimedia Web pages. Among these helpers, you will find graphics editors, video editors, sound editors, and so on.

Audio

The following are only a few of the applications on the CD-ROM that will help with the most popular audio files found on the World Wide Web:

- Cooledit
- Midigate
- Mod4Win

- WHAM
- WPLANY

HTML Editors & Utilities

Save yourself the trouble of creating HTML pages with Notepad by choosing among the following HTML editors and special-purpose utilities:

- HotDog
- HTML Assistant
- HTMLed
- HTML Notepad
- HTML Writer
- Live Markup
- WebEdit
- Webber
- Color Manipulation Device
- CrossEye
- EasyHelp/Web
- FrameGang
- Map This!
- WebForms
- Webmania

Java

Here, you find the following Java tools (and more) that help you create animated applets and design scrolling marquees. You get the HotJava browser and the Java Development Kit.

- Clikette
- Egor
- Ewgie
- Flash
- Swami
- Java Development Kit

CGI & Perl

Perl, the Practical Extraction and Report Language, is the language of choice for scripting CGI interfaces into the World Wide Web. If you don't find a version of Perl for your operating system here, check CPAN or the Perl Language Home Page, and you probably will find what you're looking for.

- Perl 4
- Perl 5
- MacPearl

VRML

The following VRML browsers are included to enable you to build "home worlds" and navigate 3-D worlds:

- NAVFlyer
- Pioneer
- VRScout
- Worldview

Web Utilities

Here you find mailing-list engines, the popular Excite search engine, Spiders, validation programs, Web stats, security programs and compression utilities. This list shows only some of the utilities on the CD-ROM. Feel free to explore and test the useful data and software this CD-ROM provides!

- Engine Mail
- HyperMail
- LISTSERV™
- LSMTP™
- LWGate
- MailServ
- Majordomo
- MHonArc
- Excite
- WebLint
- freeWAIS
- Swish
- WWWWAIS
- Get Stats
- WebPlot
- ARJ
- BinHex
- UUCode
- WinCode
- WinZip
- COPS
- CRACK
- SATAN
- SSLeay
- Tiger
- xinetd

Index

Symbols

"" (quotes), C++ header files, 44

; (semicolons), class definitions, 42

< > (angle brackets), C++ header files, 44

= assignment operator, 156

== comparison operator, 156

~charQueue( ) function, 42

16-bit applications, 416-417
  running with 32-bit applications, 424
  troubleshooting Netscape Navigator, 427-428

32-bit applications, using for Windows 3.x, 425-426

A

about:plugins, 129

abstract classes, 67-69
  defined, 495

access methods, 52, 495

accessing data, 146-147
  caching data streams, 147-148
  seekable streams, 147-150
    byte-range requests, 149
    NPP_NewStream( ) method, 149
    retrieval rates, 149-150
  streaming, 146-148
  synchronizing global data access, 357-359
    creating semaphores, 357-358
    Lock/Unlock( ) methods, 358

Acrobat Portable Document Format reader, 482

activate events, 196

ActiveX
  COM (Component Object Model), 399
  controls, 387, 392-394
    adding to Web pages, 394-395
    advantages over plug-ins, 394
    code signing, 396
    CODEBASE attribute, 395
    Java, 393
    licensing, 397
    MFC, 393
    Microsoft Internet Explorer, 395-396
    network protocol support, 397-398
    <PARAM> tag, 406-407
    scripting, 406-408
    skeleton control, 401-403
    versions, 396
    Visual C++ AppWizard, 399
    Web site, 394
  documents, 404
  scripting, 405-408
    controls, 406-408
    JavaScript, 405-406
    server scripting, 408
    VBScript, 405
  SDK, 399
  servers, 408
  Template Library (ATL), 400-404
    ATL COM AppWizard, 400-401
    interfaces, 400
    opening new projects, 400-401
    Web site, 400

adapters, 61-62
  iterator adapters, 63-64

Add Project Configuration dialog (Visual C++), 113

add( ) function, 43, 49

adjustCursorEvent, 196

Adobe PDF (Portable Document Format) files, 26-27

advertising MIME media types, 162
  Macintosh, 164-167
    resource forks, 164
    .rsrc files, 164
    STR# resource, 165-166
    vers resource, 164-165
  OS/2 Warp, 163
  UNIX, 167-168
  Windows, 162-163

afx_msg keyword (message mapping), 208

AfxBeginThread( ) function, 356

AIFF (Audio Interchange File Format), 495

AKO-relationships ("A-kind of"), 40

algorithms (STL), 65
  banker's algorithm, 345-348
  two-phase locking, 348

allocating memory, 89-90

Amber plug-in (Acrobat Portable Document Format reader), 482

angle brackets (< >), C++ header files, 44

APIs (Application Program Interfaces), 82
defined, 495
plug-in API version, 247
Windows API, handling streams, 210

AppExpert (Borland), 450-451

Apple
events, 197
Macintosh, *see* Macintosh

applets
defined, 495
see also Java

Application object (OLE automation), 378

applications
classes, mapping messages, 207
defined, 496
migrating existing applications to Web, 26-27, 244-246
menus, 245
windows, 244-245
MIME subtypes, 16
moving existing applications to Web, 145

AppWizard (Visual C++)
ATL COM AppWizard, 400-401
generating project code, 103-107
building code, 106-107
MFC AppWizard dialog, 105-106
naming plug-ins, 105
shared DLLs, 106
warnings, 107
mapping messages, 207
OLE controls, 399
setting up CRecordSet-derived classes (ODBC), 384-385

arithmetic operators, 64

arrays
embeds, 489
mimeTypes, 488-489
plugins, 488

ASSERT macro, 157
MFC ASSERTs, 158

assignment operators, 55-59

AssociateInstance( ) function, 193-194

associating information with instances, 155

associative classes, 61
defined, 496

asynchronous
defined, 496
plug-ins, 98-99
processes, 99
reentrant code, 99
threads, 98-99
processing (NPN_GetURL( ) method), 246-247
routines (Macintosh multitasking), 350-351

ATL, *see* ActiveX, Template Library

atomic read-and-set operations, 343-344

audio files, MIME subtypes, 16

automation, *see* OLE, automation

AVI files, *see* npAVI plug-in

B

back end, 496

backups, 256

banker's algorithm, 345-348

BASIC programs, 27-28

BEGIN_MESSAGE_MAP( ) macro (MFC), 206, 208

BIDS (Borland International Data Structures), 448

binary
precompiled binaries, 31
trees, 260

binding, OLE automation, 378

bitmaps
compound documents, 364-365
printing from Windows, 221-222
X Bit Maps (XBM), 505

block headers, 109

Borland
AppExpert, 450-451
C++ compiler, 31

Borland International Data Structures (BIDS), 448

browsers
defined, 496
media types, 18-19
Microsoft Internet Explorer, *see* Internet Explorer

Netscape Navigator, *see* Netscape Navigator
VRML, 511
Web Explorer (IBM), 34

BrowserWatch, 251

buffers
defined, 496
fBuffer, 200
NPP_Write( ) function, 179
sending (NPN_PostURL( ) method), 250

building
configurations (DLL), 113
plug-ins SDK (Software Developing Kit), 28-29, 128-129
C++ compilers, 31-33
configuring, 31-33
downloading, 29-30
unpacking, 30
project code (AppWizard), 106-107

buttons
activating, 121-123
connecting resources to code, 123-124

byte-range requests, 149

C

C++
case-sensitivity, 105
classes, 41-47
~charQueue( ) function, 42
add( ) function, 43, 49
charQueue( ) function, 42-44
constructors, 42, 46
exception handling, 45-46
header files, 42, 44
I/O, 47
main( ) routine, 44-45
member functions, 46
remove( ) function, 43, 50
source files, 42
compilers, 31-33
object files, 33
constants, declaring, 44
design issues, 67
abstract classes, 67-69
GUIs, 72
instances as class members, 70-71
public versus private inheritance, 69-70

style/naming
conventions, 71
virtual methods, 67-69
function objects, 64-65
methods, 47-50
operators, 55-56
overloaded methods, 472-473
templates, 57-59
instantiating template
classes, 58-59
Visual C++
4.0 Standard Edition, 102
AppWizard, 103-107
mapping messages,
206-207
see also Visual C++

caches
caching data streams, 147-148
defined, 496

callback functions
AssociateInstance( ) function,
193-194
callback.cpp listing, 194-195
Windows messages, 192-194
AssociateInstance( )
function, 193-194
callback.cpp listing,
194-195
installing, 193

calls
calling plug-ins, 152-153
reentrant calls, 361
Win32s unsupported calls, 426

**Cancel dialogs, full-page mode
printing, 222-223**

case-sensitivity of C++, 105

catch (...) clauses, 46

CCITT, 496

CCmdTarget class, 440

CD-ROM
audio applications, 509-510
electronic books, 508
HTML editors/utilities, 510
Index.htm file, 508
Java tools, 510-511
Perl versions, 511
plug-ins, 509
source code, 508
VRML browsers, 511
web utilities, 511-512

**CDatabase class (MFC),
ODBC, 383-384**

CDialog class, 439, 441

CEdit class, 202

CEditView class, 202

**CEvent class (thread
termination), 359-360**

CException, 46

**CGI (Common Gateway
Interface), 496**
coupling applications, 257-258

**CGM (Computer Graphics
Metafile) files, 496**

CharFlipper plug-in
calling CharFlipper, 292-293
closing down, 307
compiling, 290
copying files to plug-ins
directory, 290
flow of control
NP_Initialize( ) method,
293-294
NPP_GetJavaClass( )
method, 295
NPP_New( ) method,
295-297
NPP_NewStream( )
method, 299-301
NPP_SetWindow( )
method, 297-299
NPP_Write( ) method,
299-301
NPP_WriteReady( )
method, 299-301
LiveConnect, 302-307
closing down, 307
Java code, 302-304
JavaScript/HTML
connection, 306
triggering with periodic
events, 304-306
NPP_Print( ) method, 301
running, 290-291

charQueue
charQueue( ) method, 42-44
charQueue.cpp, 47-49
charQueue.h (complete
charQueue class
specification), 50-51
charQueue.H
(parameterized Queue class
specification), 58
main.cpp—demo of
charQueue, 43-44

class libraries, 438
deriving new classes, 442-444
Microsoft Foundation Classes
document classes, 445-446
view classes, 446
see also MFC

ObjectWindows Library
(Symantec), 446-448
TGauge class, 447-448
THINK Class Library
(TCL), 450
UNIX, 449
using, 438-445
CCmdTarget, 440
CDialog, 441
CObject, 439-440
CWnd, 440-441
introducing CDialog,
438-439
see also frameworks

Class Wizard (Visual C++)
DDX (dialog data
exchange), 386
OLE automation clients, 376
setting up CRecordSet-derived
classes (ODBC), 385

**classes (object-oriented
programming), 40-47**
abstract, 67-69
defined, 495
associative classes, 61
defined, 496
C++, 41-47
add( ) function, 43, 49
charQueue( ) function,
42-44
~charQueue( ) function, 42
constructors, 42, 46
exception handling, 45-46
header files, 42, 44
I/O, 47
main( ) routine, 44-45
member functions, 46
remove( ) function, 43, 50
source files, 42
concrete, defined, 497
constructors, 52-55
copy constructor, 52-55
operators, 55-56
containers, 59-66
adapters, 61-62
algorithms, 65
associative, 61
defined, 497
function objects, 64-65
iterators, 62-64
sequence, 60-61
data, 50-56
deriving new classes, 442-444
design issues, 67
abstract classes, 67-69
GUIs, 72
instances as class
members, 70-71

public versus private
inheritance, 69-70
style/naming
conventions, 71
virtual methods, 67-69
destructors, 52-55
inheritance, 40
libraries, *see* class libraries
listNode, 52
members
access methods, 52
access restrictions, 51
friends, 51
instances, 70-71
variables, 52
see also methods
methods, 50-56
access methods, 52
friends, 51
remove( ), 57-58
mix-in classes, 500
PluginInstance
keyboard events, 200
mouse events, 204-205
polymorphism, 41
variables, 52
defined, 496

**classic Windows,
see Windows 3.x**

clients
OLE automation, 376-378
COleDispatchDriver, 376
dynamic (late) binding, 378
interfaces, 377-379
static (ID) binding, 378
pull, defined, 496

clipboard transfers, 366-370
delayed rendering, 367
MFCs, 369
objects, 367-368

**CMM (Capability Maturity
Model), 496**

CObject class, 439-440

code
generating project code,
103-107
building code, 106-107
MFC AppWizard dialog,
105-106
naming plug-ins, 105
shared DLLs, 106
Single Document Interface
(SDI), 105
warnings, 107
reducing code defects, 155-158
ASSERT macro, 157
flagging defects with
compilers, 156-157

lint, 157
MFC ASSERTs, 158
warnings, 157
reentrant code (asynchronous
plug-ins), 99
signing, 396

code listings
baz.cpp (skeleton ActiveX
control), 401-403
baz.def (skeleton ActiveX
control definition file), 401
callback.cpp, 194-195
CharFlipper plug-in,
see CharFlipper plug-in
charQueue.cpp, 47-49
charQueue.h (complete
charQueue class
specification), 50-51
charQueue.H
(parameterized Queue class
specification), 58
count.java, 467
double.html file
(zero plug-in), 138
hello.java (Java Hello, world!
program), 464
hidden.html file
(zero plug-in), 139
implementing
NPP_HandleEvent( ),
197-198
main.cpp—demo of
charQueue, 43-44
main.h—the main
specification, 45
mkfp.c (far pointers), 419
msg1.cpp (Windows message
handling), 191-192
noExtent.htm, 431
npAVI plug-in,
see npAVI plug-in
npChap04.cpp (modified
version), 120-121
npChap04.def file, 127-128
npChap04Dlg.h (modified
version), 121-122
npChap04.h file (modified
version), 119
npCount.java, 474
npshell.cpp file (modified
version), 116-118
objecttg.htm, 395
Simple plug-in,
see Simple plug-in
single.html file
(zero plug-in), 138
stlMain.cpp, 65-66
twoInst.htm, 431

**CODE resources
(Macintosh), 36**

**COM (Component Object
Model), 399**

CommonPoint, 451-454
Web site, 453

comparison operators, 64

compilers, 31-33
flagging defects, 156-157
Microsoft Foundation Classes
(MFC), 31-32
object files, 33
RTTI (Runtime Type
Identification), 356

components, 27-28

**compound documents,
364-365**
document-centric
computing, 456
Microsoft, 457-458
UNIX, 457
VBScript, 458-459
editing data, 373-375

compression
utilities, 30
Web sites, 103

concrete classes, defined, 497

const variables, 156-157

constants (C++), declaring, 44

**constructors (C++ classes),
42, 52-55**
calling, 46
copy constructors, 52
deep, 55
defined, 497
operators, 55-56
shallow, 53
default constructors,
defined, 497
instantiating copies of plug-ins,
176-177

container classes, 59-66
adapters, 61-62
algorithms, 65
associative, 61
defined, 497
function objects, 64-65
iterators, 62-64
sequence containers, 60-61
defined, 503

**controls, ActiveX (OLE),
see ActiveX controls**

cooperative multitasking, 339

copy constructors, 52
defined, 497
operators, 55-56
shallow, 53
deep, 55

CoRevokeClassObject( )
function, OLE automation
servers, 380

coupling applications with
CGI, 257-258

.cpp file extension, 42

CProgressCtrl, 447

CRecordSet-derived classes
(ODBC), 384-385
members, 385-386

CRichEditView class, 202

CSemaphore class, 357

cutting data,
see clipboard transfers

CView class (MFC)
OnPrint( ) function, printing
from full-page plug-ins, 221
WM_PAINT message
message mapping, 208-209
stream handling, 213

CWinApp class, 208

CWnd class, 440-441

D

daemons
defined, 497
UNIX daemon processes, 349

data
accessing, 146-147
caching data streams,
147-148
retrieval rates, 150
seekable streams, 147-150
streaming, 146-148
synchronizing global data
access, 357-359
editing (compound
documents), 373-375
presenting, 181-186
Macintosh GrafPorts,
182-183
NPP_SetWindow( )
method, 181, 186
NPWindows, 182
UNIX (X Window System),
183-185

reading
files, 180
streams, 179
saving instance data, 231-234
destroying windows, 234
how to use
NPP_Destroy( ), 232-234
save parameter, 232
when to use
NPP_Destroy( ), 232
sending, NPN_PostURL( )
method, 249
streams, plug-in objects, 85-86
transferring
clipboard transfers, 366-370
drag-and-drop transfers,
370-372
see also ODBC

DBMS (Database Management
System), 497

DDX (dialog data
exchange), 386

deadlocks (deadly embraces),
344-348
banker's algorithm, 345-348
dealing with, 344-345
resource-numbering, 345
two-phase locking, 348

debugging, 28
reducing code defects, 155-158
ASSERT macro, 157
flagging defects with
compilers, 156-157
lint, 157
MFC ASSERTs, 158
warnings, 157

DECLARE_MESSAGE_MAP( )
macro (MFC), 206-207

default
constructors, defined, 497
icons (dialogs), 124

definition files, 127-128
creating, 127-128
skeleton ActiveX control, 401

delayed rendering, 367

delete operator, 143

dependencies, header files,
updating, 115

destroying
instances (NPP_Destroy( )
method), 155, 230-234
freeing dynamic
memory, 230
destroying windows,
234-235

how to use
NPP_Destroy( ), 232-234
save parameter, 232
when to use
NPP_Destroy( ), 232
streams,
NPN_DestroyStream( )
method, 264

destructors, 52-55

Developer Studio (Visual C++)
DLL configuration, 113-114
inserting files into
projects, 108
new projects, 103
Resource view, 109-110

developers licenses
(ActiveX controls), 397

dialog boxes
activating buttons, 121-123
Add Project Configuration
(Visual C++), 113
Cancel, full-page mode
printing, 222-223
connecting resources to
message handlers, 123-124
default icons, 124
DoDataExchange( )
method, 123
MFC AppWizard (Visual C++),
105-106
New Project Workspace
(Visual C++), 103-105
Unknown File Type
(Navigator), 13, 168-169, 481

dialog data exchange
(DDX), 386

directories, header files, 108

DisplayJavaMessage( )
function (Simple plug-in),
278-279

distributed systems, 252-256
backups, 256
coupling applications with
CGI, 257-258
downloading additional files,
254-255
file transmissions, 252-253
final updates, 256
updating files, 253
user interaction, 255

DllEntryPoint( ) function,
loading plug-ins, 170-171

DllMain( ) function, 113

DLLs (Dynamic Link Libraries), 34
configuring, 113-114
DllMain( ) function, 113
preprocessor definitions
(Project Settings
dialog), 114
shared, 106

DNS (Domain Name System), defined, 497

documents
ActiveX documents, 404
classes (MFC), 445-446
document-centric
computing, 456
Microsoft, 457-458
UNIX, 457
VBScript, 458-459
roots, defined, 497
viewer plug-ins, 91

DoDataExchange( ) method (dialog boxes), 123

DoDragDrop( ) function, 371-372

doit( ) function (Java), 284-285

DOS Protected Mode Interface, 423-424

double.html file, 138

downloading
code signing, 396
plug-ins
auto-downloading
(Navigator 4.0), 490
download pages, 483
Navigator 4.0, 29, 490
system requirements, 484
up-to-date versions, 483-484
see also installing plug-ins
SDK (Software Development
Kit), 29-30
status line progress indicators
(NPN_Status( )
method), 265
reporting time remaining,
266-267

DPtoLP( ) method, 87

drag-and-drop transfers, 370-372
DoDragDrop( ) function,
371-372
IDropSource interface, 370
IDropTarget interface, 371

DragEnter( ) function, 371

DragLeave( ) function, 371

DragOver( ) function, 371

Drop( ) function, 371

duplicate instances, troubleshooting, 431-432

dynamic
binding (late), OLE
automation, 378
generation, defined, 497
libraries, *see* dynamic libraries
linking, ActiveX controls, 397
memory, freeing, 230
memory (C++), 143

dynamic libraries, 33-34
defined, 497
DLLs (Dynamic Link
Libraries), 34
configuring, 113-114
shared, 106

E

Early Program pattern, 95

EatDialog( ) method, 125

editing embedded data, 373

<EMBED> tag, 81, 83
integrating plug-ins, 459-460
multimedia plug-ins, 90-91
NPP_New( ) function,
instantiating copies of
plug-ins, 175
PLUGINSPAGE attribute,
481, 490
TYPE attribute, 177

embedded plug-ins, 81, 152-153
document-centric
computing, 456
printing, 216-219
defining NPP_Print( ), 216
DPtoLP( ) calls, 218
embedPrint structure, 217
Macintosh features,
218-219
MM_TWIPS mapping
mode, 217
NPWindow, 217
platformPrint, 216-217
Single Document Interface
(SDI), 105
zero plug-in, 137-138

embeds array, 489

environments
defined, 498
variables, defined, 497

EPS (Encapsulated PostScript), 498

errors
NP_Initialize( ) function,
173-174
NPERR codes, loading
plug-ins, 172

events, 190
Apple events, 197
Macintosh, 195-198
adjustCursorEvent, 196
getFocusEvent, 196
loseFocusEvent, 196
NPP_HandleEvent( )
method, 195, 197-198
updateEvt, 198
thread termination, 359-360
Windows messages, 190-195
callback function, 192-194
handling, 191-192
keyboard events, 198-202
mapping, 206-209
message types, 191
mouse events, 202-205
parameters, 191
queue, 190-191
WindowProc functions, 192
WM_PAINT, 195
X Windows System
(UNIX), 198
see also messages

existing applications
migrating to Web, 145, 244-246
menus, 245
windows, 244-245

expanded/extended memory (Windows 3.x), 420-422
configuring expanded
memory, 422
page frames, 420-421
XMS (Extended Memory
Standard), 420-422

Expose event (X Windows System), 198

external viewers, *see* helper applications

F

fact( ) function (Java), 283

FAQs (Frequently Asked Questions)
g++ FAQ Web site, 31
MIME FAQ Web site, 16

far pointers (Windows 3.x), 418-420

fBuffer, 200

FileExtents field (version information), 111

FileOpenName resource, 428

files
associations, 17-18
definition files, 127-128
double.html (zero plug-in), 138
filtering (version information), 111
header files, (C++), 42, 44
moving to project directory, 108
hidden.html (zero plug-in), 139
mime.types, 17
npapi.h, 82
npChap04.cpp, modifying (Hello, world! plug-in), 120-121
npChap04.def (Hello, world! plug-in), 127-128
npChap04.exe, building (Hello, world! plug-in), 106
npChap04.h, modifying (Hello, world! plug-in), 118-119
npChap04Dlg.cpp, modifying (Hello, world! plug-in), 124-127
npChap04Dlg.h, modifying (Hello, world! plug-in), 121-123
npshell.cpp, modifying (Hello, world! plug-in), 114-118
adding plug-in specific code, 115
casting functions, 117
GetJavaClass() function, 118
header file dependencies, 115
NPP_GetJavaClass() function, 118
npwin.cpp, adding (Hello, world! plug-in), 108
object files, 32-33
PDF (Portable Document Format), 26-27
.rsrc file extension (Macintosh), 164
sending (NPN_PostURL() method), 249
single.html (zero plug-in), 138
source files (C++), 42

filters
defined, 498
filtering files (version information), 111

flat files, defined, 498

flipper, see CharFlipper plug-in

flushing, defined, 498

focus (keyboard), 190
getFocusEvent, 196
getting events, see events
loseFocusEvent, 196

fonts, printing from Windows, 223-225

fork() function (UNIX), 341

forks
forking processes, 146, 341
Macintosh, 164

forward iterators, 63

frames
stream targets, 239-240
Web site, 240

frameworks, 450-453
MacApp, 451
Taligent CommonPoint, 451-454
Web site, 453
see also class libraries

friends (classes), 51

fseek() method, 149

full-page plug-ins, 81, 91, 152-153
printing, 154-155, 219-229
bitmaps, 221-222
Cancel dialogs, 222-223
customizing Print dialog, 225-227
fonts, 223-225
Macintosh Print... dialog, 227-229
platformPrint member, 220
pluginPrinted, 220-221
PrValidate(), 221
Windows, 221-225
troubleshooting, 429
zero plug-in, 136-137

function objects, 64-65

functions
add(), 43, 49
AfxBeginThread(), 356
AssociateInstance(), 193-194
callback functions
AssociateInstance() function, 193-194
callback.cpp listing, 194-195
Windows messages, 192-194
charQueue(), 42-44

~charclassesQueue(), 42
CoRevokeClassObject() (OLE automation servers), 380
DisplayJavaMessage() (Simple plug-in), 278-279
DllEntryPoint(), loading plug-ins, 170-171
DllMain(), 113
DoDragDrop(), 371-372
doit() (Java), 284-285
DragEnter(), 371
DragLeave(), 371
DragOver(), 371
Drop(), 371
fact() (Java), 283
fork() (UNIX), 341
GetJavaClass(), modifying npshell.cpp files, 118
GiveFeedback(), 370
InvalidateRect() (mouse events), 203
member functions, calling, 46
OleUninitialize(), 380
OnDraw() (WM_PAINT message), 209
OnPaint() (WM_PAINT message), 206
Open() (ODBC), 383-384
PluginWindowProc() (Simple plug-in), 281
PolyLine(), 426
printToStdout() (Java), 283-284
QueryContinueDrag(), 370
QueryInterface(), 366
RegDeleteKey() (OLE automation servers), 380
ReleaseCapture() (mouse events), 205
remove(), 43, 50
RevokeActiveObject() (OLE automation servers), 380
SetCapture() (mouse events), 205
SetFocus(), assigning keyboard focus to WindowProc functions, 198-199
SetWindowLong(), 193
signatures, defined, 503
UpdateWindow() (mouse events), 203
WindowProc, 192, 194
assigning keyboard focus, 198-201
yield(), lack of in multitasking, 355-356
see also methods

G

g++ compiler, 31

Galileo, *see* **Netscape Navigator, 4.0**

General Protection Faults (GPFs) Windows 3.x
NPN_PostURL( ) method, 250
NPN_UserAgent( ) method, 248

GET method (HTML), 249

getFocusEvent, 196

GetJavaClass( ) function, modifying npshell.cpp files, 118

getting events, *see* **events**

GetVersion( ) method (16/32-bit plug-ins), 428

GiveFeedback( ) function, 370

global memory (Windows 3.x), 424

GNU tar, 30

GPFs (General Protection Faults) Windows 3.x
NPN_PostURL( ) method, 250
NPN_UserAgent( ) method, 248

GrafPorts (Macintosh), 182-183

graphics, (MIME subtypes), 16

GUIs, (Graphical User Interfaces), 72
building plug-ins, 28

gzip compression utility, 30

H

.h file extension, 42

handles, defined, 498

handling
events, *see* events
streams
MFC, 213
Windows API, 210
Windows messages, 191-192

headers
block headers, 109
C++, 42, 44
moving to project
directory, 108

npChap04.h (modified
version), 119
npChap04Dlg.h file
(dialog header)
modifying, 121-123
peer objects, 88-89
updating dependencies, 115

Hello, world! plug-in
adding files from SDK, 108
building, 128-129
connecting dialog resources to
message handlers, 123-124
DLL configuration, 113-114
generating project code,
103-107
Java version, 464
modifying version information
resource, 109-112
module definition file, 127-128
npChap04.cpp file, modifying,
120-121
npChap04.h file, modifying,
118-119
npChap04Dlg.cpp file,
modifying, 124-127
npChap04Dlg.h file,
modifying, 121-123
npshell.cpp file, modifying,
114-118
testing, 129-130

helper applications
advantages/disadvantages,
14, 20-22
defined, 498
media types (MIME types), 15
MIME, 15-17
Web servers, 17-18

hidden plug-ins, 81, 83, 152-153
zero plug-in, 138-139

hidden.html file (zero plug-in), 139

Hollywood Principle, 150-152

HTML (HyperText Markup Language), 11
editors, 510
GET method, 249
integrating plug-ins, 459
JavaScript
CharFlipper plug-in, 306
npAVI plug-in, 333
multitasking, 353-354
plug-ins as components, 27-28
POST method, 249
Simple plug-in, 284-285
static HTML files, defined, 504

tags
<EMBED>, 81-83, 90-91,
175-177, 459-460,
481, 490
<OBJECT>, 394
<PARAM>, 406-407
<SELECT>, 485

HTTP (HyperText Transport Protocol), byte-range requests, 149
httpd, defined, 499

Hungarian notation, 71

hyperlinking, 241
loading URLs, 241-244
current window, 242-243
other targets, 243-244
sending to current
instance, 244

HyperText Markup Language, *see* **HTML**

I

I/O (Input/Output), 47

IANA (Internet Assigned Numbers Authority), 25-26

icons, default (dialogs), 124

ID binding, 378

IDispatch interface (OLE automation), 377-379

IDropSource interface (drag-and-drop transfers), 370

IDropTarget interface (drag-and-drop transfers), 371

imagemaps, defined, 499

images (MIME subtypes), 16

indexed sequential access method (ISAM), 260

inheritance (object-oriented programming), 40
public versus private, 69-70

init( ) method (Java), 463

input
I/O (Input/Output), 47
iterators, 62
see also events

insert iterators, 63

installing callback functions (Windows messages), 193

installing plug-ins, 480
  assisted installation, 481-485
    <EMBED>
      PLUGINSPAGE
      attribute, 481
  auto-downloading
    (Navigator 4.0), 490
  download pages, 483, 486
    intranational
      considerations, 485
    licensing agreements, 484
    system requirements, 484
    up-to-date versions, 483-484
  installation scripts, 485-486
  LiveConnect, 486-489
    embeds array, 489
    MIME type conflict,
      487-489
    plug-ins array, 488
  manual installation, 480-481
  missing plug-in icons, 482

instances, 40-47
  associating information, 155
  class members, 70-71
  copies of plug-ins, 174
    NPN_MemAlloc()
      function, 176-177
    NPP_New() function,
      174-176
  destroying (NPP_Destroy()
    method), 155, 230-234
    destroying windows,
      234-235
    freeing dynamic
      memory, 230
    saving instance data,
      231-234
  duplicate instances,
    troubleshooting, 431-432
  inheritance, 40
  template classes, 58-59
  variables
    defined, 499
    initialization code for
      keyboard events, 200-201

instantiating, see instances

integrating plug-ins
  HTML, 459
  LiveConnect, 460-461
    calling Java from
      JavaScript, 466-468
    calling JavaScript from
      Java, 464-466
    Java, 462

**interaction between
  plug-ins, 154**

interfaces
  Application Program
    Interfaces (APIs), 82
    defined, 495
    plug-in API version, 247
    Windows API, handling
      streams, 210
  CGI (Common Gateway
    Interface), 496
  DOS Protected Mode
    Interface, 423-424
  graphical user interfaces,
    see GUIs
  IDispatch (OLE automation),
    377-378, 379
  IDropSource (drag-and-drop
    transfers), 370
  IDropTarget (drag-and-drop
    transfers), 371
  Internet Server Application
    Programming Interface
    (ISAPI), 408
  IUnknown (OLE), 366
  Java Runtime Interface (JRI),
    470-471
  OLE automation, 379
    ActiveX Template Library
      (ATL), 400
  Single Document Interface
    (SDI), 105
  threads, 356
  virtual function table (VTBL),
    OLE automation, 377-379
  Xlib (UNIX), 183-184

**Internet Assigned Numbers
  Authority (IANA), 25-26**

**Internet Engineering Task
  Force, 26**

Internet Explorer
  ActiveX controls, 395-396
  VBScript, 398

**Internet Server Application
  Programming Interface
  (ISAPI), 408**

**interrupt reasons,
  troubleshooting, 431**

**InvalidateRect() function
  (mouse events), 203**

invoking plug-ins, 80-81

IP addresses, defined, 499

**IPC (Inter-Process
  Communication),
  defined, 499**

IS-A relationships, 40

**ISAM, (indexed sequential
  access method), 260**

**ISAPI, (Internet Server
  Application Programming
  Interface), 408**

iterators, 62-64

**IUnknown interface
  (OLE), 366**

J

Java, 22-23, 461-463
  ActiveX controls, 393
  applets, defined, 495
  CharFlipper plug-in Java code,
    302-304
  Hello, world! program, 464
  init() method, 463
  javah, 470-471
    C stubs, 474
    naming conventions, 475
    public methods, 471
  LiveConnect, 462
    calling Java methods from
      JavaScript, 466-468
    calling JavaScript from Java
      methods, 464-466
  native methods, 302
  npAVI plug-in Java code,
    331-332
  paint() method, 463
  primitive types, 471
  SDK, 462
  Simple plug-in Java code,
    282-284
    count, 283
    doit(), 284-285
    fact() function, 283
    printToStdout() function,
      283-284
  talking to plug-ins, 468-469
    calling Java methods from
      plug-ins, 470-473
    calling plug-ins from Java
      methods, 473-475
    Java peer classes, 473-474
    overloaded methods,
      472-473

Java Console, 271

**Java Developers Kit
  (JDK), 310**

**Java Runtime Interface (JRI),
  470-471**
  Java primitive types, 471

JavaScript, 22-23, 461
ActiveX, 405-406
CharFlipper plug-in, 306
LiveConnect, 23
calling Java methods from
JavaScript, 466-468
calling JavaScript from Java
methods, 464-466
Netscape Navigator, 398
npAVI plug-in, 333
plug-ins as components, 27-28
plugins array, 488
Simple plug-in, 284-285

**JDK (Java Developers Kit),
310**

JFIF, defined, 500

**JRI (Java Runtime Interface),
470-471**
Java primitive types, 471

K-L

key events, 196

keyboard
events
assigning keyboard focus,
198-201
MFC, 202
Windows, 198-202
focus, 190
assigning to WindowProc
functions, 198-201
getFocusEvent, 196
getting events, *see* events
loseFocusEvent, 196

**keywords, afx_msg (message
mapping), 208**

late binding, 378

**LaunchApplication( ) methods
(Macintosh multitasking),
349-350**

launching plug-ins, 162
advertising MIME media
types, 162
Macintosh, 164-167
OS/2 Warp, 163
UNIX, 167-168
Windows, 162-163

libraries, 33
ActiveX Template Library
(ATL), 400-401
class libraries,
see class libraries
dynamic, *see* dynamic libraries

Standard Template Library,
see STL
static libraries, 33
defined, 504
type libraries (OLE automation
servers), 379

licensing
ActiveX controls, 397
download pages, linking to
licensing agreements, 484

linking
dynamic (ActiveX
controls), 397
hyperlinking, 241
loading URLs, 241-244
linked lists (WindowProc
pointers), 192-193
static (ActiveX controls), 397
to plug-ins, 81

lint, 157

listNode class, 52

**lists, linked (WindowProc
pointers), 192-193**

LiveConnect, 22-23, 461-462
CharFlipper plug-in, 302-307
closing down, 307
Java code, 302-304
JavaScript/HTML
connection, 306
triggering with periodic
events, 304-306
installing plug-ins, 486-489
embeds array, 489
MIME type conflict,
487-489
plug-ins array, 488
integrating plug-ins, 460-461
Java, 462
calling Java methods from
plug-ins, 470-473
calling plug-ins from Java
methods, 473-477
overloaded methods,
472-473
peer classes, 473-474
talking to plug-ins, 468-469
JavaScript
calling Java from
JavaScript, 466-468
calling JavaScript from
Java, 464-466
npAVI plug-in, 330-333
closing down, 333
Java code, 331-332
JavaScript/HTML
connection, 333

Simple plug-in, 282-287
Java code, 282-284
JavaScript/HTML
connection, 284-285
NPP_Destroy( )
method, 286
NPP_Shutdown( ), 287

LiveWire
coupling applications, 257-258
toolset, 23

loading plug-ins, 168
DllEntryPoint( ) function,
170-171
finding media types, 168
main( ) calls, 169-170
NP_GetEntryPoints( )
function, 171
NP_Initialize( ) function,
171-173
error codes, 173-174
specification, 173

local
guides, defined, 500
memory (Windows 3.x), 424

**Lock( ) method (semaphore
access), 358-359**

logical operators, 64

loseFocusEvent, 196

M

MacApp framework, 451

Macintosh
advertising media types,
164-167
resource forks, 164
.rsrc files, 164
STR# resource, 165-166
vers resource, 164-165
building plug-ins, 28
CDEFs (Control Definition
Functions), 36
configuring SDK, 36-37
download page
considerations, 486
events, 195-198
adjustCursorEvent, 196
Apple events, 197
getFocusEvent, 196
loseFocusEvent, 196
NPP_HandleEvent( )
function, 195, 197-198
updateEvt, 198
forks, 164
GrafPorts, 182-183
Helpers screen, 487-488

MacApp framework, 451
main() calls (loading plug-ins), 169-172
MDEFs (Menu Definition Functions), 37
MIME media type
    associations, 19, 487-488
    determining, 488-489
multitasking, 349-351
    asynchronous routines, 350-351
    foreground processes, 349
    LaunchApplication() method, 349-350
Navigator memory cache, 90
NPP_HandleEvent() method, 85
OpenDoc, 388-389
PDEFs (Printer Drivers), 37
plug-ins subdirectory, 480
printing
    embedded plug-ins, 218-219
    full-page plug-ins, 221, 227-229
ResEdit utility, 164-167
System 8, 350-351
THINK Reference, 229

main( ) routine, 44-45
    calling (Navigator), 169-170
    loading plug-ins (Macintosh), 169-172

make utility, 500

mapping
    messages, 206-209
        afx_msg keyword, 208
        application classes, 207
        BEGIN_MESSAGE_
            MAP() macro (MFC), 206, 208
        DECLARE_MESSAGE_
            MAP() macro (MFC), 206-207
        MFC message-handling hierarchy, 208
        ON_WM_PAINT macro (MFC), 206, 208
    MM_TWIPS mapping mode (printing), 217

media types, 15, 24-26
    advertising, 162
        Macintosh, 164-167
        OS/2 Warp, 163
        UNIX, 167-168
        Windows, 162-163
    configuring SDK for OS/2 Warp, 35-36

file associations, 17-18
finding (Netscape Navigator), 168
NPMIMEType, 263
private, 24
registering, 24-26
specifying in version information, 111-112
stream size, 238
subtypes, 16
Web
    browsers, 18-19
    servers, 17-18
    see also MIME types

member functions (C++), calling, 46

memory
    allocating, 89-90
    delete operator, 143
    dynamic memory, freeing, 230
    new operator, 143
    NPN_MemAlloc() method, 142-144
    NPN_MemFlush() method, 143
    NPN_MemFree() method, 143
    Windows 3.x, 417
        DOS Protected Mode Interface, 423-424
        extended/expanded memory, 420-422
        far pointers, 418-420
        global memory, 424
        local memory, 424
        near pointers, 417-418
        running 16- and 32-bit applications simultaneously, 424
        small memory, 417-418
        tiny memory, 418

menus (pop-up), 245

messages (Windows), 190
    callback functions, 192-194
        AssociateInstance() function, 193-194
        callback.cpp listing, 194-195
        installing, 193
    handling, 191-192
        connecting to resources (dialog boxes), 123-124
        MFC message-handling hierarchy, 208
    keyboard events, 198-202
        assigning keyboard focus to WindowProc functions, 198-201

mapping, 206-209
    afx_msg keyword, 208
    application classes, 207
    BEGIN_MESSAGE_
        MAP() macro (MFC), 206, 208
    DECLARE_MESSAGE_
        MAP() macro (MFC), 206-207
    MFC message-handling hierarchy, 208
    ON_WM_PAINT macro (MFC), 206, 208
message types, 191
mouse events, 202-205
    WM_LBUTTONDOWN, 202-203
    WM_LBUTTONUP, 202
    WM_MOUSEMOVE, 202
parameters, 191
queue, 190-191
WindowProc functions, 192
WM_KEYDOWN, 199-200
WM_PAINT, 195
    OnDraw() function, 209
see also events

methods, 47-50
    access methods, 495
    add(), 49
    defined, 500
    DoDataExchange(), dialog boxes, 123
    DPtoLP(), 87
    EatDialog(), 125
    fseek(), 149
    GET (HTML), 249
    GetVersion(),
        16/32-bit plug-ins, 428
    init() (Java), 463
    Java native methods, 302
    LaunchApplication()
        (Macintosh multitasking), 349-350
    Lock(), semaphore access, 358-359
    Notify() methods, 145
    NP_GetEntryPoints(), loading plug-ins, 171
    NP_Initialize(), 171-173
        CharFlipper plug-in, 293-294
        npAVI plug-in, 318
        Simple plug-in, 273-274
    NPN methods, 139-145
    NPN_DestroyStream(), 89, 264
    NPN_GetURL(), 88, 91, 139-140, 145, 238-240
        additional streams, 214

asynchronous processing,
246-247
hyperlinking, 241
loading URLs, 241-244
migrating existing
applications, 244-246
NPN_GetURLNotify( )
method, 246-247
sending streams to targets,
239-240
specification, 239
NPN_GetURLNotify( ), 88
additional streams, 214
reason parameter, 246-247
specification, 246
syntax, 246
NPN_MemAlloc( ), 90,
142-144, 267-268
associating information
with instances, 155
instantiating copies of
plug-ins, 176-177
NPN_MemFlush( ), 90, 143
NPN_MemFree( ), 90, 143,
267-268
NPN_NewStream( ), 91, 144,
262-264
additional streams, 213
NPN_DestroyStream( )
method, 264
NPN_Write( ) method, 263
plug-in interaction, 154
specification, 262
streaming into
Navigator, 263
NPN_PostURL( ), 88-89,
141-142, 145, 249-258
additional streams, 214
distributed systems,
252-256
non-HTTP URLs, 250
older Navigator versions,
250-252
sending buffers, 250
sending files, 249
NPN_PostURLNotify( ), 89
additional streams, 214
NPN_RequestRead( ), 89, 145,
180-181, 259-262
NPByteRange
structure, 262
seekable streams, 149,
259-261
syntax, 262
NPN_Status( ), 88, 91, 144-145,
264-267
download progress
indicators, 265

reporting time remaining,
266-267
specification, 265
NPN_UserAgent( ), 87,
142, 248
16-bit Navigator, 427
NPN_Version( ), 87, 142,
247-248
NPN_UserAgent( )
method, 248
NPN_Write( ), 263
NPP methods, 136-139
prototypes, 173
NPP_Destroy( ), 83-84, 89,
137, 155, 230-234
CharFlipper plug-in, 307
destroying windows,
234-235
events, 359
freeing dynamic
memory, 230
npAVI plug-in, 333
saving instance data,
231-234
Simple plug-in, 286
NPP_DestroyStream( ), 85
NPP_GetJavaClass( )
CharFlipper plug-in, 295
modifying npshell.cpp
files, 118
npAVI plug-in, 318-319
Simple plug-in, 274-275
NPP_HandleEvent( ), 85
Macintosh events, 195-198
NPP_Initialize( ), 83, 136-137
NPP_Initialization( ) (OLE
automation servers), 380
NPP_New( ), 83, 136-137, 139
CharFlipper plug-in,
295-297
initialization code for
instance variables,
200-201
instantiating copies of
plug-ins, 174-176
npAVI plug-in, 319-320
plug-in types, 152
Simple plug-in, 275-278
specification, 174
stream handling, 210, 213
NPP_NewStream( ), 85,
89, 137, 177-181
CharFlipper plug-in,
299-301
NP_ASFILE
parameter, 148
NP_ASFILEONLY
parameter, 148

NP_NORMAL
parameter, 147
NP_SEEK parameter
(seekable streams), 149
npAVI plug-in, 327-328
reading data as files, 180
reading data as
streams, 179
seekable streams, 180-181
specification, 177
stream handling, 210
NPP_Print( ), 86-87, 137, 154
CharFlipper plug-in, 301
embedded plug-ins, 216
full-page plug-ins, 219
npAVI plug-in, 328-330
Simple plug-in, 281-282
see also NPP_Print( )
method
NPP_SetWindow( ), 85,
137, 139
assigning keyboard focus
to WindowProc
functions, 198
callback functions, 193
CharFlipper plug-in,
297-299
initialization code for
instance variables,
200-201
npAVI plug-in, 321-327
presenting data, 181, 186
Simple plug-in, 280-281
specification, 181
stream handling, 210, 213
NPP_Shutdown( ), 137,
234-235
CharFlipper plug-in, 307
npAVI plug-in, 333
OLE automation
servers, 380
Simple plug-in, 287
NPP_StreamAsFile( ), 86,
148, 180
npAVI plug-in, 328
NPP_URLNotify( ), 87-88, 145
additional streams, 214
NPP_Write( ), 85, 147-148
buffers, 179
CharFlipper plug-in,
299-301
seekable streams, 149
stream handling, 210
NPP_WriteReady( ), 85,
147-148, 179
CharFlipper plug-in,
299-301
stream handling, 210

OleInitialize( ), 368
OnDraw( ), view classes, 446
OnPaint( ), 127
overloaded methods, 472-473
paint( ) (Java), 463
plug-in objects, 85
POST (HTML), 249
post( ) (Java), 473
remove( ), 50, 57-58
SetTimer( ), 361
system( ), 99
Unlock( ), semaphore access,
    358-359
virtual, 67-69
see also functions

**MFC (Microsoft Foundation
Classes), 31-32**
accessing, 445
    document classes, 445-446
    view classes, 446
ActiveX controls, 393
    dynamic linking, 397
    static linking, 397
ASSERTs, 158
casting functions, 117
CEvent class (thread
    termination), 359-360
CException, 46
clipboard data transfers, 369
COleDispatchDriver, OLE
    automation clients, 376
CView, 208-209, 213
    printing from full-page
        plug-ins, 221
CWinApp, 208
dynamic linking, ActiveX
    controls, 397
keyboard events, 202
mapping messages, 206-209
    BEGIN_MESSAGE_
        MAP( ) macro, 206
    DECLARE_MBEGIN_
        MESSAGE_MAP( )
        macro, 208
    DECLARE_MESSAGE_
        MAP( ) macro, 206-207
    message-handling
        hierarchy, 208
    ON_WM_PAINT macro,
        206, 208
ODBC, 383
    CDatabase class, 383-384
static linking, ActiveX
    controls, 397
STL, 66
stream handling, 213
tree views, 241-244
Visual C++ 4.0 Standard
    Edition, 102

**MFC AppWizard dialog,
105-106**
Microsoft
ActiveX, see ActiveX
code signing, 396
document-centric computing,
    457-458
Internet Explorer
    ActiveX controls, 395-396
    VBScript, 398
Internet products, 392
ODBC, see ODBC
OLE, see OLE
Window, see Windows

**Microsoft Foundation Classes,
see MFC**

**migrating existing applications
to Web, 244-246**
menus, 245
windows, 244-245

**MIME (Multimedia Internet
Message Extensions), 15-17**
FAQ (Frequently Asked
    Questions) Web site, 16
types, 24-26
    advertising, 162
    conflict during plug-in
        installation, 487-489
    configuring SDK for, 35-36
    finding (Netscape
        Navigator), 168
    MIMEType strings, adding
        to version information,
        111-112
    mimeTypes array, 488-489
    NPMIMEType, 263
    private, 24
    registering, 24-26
    stream size, 238
    subtypes, 16
    see also media types

mime.types files, 17

mix-in classes, defined, 500

**MM_TWIPS mapping
mode, 217**

**module definition files,
127-128**

mouse
drag-and-drop transfers, 371
events, 196
    adjustCursorEvent, 196
    Windows, 202-205

WM_LBUTTONDOWN
    message, 202-203
WM_LBUTTONUP, 202
WM_MOUSEMOVE, 202
hyperlinks, 242-244

**MoveTo( )/LineTo( ) function
sequence, 426**

Mozilla, 500

**MPEG (Moving Pictures
Experts Group),
defined, 501**

msg1.cpp listing, 191-192

**Multimedia Internet Message
Extensions, see MIME**

multimedia plug-ins, 90-91

multitasking, 338-339
background processing, 355
cooperative, 339
deadlocks (deadly embraces),
    344-348
    banker's algorithm, 345-348
    dealing with, 344-345
    resource-numbering, 345
    two-phase locking, 348
defined, 501
HTML, 353-354
Macintosh, 349-351
    asynchronous routines,
        350-351
    foreground processes, 349
    LaunchApplication( )
        method, 349-350
    Notify( ) methods, 355
    NPP_New( ) method, 354
preemptive, 339-340
processes, 340-341
reentrant calls, 361
semaphores (p-v), 342-344
separate threads, 356-357
    priorities, 357
    Runtime Type
        Identification (RTTI), 356
    starting threads
        (AfxBeginThread( )
        function), 356
threads, 341-342
    terminating, 359-360
timers, 361
UNIX, 349
Windows, 351-353
    Windows 3.x, 425
yield( ) function, lack of,
    355-356
yielding, 339

N

naming
C++ naming conventions, 71
plug-ins, 105

navigation, defined, 501

Navigator,
see Netscape Navigator

NCSA (National Center for Supercomputer Applications), 501

near pointers (Windows 3.x), 417-418

Netscape Navigator
3.0, 12
plug-ins, 22
SDK Web site, 103
4.0 (Galileo)
downloading plug-ins, 29, 490
OS/2 Warp, 35
finding MIME media types, 168
frames, *see* frames
Helpers tab (General Preferences), 18-19
JavaScript, 398
loading plug-ins,
see loading plug-ins
media types, 18-19
plugins array, 488
troubleshooting
16-bit version, 427-428
duplicate instances, 431-432
interrupt reasons, 431
NPN_GetURL( ), 430-431
NPN_PostURL( ), 430-431
NPN_RequestRead( ), 432
NPP_New( ) errors, 430-431
NPP_StreamAsFile( ), 430
resizing windows, 430-431
versions
BrowserWatch, 251
determining, 247
NPN_PostURL( ) method, 250-252
NPN_UserAgent( ) method, 248
Web site, 12

networking, *see* multitasking

new operator, 143

New Project Workspace dialog box (Visual C++), 103-105

Notify( ) methods, 145
multitasking, 355

np prefix, 105

NP_GetEntryPoints( ) function, loading plug-ins, 171

NP_Initialize( ) method
CharFlipper plug-in, 293-294
loading plug-ins, 171-173
error codes, 173-174
specification, 173
npAVI plug-in, 318
Simple plug-in, 273-274

npapi.h files, 82

npAVI plug-in, 310
closing down, 333
compiling, 310-313
building
.\objs\$(TARGET).dll, 312-313
building all, 311
building java, 311-312
flow of control
calling, 317
NP_Initialize( ) method, 318
NPP_GetJavaClass( ) method, 318-319
NPP_New( ) method, 319-320
NPP_NewStream( ) method, 327-328
NPP_Print( ) method, 328-330
NPP_SetWindow( ) method, 321-327
NPP_StreamAsFile( ) method, 328
Java Developers Kit installation, 310
LiveConnect, 330-333
closing down, 333
Java code, 331-332
JavaScript/HTML connection, 333
moving files to plug-ins directory, 313
putting into a project, 314-315
running, 313-314

NPByteRange structure, 262

npChap04.cpp file, modifying (Hello world! plug-in), 120-121

npChap04.def file (Hello world! plug-in), 127-128

npChap04.exe file (Hello world! plug-in), 106

npChap04.h file, modified version (Hello world! plug-in), 118-119

npChap04Dlg.cpp file, modifying (Hello world! plug-in), 124-127

npChap04Dlg.h file, modifying (Hello world! plug-in), 121-123

npCount.java, 474

NPERR codes, loading plug-ins, 172

NPFullPrint, 220

NPMIMEType, 263

NPN methods, 139-145
NPN_ prefix, 136

NPN_DestroyStream( ) method, 89, 264

NPN_GetURL( ) method, 88, 91, 139-140, 145, 238-240
additional streams, 214
asynchronous processing, 246-247
hyperlinking, 241
loading URLs, 241-244
migrating existing applications, 244-246
menus, 245
windows, 244-245
specification, 239

NPN_GetURLNotify( ) method, 88, 246-247
additional streams, 214
reason parameter, 246-247
sending streams to targets, 239-240
specification, 246
syntax, 246
troubleshooting, 430-431

NPN_MemAlloc( ) method, 90, 142-144, 267-268
associating information with instances, 155
instantiating copies of plug-ins, 176-177

NPN_MemFlush( ) method, 90, 143

NPN_MemFree( ) method, 90, 143, 267-268

NPN_NewStream( ) method,
91, 144, 262-264
   additional streams, 213
   NPN_DestroyStream( )
      method, 264
   NPN_Write( ) method, 263
   plug-in interaction, 154
   specification, 262
   streaming into Navigator, 263

NPN_PostURL( ) method,
88-89, 141-142, 145,
249-258
   additional streams, 214
   distributed systems, 252-256
      backups, 256
      downloading additional
         files, 254-255
      file transmissions, 252-253
      final updates, 256
      updating files, 253
      user interaction, 255
   non-HTTP URLs, 250
   older Navigator versions,
      250-252
   sending buffers, 250
   sending files, 249
   troubleshooting, 430-431

NPN_PostURLNotify( )
method, 89
   additional streams, 214

NPN_RequestRead( ) method,
89, 145, 180-181, 259-262
   NPByteRange structure, 262
   seekable streams, 149, 259-261
      binary trees, 260
      indexed sequential access
         method (ISAM), 260
   syntax, 262
   troubleshooting, 432

NPN_Status( ) method, 88,
91, 144-145, 264-267
   download progress
      indicators, 265
      reporting time remaining,
         266-267
   specification, 265

NPN_UserAgent( ) method,
87, 142, 248
   16-bit Navigator, 427

NPN_Version( ) method, 87,
142, 247-248
   NPN_UserAgent( )
      method, 248

NPN_Write( ) method, 263

NPP methods, 136-139
   NPP_ /NPN_ calls, 82
   NPP_ prefix, 136
   prototypes, 173

NPP_Destroy( ) method,
83-84, 89, 137, 155,
230-234
   CharFlipper plug-in, 307
   events, 359
   freeing dynamic memory, 230
   npAVI plug-in, 333
   saving instance data, 231-234
      destroying windows,
         234-235
      how to use
         NPP_Destroy( ), 232-234
      save parameter, 232
      when to use
         NPP_Destroy( ), 232
   Simple plug-in, 286

NPP_DestroyStream( )
method, 85

NPP_GetJavaClass( ) method
   CharFlipper plug-in, 295
   modifying npshell.cpp
      files, 118
   npAVI plug-in, 318-319
   Simple plug-in, 274-275

NPP_HandleEvent( )
method, 85
   Macintosh events, 195
      event types, 196
      implementing, 197-198

NPP_Initialization( ) method,
OLE automation
servers, 380

NPP_Initialize( ) method, 83,
136-137

NPP_New( ) method, 83,
136-137, 139
   CharFlipper plug-in, 295-297
   initialization code for instance
      variables, 200-201
   instantiating copies of plug-ins,
      174-176
         <EMBED> tag, 175
         NPSavedData type, 175-176
         specification, 174
   multitasking, 354
   npAVI plug-in, 319-320
   plug-in types, 152
   Simple plug-in, 275-278

stream handling
   MFC, 213
   Windows API, 210
troubleshooting, 430

NPP_NewStream( ) method,
85, 89, 137, 177-181
   CharFlipper plug-in, 299-301
   NP_ASFILE parameter, 148
   NP_ASFILEONLY
      parameter, 148
   NP_NORMAL parameter, 147
   NP_SEEK parameter
      (seekable streams), 149
   npAVI plug-in, 327-328
   reading data
      as files, 180
      as streams, 179
   seekable streams, 180-181
   specification, 177
   stream handling (Windows
      API), 210

NPP_Print( ) method, 86-87,
137, 154
   CharFlipper plug-in, 301
   embedded mode, 216-219
      defining NPP_Print( ), 216
      DPtoLP( ) calls, 218
      embedPrint, 217
      Macintosh features,
         218-219
      MM_TWIPS mapping
         mode, 217
      NPWindow, 217
      platformPrint, 216-217
   full-page mode, 219-229
      bitmaps, 221-222
      Cancel dialogs, 222-223
      customizing Print dialog,
         225-227
      fonts, 223-225
      Macintosh Print... dialog,
         227-229
      platformPrint member, 220
      pluginPrinted, 220-221
      PrValidate( ), 221
      Windows, 221-225
   npAVI plug-in, 328-330
   Simple plug-in, 281-282

NPP_SetWindow( ) method,
85, 137, 139
   assigning keyboard focus to
      WindowProc functions, 198
   callback functions, 193
   CharFlipper plug-in, 297-299
   initialization code for instance
      variables, 200-201
   npAVI plug-in, 321-327

presenting data, 181, 186
Simple plug-in, 280-281
specification, 181
stream handling
MFC, 213
Windows API, 210
troubleshooting, 430

NPP_Shutdown( ) method, 137, 234-235
CharFlipper plug-in, 307
npAVI plug-in, 333
OLE automation servers, 380
Simple plug-in, 287

NPP_StreamAsFile( ) method, 86, 148, 180
npAVI plug-in, 328
troubleshooting, 430

NPP_URLNotify( ) method, 87-88, 145
additional streams, 214

NPP_Write( ) method, 85
CharFlipper plug-in, 299-301

NPP_Write( ) method, 147-148
buffers, 179
seekable streams, 149
stream handling (Windows API), 210

NPP_WriteReady( ) method, 85, 147-148, 179
CharFlipper plug-in, 299-301
stream handling (Windows API), 210

NPSavedData type
instantiating copies of plug-ins, 175-176
troubleshooting, 429

npshell.cpp file, modifying (Hello world! plug-in), 114-118
adding plug-in specific code, 115
casting functions, 117
GetJavaClass( ) function, 118
header file dependencies, 115
NPP_GetJavaClass( ) function, 118

npsimple.c, *see* **Simple plug-in**

npwin.cpp file, adding (Hello world! plug-in), 108

NPWindows
presenting data, 182
UNIX, 183
printing, embedded plug-ins, 217

null events, 196

O

.obj (object) files extension, 32-33

Object Identifiers (OIDs), 26

Object Linking and Embedding, *see* **OLE**

object-oriented programming
Active X (OLE) controls, 387
classes, 40-47
C++, *see* C++, classes
inheritance, 40
polymorphism, 41
design issues, 67
abstract classes, 67-69
GUIs, 72
instances as class members, 70-71
public versus private inheritance, 69-70
style/naming conventions, 71
virtual methods, 67-69
Hollywood Principle, 150-152
instances, 40-47
methods, 47-50
see also ODBC (Open DataBase Connectivity); OLE (Object Linking and Embedding)

<OBJECT> tag, ActiveX controls, 394-395

objects
function objects, 64-65
object-oriented programming, *see* object-oriented programming
plug-in objects, 84-87
data streams, 85-86
methods, 85

objecttg.htm listing, 395

ObjectWindows Library, 446-448
TGauge class, 447-448

octet-stream MIME type, 16

OCXs, *see* **OLE, controls**

ODBC (open database connectivity), 381-383
connecting to data sources, 383-384
associating connection with different URLs, 384

exceptions, 384
sharing connections across all instances, 384
driver packs, 383
MFC, 383
selecting records, 384-386
CRecordSet-derived classes, 384-386
SQL queries, 384
shutting down connections, 386-387

OIDs (Object Identifiers), 26

OLE (Object Linking and Embedding), 364-365
automation, 375-380
Application object, 378
cancelling connections, 380
clients, 376-378
COleDispatchDriver, 376
constants in registration routines, 380
dynamic (late) binding, 378
interfaces, 377-379
NPP_Shutdown( ), 380
servers, 378-380
static (ID) binding, 378
temporary plug-in registration, 380
type libraries, 379
UNIX, 375-376
clipboard transfers, 366-370
delayed rendering, 367
MFCs, 369
objects, 367-368
COM (Component Object Model), 399
component object model, 366
controls, 393
see also ActiveX, controls
drag-and-drop transfers, 370-372
DoDragDrop( ) function, 371-372
IDropSource interface, 370
IDropTarget interface, 371
OpenDoc, 388-389

OleInitialize( ) function, 368

OleUninitialize( ) function, 380

ON_WM_PAINT macro (MFC), 206, 208

OnDraw( ) method
view classes, 446
WM_PAINT message, 209

OnPaint( ) method, 127
WM_PAINT, 206

OnPrint( ) function, full-page plug-ins, 221

open database connectivity, *see* ODBC

Open( ) function, ODBC, 383-384

OpenDoc, 388-389

operating systems, 28, 30
ActiveX controls, 393
defined, 501
Macintosh, 36-37
advertising media types, 164-167
download page considerations, 486
GrafPorts, 182-183
MacApp framework, 451
MIME type association (Helpers screen), 487-489
multitasking, 349-351
OpenDoc, 388-389
plug-ins subdirectory, 480
printing, 218-219
System 8, 350-351
see also Macintosh
OS/2 Warp, 34-36
advertising media types, 163
configuring SDK, 34-36
Netscape 4.0 (Galileo), 35
plug-ins subdirectory, 480
SDK Web site, 35
UNIX
advertising media types, 167-168
class libraries, 449
configuring SDK, 37
document-centric computing, 457
download page considerations, 486
MIME type association (Helpers screen), 487-489
multitasking, 349
OLE automation, 375-376
plug-ins subdirectory, 480-481
see also UNIX
Windows, *see* Windows; Windows 3.x

operators, 55-56
arithmetic, 64
comparison, 64
delete, 143
logical, 64
new, 143

OS/2 Warp
advertising media types, 163
configuring SDK, 34-36
MIME media types, 35-36
Netscape 4.0 (Galileo), 35
plug-ins subdirectory, 480
SDK Web site, 35

output iterators, 63

overloading
defined, 501
overloaded methods, 472-473

OWL (ObjectWindows Library), 446-448
TGauge class, 447-448

P

p-v semaphore, 343

paint( ) method (Java), 463

<PARAM> tag, ActiveX controls, 406-407

pasting data, *see* clipboard transfers

PATH variable, defined, 501

patterns, 76-80
Christopher Alexander, 76-78
Early Program, 95
Gang of Four, 77
Gang of Four template, 78-80
Portland Pattern Repository, 95
Story pattern, 91-93
Task, 94
Task Window, 94-95
User Decision, 93-94

PCL (Printer Control Language), defined, 501

PDF files (Portable Document Format), 26-27
Acrobat Portable Document Format reader, 482

PDL (Page Description Language), 501

peer objects, 87-90
allocating memory, 89-90
headers, 88-89

opening new streams, 88
opening URLs for writing, 89
seeking streams, 89
status lines, 88

Perl (Practical Extraction and Report Language), 501

PKUNZIP, 30

platformPrint member
embedded plug-ins, 216-217
full-page plug-ins, 220

platforms, 28, 30
ActiveX controls, 393
Macintosh, 36-37
advertising media types, 164-167
download page considerations, 486
GrafPorts, 182-183
MacApp framework, 451
MIME type association (Helpers screen), 487-489
multitasking, 349-351
OpenDoc, 388-389
plug-ins subdirectory, 480
printing, 218-219
System 8, 350-351
OS/2 Warp, 34-36
advertising media types, 163
plug-ins subdirectory, 480
UNIX
advertising media types, 167-168
class libraries, 449
configuring SDK, 37
document-centric computing, 457
download page considerations, 486
MIME type association (Helpers screen), 487-489
multitasking, 349
OLE automation, 375-376
plug-ins subdirectory, 480-481
Windows, 34
multitasking, 351-353
Win32 API, 353

plug-ins, 22-23
Acrobat Portable Document Format reader (Amber), 482
API version, 247
architecture, 82-84
npapi.h files, 82
NPP_ /NPN_ calls, 82
bugs, 28

building, 28-29, 128-129
calling, 152-153
CharFlipper plug-in
  calling CharFlipper,
    292-293
  closing down, 307
  compiling, 290
  copying files to plug-ins
    directory, 290
  Java code, 302-304
  JavaScript/HTML
    connection, 306
  LiveConnect, 302
  NP_Initialize( ) method,
    293-294
  NPP_GetJavaClass( )
    method, 295
  NPP_New( ) method,
    295-297
  NPP_NewStream( )
    method, 299-301
  NPP_Print( ) method, 301
  NPP_SetWindow( )
    method, 297-299
  NPP_Write( ) method,
    299-301
  NPP_WriteReady( )
    method, 299-301
  running, 290-291
  triggering with periodic
    events, 304-306
code, 28
components, 27-28
defined, 502
document viewers, 91
downloading
  auto-downloading
    (Navigator 4.0), 490
  download pages, 483
  Navigator 4.0, 29
  system requirements, 484
  up to date versions, 483-484
embedded, see embedded
  plug-ins
full-page, see full-page plug-ins
getting events, see events
hidden, 81
installing, 480
  assisted installation,
    481-485
  download pages, 483
  embeds array, 489
  installation scripts, 485-486
  LiveConnect, 486-489
  manual installation, 480-481
  MIME type conflict,
    487-489
  missing plug-in icons,
    482-485

Navigator 4.0 (Galileo), 490
plug-ins array, 488
system requirements, 484
up to date versions, 483-484
integrating
  HTML, 459
  LiveConnect,
    see LiveConnect,
    integrating plug-ins
interaction, 154
invoking, 80-81
launching, see launching
  plug-ins
LiveConnect, 22-23
loading, see loading plug-ins
MIME media types, 24-26
  private, 24
  registering, 24-26
multimedia, 90-91
naming, 105
np prefix, 105
npAVI plug-in, 310
  calling, 317
  closing down, 333
  compiling, 310-313
  Java code, 331-332
  Java Developers Kit
    installation, 310
  JavaScript/HTML
    connection, 333
  LiveConnect, 330
  moving files to plug-ins
    directory, 313
  NP_Initialize( )
    method, 318
  NPP_GetJavaClass( )
    method, 318-319
  NPP_New( ) method,
    319-320
  NPP_NewStream( )
    method, 327-328
  NPP_Print( ) method,
    328-330
  NPP_SetWindow( )
    method, 321-327
  NPP_StreamAsFile( )
    method, 328
  putting into a project,
    314-315
  running, 313-314
NPP_ /NPN_ calls, 82-84
objects, 84-87
  data streams, 85-86
  methods, 85
printing, 86-87, 154-155
Simple plug-in, 270-271
  calling Simple, 272-273
  compiling, 270
  copying files to plug-ins
    directory, 270

DisplayJavaMessage( )
  function, 278-279
doit( ) function, 284-285
Java code, 282-284
JavaScript/HTML
  connection, 284-285
LiveConnect, 282
NP_Initialize( ) method,
  273-274
NPP_Destroy( )
  method, 286
NPP_GetJavaClass( )
  method, 274-275
NPP_New( ) method,
  275-278
NPP_Print( ) method,
  281-282
NPP_SetWindow( )
  method, 280-281
NPP_Shutdown( ), 287
PluginWindowProc( )
  function, 281
running, 270-271
TextOut defect, 281
Software Development Kit,
  see SDK
subdirectory, 480-481
testing
  about:plugins, 129
  sample data, 129-130
troubleshooting Windows
  plug-ins, 427-432
  16-bit Navigator, 427-428
  FileOpenName
    resource, 428
  full-page plug-ins, 429
  Netscape Navigator
    problems, 429-432
  unregistering failed
    plug-ins, 428

PluginInstance class
  keyboard events, 200
  mouse events, 204-205
  Simple plug-in, 276

plugins array, 488

**PluginWindowProc( ) function
  (Simple plug-in), 281**

pointers
  WindowProc pointers, 192-193
  Windows 3.x
    far, 418-420
    near, 417-418

PolyLine( ) function, 426

**polymorphism (object-oriented
  programming), 41**
  defined, 502

pop-up menus, 245

Portable Document Format, *see* **PDF files**

Portland Pattern Repository Web site, 95

POST method (HTML), 249

post( ) method (Java), 473

PostScript, defined, 502

precompiled binaries, 31

preemptive multitasking, 339-340

preprocessor definitions (Project Settings dialog), 114

presenting data, 181-186
  Macintosh GrafPorts, 182-183
  NPP_SetWindow( ) method, 181, 186
  NPWindows, 182-183
  UNIX (X Window System), 183-185
    callback structure, 183
    colormaps, 184-185
    hierarchy, 184-185
    X Toolkit, 183-184
    Xlib interface, 183-184

printing, 86-87, 154-155
  embedded mode, 216-219
    defining NPP_Print( ), 216
    DPtoLP( ) calls, 218
    embedPrint, 217
    Macintosh features, 218-219
    MM_TWIPS mapping mode, 217
    NPWindow, 217
    platformPrint, 216-217
  full-page mode, 219-229
    bitmaps, 221-222
    Cancel dialogs, 222-223
    customizing Print dialog, 225-227
    fonts, 223-225
    Macintosh Print... dialog, 227-229
    platformPrint member, 220
    pluginPrinted, 220-221
    PrValidate( ), 221
    Windows, 221-225
  Print dialog, customizing, 225-227
    Macintosh Print... dialog, 227-229
  troubleshooting full-page plug-ins, 429
  see also NPP_Print( ) method

printToStdout( ) function (Java), 283-284

private
  inheritance, 69-70
  members (classes), 51

processes, 146
  asynchronous plug-ins, 99
  daemon processes
    UNIX, 349
  forking (spawning), 146, 341
  multiprocessing, 340-341
  process ID, defined, 502
  Symmetric Multiprocessors (SMPs), 341

program design, Hollywood Principle, 150-152

progress indicators, 265
  reporting time remaining, 266-267

projects
  copying SDK files, 108
  generating code, 103-107
    building code, 106-107
    MFC AppWizard dialog, 105-106
    naming plug-ins, 105
    shared DLLs, 106
    Single Document Interface (SDI), 105
    warnings, 107

proof of concept, defined, 502

protected members (classes), 51

protocols, byte-oriented, 21

PrValidate( ) function, full-page plug-ins, 221

public
  inheritance, 69-70
  members (classes), 51

pure virtual, defined, 502

Q

QUERY_STRING environment variable, defined, 502

QueryContinueDrag( ) function, 370

QueryInterface( ) function, 366

QuickTime, 502

quotes (""), C++ header files, 44

R

random access iterators, 63

raw storage iterators, 63

RDBMS (Relational Database Management System), defined, 502

reading, 86
  data
    files, 180
    streams, 179
  keyboard events
    assigning keyboard focus, 198-201
    MFC, 202
    Windows, 198-202
  mouse events
    Windows, 202-205
    WM_LBUTTONDOWN message, 202-203
    WM_LBUTTONUP, 202
    WM_MOUSEMOVE, 202
  NPN_RequestRead( ) method, 145, 259-262
    NPByteRange structure, 262
    seekable streams, 259-261
    syntax, 262
  opening new streams, 88
  read-and-set operations, 343-344

Ready-to-Run Software, Inc., 31

real-time, defined, 502

RealAudio, 21

reentrant
  calls, 361
  code, asynchronous plug-ins, 99

RegDeleteKey( ) function, OLE automation servers, 380

registering
  MIME media types, 24-26
  plug-ins, temporary registration (OLE automation servers), 380

ReleaseCapture( ) function, mouse events, 205

reloading, defined, 503

remove( ) method, 43, 50, 57-58

rendering
  delayed rendering, 367
  separate threads, 356-357

priorities, 357
Runtime Type
Identification (RTTI), 356
starting threads
(AfxBeginThread( )
function), 356

ResEdit utility (Macintosh), 164-167

Resource Editor (Visual C++), 112

resources
connecting to message
handlers (dialog boxes),
123-124
forks (Macintosh), 164
numbering, 345
ResEdit utility (Macintosh),
164-167
version information, 109-112
block headers, 109
FileExtents field, 111
filtering files, 111
MIMEType string, 111-112

reverse iterators, 63

RevokeActiveObject( ) function, OLE automation servers, 380

RFC (Request for Comments), 15
defined, 503
RFC 1590 (MIME), 15
MIME media type
registration, 24

Rogue Wave, 449

routines, asynchronous (Macintosh multitasking), 350-351

.rsrc file extension (Macintosh), 164

RTTI (Runtime Type Identification), 356

runtime licenses, ActiveX controls, 397

S

saving instance data, 231-234
destroying windows, 234-235
how to use NPP_Destroy( ),
232-234
NPP_Destroy( ) save
parameter, 232
when to use NPP_Destroy( ),
232

scripting, ActiveX, 405-408
controls, 406-408
JavaScript, 405-406
server scripting, 408
VBScript, 405

SDI (Single Document Interface), 105

SDK (Software Development Kit)
configuring, 31-33
libraries, 33
Macintosh, 36-37
OS/2 Warp, 34-36
UNIX, 37
Windows, 34
copying files to project
directories, 108
downloading, 29-30
installing, 102-103
Java SDK, 462
npChap04.cpp file, modifying,
120-121
npChap04.h file, modified
version, 118-119
npChap04Dlg.h file,
modifying, 121-123
npshell.cpp file, modifying,
114-118
adding plug-in specific
code, 115
casting functions, 117
GetJavaClass( )
function, 118
header file
dependencies, 115
NPP_GetJavaClass( )
function, 118
Simple plug-in, 270-271
calling Simple, 272-273
compiling, 270
copying files to plug-ins
directory, 270
DisplayJavaMessage( )
function, 278-279
doit( ) function, 284-285
Java code, 282-284
JavaScript/HTML
connection, 284-285
LiveConnect, 282
NP_Initialize( ) method,
273-274
NPP_Destroy( )
method, 286
NPP_GetJavaClass( )
method, 274-275
NPP_New( ) method,
275-278
NPP_Print( ) method,
281-282

NPP_SetWindow( )
method, 280-281
NPP_Shutdown( ), 287
PluginWindowProc( )
function, 281
running, 270-271
TextOut defect, 281
unpacking, 30
Web site, 29

seekable streams, 147-150
byte-range requests, 149
NPN_RequestRead( ) method,
259-261
binary trees, 260
indexed sequential access
method (ISAM), 260
NPP_NewStream( ) method,
149, 180-181
retrieval rates, 149-150

<SELECT> tag, international plug-in versions, 485

semaphores, 357-359
controlling access (Lock/
Unlock( ) methods), 358
creating, 357-358
defined, 503
p-v semaphore, 342-344

semicolons (;), class definitions, 42

sending
buffers (NPN_PostURL( )
method), 250
files (NPN_PostURL( )
method), 249

sequence containers, 60-61
defined, 503

servers
ActiveX, 408
OLE automation servers,
378-380
Application object, 378
cancelling connections, 380
constants in registration
routines, 380
interfaces, 377-378, 379
NPP_Shutdown( ), 380
temporary plug-in
registration, 380
type libraries, 379
server push, defined, 503
Web servers, defined, 505

SetCapture( ) function, mouse events, 205

SetFocus( ) function, assigning keyboard focus to WindowProc functions, 198-199

SetTimer( ) method, 361

SetWindowLong( ) function, 193

shared DLLs, 106

shutting down streams, *see* NPP_Shutdown( ) method

SIGHUP, defined, 503

signatures, defined, 503

Simple plug-in, 270-271
  closing down, 286-287
    NPP_Destroy( ) method, 286
    NPP_Shutdown( ), 287
  compiling, 270
  copying files to plug-ins directory, 270
  doit( ) function (Java), 284-285
  flow of control
    calling Simple, 272-273
    DisplayJavaMessage( ) function, 278-279
    NP_Initialize( ) method, 273-274
    NPP_GetJavaClass( ) method, 274-275
    NPP_New( ) method, 275-278
    NPP_SetWindow( ) method, 280-281
    PluginWindowProc( ) function, 281
    TextOut defect, 281
  LiveConnect, 282
    closing down, 286-288
    Java code, 282-284
    JavaScript/HTML connection, 284-285
    NPP_Print( ) method, 281-282
  running, 270-271

Single Document Interface (SDI), 105

single.html file (zero plug-in), 138

skeleton programs, defined, 503

SLOC (Source Line of Code), defined, 503

SMPs (Symmetric Multiprocessors), 341

Software Development Kit, *see* SDK

source
  code locations, 169
  files (C++), 42

spawning processes, 146

SQL (Structured Query Language), ODBC, 384

SSIs (Server-side includes), defined, 504

Standard Template Library, *see* STL

static
  binding (ID) , OLE automation, 378
  HTML files, defined, 504
  libraries, 33
    defined, 504
  linking, ActiveX controls, 397

status bars
  hyperlinks, 242
  NPN_GetURL( ) method, 139-140
  NPN_Status( ) method, 144-145, 264-267
    download progress indicators, 265
    reporting time remaining, 266-267
    specification, 265
  peer objects, 88

STDERR (Standard Error), defined, 504

STDIN (Standard Input), defined, 504

STDOUT (Standard Output), defined, 504

STL (Standard Template Library), 59-66
  container classes, 60-61
    adapters, 61-62
  algorithms, 65
  function objects, 64-65
  iterators, 62-64
  MFC, 66
  sequences classes, 60

Story pattern, 91-93

STR# resources (Macintosh), 165-166

streams
  data streams, 85-86, 146-148
  destroying (NPN_DestroyStream( ) method), 264
  example, 210-212
  handling
    MFC, 213
    Windows API, 210

new (additional) streams, 213-214
  NPN_NewStream( ) method, 144, 177-181, 262-264
    NPN_DestroyStream( ) method, 264
    NPN_Write( ) method, 263
  reading data as files, 180
  reading data as streams, 179
  seekable streams, 180-181
  specification, 177, 262
  streaming into Navigator, 263
opening new streams, peer objects, 88
seekable streams, 147-150
  byte-range requests, 149
  NPN_RequestRead( ) method, 259-261
  NPP_NewStream( ) method, 149, 180-181
  retrieval rates, 149-150
seeking, peer objects, 89
sending to targets (Navigator frames), 239-240
size, 238

strings, MIMEType strings, adding to version information, 111-112

StuffIt Expander, 30

suspend/resume events, 196

Symantec
  C++ compiler, 31
  ObjectWindows Library (OWL), 446-448
  THINK Class Library (TCL), 450

Symmetric Multiprocessors (SMPs), 341

synchronizing tasks, 342-344
  deadlocks, 344-348
    banker's algorithm, 345-348
    dealing with, 344-345
    resource-numbering, 345
    two-phase locking, 348
  global data access, 357-359
    creating semaphores, 357-358
    Lock/Unlock( ) methods, 358

System 8 (Macintosh), 350-351

system( ) method, 99

T

tags
    <EMBED>, 81, 83
        NPP_New( ) function, 175
        multimedia plug-ins, 90-91
        integrating plug-ins,
        459-460
        PLUGINSPAGE attribute,
        481, 490
        TYPE attribute, 177
    <OBJECT>, ActiveX controls,
    394-395
    <PARAM>, ActiveX controls,
    406-407
    <SELECT>, international
    plug-in versions, 485

**Taligent CommonPoint,
451-454**
    Web site, 453

tar compression utility, 30
    GNU tar, 30

targets
    Navigator frames, 239-240
    NPN_NewStream( )
    method, 263

Task pattern, 94

Task Window pattern, 94-95

**TCL (THINK Class
Library), 450**

**TCP (Transmission Control
Protocol), defined, 504**

templates, 57-59
    ActiveX Template Library
    (ATL), 400-401
    instantiating template classes,
    58-59
    Standard Template Library,
    see STL

testing plug-ins
    about:plugins, 129
    sample data, 129-130

text boxes
    defined, 504
    MIME subtypes, 16

TGauge class (OWL), 447-448

THINK Reference, 229

threads, 146
    asynchronous plug-ins, 98-99
    defined, 504
    multithreading, 341-342
        terminating threads,
        359-360

    separate threads, 356-357
        priorities, 357
        Runtime Type
        Identification (RTTI), 356
        starting threads
        (AfxBeginThread( )
        function), 356

time
    remaining, reporting, 266-267
    stamp, defined, 504
    timers, 361

toolbars, defined, 504

**TPrint structure (Macintosh),
embedded plug-ins, 218-219**

transferring data
    clipboard transfers, 366-370
        delayed rendering, 367
        MFCs, 369
        objects, 367-368
    drag-and-drop transfers,
    370-372
        DoDragDrop( ) function,
        371-372
        IDropSource interface, 370
        IDropTarget interface, 371

trees
    binary trees, 260
    views, 241-244

troubleshooting
    Netscape Navigator, 429-432
    NPN_UserAgent( ) method
    GPFs (General Protection
    Faults), 248
    Windows plug-ins, 427-432
        16-bit Navigator, 427-428
        FileOpenName
        resource, 428
        full-page plug-ins, 429
        unregistering failed
        plug-ins, 428

TWIPs, 87
    printing, embedded
    plug-ins, 217

**two-phase locking
algorithm, 348**

**type libraries, OLE automation
servers, 379**

U

UNIX
    advertising media types,
    167-168
    class libraries, 449
    configuring SDK, 37

    document-centric
    computing, 457
    download page
    considerations, 486
    fork( ) function, 341
    g++ compiler, 31
    Helpers screen, 487-488
    media types, 17-18
    MIME type association,
    487-488
        determining, 488-489
    multitasking, 349
    NPWindows, 183
    OLE automation, 375-376
    plug-ins subdirectory, 480-481
    processes, 340-341
    SIGHUP, defined, 503
    X Window System, 183-185
        callback structure, 183
        colormaps, 184-185
        events, 198
        hierarchy, 184-185
        X Toolkit, 183-184
    Xlib interface, 183-184
        event model, 198

**Unknown File Type dialog box
(Navigator), 13,
168-169, 481**

**Unlock( ) method, semaphore
access, 358-359**

**unregistering failed
plug-ins, 428**

**UpdateWindow( ) function,
mouse events, 203**

updating
    embedded objects, 373
    header file dependencies, 115
    update events, 196
        updateEvt event
        (Macintosh), 198

URLs
    defined, 504
    hyperlinking, 241
        loading URLs, 241-244
    NPN_GetURL( ) method,
    139-140, 238-240
        asynchronous processing,
        246-247
        migrating existing
        applications, 244-246
        NPN_GetURLNotify( )
        method, 246-247
        sending streams to targets,
        239-240
        specification, 239

NPN_PostURL() method,
141-142, 249-258
distributed systems,
252-256
non-HTTP URLs, 250
older Navigator versions,
250-252
sending buffers, 250
sending files, 249
opening for writing, 89

User Decision pattern, 93-94

V

variables
class variables, 52
defined, 496
const variables, 156-157
environment variables,
defined, 497
instances
defined, 499
initialization code for
keyboard events, 200-201
PATH, defined, 501

VBScript, 398
ActiveX, 405
document-centric computing,
458-459

versions
ActiveX controls, 396
information resources, 109-112
block headers, 109
FileExtents field, 111
FileOpenName, 428
filtering files, 111
MIMEType strings,
111-112
Netscape Navigator versions
BrowserWatch, 251
determining, 247
NPN_PostURL() method,
250-252
NPN_UserAgent()
method, 248
NPN_Version() method, 142

video
MIME subtypes, 16
see also npAVI plug-in

view classes (MFC), 446
CView, WM_PAINT message,
208-209, 213

virtual
defined, 505
function table (VTBL)
interface, OLE automation,
377-379
methods, 67-69

Visual C++
ActiveX controls, 399
AppWizard
ATL COM AppWizard,
400-401
generating project code,
103-107
mapping messages, 207
OLE controls, 399
setting up
CRecordSet-derived
classes (ODBC), 384-385
Class Wizard
DDX (dialog data
exchange), 386
OLE automation
clients, 376
setting up CRecordSet-
derived classes
(ODBC), 385
Developer Studio
DLL configuration, 113-114
inserting files into
projects, 108
new projects, 103
Resource view, 109-110
mapping messages, 206-207
Resource Editor, 112

VRML browsers, 511

W

warnings, 157

**Web Explorer browser
(IBM), 34**

Webmasters, defined, 505

Win32/Win32s
unsupported calls, 426
using for Windows 3.x, 425-426
Win32 API, 353

window procedures, 125

**WindowProc functions,
192, 194**
assigning keyboard focus,
198-199
adding fBuffer to
PluginInstance, 200
callback function, 199-200
calling SetFocus(), 198-199
initializing fBuffer, 200-201

Windows
advertising media types,
162-163
API, handling streams, 210

DLLs (Dynamic Link
Libraries), 34
download page
considerations, 486
messages (getting events),
190-195
callback functions, 192-194
handling, 191-192
keyboard events, 198-202
mapping, 206-209
message types, 191
mouse events, 202-205
parameters, 191
queue, 190-191
WindowProc functions, 192
WM_KEYDOWN, 199-200
WM_PAINT, 195
multitasking, 351-353
plug-ins subdirectory, 480
printing
bitmaps, 221-222
Cancel dialogs, 222-223
fonts, 223-225
full-page plug-ins, 221-225
Print dialog, 225-227
SDK, 34
troubleshooting plug-ins,
427-432
16-bit Navigator, 427-428
FileOpenName
resource, 428
full-page plug-ins, 429
Netscape Navigator
problems, 429-432
unregistering failed
plug-ins, 428
WindowProc functions,
see WindowProc functions
see also Windows 3.x

windows
destroying, 234
NPP_SetWindow() function,
presenting data, 181
see also NPP_SetWindow()
method

Windows 3.x, 412-413
16-bit programing, 416-417
disadvantages, 414-415
int specifier, 417
memory, 417
DOS Protected Mode
Interface, 423-424
extended/expanded
memory, 420-422
far pointers, 418-420
NEAR and FAR
macros, 420
near pointers, 417-418

running 16- and 32-bit
applications
simultaneously, 424
small memory, 417-418
tiny memory, 418
multitasking, 425
using 32-bit applications,
425-426
Win32s unsupported calls, 426
WinZip, 30
Web site, 103
WM_ prefix, 191
**WM_KEYDOWN message,
199-200**
**WM_LBUTTONDOWN
message, 202-203**
**WM_LBUTTONUP
message, 202**
**WM_MOUSEMOVE
message, 202**
WM_PAINT message
CView (MFC)
message mapping, 208-209
stream handling, 213
mouse events, 203-204
OnDraw( ) function, 209
OnPaint( ) handler
function, 206
Simple plug-in, 281
worker threads, 356
World Wide Web (WWW)
browsers
BrowserWatch, 251
defined, 496
media types, 18-19
Microsoft Internet
Explorer,
see Internet Explorer
Netscape Navigator,
see Netscape Navigator
VRML, 511
Web Explorer (IBM), 34
document-centric
computing, 456
servers
defined, 505
media types, 17-18
sites
ActiveX, 394
ActiveX Gallery, 396
ActiveX SDK, 399-400
ActiveX Template Library
(ATL), 400

Amber (Acrobat Portable
Document Format
reader, 482
BrowserWatch, 251
CommonPoint, 453
compression, 103
frames, 240
Java Developers Kit
(JDK), 310
Java Runtime Interface
(JRI), 470
Macintosh System 8, 351
MIME FAQ (Frequently
Asked Questions)
Web site, 16
NCSA (National Center for
Supercomputer
Applications), 501
Netscape Navigator, 12
OpenDoc, 388
Portland Pattern
Repository, 95
Ready-to-Run Software,
Inc., 31
Rogue Wave, 449
SDK (Software
Development Kit), 29
Taligent, 453
THINK Reference, 229
WinZip, 103
Web utilities on included
CD-ROM, 511-512
writing, 85-86
opening URLs for writing, 89
WWW, *see* **World Wide Web**

X-Y-Z

x MIME subtypes, 24
X, *see* **X Windows System**
**X Toolkit (UNIX X Window
System), 183-184**
X Window System (UNIX)
callback structure, 183
colormaps, 184-185
events, 198
hierarchy, 184-185
X Toolkit, 183-184
Xlib interfaces, 183-184
see also UNIX
**XBM (X Bit Maps),
defined, 505**
**Xlib interface (UNIX),
183-184**
event model, 198

**XMS (Extended Memory
Standard), 420**
**yield( ) function, lack of in
multitasking, 355-356**
yielding, multitasking, 339
zero plug-in
calling as full-page, 136-137
double.html file, 138
embedded
single instance, 137-138
two instances, 138
hidden, 138-139
hidden.html file, 139
single.html file, 138

Licensing Agreement